LIBERTY

and the

Great Libertarians

An Anthology on Liberty
A Hand-book of Freedom

Edited and compiled, with preface, introduction,
and index, by

CHARLES T. SPRADING

Published for the author
LOS ANGELES
1913

Dedicated to all Lovers of Liberty.

Reprinted 2015
The Ludwig von Mises Institute
ISBN: 978-1-61016-107-7

PREFACE

Libertarian: One who upholds the principle of liberty, especially individual liberty of thought and action.—*Webster's New International Dictionary.*

It is in the sense defined above that the word Libertarian is used throughout this book. In Metaphysics, a Libertarian is one who believes in the doctrine of freedom of the will, as opposed to necessitarianism. As the Libertarians quoted are nearly all believers in determinism (the opposite of the theory of "free will"), and as the questions they discuss are all sociological, they must not be confounded with the advocates of "free will" in metaphysical discussions.

It will be noticed that the Libertarians cited are chosen from different political parties and economic schools; there are Republicans, Democrats, Socialists, Single-Taxers, Anarchists, and Woman's Rights advocates; and it will be perceived, also, that these master minds are in perfect accord when treating of liberty. To point out that some of them are not always consistent in their application of the principles of liberty is no valid argument against it, but merely shows that they did not accept liberty as their guiding principle, nor perhaps believe in its universal application. The principle of equal liberty has been approached from many standpoints by these writers and applied to various fields. The only question we have here to consider is whether they have proved that liberty in particular human relations is a logical deduction from correct reasoning; and this the writer maintains they have done.

It is shown by the writers quoted that liberty has been applied to various fields, and has proved successful wherever tried. Many of the earlier Libertarians, living in different countries, wrote without knowledge of the others; yet the reader will detect a note of harmony between them. Some of them believed freedom would work in this or that field, some believed it would work in other fields; each had confidence in it in his own particular sphere and encouraged its application. We find the theory has been applied to many social relations, and that when these instances of its application are brought together, as they are in this book, they demonstrate conclusively that the extension of the principle of equal liberty to all social relations is not only feasible, but necessary.

It will also be observed that extremes meet here, and are equally provided for by liberty. The Individualist and the Communist, each advocating his own ideas, are both within the scope of equal liberty, and there is no conflict between them when the principle of liberty is adhered to; that is, if they produce and distribute among themselves. Plans voluntarily accepted by individuals or groups of individuals and not forced upon others are in no way a violation of liberty. They would be if others were forced to do so by the seizure of "all means of production and distribution," as the State Socialists purpose to do, thereby excluding non-conformers from their use. It is not the difference in taste between individuals that Libertarians object to, but the forcing of one's tastes upon another. Individualists believe in common ownership of such things as roads, streets and waterways, and Communists believe in individual ownership of such things as clothes and personal effects. They really merge into one another; but there is no need for either to conform to the other's taste or to be deprived of its own liberty.

There is an admirable *Free Press Anthology*, by Theodore Schroeder, but this is the only anthology on the general subject of liberty known to its compiler, who has made a very close study of libertarian literature.

The present volume is not limited to a few fields, as the excellent work of Mr. Schroeder's necessarily is, but covers the entire scope of social activity. A search of the public libraries gives evidence that comparatively little has been written on the subject of Liberty—and there are more presentations of and arguments for Liberty in this one volume than can be found in a dozen average public libraries. A revival of interest in the subject is manifesting itself now and the purpose of this book is to furnish the worker for liberty, or the lover of liberty, a handbook containing every important contribution to that subject. The writer has often felt the need of such a work when lecturing or debating. This volume represents five years of research and arrangement of material and gives the reader, in one volume, what he hopes will prove to be a useful and comprehensive library on the subject of Liberty.

A portion of the literature in this book is now available to readers for the first time in many years, as some of it was withdrawn by the authors after much persecution; some was suppressed by publishers, owing to opposition from influential conservatives, and a considerable part of it is literature that has been neglected and not republished, because its thought was too far ahead of its time. The general reader will find the writers of a century ago perhaps as radical as he can tolerate; while the real progressive thinker will appreciate the more advanced thought of the libertarian writers of his own age.

Opportunity is here taken to thank the publishers of copyrighted books for their kind permission to quote from them, not one having refused such request; and detailed acknowledgement of them is given in the chapter headings.

Indebtedness is also acknowledged to Hans and Ollie Steedman Rossner for proof-reading and the Index.

CHARLES T. SPRADING.

Los Angeles, May 1, 1913.

CONTENTS

INTRODUCTION. Rights. Justice. Law. Equal Liberty. Natural Law and Statute Law. Government. Crimes and Criminals. Majority Rule. War. Industrial vs. Militant Type. Flags... 11

LACONICS OF LIBERTY... 33

EDMUND BURKE. Bio-bibliography. A Vindication of Natural Society... 60

THOMAS PAINE. Bio-bibliography. Reason. Negro Slavery. War. Society and Civilization... 74

THOMAS JEFFERSON. Bio-bibliography. Government. Law and Judges. War. Trial by Jury. Capital Punishment. Slavery. Land. Religious Freedom... 82

WILLIAM GODWIN. Bio-bibliography. Political Justice. Wealth. Crime. War. Government. Law... 93

WILHELM VON HUMBOLDT. Bio-bibliography. Selections from *The Sphere and Duty of Government*. State... 105

JOHN STUART MILL. Bio-bibliography. Liberty of Thought, Speech and Press. Majority Rule. Religious Intolerance. Social Freedom. Originality... 118

RALPH WALDO EMERSON. Bio-bibliography. Ethics. Politics. Self-Reliance... 142

WILLIAM LLOYD GARRISON. Bio-bibliography. Liberty. Free Speech. Moderation. War. Non-resistance... 154

WENDELL PHILLIPS. Bio-bibliography. Liberty. Free Speech. Church. Government. Labor. Address to Boys... 160

JOSIAH WARREN. Bio-bibliography. Liberty. Individuality. Children... 168

MAX STIRNER. Bio-bibliography. Egoism. The State. Labor... 174

HENRY D. THOREAU. Bio-bibliography. On the Duty of Civil Disobedience... 191

HERBERT SPENCER. Bio-bibliography. Equal Freedom. The Right to Ignore the State. Militarism. Land Titles... 210

STEPHEN PEARL ANDREWS. Bio-bibliography. The Sovereignty of the Individual. Internationalism. Government. Products of Labor. Land. Prisons... 236

ABRAHAM LINCOLN. Bio-bibliography. Slavery. Church and Ministers. Labor and Capital... 253

LYSANDER SPOONER. Bio-bibliography. Trial by Jury... 258

ROBERT G. INGERSOLL. Bio-bibliography. Individuality. Egoism. My Religion. Church and State. Law. War. Vision of the Future. Criminals. Labor. Land... 272

HENRY GEORGE. Bio-bibliography. Liberty. Land. Single Tax. Patent Rights. Freedom in Trade... 291

LYOFF N. TOLSTOY. Bio-bibliography. War. Slavery. Land. Money. Slaves. How Can Governments Be Abolished?.....313
BENJAMIN R. TUCKER. Bio-bibliography. Relation of the State to the Individual. Value. Voluntary Co-operation. The Proletaire and Strikes. The Ballot. Methods of Anarchists. Passive and Non-resistance. Trial by Jury......334
PIERRE A. KROPOTKIN. Bio-bibliography. Mutual Aid. Social Bonds. Voluntary Associations. Communism..........359
WILLIAM B. GREENE. Bio-bibliography. Freedom in Money. Usury Laws. Credit. Measure of Value. Mutual Currency..382
AUBERON HERBERT. Bio-bibliography. Liberty and Majority Rule. Force and Power. Liberty and Society...........398
G. BERNARD SHAW. Bio-bibliography. How to Beat Children. The Perfect Gentleman. The Golden Rule. Idolatry. Democracy. Women. Duty. Love and Marriage.............416
THEODORE HERTZKA. Bio-bibliography. Economics. Labor. Value. Capital. Interest. Machinery. Land.............424
EDWARD CARPENTER. Bio-bibliography. Woman in Freedom. Marriage..442
OLIVE SCHREINER. Bio-bibliography. Freedom and Woman..458
OSCAR WILDE. Bio-bibliography. Liberty in Art...............472
FRANCISCO FERRER. Bio-bibliography. The Modern School..487
MARIA MONTESSORI. Bio-bibliography. Education of Children. Discipline. Independence....................................494
OTHER LIBERTARIANS. The International. Economic Interpretation of History. Syndicalism. Freedom in Music. Obscenity Laws. Liberty and the State. Majority vs. Minority. Optional Single Tax. Mr. Dooley on Liberty. Liberty in Art. Medical Freedom. Libel. Liberty and Duty. Land. Liberty and Justice. Egoism...............501
LACONICS..529

INTRODUCTION

The history of civilized man is the history of the incessant conflict between liberty and authority. Each victory for liberty marked a new step in the world's progress; so we can measure the advance of civilization by the amount of freedom acquired by human institutions.

The first great struggle for liberty was in the realm of thought. The Libertarians reasoned that freedom of thought would be good for mankind; it would promote knowledge, and increased knowledge would advance civilization. But the Authoritarians protested that freedom of thought would be dangerous; that people would think wrong; that a few were divinely appointed to think for the people, that these had books which contained the whole truth, and that further search was unnecessary and forbidden. The powers of Church and State were arrayed against the Libertarians; but, after the sacrifice of many great men, freedom in thought was won.

The second momentous contest was for the liberty to speak. The enemies of liberty, those possessing power and privilege, opposed freedom of speech, just as they had opposed freedom of thought. The Church said it was perilous to permit people to speak their minds;—they might speak the truth. The State said free speech was dangerous; it was not the duty of citizens to think and speak, but to obey. After much persecution the Libertarians were victorious, although such authoritarian institutions as the Catholic Church and the Spanish and Russian States do not even now concede freedom of thought and speech.

The third contest was for liberty of the press. The same old enemies who had so much to conceal opposed it, and their repressive measures added a long list of martyrs to the cause of freedom. Like free thought and free speech, free press has proved to be a powerful factor in human progress. It still has its enemies as of old, but their number and influence are dwindling.

The fourth struggle was for the liberty of assembly. Here again Libertarians met the same old enemies using the same old arguments. The people could not be permitted to assemble freely because they might come together and discuss matters relating to Church or State or plan treason and revolution. But again liberty was victorious, and free assembly has been found to be beneficial to the people, if not to some institutions.

The fifth important contest for liberty was in the field of religion. The Libertarians argued that freedom was as necessary and desirable in religion as in other human relations; that man should be free to worship at any shrine he pleased, or at no shrine; to worship as his reason and conscience dictated, or even not to worship at all. An infallible church could never permit fallible human beings to choose their own religion, but a succession of conflicts opened the gates of religious liberty.

In these five important spheres of human action there have been, against a sea of ignorance and tradition, five great victories for freedom. Liberty, wherever applied, has proved a benefit to the race; furthermore, the most important steps in human progress would have been impossible without it; and if civilization is to advance, that advance can come only as a result of a broader and more complete freedom in all human relations. A principle that has proved its workability in five such important and vital phases of social evolution should prove desirable in all the affairs of man.

And here is the difference between the Libertarians and the Authoritarians: the latter have no confidence in liberty; they believe in compelling people to be good, assuming that people are totally depraved; the former believe in letting people be good, and maintain that humanity grows better and better as it gains more and more liberty. If Libertarians were merely to ask that liberty be tried in any one of the other fields of

Introduction 13

human expression they would meet the same opposition as their pioneer predecessors; but such is their confidence in the advantages of liberty that they demand, not that it be tried in one more instance only, but that it be universally adopted.

Their demand is for equal liberty, which denies all privileges and permits no other restrictions than those imposed by social conditions. As it is their relation to their fellowmen with which they are concerned, Libertarians seek to promote equal liberty, and not absolute liberty. "Absolute liberty" means that liberty which disregards the liberty of others. Some extreme individualists like Nietzsche believe in it; but absolute liberty, as the word implies, is unsocial, because it is unrelated. If there is an absolute, it is not a social law, for all social laws are relative. Equal liberty is bounded by the like liberty of all.

Mere equality does not imply equal liberty, however, for slaves are equal in their slavery. Equal opportunity to rob others is not equal liberty, but its violation; it abridges "liberty to possess," and the "liberty to produce and to own the product." These liberties are implied by equality of liberty, just as equal opportunity is; equal robbery or equal slavery have no relation to equal liberty, but are its opposite. There are but two positions from which to choose, equal liberty or unequal liberty. Most persons believe in liberty for themselves, but not for others. Some Christians believe in hell for others, but not for themselves. Libertarians are not like either, for they demand the same liberty for others that they ask for themselves.

Its enemies deride liberty as an abstraction. It is abstract, but so are most of the sciences. Mathematics, for instance, is abstract, but we find that this abstraction fits every concrete fact in the universe. So it is with abstract liberty. It will fit every concrete social fact; it will solve every social ill.

Liberty has its positive and its negative side—it negates authority and tyranny, but it affirms equity and justice; that is, it negates the bad and affirms the good. Destruction is necessary, but construction is equally so; it is essential to tear away the old building in order to erect the new in its place, but before consenting to its demolition the occupant may demand to know what is to take its place, and the architect should furnish him specifications of the proposed structure. There are those who are most successful in tearing down the old building, who, however, may not have the abstract idea of the new structure in their minds, while there are others who excel in building up the new. Both are essential. It is absurd to say that clearing the ground is sufficient, for tomorrow's weeds will grow where they are cleared today. How often is one superstition overthrown only to be replaced by a different one! Truth must be substituted for error,—and this is the work of the positive side of liberty. Liberty means freedom to construct the new as well as freedom to destroy the old. A society of Libertarians will destroy the old, but they will also build the new, and whatever ground they clear of weeds will be sown with seeds of progress.

Rights.—The word "Right" has many meanings; and unfortunately it has two contradictory ones—legal rights and ethical right—that lead to much confusion of thought. Legal rights are: "Any power or privilege vested in a person by the law;" "A claim or title to or interest in anything whatsoever that is enforcible by law;" "A franchise—a specific right or privilege granted or established by governmental authority;" "A capacity or privilege the enjoyment of which is secured to a person by law, hence the interest or share which anyone has in a piece of property, title, claim, interest." It will be seen from these accepted definitions that legal right is synonymous with power; whoever or whatsoever has the power, has the right. Now, governments have most power, therefore have most rights. If individuals have any legal rights, it is because governments have granted them in the way of "franchise," "title," "privilege," etc. Legal right means to take, to have

Introduction

and to hold. There is no sentiment in legal right; it is the offspring of power only—"Might is right!"

Right in its ethical sense is defined thus: "Right is in accordance with equity;" "Conformity to the standard of justice;" "Right is identical with the good, not deviating from the true and just;" "Freedom from guilt." A comparison of these two conceptions of right will disclose the fundamental disagreement between them. Although the legal and ethical definitions of right are the antithesis of each other, most writers use them as synonyms. They confuse power with goodness, and mistake law for justice.

Ethical right is largely abstract; legal right is mostly concrete. Ethical right the just man wishes to be established; legal right is already established. Ethical right and legal right mutually exclude each other; where one prevails, the other cannot endure. One is founded on power, on might; the other on justice, on equality. One appeals to the sword to settle matters, the other appeals to the judgment of men. For illustration: Governments have the right to do wrong; that is, they have the power, the legal right, to do anything they choose, regardless of whether it is good or bad—and their choice is usually bad from the ethical standpoint. Governments can and do invade nations, rob the people of their property, enslave or kill the inhabitants; all in perfect accord with legal rights, but in gross violation of ethical right. Let it be understood that the right of a government is coextensive with its power; it has not the right to invade, enslave or kill the people of a stronger nation or government, for it lacks the power on which this right is based; but, having the power, it has the right to commit these acts against a weaker nation. Let us not mistake things as they are for things as they ought to be.

It is absurd to speak of the slave having the "right" to liberty. It is a curious sort of right that could in no way be exercised during the thousands of years in which slavery existed; surely not a legal right, for slavery was legal then. Neither had the slave an ethical right; for ethical right means "justice," "equity," "liberty," the very things he did not have: it is even doubtful if many of the slaves had the least idea of justice and liberty. It is only correct to say that they should have had such a right. To say they had it, is like saying one already has a fortune that he is hoping to acquire.

Justice.—Some of the accepted definitions of Justice are: "Conformity to truth, fact or right reason; fairness; rightfulness; truth; impartiality;" "The rendering to everyone his due or right; just treatment;" "To do justice to; to treat with fairness or according to merit; to render what is due to;" "Rightfulness; uprightness; equitableness, as the justice of a cause." These definitions are accepted by Libertarians, who believe that justice is that which ought to be done by one to another. But what is the true criterion of the conduct we expect from another? How are we to know it is just? by what standard is justice to be judged? Authorities on law answer, "Custom": whatever is customary is just. Therefore the lawyer looks for "precedents." No lawyer will declare, "My client broke this law, and he did right, for it is a bad law": that would be in violation of custom and precedent, and he dare not say it; but he will ransack the maze of law for a precedent—and will find one, too!

To quote only one of the great authorities on law: James Coolidge Carter in his *Law: Its Origin, Growth and Function*, page 163, says, "Justice consists in the compliance with custom in all matters of difference between men," and he tells us on the same page that "This accords with the definition of the Roman law." But custom and precedent are defective as a basis for that conception of justice which recognizes good acts only; for custom and precedent can be found for all kinds of acts, good, bad and indifferent. Some of our savage ancestors had the habit, or "custom," of eating their dead parents; so, by proving the precedent or custom, we can prove that cannibalism is just! Custom may suffice as the basis of law, but is inadequate as the basis of justice. Tyranny, not liberty, has been the custom in the past; and so Libertarians reject custom as a guiding principle, just as they reject power or might. They know that justice is not something that was, or is, but that is to be. Pascal saw the absurdity of law and justice that have their source in custom, for he says: "In the just and unjust we find hardly anything which does not change its character in changing its climate. Three degrees of elevation of the pole reverse the whole of jurisprudence. A meridian is decisive of truth, or a few years of possession. Fundamental laws change! Right has its epochs! A pleasant justice that, which a river or a mountain limits! Truth on this side the Pyrenees, error on the other!"

And who can know what the law really is? In the United States we have over 50,000 laws, most of which conflict with each other, and to interpret them we employ an army of lawyers and judges, who disagree as to the intent or applicability of every law. The writers on the theory of law are equally perplexed. Sir Henry Maine says: "There is much widespread dissatisfaction with existing theories of jurisprudence, and so general a conviction that they do not really solve the questions they pretend to dispose of, as to justify the suspicion that some line of inquiry necessary to a perfect result has been incompletely followed or altogether omitted by their authors." Perceiving, like Sir Henry Maine and other honest writers on law and justice, the "widespread dissatisfaction with existing theories of jurisprudence," Libertarians reject them altogether as the basis of justice.

Law.—Some writers on this subject have made justice the basis of law, while others have made law the basis of justice; but, as a matter of fact, statute law did not have its source in justice nor is justice the outcome of such law. Lawmakers are not imbued with the idea of arriving at justice. The motive most prevalent among them is that of personal or class benefit, benefit to the makers of law or to the makers of the lawmakers. Benefit to them means property-getting. They find that the State is of great assistance both in this property-getting and in the property-holding part of the game, so they seize the State and use it as their instrument in acquiring and defending property. These lawmakers believe that the law should reflect their interests; and as they enact nearly all laws they see to it that the law represents their desires and not the ideas of equity.

If all men had the same interests, there would be less harm in permitting a part of the people to legislate for all; but this is not the case. There is a great conflict of interests between the possessed and the dispossessed, between the poor and the rich, between the weak and the strong, between the ruler and the ruled, between the worker and the shirker, between the producer and the appropriator, which is apparent in existing laws, always made by those powerful enough to take advantage of the State and of the law-abiding sentiment of the people. That their laws conflict with justice is no concern of theirs, for profit and not justice is their object. The object is legitimate because they make it legitimate. The game they play is lawful because they make the law to uphold their game; but they raise a hue and cry for "law and order" if they find any game conflicting with theirs, and declare it unlawful. It is easy to see that laws thus enacted are unjust, for to be just a law must be enacted for the benefit of all; thus it is in no wise logical to presume that the "legal" is the just.

When we compare the laws made today and the method and purpose of their making, with those of the past, we find them to be in perfect harmony. It was the law and custom of the past to provide for a class of idlers, it was customary for the powerful to enslave the weak, for the rich to rob the poor, for the unscrupulous to make laws in their own interests, even as it is the law and custom today. Surely it must be evident that law does not have its basis in justice, but rather in custom. To both law and custom, justice is a total stranger.

When we know the source of law, we cease to wonder at the conduct of those who accept law as a guiding principle; we understand why they conduct themselves so badly from the standpoint of justice and still keep out of jail; we also understand why some who have violated no rule of justice go to jail. Most people accept law as their guide to conduct; they find it to be more profitable than following the rules of justice. They are always asking, "What is the law?" "Can I do that and not be arrested?" To them anything within the law is right; yet we know that the greatest injustices are committed within the law. They would see nothing wrong in murder, if it was lawful; but murder is lawful only to the makers of law, to the State or the Government, which indulges its own murderous inclinations, legitimately, by capital punishment and by war.

Equal Liberty.—The Law of Equal Liberty is the principle that is offered by Libertarians as a substitute for these conflicting and unjust customs of the past. This law has been well formulated by that great philosopher and sociologist, Herbert Spencer. Here it is in brief: "That every man may claim the fullest liberty to exercise his faculties compatible with the possession of like liberty by every other man." This gives us a basis for justice in perfect harmony with the idea of equity. Equal liberty is the essence of equity, and is not equity just? If there are to be laws in a free society, they must be based upon equal liberty or they will be unjust.

Natural Law and Statute Law.—Some authorities on law hold that statute law is based on natural law and therefore in perfect harmony with it, but this will not bear analysis. The natural law of evolution, of development, is variation, differentiation; statute law is intended to produce similarity and uniformity. The first depends upon dynamic forces, the second upon customs of the dead. The first is the law of the new; the second, the law of the old. The first does its own enforcing; the second needs to be enforced. The first cannot be suspended; the second is changed to suit the lawmakers. The law of variation has guided us in the path of progression, while statute law has tended only toward retrogression.

In the animal world, when the law of variation produces an animal differing somewhat from its kind, whether it be in different physical characteristics, to more perfectly adapt it to its environment, or in the addition of new organs to adapt it to a different environment, it is permitted by others of its species to live and propagate its kind, and often produces an entirely new and higher type of animal. But how do upholders of statute law act toward those who differ from them? Let the treatment accorded a Jesus, a Bruno, a Ferrer, be the answer. Statute law is not based on natural law; they are the antithesis of each other.

Government.—The greatest violator of the principle of equal liberty is the State. Its functions are to control, to rule, to dictate, to regulate, and in exercising these functions it interferes with and injures individuals who have done no wrong. The objection to government is, not that it controls those who invade the liberty of others, but that it controls the non-invader. It may be necessary to govern one who will not govern himself, but that in no wise justifies governing one who is capable of and willing to govern himself. To argue that because some need restraint all must be restrained is neither consistent nor logical.

Governments cannot accept liberty as their fundamental basis for justice, because governments rest upon authority and not upon liberty. To accept liberty as the fundamental basis is to discard authority; that is, to discard government itself; as this would mean the dethronement of the leaders of government, we can expect only those who have no economic compromise to make to accept equal liberty as the basis of justice.

If a person accepts the standard of might or power as the correct guiding principle, as the State does, then he can have no reasonable complaint against the unjust conditions that prevail, for they are the logical outcome of the existing principle of government. One must not complain against powerful corporations, for they are the acme of power; by the power of the State they have been granted special "privileges," such as franchises, large land grants, the use and control of public utilities, etc., all of which add to their power by adding to their wealth. In order to oppose logically this inequitable condition, it is necessary to adopt a different standard from that of *might* or *power*.

It is the nature of government to invade. It will impose itself upon the non-invasive individual as readily as it will upon the invasive one, It will seize his property through taxation, or otherwise, and use it for purposes of which the individual does not approve—for going to war, for instance, or building warships (things obnoxious to the peaceful man). It makes so many complicated laws that the individual is bound to break some of them. There are innumerable laws on our statute books, and no lawyer or judge pretends that he knows ten per cent of them; yet the layman may be held to a strict obedience of any or all of them, and if he pleads that he did not know the law he is told that ignorance of the law is no excuse for its breach. He is supposed to know ninety per cent more of law than its students, practitioners, and makers. The more laws, the more ignorance of them; the more ignorance of the law, the more the laws are broken; the more the laws are broken, the more criminals there are; and the more criminals, the more policemen, detectives, lawyers, judges, and other officials that go to make up a strong and expensive government. All of this is good for government officials, but bad for the citizens who carry the load. Rulers have always profited by the mistakes of individuals, and have always made conditions such that mistakes were unavoidable.

The State is even more unfair than the law it pretends to enforce. It never enforces the law equitably, but always favors the rich and the powerful. When it so happens that the law conflicts with the interests of the powerful, it is invariably interpreted in their favor.

The protective part of government is greatly exaggerated. It collects taxes on the theory that it renders an equivalent in protection, but if a crime is committed and a poor man is accused, instead of protecting him, it turns all of its machinery against him; instead of presenting both sides, so that justice may be arrived at, it presents one side and leaves it to the unfortunate one to present the other side if he can. It suppresses all evidence in its possession favorable to the individual, and conceals all evidence against him until the day of trial and then presents it: and all under the pretense of protecting the individual! The fact is, the government is a prosecutor and not a defender; it is an invader and not a protector.

The Libertarians say: Let those who believe in religion have religion; let those who believe in government, have government; but also let those who believe in liberty, have liberty, and do not compel them to accept a religion or a government they do not want. It is as unjust to force one's government upon another, as it is unjust to force one's religion upon another. This was done in the past; but we have won religious freedom, and must now work toward political freedom. We no longer believe that it is just for one man to govern two men, but we have yet to outgrow the absurd belief that it is just for two men to govern one man. To govern a man—that is, to control him, to dictate to him, to rule him—is to violate the principle of equal liberty, for there is the same inequality between the governor and the governed, between the dictator and those dictated to, between the ruler and the ruled, that there was between the master and his slave. The power to command and the weakness to obey are the essence of government and the quintessence of slavery.

It is not even just to restrain the invader, but it seems expedient to do so, since he fails to restrain himself. He has violated the principles of justice and liberty, but we are doing likewise when we take his liberty from him. However, it seems necessary to do so for self-protection against an invader who will not recognize the principle of equal liberty. It is like going to war in self-defense: it is not just, but it may be expedient to do so. It is not just, because war of any kind is not just; but in the extreme alternative of going to war or being exterminated, we will choose the lesser of the two evils. So if we are compelled to restrain the invader to prevent invasive acts, why not be honest and admit that it is a bad state of affairs which necessitates it, and one to be dispensed with just as soon as the invader is cured? The principle of equal liberty, which implies equal opportunity, will cure all but the insane.

Humane men look forward to the day when all of the aggressive and violent parts of the government will cease and only the defensive part remain. "But," say men like Tucker, "that will be the end of government." Very well, let what he calls government go. "But how will you abolish it?" will be asked. It may be answered by asking another: How was slavery abolished? Was it abolished by all the people going into the slave-owning business? Certainly not. It was abolished because the people disliked it and opposed it; because they would not support the business and the people in the business. So it will be with government, or that part of it that is not protective, but invasive; when the people withdraw their support from it, when they oppose it and refuse to pay taxes, when they refuse to go to war, refuse to accept office to enforce unjust laws, then the end will come, and a voluntary co-operative society of free people will take its place, and nothing of the invasive nature of the State will remain.

Crimes and Criminals.—Most crimes are offenses against property. The struggle for property leads to depredations and infractions of the principles of equal liberty in various ways. Greed on the one side and poverty on the other, is the cause of so-called crime. To cure crime, it is necessary to remove its cause. The disease of greed may not be curable, but its baneful results can be obviated by destroying special privileges, out of which ensues poverty, that in turn breeds crime.

Economists are agreed that there are four methods by which wealth is acquired by those who do not produce it. These are, interest, profit, rent and taxes, each of which is based upon special privilege, and all are gross violations of the principle of equal liberty.

First, Interest arises from the special privilege granting to a favored few, known as national bankers, the exclusive right of issuing money. The liberty to establish mutual banks or other free systems of issuing money would abolish interest.

Second, Profits arise from such special privileges as copyrights, patent rights, franchises, grants, etc., all of which violate the principle of equal liberty.

Third, Rent arises from the special privilege of land titles, land grants, the right by deed to hold land and compel others to pay for its use. Equal liberty to use land would eliminate rent.

Fourth, Taxation is a special privilege assumed by the ruling class to levy tribute on their subjects, and is a violation of the liberty of those who do not want a ruling class.

Thus it is seen that the four methods of acquiring wealth and producing poverty rest upon special privileges granted by government. Thus government, producing the criminal rich and the criminal poor, is itself the cause of crime, and not its prevention, as stupid people believe. In order to perpetuate itself government must manufacture criminals; it rests on their backs and without them it would fall. If there were no criminals there would be no policemen, no detectives, no lawyers, no judges, no courts, no legislatures, no penitentiaries —no government, in fact. Government would cease without "criminals" to sustain it, and to expect the government to remove its own foundation is idle.

If the cause of crime is removed it will be by Libertarians and not by Authoritarians. It will be by those who hate it, not by those who profit by it.

Majority Rule.—Majority rule, like every other rule, is a violation of the principle of equal liberty. Like all other rules it rests on power. This power is the power of numbers; not the power of extermination by means of the bullet and the war club, as in ages past, but of the same nature, having neither regard for justice nor for reason. For centuries the only means at the disposal of power by which it might acquire its ends was the bullet. All its conquest, its means of securing the subserviency and exploitation of the weak, was by the method of extermination—the bullet. But, finally, the observation that a large army could conquer a small one led to the method of enumeration to settle a dispute instead of the old one of extermination: the ballot instead of the bullet. The ballot is more economical of human life—but to use enumeration as the means of arriving at justice is a poor substitute for reason.

A reasonable action on the part of the majority is very rare, while the evidence of mob stupidity and brutality is overwhelming. The majority in power make laws for their own financial benefit, disregarding the interests of the minority, and when the weak minority, by adding to its numbers, becomes powerful, it, in turn, does the same thing; thus, by appealing to power to settle their conflicting interests, the conflict would go on forever.

Does it not seem a vast waste of valuable human material that the pioneers of thought, those who by their genius dare to clear unknown paths in the arts and sciences and in government, should have to conform to the dictates of that non-creative, slow-moving mass, the majority? An appeal to the majority is a resort to force and not an appeal to intelligence; the majority is always ignorant, and by increasing the majority we multiply ignorance. The majority is incapable of initiative, its attitude being one of opposition toward everything that is new. If it had been left to the majority, the world would never have had the steamboat, the railroad, the telegraph, or any of the conveniences of modern life.

We are required to accept the decision of the majority as final, although the majority does and always has decided against the very things which have proved themselves most useful to society. In fact, every advance in civilization—in the arts, in language, in science, in invention and discovery—has been achieved, not because of the wish of the majority, but by the constant work and urgent demands of a persistent few. It took Voltaire and others of his kind half a century to convince the majority that it was being robbed and enslaved; and when a part of that majority was at last convinced, it did not use the educational method that had convinced them, but resorted to force to convince the rest. War, not logic, is the method of the mob.

If majority rule is right, then we have no just complaint to make against existing conditions, for the majority favors them or it surely would change them. The majority looks to its politicians for guidance. The successful politicians never advance new ideas, knowing that they must stay by the majority, echoing only the sentiment of the majority, or they will lose their jobs. The real educator does his work at his own expense, sows the seed, builds up a movement, perhaps; the politician snatches his idea and reaps the harvest, loudly declaring himself the author of the idea, and the majority accepts his assertion and follows him.

A political convention illustrates the workings of majority rule: If the minority in a party advocate a progressive move which is defeated when put to a vote in the convention, the minority are prohibited from advancing it during the campaign; if this minority refuse to advocate what the convention has decided to be right, they are barred from the platform and press, the cry of majority rule is raised against them, and they are called "traitors to the party;" but if they abandon their progressive ideas and advocate the wishes of the majority they are rewarded with office. Thus majority rule develops the dishonest politician: in order to rule sometime, he consents to being ruled at other times. The desire to rule and the willingness to be ruled ends in degradation; and no one who accepts the principles of equal liberty can indorse majority rule.

War.—War is a violation of the principle of liberty as well as of justice. It is founded on force; its method is violence; its theory is "Might is right;" its purpose is to conquer or destroy. Its greatest heroes are those who have slaughtered the greatest number of people; its Alexanders, its Napoleons. Napoleon said that "God is always on the side of the strong battalions." When differences between nations are settled by appeals to force, and not to justice, the stronger nations soon demonstrate that they are right. While the majority of men have outgrown the notion that a pugilist is in the right and an invalid is in the wrong because the former can thrash the latter, an analogous opinion is still entertained by those nations that rely solely on arms to vindicate the right.

Wars have been profitable to the military class and some of the capitalist class. The military class obtain salaries, positions and honors; the capitalist class receive interest on war debts, and profits from making guns and battleships and furnishing supplies. But the great body of a nation does not profit by war. A nation that conquers another by invasion never receives an indemnity equal to the expense of the war, or the conquering nation would have no war debt; and the victorious nations have the largest war debts, while the conquered nations have the smallest war debts. The nations that have the largest armies and make the most conquests have less wealth per capita than the nations which have small armies or none at all. This proves that war is not profitable to nations, and it also proves that in going to war nations do not act from motives of "economic interests," as is claimed by those who try to explain all human phenomena by "economic interests." It is only a few who profit by war; "economic interests" do not control the majority, or there would have been no war.

One of the favorite arguments in this country in defense of

war is that we owe to it the freeing of the slaves. But such is not the case. Thirty years before the war William Lloyd Garrison, Wendell Phillips, and a few co-workers, without money or followers, in 1830 started the abolition movement, which gathered force by years of work until, in 1860, about half the people of the United States were converted to their cause. When abolition was in the air, when it was very apparent that it was to be accomplished by the educational method, that happened which has always happened in great world movements: the military class rushed in and said, We will settle this question with the sword; we will convert the other half of the people, not by arguments, as was the first half, but by force; if any are killed they will not need to be converted. It is reasonable to infer that if the same process that had converted the first half of the nation had been permitted to continue, it would have converted the rest of the people or enough to assure the success of the abolition of slavery without war. The educational work of Garrison, Phillips and others did not cost the nation a dollar, but the war cost thousands of lives and incurred a war debt of millions of dollars, the interest on which our children's children will pay forever.

How is war to be abolished? By going to war? Is bloodshed to be stopped by the shedding of blood? No; the way to stop war is to stop going to war; stop supporting it and it will fall, just as slavery did, just as the Inquisition did. The end of war is in sight; there will be no more world wars. The laboring-man, who has always done the fighting, is losing his patriotism; he is beginning to realize that he has no country or much of anything else to fight for, and is beginning to decline the honor of being killed for the glory and profits of the few. And those who profit by war, those who own the country, will not fight for it; that is, they are not patriotic if it is necessary for them to do the killing or to be killed in war. In all the wars of history there are very few instances of the rich meeting their death on the battlefield.

Soon there will be no poor so foolish as to go to war; not because it has become unprofitable, for it has never been profitable; but because social consciousness has been developed by the teachings of the great Libertarians, who have always stood for peace. Liberty leads to peace, while authority necessarily leads to war. Lovers of liberty are willing to compare the lives of those who stood for liberty with those who have stood for authority, of those who have tried to save with those who have tried to destroy.

Industrial vs. Militant Type.—Those who would rather fight than work are of the Militant type; those who would rather work than fight are of the Industrial type, and now outnumber the former more than a hundred to one. Savagery and barbarism developed the Militant type; civilization introduced the Industrial type. Herbert Spencer has traced the origin, development, functions and decline of the Militant type; he has described the origin, development and functions of the Industrial type, and the evidences of its ultimate supremacy. There was a time when most men were warriors; but as industry developed, fewer and fewer went to war, until only a small minority did so, and governments were forced to draft men to serve; and of late years governments have to instill ideas of war into the plastic minds of school children in order to keep alive the dying embers of militancy. The United States government spends millions of dollars yearly in luring,—by means of advertisements in newspapers, on billboards and moving pictures,—young men to enlist in sufficient numbers to keep its standing army fully recruited.

The distinguishing characteristic of the militant class is parasitism: the power and ability to destroy, to wage war and levy tribute, to impose arbitrary restrictions and collect taxes, to take and to consume; in short, to govern.

For countless ages the industrial class has been oppressed and despoiled by the militant class, but now it is coming into its own, and holds the future of the race in its hands. The industrial class possesses one power that is distinctively and exclusively its own: it is an economic power: the industrial class produces all, builds all, exchanges all. The realization of its irresistible power and the knowledge of how to use it will bring its emancipation.

When the workingman realizes that war does not benefit him, but robs him, the militant class will not be able to hire him or force him to go to war; and if the industrial class refuses to use its economic power for the benefit of the militant parasites, one of these classes must disappear—and it will not be the industrial! Only so long as the militant class can induce the industrial class to support it will it survive. When the worker learns that he belongs to the industrial class and not to the militant class, that his power is economic and not military, the economic problem will be solved.

The laboring-men who still prattle of revolution, meaning by that term warfare, and those labor "leaders" who imagine they can gain something for their cause by violence, are half a century behind the times. Can they not see that violence is the game of their oppressors? and do they hope to beat them at their own game? They might be able to throw a few dynamite bombs by hand, but the war-machines of the soldiers can throw them at the rate of twenty per second. The industrial class cannot compete with the military class in the art of war; if it could, it would cease to be industrial and become militant.

Individuals may do this, but the race has passed that period of its development. The man who thinks the industrial class can progress by any other then industrial methods does not understand economic forces; he is in the wrong class; he should join the army; he is betraying the laboring class when he advocates militant measures. In this country not one workingman in a hundred can handle a gun as well as a soldier can, and yet some labor leaders insist on war talk and the singing of war songs like the "Marseillaise" and "The Red Flag."

Flags.—A flag is an emblem of warfare; when unfurled, it is a challenge to combat. Are the laboring-men able and willing to defend a war emblem on the battlefield? If so, then they are of the Militant type and not of the Industrial type. But the fact is they cannot successfully defend their flag in battle. They must cure themselves of this war disease, and learn to use their industrial power instead. The economic or industrial power is sufficient if intelligently used. It is industrial freedom that the laboring man needs, not military despotism, and industrial freedom must come from industrial action and not from military action.

The Mexican Revolution is an attempt by many of the dispossessed to regain the lands taken from them by their government and given or sold cheaply to big corporations. Their cause is just, but their method of war is the worst that could be chosen, for if it succeeds it will only convert an agricultural class into a military class, without any gain to the workingman. Just follow the history of these military movements. Porfirio Diaz by military power overthrew the ruler before him, and continued his reign by this power; then Francisco Madero overthrew Diaz by military power, and the laboringman was as bad off as before; then Madero was overthrown by Felix Diaz by military power; and thus the game would go on forever if the deluded laboring-man would continue to furnish the wealth and lives necessary to play it.

On the other hand, a few wise laboring-men in Mexico have used the industrial or economic method, and if anything is gained in this revolution, it will be due to this small peaceable minority. They have taken possession of land, and refused to pay rent for it. This is the passive method, so effective in the hands of intelligent men. It is the opposite of the military method, which is active. The passive method is suitable to the Industrial type, but is fatal to the Militant type; the difference in method arises from the difference in type. The military class can take, but cannot give; it can consume, but it cannot produce; it can destroy, but it cannot build; it can kill, but it cannot create. The industrial class possesses the economic power to produce, to create, to build. The laboring-man must realize that his only power is industrial, and rely on it to win his cause.

War will cease, and this will be due to intellectual development and the acceptance of the principle of liberty, which leads to justice. The humane spirit is at last coming uppermost, and the men who have brought this about are the great educators of the race—the great Libertarians whose arguments constitute this book, and whose names will live as long as men love liberty.

Laconics of Liberty

Force is no remedy.—*John Bright.*

Freedom is a new religion, the religion of our time.—*Heine.*

Force and fraud are in war the two cardinal virtues.—*Hobbes.*

It is difficult to free fools from the chains they revere.—*Voltaire.*

When the state is corrupt then the laws are most multiplied.—*Tacitus.*

Law grinds the poor, and the rich men rule the law.—*Oliver Goldsmith.*

The free man is as courageous in timely retreat as in combat.—*Spinoza.*

Desire nothing for yourself which you do not desire for others.—*Spinoza.*

Liberty is rendered even more precious by the recollection of servitude.—*Cicero.*

I wish men to be free, as much from mobs as kings,—from you as me.—*Byron.*

Freedom degenerates unless it has to struggle in its own defence.—*Lord Acton.*

The liberty of the individual is a necessary postulate of human progress.—*Ernest Renan.*

We have all of us sufficient fortitude to bear the misfortunes of others.—*Rochefoucauld.*

Men in earnest have no time to waste in patching fig leaves for the naked truth.—*Lowell.*

The concealment of truth is the only indecorum known to science.—*Edward Westermarck.*

Liberty of thought is a mockery if liberty of speech and action is denied.—*Rev. Sidney Holmes.*

Liberty is not a means to a higher political end. It is itself the highest political end.—*Lord Acton.*

Where slavery is there liberty cannot be, and where liberty is there slavery cannot be.—*Charles Sumner.*

God grants liberty only to those who live it, and are always ready to guard and defend it.—*Daniel Webster.*

Man has a right to think all things, speak all things, write all things, but not to impose his opinions.—*Machiavelli.*

If you would achieve undying fame, attach yourself to the most unpopular righteous cause.—*George William Curtis.*

Society can overlook murder, adultery or swindling; it never forgives the preaching of a new gospel.—*Frederick Harrison.*

I don't believe in capital punishment, Hinnissy, but 'twill never be abolished while th' people injie it so much.—*Mr. Dooley.*

There is one thing in the world more wicked than the desire to command, and that is the will to obey.—*William Kingdon Clifford.*

All our liberties are due to men who, when their conscience has compelled them, have broken the laws of the land.—*Dr. Clifford.*

They that can give up essential liberty to obtain a little temporary safety deserve neither liberty nor safety.—*Benjamin Franklin.*

It will be found an unjust and unwise jealousy to deprive a man of his natural liberty upon a supposition he may abuse it. —*Cromwell.*

It is doubtful whether any tyranny can be worse than that exercised in the name of the sovereignty of the people.—*George L. Scherger.*

It is not the disease, but the physician; it is the pernicious hand of government alone which can reduce a whole people to despair.—*Junius.*

Rayformers, Hinnissy, is in favor iv suppressin' iverything, but rale pollyticians believes in suppressin' nawthin' but ividence.—*Mr. Dooley.*

Every citizen may freely speak, write or print on any subject, being responsible for the abuse of that liberty.—*Constitution of Pennsylvania.*

Liberty which is the nurse of all great wits. . . . Give me the liberty to know, to utter, and to argue freely according to conscience, above all liberties.—*Milton.*

An ambassador is a man who goes abroad to lie for the good of his country. A journalist is a man who stays at home to pursue the same vocation.—*Dr. S. Johnson.*

To argue against any breach of liberty from the ill use that may be made of it, is to argue against liberty itself, since all is capable of being abused.—*Lord Lyttleton.*

I'll niver go down again to see sojers off to th' war. But ye'll see me at th' depot with a brass band whin th' men that causes wars starts f'r th' scene iv carnage.—*Mr. Dooley.*

Did the mass of men know the actual selfishness and injustice of their rulers, not a government would stand a year; the world would ferment with Revolution.—*Theodore Parker.*

It takes great strength to live where you belong
When other people think that you are wrong.
—*Charlotte Perkins Gilman.*

All of our greatness was born of liberty, even our commercialism was rocked in the cradle of democracy, and we cannot strangle the mother without destroying her children.—*Altgeld*.

We crave for the good opinion of the world, in which we don't believe, and tremble in face of its condemnation, which we despise and condemn in our hearts.—*Hermann Sudermann*.

A temporal government in the hands of ecclesiastics develops into a mild, petty, listless, respectable, monkish, invincible despotism just as any plant develops into its flower.—*Taine*.

Is life so dear, or peace so sweet, as to be purchased at the price of chains and slavery? I know not what course others may take, but as for me. give me liberty or give me death!—*Patrick Henry*.

All truth is safe, and nothing else is safe; and he who keeps back the truth or withholds it from men, from motives of expediency, is either a coward, or a criminal, or both.—*Max Muller*.

Everywhere the strong have made the laws and oppressed the weak; and, if they have sometimes consulted the interests of society, they have always forgotten those of humanity. —*Turgot*.

The persecuting spirit has its origin morally in the disposition of man to domineer over his fellow creatures; intellectually, in the assumption that one's own opinions are infallibly correct.—*John Fiske*.

The freest government cannot long endure when the tendency of the law is to create a rapid accumulation of property in the hands of a few, and to render the masses poor and dependent.—*Daniel Webster*.

The fancy that war is necessary to maintain the ideals of manly courage is as mistaken as is the notion that the system of the duel was required to uphold the sense of personal honor. —*Nathaniel Southgate Shaler*.

Every citizen may freely speak, write and publish his sentiments on all subjects, being responsible for the abuse of that liberty. No law shall ever be passed to curtail or restrain the liberty of speech or of the press.—*Constitution of Connecticut.*

The good of mankind is a dream if it is not to be secured by preserving for all men the possible maximum of liberty of action and of freedom of thought.—*John M. Robertson.*

> For always in thine eyes, O Liberty!
> Shines that high light whereby the world is saved;
> And, though thou slay us, we will trust in thee.
> —*John Hay.*

'Tis a good thing preachers don't go to Congress. Whin they're ca'm they'd wipe out all th' laws, an' whin they're excited, they'd wipe out all th' popylation. They're niver two jumps fr'm th' thumbscrew.—*Mr. Dooley.*

> To this thought I cling, with virtue rife,
> Wisdom's last fruit profoundly true.
> Freedom alone he earns as well as life,
> Who day by day must conquer them anew.—*Goethe.*

Everyone may seek his own happiness in the way that seems good to himself, provided that he infringe not such freedom of others to strive after a similar end as is consistent with the freedom of all according to a possible general law.—*Kant.*

Although I am not such a fanatic for the liberty of the subject as to plead that interfering with the way in which a man may choose to be killed is a violation of that liberty, yet I do think that it is far better to let everybody do as he likes.—*Huxley.*

To mind your own business and do the square thing with your neighbors is an extremely high order of patriotism. If every man were to do this, flags, governments, powers, dominations and thrones might all take an indefinite vacation.—*Puck.*

And this is Liberty—that one grow after the law of his own life, hindering not another; and this is Opportunity; and the fruit thereof is Variation; and from the glad growing and the fruit-feasting comes Sympathy, which is appreciative and helpful good-fellowship.—*J. Wm. Lloyd.*

He's true to God who's true to man; where ever wrong is done,
To the humblest and the weakest, 'neath the all-beholding sun,
That wrong is also done to us, and they are slaves most base,
Whose love of right is for themselves and not for all the race.
—*Lowell.*

Let us all seek truth as if none of us had possession of it. The opinions which to this day have governed the earth, produced by chance, disseminated in obscurity, admitted without discussion, credited from a love of novelty and imitation, have in a manner clandestinely usurped their empire.—*Volney.*

There is tonic in the things that men do not love to hear; and there is damnation in the things that wicked men love to hear. Free speech is to a great people what winds are to oceans and malarial regions, which waft away the elements of disease, and bring new elements of health; and where free speech is stopped miasma is bred, and death comes fast.—*Henry Ward Beecher.*

In Russia, whenever they catch a man, woman, or child that has got any brains or education or character, they ship that person straight to Siberia. It is admirable, it is wonderful. It is so searching and so effective that it keeps the general level of Russian intellect and education down to that of the czar. —*Mark Twain.*

The great truth has finally gone forth to all the ends of the earth that man shall no more render account to man for his belief, over which he has himself no control. Henceforward nothing shall prevail upon us to praise or to blame any one for that which he can no more change than he can the hue of his skin or the height of his stature.—*Lord Brougham.*

In those days there was no king in Israel, but every man did that which was right in his own eyes.

And as ye would that men should do to you, do ye also to them likewise. If the truth shall make you free, ye shall be freed indeed. He that knoweth to do good and doeth it not, to him it is sin.—*Bible.*

The constitution of man is such that for a long time after he has discovered the incorrectness of the ideas prevailing around him, he shrinks from openly emancipating himself from their domination; and constrained by the force of circumstances, he becomes a hypocrite, publicly applauding what his private judgment condemns.—*Dr. J. W. Draper.*

The whole progress of society consists in learning how to attain, by the independent action or voluntary association of individuals, those objects which are at first attempted only through the agency of government, and in lessening the sphere of legislation and enlarging that of the individual reason and conscience.—*Samuel J. Tilden.*

> Open thine eyes to see,
> Slave, and thy feet are free.
> Thy bonds, and thy beliefs are one in kind,
> And of thy fears thine irons wrought.
> Hang weights about thee fashioned out of thine own thought.—*Swinburne.*

Of what use is freedom of thought, if it will not produce freedom of action, which is the sole end, how remote soever in appearance, of all objections against Christianity? And therefore the free thinkers consider it an edifice where all the parts have such a mutual dependence on each other, that, if you pull out one single nail, the whole fabric must fall to the ground.—*Swift.*

The modern reformist, Philosophy, which annihilates the individual by way of aiding the mass, and the late reformist, Legislation, which prohibits pleasure with the view of advancing happiness, seem to be chips of that old block of a French feudal law which, to prevent young partridges from being disturbed, imposed penalties upon hoeing and weeding.—*Edgar Allen Poe.*

The law of nature, being co-eval with mankind, and dictated by God himself, is superior in obligation to every other. It is binding all over the globe, in all countries, and at all times; no human laws are of any validity if contrary to this, and such of them as are valid derive their force and all their authority, mediately or immediately, from the original.—*Blackstone.*

> O sorrowing hearts of slaves,
> We heard you beat from far!
> We bring the light that saves,
> We bring the morning star;
> Freedom's good things we bring you,
> Whence all good things are.
> —*Algernon Charles Swinburne.*

In the twentieth century war will be dead, the scaffold will be dead, royalty will be dead, and dogmas will be dead; but man will live. For all, there will be but one country—that country the whole earth; for all, there will be but one hope—that hope the whole heaven. All hail, then, to that noble twentieth century, which shall own our children, and which our children shall inherit.—*Victor Hugo.*

Over against Nature stands the Man, and deep in his heart is the passion for liberty. For the passion for liberty is only another name for life itself. Liberty is a word of much sophistication, but it means, when it means anything, opportunity to live one's own life in one's own way. . . . The original sin of the world is not contempt for arbitrary laws, but respect for them. . . . —*Rev. Charles Ferguson.*

Without free speech no search for truth is possible; without free speech no discovery of truth is useful; without free speech progress is checked and the nations no longer march forward toward the nobler life which the future holds for man. Better a thousand fold abuse of free speech than denial of free speech.

The abuse dies in a day, but the denial slays the life of the people and entombs the hope of the race.—*Charles Bradlaugh.*

Bigotry has no head and cannot think, no heart and cannot feel. When she moves it is in wrath; when she pauses it is amid ruin. Her prayers are curses, her God is a demon, her communion is death, her vengeance is eternity, her decalogue written in the blood of her victims, and if she stops for a moment in her infernal flight it is upon a kindred rock to whet her vulture fang for a more sanguinary desolation.—*Daniel O'Connell.*

> The man of virtuous soul commands not, nor obeys.
> Power, like a desolating pestilence,
> Pollutes whate'er it touches;
> .... and obedience,
> Bane of all genius, virtue, freedom, truth,
> Makes slaves of men, and, of the human frame,
> A mechanized automaton.—*Shelley.*

Self-love is a necessary, indestructible, universal law and principle, inseparable from every kind of love. Religion must and does confirm this on every page of her history. Wherever man tries to resist that human egoism, whether in religion, philosophy, or politics, he sinks into pure nonsense and insanity; for the sense which forms the egoism of all human instincts, desires and actions, is the satisfaction of the human being, the satisfaction of human egoism.—*Feuerbach.*

I say discuss all and expose all–I am for every topic openly;
I say there can be no safety for these States without innovators—without free tongues, and ears willing to hear the tongues;
And I announce as a glory of these States, that they respectfully listen to propositions, reforms, fresh views and doctrines, from successions of men and women.
Each age with its own growth!—*Walt Whitman.*

Of all the miserable, unprofitable, inglorious wars in the

world is the war against words. Let men say just what they like. Let them propose to cut every throat and burn every house—if so they like it. We have nothing to do with a man's words or a man's thoughts, except to put against them better words and better thoughts, and so to win in the great moral and intellectual duel that is always going on, and on which all progress depends.—*Auberon Herbert.*

And this freedom will be the freedom of all. It will loosen both master and slave from the chain. For, by a divine paradox, wherever there is one slave there are two. So in the wonderful reciprocities of being, we can never reach the higher levels until all our fellows ascend with us. There is no true liberty for the individual except as he finds it in the liberty of all. There is no true security for the individual except as he finds it in the security of all.—*Edwin Markham.*

It is the greatest of all inconsistencies to wish to be other than we are.

The more a man has in himself, the less he will want from other people—the less, indeed, other people can be to him. This is why a high degree of intellect tends to make a man unsocial.

A man can be himself only so long as he is alone; and, if he does not love solitude, he will not love freedom; for it is only when he is alone that he is really free.—*Schopenhauer.*

Would to God that this hot and bloody struggle was over, and that peace may come at last to the world! And yet I invoke no seeming peace that the weaker may ever anon be plundered, but a peace with liberty, equality, and honest man's and not robber's order for its condition. . . . Let others give aid and comfort to despots. Be it ours to stand for liberty and justice, nor fear to lock arms with those who are called hot-heads and demagogues, when the good cause requires.
—*Chas. A. Dana.*

> They are slaves who fear to speak
> For the fallen and the weak;
> They are slaves who will not choose
> Hatred, scoffing, and abuse
> Rather than in silence shrink
> From the truth they needs must think;
> They are slaves who dare not be
> In the right with two or three.—*Lowell*.

If governments are to accept the principle that the only limits to the enforcement of the moral standard of the majority are the narrow expediencies of each special case, without reference to any deep and comprehensive principle covering all the largest considerations, why, then, the society to which we ought to look with most admiration and envy is the Eastern Empire during the ninth and tenth centuries, when the Byzantine system of a thorough subordination of the spiritual power had fully consolidated itself.—*John Morley*.

> Power usurped
> Is weakness when opposed; conscious of wrong
> 'Tis pusillanimous and prone to flight.
> But slaves that once conceive the glowing thought
> Of freedom, in that hope itself possess
> All that the contest calls for—spirit, strength.
> The scorn of danger and united hearts,
> The surest presage of the good they seek.—*Cowper*.

There was once a discussion between Mr. Pitt and some of his friends on what were the qualities most needed in politics. Was it knowledge, patience, courage, eloquence, or what was it? Mr. Pitt said, "Patience." We liberals have tried patience for twenty years. I vote we now try "courage." I say again, don't let us be afraid of our own shadows. We have principles we believe in, we have faith, we have great traditions, and we have a great cause behind us and before us. Let us not lose courage and straightforwardness.—*John Morley*.

> What greater life, what grander claim,
>   Than that which bids you to be just?
> What brighter halo, fairer fame,
>   Than shines above the sacred dust
> Of him who, formed of finer clay,
>   Stood firm, a hero of revolt
> Against the weakness of his day,
>   The traitor's trick, the pander's fault?—*Gordak.*

The enlargement of freedom has always been due to heretics who have been unrequited during their day and defamed when dead. No (other) publisher in any country ever incurred so much peril to free the press as Richard Carlile. Every British bookseller has profited by his intrepedity and endurance. Speculations of philosophy and science, which are now part of the common intelligence, power and profit, would have been stifled to this day but for him.—*George Jacob Holyoake.*

> Fear not the tyrants shall rule forever,
> Or the priests of the evil faith;
> They stand on the brink of that mighty river
> Whose waves they have tainted with death;
> It is fed from the depths of a thousand dells,
> Around them it foams and rages and swells,
> And their swords and their scepters I floating see,
> Like wrecks on the surge of eternity.—*Shelley.*

The idea of governing by force another man, who I believe to be my equal in the sight of God, is repugnant to me. I do not want to do it. I do not want any one to govern me by any kind of force. I am a reasoning being, and I only need to be shown what is best for me, when I will take that course or do that thing simply because it is best, and so will you. I do not believe that a soul was ever forced toward anything except toward ruin.

Liberty for the few is not liberty. Liberty for me and slavery for you means slavery for both.—*Samuel M. Jones.*

Wherever bibliolatry has prevailed, bigotry and cruelty have accompanied it. It lies at the root of the deep-seated, sometimes disguised, but never absent, antagonism of all the varieties of ecclesiasticism to the freedom of thought and to the spirit of scientific investigation. To those who look upon ignorance as one of the chief sources of evil, and hold veracity, not merely in act, but in thought, to be the one condition of true progress, whether moral or intellectual, it is clear that the biblical idol must go the way of all other idols, of infallibility in all shapes, lay or clerical.—*Thomas Henry Huxley.*

> Yet let us ponder boldly—'tis a base
>   Abandonment of reason to resign
> Our right of thought—our last and only place
>   Of refuge; this, at least, shall still be mine:
> Though from our birth the faculty divine
>   Is chain'd and tortured—cabin'd, cribb'd, confined,
> And bred in darkness, lest the truth should shine
>   Too brightly on the unprepared mind,
> The beam pours in, for time and skill will couch the
>   blind.—*Byron.*

Do nothing to others which you would not have them do to you. Now I cannot see how, on this principle, one man is authorized to say to another, Believe what I believe, and what you cannot, or you shall be put to death. And yet this is said in direct terms in Portugal, Spain, and at Goa. In some other countries, indeed, they now content themselves with saying only, Believe as I do, or I shall hate you, and will do you all the mischief in my power. What an impious monster thou art! Not to be of my religion is to be of none. You ought to be held in abhorrence by your neighbors, your countrymen, and by all mankind.—*Voltaire.*

No revolution ever rises above the intellectual level of those who make it, and little is gained where one false notion supplants another. But we must some day, at last and forever, cross the line between nonsense and common sense. And on that day we shall pass from class paternalism, originally derived from the fetich fiction in times of universal ignorance, to human brotherhood in accordance with the nature of things and our growing knowledge of it; from political government to industrial administration; from competition in individualism to individuality in co-operation; from war and despotism in any form to peace and liberty.—*Carlyle.*

The State makes use of the money which it extorts from me to unjustly impose fresh constraints upon me; this is the case when it prescribes for me its theology or its philosophy, when it prescribes for me or denies me a special form of religious observance, when it pretends to regulate my morals and my manners, to limit my labor or my expenditure, to fix the price of my merchandise or the rate of my wages. With the coin which I do not owe it and which it steals from me it defrays the expense of the persecution which it inflicts upon me. Let us beware of the encroachments of the State, and suffer it to be nothing more than a watch-dog.—*Taine.*

Now for the promised test, by which, when applied to a man, it may be seen whether the government he means to give his support to is of the one sort or of the other. Put him to this question: Will you, sir, or will you not, concur in putting matters on such a footing, in respect to the liberty of the press, and the liberty of public discussion, that, at the hands of the persons exercising the powers of government, a man shall have no more fear from speaking and writing against them, than from speaking and writing for them? If his answer be yes, the government he declares in favor of, is an undespotic one; if his answer be no, the government he declares in favor of, is a despotic one.—*Jeremy Bentham.*

Ideas are always liveliest when attempts are made to suppress them. The very worst way to suppress an idea is to attempt to suppress it. For, if an idea is true, you can't suppress it, and if it is false it does not need to be suppressed—it will suppress itself. If we all agreed finally and for good, talking would be nonsense. But because we disagree talking is the part of wisdom. The wise men who made the Constitution of the State of Pennsylvania knew this. So they advocated free speech. The men who today in Philadelphia make the administration of the laws foolish don't know it. So they advocate a despotism.—*Horace Traubel.*

Liberty of thought and speech have, after a prolonged struggle, been conceded, although there may be found people who, on their own pet failings, even yet refuse to allow the right unreservedly. Liberty of speech is justified on three grounds: First, if the opinion be true, the world reaps a benefit to be derived from the truth; secondly, if the opinion be false, truth is the more strengthened by contest with it, and lastly, if it be partly true and partly false, our opinions, if they do not entirely lose their weakness, at any rate gain the corrections which have greatly improved them. The commencement of the struggle was due to religion, and the man who brought the long fight to a close and finally settled that matter was Charles Bradlaugh.—*J. P. Poole.*

There are no specious pretexts with which hypocrisy and tyranny have not colored their desire of imposing silence on men of discernment; and there is no virtuous citizen that can see in the pretexts any legitimate reason for their remaining silent. . . .

To limit the press is to insult the nation; to prohibit the reading of certain books is to declare the inhabitants to be either fools or slaves.

Should we to destroy error compel it to silence? No. How then? Let it talk on. Error, obscure of itself, is rejected by every sound understanding. If time have not given it credit, and it be not favored by government, it cannot bear the eye of examination. Reason will ultimately direct wherever it be freely exercised.—*Helvetius*.

I care not for the truth or error of the opinions held or uttered, nor for the wisdom of the words or time of their attempted expression, when I consider this great question of fundamental significance, this great fight which must first be secure before free society can be said to stand on any foundation, but only on temporary or capricious props.

Rich or poor, white or black, great or small, wise or foolish, in season or out of season, in the right or in the wrong, whosoever will speak, let him speak, and whosoever will hear, let him hear. And let no one pretend to the prerogative of judging another man's liberty. In this respect there is, and there can be, no superiority of persons or privileges, nor the slightest pretext for any.—*J. A. Andrews, Governor of Massachusetts.*

> We will speak out, we will be heard,
>   Though all earth's systems crack;
> We will not bate a single word,
>   Nor take a letter back.
> Let liars fear, let cowards shrink,
>   Let traitors turn away;
> Whatever we have dared to think
>   That dare we also say.
> We speak the truth, and what care we
>   For hissing and for scorn,
> While some faint gleamings we can see
>   Of Freedom's coming morn.—*James R. Lowell.*

It is apprehended that arbitrary power would steal in upon us, were we not careful to prevent its progress, and were there not an easy method of conveying the alarm from one end of the kingdom to another. The spirit of the people must frequently be roused, in order to curb the ambition of the court, and the dread of rousing this spirit must be employed to pre-

vent that ambition. Nothing is so effectual to this
purpose as the liberty of the press, by which all the learning,
wit, and the genius of the nation may be employed on the side
of freedom, and every one be animated to its defense. As
long, therefore, as the republican part of our government can
maintain itself against the monarchical, it will naturally be
careful to keep the press open, as of importance to its own
preservation.—*Hume.*

Once to every man and nation comes the moment to decide,
In the strife of truth with Falsehood, for the good or evil side;
Some great cause, God's new Messiah, offering each the bloom
  or blight,
Parts the goats upon the left hand, and the sheep upon the right,
And the choice goes by forever 'twixt that darkness and that
  light.

New occasions teach new duties; Time makes ancient good
  uncouth;
They must upward still, and onward, who keep abreast of Truth;
Lo, before us gleam her camp-fires! we ourselves must Pilgrims be,
Launch our Mayflower and steer boldly through the desperate
  winter sea,
Nor attempt the Future's portal with the Past's blood-rusted
  key.—*James Russell Lowell.*

When for the free human beings of the future it will no
longer be the purpose of life to obtain the means of subsistence,
but, as a result of a new belief, or rather knowledge, they will
be certain of obtaining the means of subsistence in return for
an appropriate natural activity, when in short, industry will
no longer be our mistress, but our servant, the true purpose
of life will become the enjoyment of life, and by education we
will endeavor to make our children capable of its real enjoyment. An education, founded on the exercise of strength and

the care of physical beauty, will, owing to the love for the child and the joy at the development of its beauty, become a purely artistic one, and every human being will in some way be a true artist. The diversity of natural inclinations will develop the most manifold tendencies in an unthought-of wealth.
—*Richard Wagner.*

"Educate women like men," says Rousseau, "and the more they resemble our sex the less power will they have over us." This is the very point I aim at. I do not wish them to have power over men, but over themselves. It is not empire, but equality and friendship, which women want. Speaking of women at large, their first duty is to themselves as rational creatures, and the next, in point of importance, as citizens.

Men submit everywhere to oppression, when they have only to lift their heads to throw off the yoke; yet, instead of asserting their birthright, they quietly lick the lust and say, Let us eat and drink, for tomorrow we die. Women, I argue from analogy, are degraded by the same propensity to enjoy the present moment; and, at last, despise the freedom which they have not sufficient virtue to struggle to attain.—*Mary Wollstonecraft.*

I think the religious tests were invented not so much to secure religion as the emoluments of it. When a religion is good, I conceive that it will support itself; and when it does not support itself, and God does not take care to support it, so that its professors are obliged to call for help of the civil power, 'tis a sign, I apprehend, of its being a bad one.

If we look back into history for the character of the present sects in Christianity, we shall find few that have not in their turns been persecutors, and complainers of persecution. The primitive Christians thought persecution extremely wrong in the Pagans, but practiced it on one another. The first Protestants of the Church of England blamed persecution in the Romish church, but practiced it upon the Puritans. These found it wrong in the Bishops, but fell into the same practice themselves both here (England) and in New England.—*Benjamin Franklin.*

Every new truth which has ever been propounded has, for a time, caused mischief; it has produced discomfort, and often unhappiness; sometimes by disturbing social or religious arrangements, and sometimes merely by the disruption of old and cherished association of thoughts. It is only after a certain interval, and when the frame-work of affairs has adjusted itself to the new truth, that its good effects preponderate; and the preponderance continues to increase, until, at length, the truth causes nothing but good. But, at the outset there is always harm. And if the truth is very great as well as very new the harm is serious. Men are made uneasy; they flinch; they cannot bear the sudden light; a general restlessness supervenes; the face of society is disturbed, or perhaps convulsed; old interests and old beliefs have been destroyed before new ones have been created. These symptoms are the precursors of revolution; they have preceded all the great changes through which the world has passed.—*Buckle's " History of Civilization."*

We do not mean merely freedom from restraint or compulsion. We do not mean merely freedom to do as we like, irrespectively of what it is that we like. We do not mean a freedom that can be enjoyed by one man or one set of men at the cost of a loss of freedom to others. When we speak of freedom as something to be highly prized, we mean a positive power or capacity of doing or enjoying something worth doing or enjoying, and that, too, something that we do or enjoy in common with others. We mean by it a power which each man exercises through the help or security given him by his fellowmen, and which he in turn helps to secure for them. When we measure the progress of a society by the growth in freedom, we measure it by the increasing development and exercise on the whole of those powers of contributing to social good with which we believe the members of the society to be endowed; in short, by the greater power on the part of the citizens as a body to make the most and best of themselves.—*Prof. T. H. Green.*

There is only one cure for evils which newly-acquired freedom produces, and that cure is freedom. When a prisoner first leaves his cell, he cannot bear the light of day, he is unable to discriminate colors, or recognize faces. The remedy is, to accustom him to the rays of the sun.

The blaze of truth and liberty may at first dazzle and bewilder nations which have become half blind in the house of bondage. But let them gaze on, and they will soon be able to bear it. In a few years men learn to reason. The extreme violence of opinions subsides. Hostile theories correct each other. The scattered elements of truth cease to contend, and begin to coalesce. And, at length, a system of justice and order is educed out of the chaos.

Many politicians of our time are in the habit of laying it down as a self-evident proposition, that no people ought to be free till they are fit to use their freedom. The maxim is worthy of the fool in the old story, who resolved not to go into the water till he had learned to swim. If men are to wait for liberty till they become wise and good in slavery, they may indeed wait forever.—*Macauley.*

Indeed, no opinion or doctrine, of whatever nature it be, or whatever be its tendency, ought to be suppressed. For it is either manifestly true, or it is manifestly false, or its truth or falsehood is dubious. Its tendency is manifestly good, or manifestly bad, or it is dubious and concealed. There are no other assignable conditions, no other functions of the problem.

In the case of its being manifestly true, and of good tendency; there can be no dispute. Nor in the case of its being manifestly otherwise; for by the terms it can mislead nobody. If its truth or its tendency be dubious, it is clear that nothing can bring the good to light, or expose the evil, but full and free discussion. Until this takes place, a plausible fallacy may do harm; but discussion is sure to elicit the truth, and fix public opinion on a proper basis; and nothing else can do it.

Criminality can only be predicated where there is an obstinate, unreasonable refusal to consider any kind of evidence but what exclusively supports one side of a question.

It follows that errors of the understanding must be treated by appeals to the understanding. That argument should be opposed by argument, and fact by fact. That fine and imprisonment are bad forms of syllogism, well calculated to irritate, but powerless for refutation. They may suppress truth, they can never elicit it.—*Thomas Cooper*.

If I could have entertained the slightest apprehension that the Constitution framed in the Convention when I had the honor to preside, might possibly endanger the religious rights of any ecclesiastical society, certainly I would never have placed my signature to it; and if I could now conceive that the general government might be so administered as to render the liberty of conscience insecure, I beg you will be persuaded that no one would be more zealous than myself to establish effectual barriers against the horrors of spiritual tyranny and every specious of religious persecution.

Of all the animosities which have existed among mankind, those which are caused by a difference of sentiments in religion appear to be the most inveterate and distressing, and ought most to be deprecated. I was in hopes that the enlightened and liberal policy, which has marked the present age, would at least have reconciled Christians of every denomination so far that we should never again see their religious disputes carried to such a pitch as to endanger the peace of society.

Government is not reason, it is not eloquence—it is force! Like fire it is a dangerous servant and a fearful master; never for a moment should it be left to irresponsible action.

The government of the United States of America is not, in any sense, founded upon the Christian religion.—*George Washington.*

THE SOLDIER'S CREED
By Ernest Crosby

"Captain, what do you think," I asked,
"Of the part your soldiers play?"
But the captain answered, "I do not think;
I do not think, I obey!"

"Do you think you should shoot a patriot down,
Or help a tyrant slay?"
But the captain answered, "I do not think;
I do not think, I obey!"

"Do you think your conscience was made to die,
 And your brain to rot away?"
But the captain answered, "I do not think;
 I do not think, I obey!"

"Then if this is your soldier's creed," I cried,
 "You're a mean unmanly crew;
And for all your feathers and gilt and braid
 I am more of a man than you!

"For whatever my place in life may be,
 And whether I swim or sink,
I can say with pride, 'I do not obey;
 I do not obey, I think!'"

NO MASTER
By William Morris

Saith man to man, We've heard and known
 That we no master need
To live upon this earth, our own,
 In the fair and manly deed;

The grief of slaves long passed away
    For us hath forged the chain,
Till now each worker's patient day
    Builds up the House of Pain.

And we, shall we too crouch and quail,
    Ashamed, afraid of strife;
And lest our lives untimely fail
    Embrace the death in life?
Nay, cry aloud and have no fear;
    We few against the world;
Awake, arise! the hope we bear
    Against the curse is hurl'd.

It grows, it grows: are we the same,
    The feeble band, the few?
Or what are these with eyes aflame,
    And hands to deal and do?
This is the host that bears the word,
    No Master, High or Low,
A lightning flame, a shearing sword,
    A storm to overthrow.

    Let us all labor to add all needful guarantees for the more perfect security of free thought, free speech, and free press, pure morals, unfettered religious sentiments, and of equal rights and privileges to all men, irrespective of nationality, color, or religion. Encourage free schools, and resolve that not one dollar of money shall be appropriated to the support of any sectarian school. Resolve that neither the state nor nation, or both combined, shall support institutions of learning other than those sufficient to afford every child growing up in the land the opportunity of a good common school education, unmixed with sectarian, pagan, or atheistical tenets. Leave the matter of religion to the family altar, the church, and the private schools, supported entirely by private contributions. Keep the church and the state forever separate.

I would call your attention to the importance of correcting an evil that, if permitted to continue, will probably lead to great trouble in our land before the close of the nineteenth century. It is the acquisition of vast amounts of untaxed church property. In 1850, I believe, the church property of the United States, which paid no tax, municipal or state, amounted to about $83,000,000. In 1860 the amount had doubled. In 1875 it is about $1,000,000,000. By 1900, without check, it is safe to say this property will reach a sum exceeding $3,000,000,000. So vast a sum, receiving all the protection and benefits of government without bearing its proportion of the burdens and expenses of the same, will not be looked upon acquiescently by those who have to pay the taxes. In a growing country, where real estate enhances so rapidly with time as in the United States, there is scarcely a limit to the wealth that may be acquired by corporations, religious or otherwise, if allowed to retain real estate without taxation. The contemplation of so vast a property as here alluded to, without taxation, may lead to sequestration without constitutional authority, and through blood. I would suggest the taxation of all property equally, whether church or corporation.—*U. S. Grant.*

In a word, there is scarcely a disposition that marks the love of abstract truth and scarcely a rule which reason teaches as essential for its attainment, that theologians did not, for centuries, stigmatize as offensive to the Almighty. By destroying every book that could generate discussion, by diffusing through every field of knowledge a spirit of boundless credulity, and, above all, by persecuting with atrocious cruelty those who differed from their opinions, they succeeded for a long period in almost arresting the action of the European mind, and in persuading men that a critical, impartial, and enquiring spirit was the worst form of vice. From this frightful condition Europe was at last rescued by the intellectual influences that produced the Reformation, by the teaching of those great philosophers who clearly laid down the conditions of enquiry, and by those bold innovators who, with the stake of Bruno and Vanini before their eyes, dared to challenge directly the doctrines of the past. By those means the spirit of philosophy or of truth became prominent, and the spirit of dogmatism, with all its consequences, was proportionately weakened. As long as the latter spirit possessed an indisputable ascendency, persecution was ruthless, universal, and unquestioned. When the former spirit became more powerful, the language of anathema grew less peremptory. Exceptions and qualifications were introduced; the full meaning of the words was no longer realized; persecution became languid; it changed its character; it exhibited itself rather in a general tendency than in overt acts; it grew apologetical, timid and evasive. In one age the persecutor burnt the heretic; in another, he crushed him with penal laws; in a third, he withheld from him places of emolument and dignity; in a fourth, he subjected him to the excommunication of society. Each stage of advancing toleration marks a stage of the decline of the spirit of dogmatism and of the increase of the spirit of truth.

On the other hand, men who have been deeply imbued with the spirit of earnest and impartial enquiry, will invariably come to value such a disposition more than any particular doctrines to which it may lead them; they will deny the necessity of correct opinions; they will place the moral far above the dogmatic side of their faith; they will give free scope to every criticism that restricts their belief; and they will value men according to their acts, and not at all according to their opinions. The first of these tendencies is essentially Roman Catholic. The second is essentially rationalistic.—*W. E. H. Lecky.*

The greatest thing in the world is for a man to know that he is his own.

We ought to hold with all our force, both of hands and teeth, the use of the pleasures of life that one after another our years snatch away from us.

To speak less of one's self than what one really is, is folly, not modesty; and to take that for current pay which is under a man's value is pusillanimity and cowardice.

Retire yourself into yourself, but first prepare yourself there to receive yourself; it were folly to trust yourself in your own hands if you cannot govern yourself.

We have lived long enough for others; let us, at least, live out the small remnant of life for ourselves; let us now call in our thoughts and intentions to ourselves.

It is a wretched and dangerous thing to depend upon others; we ourselves, in whom is ever the most just and safest dependence, are not sufficiently sure. I have nothing mine but myself.

It is not enough to get remote from the public; 'tis not enough to shift the soil only; a man must flee from the popular conditions that have taken possession of his soul, he must sequester and come again to himself.

My trade and art is to live; he that forbids me to speak according to my own sense, experience and practice, may as well enjoin an architect not to speak of building according to his own knowledge, but according to that of his neighbor; according to the knowledge of another and not according to his own.

As for the fine saying, with which ambition and avarice palliate their vices, that we are not born for ourselves but for the public, let us boldly appeal to those who are in public affairs; let them lay their hands upon their hearts and then say whether, on the contrary, they do rather aspire to titles and offices and that tumult of the world to make their private advantage at the public expense.

The laws keep up their credit, not by being just, but because they are laws; 'tis the mystic foundation of their authority; they have no other, and it well answers their purpose. They are often made by fools; still oftener by men who, out of hatred to equality, fail in equity; but always by men, vain and irresolute authors. There is nothing so much, nor so grossly, nor so ordinarily faulty, as the laws. Whoever obeys them because they are just, does not justly obey them as he ought.
—*Montaigne.*

I
EDMUND BURKE

Edmund Burke, 1729-1797, orator, statesman, writer. Born in Dublin; was graduated at Trinity College, Dublin; became member of Parliment in 1766. An ardent champion of justice, he delivered his speech on *American Taxation* in 1774 and his speech on *Conciliation with America*, which has become world-famous, in 1775; was paymaster-general and privy councilor, 1782-83; conducted the impeachment of Warren Hastings, 1787-95; resigned from Parliament, 1795. A contemporary of Pitt and Fox. Chief works: *A Vindication of Natural Society*, 1756; *A Philosophical Enquiry into the Origin of Our Ideas of the Sublime and the Beautiful*, 1756; *Thoughts on the Causes of the Present Discontents*, 1770; *Reflections on the Revolution in France*, 1790; and four letters on the subject of "a regicide peace" with France, 1796-97.

This chapter is Burke's essay, *A Vindication of Natural Society*, slightly abridged but giving all of his arguments against authority and in favor of liberty. This essay is little known, as he was compelled by the storm of opposition it met with to withdraw it from publication. The reader will not find it in "Burke's Complete (?) Works."

A Vindication of Natural Society

A man is allowed sufficient freedom of thought, provided he knows how to choose his subject properly. You may criticise freely upon the Chinese constitution, and observe with as much severity as you please upon the absurd tricks or destructive bigotry of the bonzees. But the scene is changed as you come homeward, and atheism or treason may be the names given in Britain to what would be reason and truth if asserted of China.

There is a most absurd and audacious method of reasoning avowed by some bigots and enthusiasts, and, through fear, assented to by some wiser and better men; it is this: They argue against a fair discussion of popular prejudices, because, say they, though they would be found without any reasonable support, yet the discovery might be productive of the most dangerous consequences. Absurd and blasphemous notion! as if all happiness was not connected with the practice of virtue, which necessarily depends upon the knowledge of truth; that is, upon the knowledge of those unalterable relations which Providence has ordained that every thing should bear to every other. These relations, which are truth itself, the foundation of virtue, and, consequently, the only measures of happiness, should be likewise the only measures by which we should direct our reasoning. To these we should conform in good earnest; and not to think to force nature, and the whole order of her system by a compliance with our pride and folly, to conform to our artificial regulations. It is by a conformity to this method we owe the discovery of the few truths we know, and the little liberty and rational happiness we enjoy. We have somewhat fairer play than a reasoner could have expected formerly; and we derive advantages from it which are very visible.

The fabric of superstition has in this our age and nation received much ruder shocks than it had ever felt before; and, through the chinks and breaches of our prison, we see such glimmerings of light, and feel such refreshing airs of liberty, as daily raise our ardor for more. The miseries derived to mankind from superstition under the name of religion, and of ecclesiastical tyranny under the name of church government, have been clearly and usefully exposed. We begin to think and to act from reason and from nature alone. This is true of several, but still is by far the majority in the same old state of blindness and slavery; and much is to be feared that we shall perpetually relapse, whilst the real productive cause of all this superstitious folly, enthusiastical nonsense, and holy tyranny holds a reverend place in the estimation even of those who are otherwise enlightened.

The professors of artificial law have always walked hand in hand with the professors of artificial theology. As their end, in confounding the reason of man and abridging his natural freedom, is exactly the same, they have adjusted the means to that end in a way entirely similar. The divine thunders out his *anathemas,* with more noise and terror against the breach of one of his positive institutions, or the neglect of some of his trivial forms, than against the neglect or breach of those duties and commandments of natural religion which by these forms and institutions he pretends to enforce. The lawyer has his forms, and his positive institutions too, and he adheres to them with a veneration altogether as religious.

But whoever is a genuine follower of Truth keeps his eye steady upon his guide, indifferent whither he is led, provided that she is the leader. And, if it may be properly considered, it were infinitely better to remain possessed by the whole legion of vulgar mistakes than to reject some and at the same time to retain a fondness for others altogether as absurd and irrational.

Many of the greatest tyrants on the records of history have begun their reigns in the fairest manner. *But the truth is, this unnatural power corrupts both the heart and the understanding.* And to prevent the least hope of amendment, a king is ever surrounded by a crowd of infamous flatterers, who find their account in keeping him from the least light of reason, till all ideas of rectitude and justice are utterly erased from his mind.

The first accounts we have of mankind are but so many accounts of their butcheries. All empires have been cemented in blood; and, in those early periods when the races of mankind began first to form themselves into parties and combinations, the first effect of the combination, and indeed the end for which it seems purposely formed, and best calculated, is their mutual destruction. All ancient history is dark and uncertain. One thing, however, is clear. There were conquerors and conquests in those days; and, consequently, all that devastation by which they are formed, and all that oppression by which they are maintained.

How far mere nature would have carried us, we may judge by the example of those animals who still follow her laws, and even of those to whom she has given dispositions more fierce, and arms more terrible, than ever she intended we should use. It is an incontestable truth that there is more havoc made in

Edmund Burke 63

one year by men of men, than has been made by all the lions, tigers, panthers, ounces, leopards, hyenas, rhinoceroses, elephants, bears, and wolves, upon their several species, since the beginning of the world; though these agree ill enough with each other, and have a much greater proportion of rage and fury in their composition than we have. But with respect to you, ye legislators, ye civilizers of mankind! ye Orpheuses, Moseses, Minoses, Solons, Theseuses, Lycurguses, Numas! with respect to you, be it spoken, your regulations have done more mischief in cold blood, than all the rage of the fiercest animals in their greatest terrors, or furies, has ever done, or ever could do!

These evils are not accidental. Whoever will take the pains to consider the nature of society, will find they result directly from its constitution. For as subordination, or in other words, the reciprocation of tyranny and slavery, is requisite to support these societies; the interest, the ambition, the malice, or the revenge—nay, even the whim and caprice of one ruling man among them, is enough to arm all the rest, without any private views of their own, to the worst and blackest purposes; and, what is at once lamentable and ridiculous, these wretches engage under those banners with a fury greater than if they were animated by revenge for their own wrongs.

It is no less worth observing that this artificial division of mankind into separate societies is a perpetual source in itself of hatred and dissension among them. The names which distinguish them are enough to blow up hatred and rage. Examine history; consult present experience; and you will find that far the greater part of the quarrels between several nations had scarce any other occasion than that these nations were different combinations of people, and called by different names; to an Englishman, the name of a Frenchman, a Spaniard, an Italian, much more a Turk, or a Tartar, raises of course ideas of hatred and contempt. If you would inspire this compatriot of ours with pity, or regard, for one of these, would you not hide that distinction? You would not pray him to compassionate the poor Frenchman, or the unhappy German. Far from it; you would speak of him as a foreigner; an accident to which all are liable. You would represent him as a man; one partaking with us of the same common nature, and subject to the same law. There is something so averse from our own nature in these artificial political distinctions that we need no other trumpet to kindle us to war and destruction. But there is something so benign and healing in the general voice of humanity, that, maugre all our regulations to prevent it, the simple name of man, applied properly, never fails to work a salutary effect.

This natural unpremeditated effect of policy on the unpossessed passions of mankind appears on other occasions. The very name of a politician, a statesman, is sure to cause terror and hatred; it has always connected with it the ideas of treachery, cruelty, fraud, and tyranny; and those writers, who have faithfully unveiled the mysteries of state free-masonry, have ever been held in general detestation for even knowing so perfectly a theory so detestable. The case of Machiavelli seems at first sight something hard in that respect. He is obliged to bear the iniquities of those whose maxims and rules of government he published. His speculation is more abhorred than their practice.

But if there were no other arguments against artificial society than this I am going to mention, methinks it ought to fall by this one only. All writers on the science of policy are agreed, and they agree with experience, that all governments must frequently infringe the rules of justice to support themselves; that truth must give way to dissimulation, honesty to convenience, and humanity to the reigning interest. The whole of this mystery of iniquity is called the reason of state. It is a reason which I own I cannot penetrate. What sort of a protection is this of the general right, that is maintained by infringing the rights of particulars? What sort of justice is this, which is enforced by breaches of its own laws? These paradoxes I leave to be solved by the able heads of legislators and politicians. For my part, I say what a plain man would say on such occasion. I can never believe that any institution, agreeable to nature, and proper for mankind, could find it necessary, or even expedient, in any case whatsoever, to do what the best and worthiest instincts of mankind warn us to avoid. But no wonder that what is set up in opposition to the state of nature should preserve itself by trampling upon the law of nature.

To prove that these sorts of policed societies are a violation offered to nature and a constraint upon the human mind, it needs only to look upon the sanguinary measures and instruments of violence which are everywhere used to support them. Let us take a review of the dungeons, whips, chains, racks, gibbets, with which every society is abundantly stored, by which hundreds of victims are annually offered to support a dozen or two in pride and madness, and millions in an abject servitude and dependence. There was a time when I looked with a reverential awe on these mysteries of policy; but age, experience, and philosophy have rent the veil; and I view this *sanctum sanctorum*, at least, without an enthusiastic admiration. I acknowledge, indeed, the necessity of such a proceeding in such institutions; but I must have a very mean opinion of institutions where such proceedings are necessary.

Kings are ambitious; the nobility haughty; and the populace tumultuous and ungovernable. Each party, however in appearance peaceable, carries on a design upon the others; and it is owing to this that in all questions, whether concerning foreign or domestic affairs, the whole generally turns more upon some party-matter than upon the nature of the thing itself; whether such a step will diminish or augment the power of the crown, or how far the privileges of the subject are likely to be extended or restricted by it. And these questions are constantly resolved without any consideration of the merits of the cause, merely as the parties who uphold these jarring interests may chance to prevail; and as they prevail, the balance is overset, now upon one side, now upon the other. The government is, one day, arbitrary power in a single person; another, a juggling confederacy of a few to cheat the prince and enslave the people; and the third, a frantic and unmanageable democracy. The great instrument of all these changes, and what infuses a peculiar venom into all of them, is party; it is of no consequence what the principles of any party, or what their pretensions, are; the spirit which actuates all parties is the same,—the spirit of ambition, of self-interest, of oppression, and treachery. This spirit entirely reverses all the principles which a benevolent nature has erected within us; all honest, all equal justice, and even the ties of natural society, the natural affections.

Parties in religion and politics make sufficient discoveries concerning each other to give a sober man a proper caution against them all. The monarchic and aristocratical and popular partisans have been jointly laying their axes to the root of all government, and have in their turns proved each other absurd and inconvenient. In vain you tell me that artificial government is good, but that I fall out only with the abuse. The thing! the thing itself is the abuse! Observe, that grand error upon which all artificial legislative power is founded. It was observed that men had ungovernable passions, which made it necessary to guard against the violence they might offer to each other. They appointed governors over them for this reason! But a worse and more perplexing difficulty arises, how to be defended against the governors? In vain they change from a single person to a few. These few have the passions of the one; and they unite to strengthen themselves, and to secure the gratifications of their lawless passions at the expense of the general good. In vain do we fly to the many. The case is worse; their passions are less under the government of reason, they are augmented by the contagion, and defended against all attacks by their multitude.

A republic, as an ancient philosopher has observed, is not one species of government, but a magazine of every species; here you find every sort of it, and that in the worst form. As there is a perpetual change, one rising and the other falling, you have all the violent and wicked policy by which a beginning power must always acquire its strength, and all the weakness by which falling states are brought to a complete destruction.

Ask of politicans the ends for which laws were originally designed, and they will answer that the laws were designed as a protection for the poor and weak, against the oppression of the rich and powerful. But surely no pretence can be so ridiculous; a man might as well tell me he has taken off my load, because he has changed the burden. If the poor man is not able to support his suit according to the vexatious and expensive manner established in civilised countries, has not the rich as great an advantage over him as the strong has over the weak in a state of nature? But we will not place the state of nature, which is the reign of God, in competition with political society, which is the absurd usurpation of man. In a state of nature it is true that a man of superior force may beat or rob me; but then it is true that I am at full liberty to defend myself, or make reprisal by surprise, or by cunning, or by any other way in which I may be superior to him. But in political society a rich man may rob me in another way. I cannot defend myself; for money is the only weapon with which we are allowed to fight. And if I attempt to avenge myself, the whole force of that society is ready to complete my ruin.

The most obvious division of society is into rich and poor, and it is no less obvious that the number of the former bear a great disproportion to those of the latter. The whole business of the poor is to administer to the idleness, folly, and luxury of the rich, and that of the rich, in return, is to find the best methods of confirming the slavery and increasing the burdens of the poor. In a state of nature it is an invariable law that a man's acquisitions are in proportion to his labors. In a state of artificial society it is a law as constant and as invariable that those who labor most enjoy the fewest things, and that those who labor not at all have the greatest number of enjoyments. A constitution of things this, strange and ridiculous beyond expression! We scarce believe a thing when we are told it which we actually see before our eyes every day without being in the least surprised. I suppose that there are in Great Britain upwards of an hundred thousand people employed in lead, tin, iron, copper, and coal mines; these unhappy wretches scarce ever see the light of the sun; they are buried in the bowels of the earth; there they work at a severe and dismal task, without the least prospect of being delivered from it; they subsist upon the coarsest and worst sort of fare; they have their health miserably impaired, and their lives cut short, by being perpetually confined in the close vapors of these malignant minerals. An hundred thousand more at least are tortured without remission by the suffocating smoke, intense fires, and constant drudgery necessary in refining and managing the products of those mines. If any man informed us that two hundred thousand innocent persons were condemned to so intolerable slavery, how should we pity the unhappy sufferers, and how great would be our just indignation against those who inflicted so cruel and ignominious a punishment! This is an instance—I could not wish a stronger—of the numberless things which we pass by in their common dress, yet which shock us when they are nakedly represented. But this number, considerable as it is, and the slavery, with all its baseness and horror, which we have at home, is nothing to what the rest of the world affords of the same nature. Millions are daily bathed in the poisonous damps and destructive effluvia of lead, silver, copper, and arsenic; to say nothing of those other employments, those stations of wretchedness and contempt, in which civil society has placed the numerous *enfants perdus* of her army. Would any rational man submit to one of the most tolerable of these drudgeries for all the artificial enjoyments which policy has made to result from them? By no means.

Indeed, the blindness of one part of mankind, co-operating with the frenzy and villainy of the other, has been the real builder of this respectable fabric of political society: and as the blindness of mankind has caused their slavery, in return their state of slavery is made a pretence for continuing them in a state of blindness; for the politician will tell you gravely that their life of servitude disqualifies the greater part of the race of man for a search of truth, and supplies them with no other than mean and insufficient ideas. This is but true; and this is one of the reasons for which I blame such institutions.

In a misery of this sort, admitting some few lenitives, and those too but a few, nine parts in ten of the whole race of mankind drudge through life. It may be urged, perhaps, in palliation of this, that at least the rich few find a considerable and real benefit from the wretchedness of the many. But is this so in fact? Let us examine the point with a little more attention. For this purpose the rich in all societies may be thrown into two classes. The first is of those who are powerful as well as rich, and conduct the operations of the vast political machine. The other is of those who employ their riches wholly in the acquisition of pleasure. As to the first sort, their continual care and anxiety, their toilsome days and sleepless nights, are next to proverbial. These circumstances are sufficient almost to level their condition to that of the unhappy majority; but there are other circumstances which place them in a far lower condition. Not only their understandings labor continually, which is the severest labor; but their hearts are torn by the worst, most troublesome, and insatiable of all passions, by avarice, by ambition, by fear and jealousy. No part of the mind has rest. Power gradually extirpates from the mind every human and gentle virtue. Pity, benevolence, friendship, are things almost unknown in high stations.

Let us now view the other species of the rich, those who devote their time and fortunes to idleness and pleasure. How much happier are they? The pleasures which are agreeable to nature are within the reach of all, and therefore can form no distinction in favor of the rich. The pleasures which art forces up are seldom sincere and never satisfying. What is worse, this constant application to pleasure takes away from the enjoyment, or rather turns it into the nature of a very burdensome and laborious business. It has consequences much more fatal. It produces a weak valetudinary state of body, attended by all those horrid disorders, and yet more horrid methods of cure, which are the results of luxury on one hand and the weak and ridiculous efforts of human art on the other. The pleasures of such men are scarcely felt as pleasures; at the same time they bring on pain and diseases, which are felt but too severely. The mind has its share of the misfortune; it grows lazy and enervate, unwilling and unable to search for truth, and utterly uncapable of knowing, much less of relishing, real happiness. The poor by their excessive labor, and the rich by their enormous luxury, are set upon a level, and rendered equally ignorant of any knowledge which might conduce to their happiness. A dismal view of the interior of all civil society! The lower part broken and ground down by the most cruel oppression; and the rich by their artificial method of life bringing worse evils on themselves than their tyranny could possibly inflict on those below them. Very different is the prospect of the natural state. Here there are no wants which nature gives (and in this state men can be sensible of no other wants) which are not to be supplied by a very moderate degree of labor; therefore there is no slavery. Neither is there any luxury, because no single man can supply the materials of it. Life is simple, therefore it is happy.

The politician will urge in his defense that this unequal state is highly useful. That without dooming some part of mankind to extraordinary toil, the arts which cultivate life could not be exercised. But I demand of this politican, how such arts come to be necessary? He answers that civil society could not well exist without them. So that these arts are necessary to civil society, and civil society necessary again to these arts. Thus are we running in a circle, without modesty and without end, and making one error and extravagance an excuse for the other.

If political society, in whatever form, has still made the many the property of the few; if it has introduced labors unnecessary, vices and diseases unknown, and pleasures incompatible with na⁺ure; if in all countries it abridges the lives of millions, and renders those of millions more utterly abject and miserable; shall we still worship so destructive an idol, and daily sacrifice to it our health, our liberty, and our peace? Or shall we pass by this monstrous heap of absurd notions and abominable practices, thinking we have sufficiently discharged our duty in exposing the trifling cheats and ridiculous juggles of a few mad, designing, or ambitious priests?

We have shown that political society, on a moderate calculation, has been the means of murdering several times the number of inhabitants now upon the earth, during its short existence, not upwards of four thousand years in any accounts to be depended on. But we have said nothing of the other, and perhaps as bad, consequences of these wars, which have spilled such seas of blood and reduced so many millions to a merciless slavery. But these are only the ceremonies performed in the porch of the political temple. Much more horrid ones are seen as you enter it. The several species of governments vie with each other in the absurdity of their constitutions and the oppression which they make their subjects endure. Take them under what form you please, they are in effect but a despotism, and they fall, both in effect and appearance too, after a very short period, into that cruel and detestable species of tyranny; which I rather call it, because we have been educated under another form, than that this is of worse consequences to mankind. For the free governments, for the point of their space, and the moment of their duration, have felt more confusion, and committed more flagrant acts of tryanny, than the most perfect despotic governments which we have ever known. Turn your eye next to the labyrinth of the law, and the iniquity conceived in its intricate recesses. Consider the ravages committed in the bowels of all the commonwealths by ambition, by avarice, envy, fraud, open injustice, and pretended friendship; vices which could draw little support from a state of nature, but which blossom and flourish in the rankness of political society. Revolve our whole discourse; add to it all those reflections which your own understanding shall suggest, and make a strenuous effort beyond the reach of vulgar philosophy to confess that the cause of artificial society is more defenceless even than that of artificial religion; that it is as derogatory from the honor of the Creator, as subversive of human reason, and productive of infinitely more mischief to the human race.

If pretended revelations have caused wars where they were opposed, and slavery where they were received, the pretended wise inventions of politicians have done the same. But the slavery has been much heavier, the wars far more bloody, and both more universal by many degrees. Show me any mischief produced by the madness or wickedness of theologians, and I will show you an hundred resulting from the ambition and villainy of conquerors and statesmen. Show me an absurdity in religion, and I will undertake to show you an hundred for one in political laws and institutions. If you say that natural religion is a sufficient guide without the foreign aid of revelation, on what principle should political laws become necessary? Is not the same reason available in theology and in politics? If the laws of nature are the laws of God, is it consistent with the divine wisdom to prescribe rules to us, and leave the enforcement of them to the folly of human institutions? Will you follow truth but to a certain point?

We are indebted for all our miseries to our distrust of that

guide which Providence thought sufficient for our condition,—
our own natural reason, which rejecting, both in human and
Divine things, we have given our necks to the yoke of political
and theological slavery. We have renounced the prerogative
of man, and it is no wonder that we should be treated like beasts.
But our misery is much greater than theirs, as the crime we
commit in rejecting the lawful dominion of our reason is greater
than any which they can commit. If, after all, you should
confess all these things, yet plead the necessity of political institutions, weak and wicked as they are, I can argue with equal,
perhaps superior, force, concerning the necessity of artificial
religion; and every step you advance in your argument, you
add a strength to mine. So that if we are resolved to submit
our reason and our liberty to civil usurpation, we have nothing
to do but to conform as quietly as we can to the vulgar notions
which are connected with this, and take up the theology of the
vulgar as well as their politics. But if we think this necessity
rather imaginary than real, we should renounce their dreams
of society, together with their visions of religion, and vindicate
ourselves into perfect liberty.

The nearer we approach to the goal of life, the better we
begin to understand the true value of our existence and the
real weight of our opinions. We set out much in love with
both; but we leave much behind as we advance. We first
throw away the tales along with the rattles of our nurses; those
of the priest keep their hold a little longer; those of our governors the longest of all. But the passions which prop these
opinions are withdrawn one after another; and the cool light
of reason, at the setting of our life, shows us what a false splendor played upon these objects during our more sanguine seasons.

It is hard to say whether the doctors of law or divinity have
made the greater advances in the lucrative business of mystery.

II
THOMAS PAINE

Thomas Paine, 1737-1809. Born in England, of a Quaker father; attended grammar school until 13 years of age; later studied mathematics, astronomy and natural philosophy. Came to America in 1774, bringing letter of introduction from Franklin. Convinced that a reconciliation between England and the American colonies was impossible, he published *Common Sense,* 1776, advocating independence; issued the periodical *Crisis,* 1776-83, encouraging the disheartened soldiers of the Revolution. Washington and Jefferson recognized the great service Paine had rendered the Revolution, and Jefferson offered him return passage from Europe on a United States man-of-war. "Where liberty dwells, there is my country," Franklin said; but Paine said, "Where liberty dwells *not,* there is my country." He went to Europe in 1787. In answer to Burke's *Reflections on the French Revolution* he published *The Rights of Man,* 1791-2 which the British Government vainly attempted to suppress. Elected to the French National convention, 1793; opposed the execution of Louis XVI; imprisoned by the terrorists and narrowly escaped the guillotine, 1794; while in prison wrote *The Age of Reason,* published 1795. Resumed his seat in the Convention after his release from prison. Returned to the United States, 1802. Died in New York.

The first part of the following selections are from *The Age of Reason.* That on Negro slavery is from Moncure D. Conway's splendid *Life of Thomas Paine.* The rest of the chapter, *Society and Civilization,* is from *The Rights of Man,* part 2, chapters 1 and 2.

To argue with a man who has renounced his reason is like giving medicine to the dead.

The world is my country, all mankind are my brethren, and to do good is my religion.

I believe in the equality of man; and I believe that religious duties consist in doing justice, loving mercy, and endeavoring to make our fellow-creatures happy.

You will do me the justice to remember, that I have always strenuously supported the right of every man to his opinion, however different that opinion may be to mine. He who denies to another this right, makes a slave of himself to his present opinion, because he precludes himself the right of changing it. The most formidable weapon against errors of every kind is reason. I have never used any other, and I trust I never shall.

Negro Slavery.—These inoffensive people are brought into slavery, by stealing them, tempting kings to sell subjects, which they can have no right to do, and hiring one tribe to war against another, in order to catch prisoners. By such wicked and inhuman ways . . . left by Heathen nations to be practiced by Christians.

War never can be the interest of a trading nation any more than quarreling can be profitable to a man in business. But to make war with those who trade with us is like setting a bulldog upon a customer at the shop-door.

Society and Civilization.—A great part of that order which reigns among mankind is not the effect of government. It had its origin in the principles of society, and the natural constitution of man. It existed prior to government, and would exist if the formality of government was abolished. The mutual dependence and reciprocal interest which man has in man and all the parts of a civilized community upon each other, create that great chain of connection which holds it together. The landholder, the farmer, the manufacturer, the merchant, the tradesman, and every occupation prospers by the aid which each receives from the other, and from the whole. Common interest regulates their concerns, and forms their laws; and the laws which common usage ordains, have a greater influence than the laws of government. In fine, society performs for itself almost everything which is ascribed to government.

To understand the nature and quantity of government proper for man it is necessary to attend to his character. As nature created him for social life, she fitted him for the station she intended. In all cases she made his natural wants greater than his individual powers. No one man is capable, without the aid of society, of supplying his own wants; and those wants acting upon every individual impel the whole of them into society, as naturally as gravitation acts to a center.

But she has gone further. She has not only forced man into society by a diversity of wants, which the reciprocal aid of each other can supply, but she has implanted in him a system of social affections, which, though not necessary to his existence, are essential to his happiness. There is no period in life when this love for society ceases to act. It begins and ends with our being.

If we examine, with attention, into the composition and constitution of man, the diversity of talents in different men for reciprocally accommodating the wants of each other, his propensity to society, and consequently to preserve the advantages resulting from it, we shall easily discover that a great part of what is called government is mere imposition.

Government is no further necessary than to supply the few cases to which society and civilization are not conveniently competent; and instances are not wanting to show that everything which government can usefully add thereto, has been performed by the common consent of society, without government.

For upwards of two years from the commencement of the American war, and a longer period in several of the American states, there were no established forms of government. The old governments had been abolished, and the country was too much occupied in defense to employ its attention in establishing new governments; yet, during this interval, order and harmony were preserved as inviolate as in any country in Europe. There is a natural aptness in man, and more so in society, because it embraces a greater variety of abilities and resources, to accommodate itself to whatever situation it is in. The instant formal government is abolished, society begins to act. A general association takes place, and common interest produces common security.

So far is it from being true, as has been pretended, that the abolition of any formal government is the dissolution of society, it acts by contrary impulse, and brings the latter the closer together. All that part of its organization which it had committed to its government, devolves again upon itself, and acts through its medium. When men, as well from natural instinct as from reciprocal benefits, have habituated themselves to social and civilized life, there is always enough of its principles in practice to carry them through any changes they may find necessary or convenient to make in their government. In short, man is so naturally a creature of society that it is almost impossible to put him out of it.

Formal government makes but a small part of civilized life; and when even the best that human wisdom can devise is established, it is a thing more in name and idea than in fact. It is to the great and fundamental principles of society and civilization—to the common usage universally consented to, and mutually and reciprocally maintained—to the unceasing circulation of interest, which passing through its innumerable channels, invigorates the whole mass of civilized man—it is to these things, infinitely more than anything which even the best instituted government can perform, that the safety and prosperity of the individual and of the whole depends.

The more perfect civilization is, the less occasion has it for government, because the more does it regulate its own affairs, and govern itself; but so contrary is the practice of old governments to the reason of the case, that the expenses of them increase in the proportion they ought to diminish. It is but few general laws that civilized life requires, and those of such common usefulness, that whether they are enforced by the forms of government or not, the effect will be nearly the same. If we consider what the principles are that first condense man into society, and what the motives that regulate their mutual intercourse afterwards, we shall find, by the time we arrive at what is called government, that nearly the whole of the business is performed by the natural operation of the parts upon each other.

Man, with respect to all those matters, is more a creature of consistency than he is aware of, or that governments would wish him to believe. All the great laws of society are the laws of nature. Those of trade and commerce, whether with respect to the intercourse of individuals or of nations, are laws of mutual and reciprocal interest. They are followed and obeyed because it is the interest of the parties so to do, and not on account of any formal laws their governments may impose or interpose.

But how often is the natural propensity to society disturbed or destroyed by the operations of government! When the latter, instead of being engrafted on the principles of the former, assumes to exist for itself, and acts by partialities of favor and oppression, it becomes the cause of the mischiefs it ought to prevent.

If we look back to the riots and tumults which at various times have happened in England, we shall find, that they did not proceed from the want of a government, but that government was itself the generating cause; instead of consolidating society, it divided it; it deprived it of its natural cohesion, and engendered discontents and disorders, which otherwise would not have existed. In those associations which men promiscuously form for the purpose of trade or of any concern, in which government is totally out of the question, and in which they act merely on the principles of society, we see how naturally the various parties unite; and this shows, by comparison, that governments, so far from always being the cause or means of order, are often the destruction of it. The riots of 1780 had no other source than the remains of those prejudices which the government itself had encouraged. But with respect to England there are also other causes.

Excess and inequality of taxation, however disguised in the means, never fail to appear in their effect. As a great mass of the community are thrown thereby into poverty and discontent, they are constantly on the brink of commotion; and, deprived, as they unfortunately are, of the means of information, are easily heated to outrage. Whatever the apparent cause of any riots may be, the real one is always want of happiness. It shows that something is wrong in the system of government, that injures the felicity by which society is to be preserved.

Having thus endeavored to show, that the social and civilized state of man is capable of performing within itself, almost everything necessary to its protection and government, it will be proper, on the other hand, to take a review of the present old governments, and examine whether their principles and practice are correspondent thereto.

It is impossible that such governments as have hitherto existed in the world, could have commenced by any other means than a total violation of every principle, sacred and moral. The obscurity in which the origin of all the present old governments is buried, implies the iniquity and disgrace with which they began. The origin of the present governments of America and France will ever be remembered, because it is honorable to record it; but with respect to the rest, even flattery has consigned them to the tomb of time, without an inscription.

It could have been no difficult thing in the early and solitary ages of the world, while the chief employment of men was that of attending flocks and herds, for a banditti of ruffians to overrun a country, and lay it under contribution. Their power being thus established, the chief of the band contrived to lose the name of robber in that of monarch; and hence the origin of monarchy and kings.

The origin of the government of England, so far as it relates to what is called its line of monarchy, being one of the latest, is perhaps the best recorded. The hatred which the Norman invasion and tyranny begat, must have been deeply rooted in the nation, to have outlived the contrivance to obliterate it. Though not a courtier will talk of the curfew-bell, not a village in England has forgotten it.

Those bands of robbers having parcelled out the world, and divided it into dominions, began, as is naturally the case, to quarrel with each other. What at first was obtained by violence, was considered by others as lawful to be taken, and a second plunderer succeeded the first. They alternately invaded the dominions which each had assigned to himself, and the brutality with which they treated each other explains the original character of monarchy. It was ruffian torturing ruffian. The conqueror considered the conquered not as his prisoner, but his property. He led him in triumph rattling in chains, and doomed him, at pleasure, to slavery or death. As time obliterated the history of their beginning, their successors assumed new appearances, to cut off the entail of their disgrace, but their principles and objects remained the same. What at first was plunder assumed the softer name of revenue; and the power they originally usurped, they affected to inherit.

From such beginning of governments, what could be expected, but a continual system of war and extortion? It has established itself into a trade. The vice is not peculiar to one more than to another, but is the common principle of all. There does not exist within such governments a stamina whereon to ingraft reformation; and the shortest and most effectual remedy is to begin anew.

What scenes of horror, what perfection of iniquity, present themselves in contemplating the character, and reviewing the history of such governments! If we would delineate human nature with a baseness of heart, and hyprocrisy of countenance, that reflection would shudder at and humanity disown, it is kings, courts, and cabinets, that must sit for the portrait. Man, as he is naturally, with all his faults about him, is not up to the character.

Can we possibly suppose that if government had originated in a right principle, and had not an interest in pursuing a wrong one, that the world could have been in the wretched and quarrelsome condition we have seen it? What inducement has the farmer, while following the plow, to lay aside his peaceful pursuits and go to war with the farmer of another country? Or what inducement has the manufacturer? What is dominion to them or to any class of men in a nation? Does it add an acre to any man's estate, or raise its value? Are not conquest and defeat each of the same price, and taxes the never failing consequence? Though this reasoning may be good to a nation, it is not so to a government. War is the faro-table of governments, and nations the dupes of the game.

If there is anything to wonder at in this miserable scene of governments, more than might be expected, it is the progress which the peaceful arts of agriculture, manufactures, and commerce have made, beneath such a long accumulating load of discouragement and oppression. It serves to show that instinct in animals does not act with stronger impulse than the principles of society and civilization operate in man. Under all discouragements, he pursues his object, and yields to nothing but impossibilities.

Society in every state is a blessing, but government, even in its best state, is but a necessary evil; in its worst state, an intolerable one.

The trade of governing has always been monopolized by the most ignorant and the most rascally individuals of mankind.

III
THOMAS JEFFERSON

Thomas Jefferson, LL.D., 1743-1826, third President of the United States, 1801-9. Born in Virginia, of Welsh ancestry; educated at William and Mary's College; adopted the profession of law. Leader of the original Republicans as opposed to the Federalists. Delegate to the Continental Congress, 1775-6; submitted the original draft of the Declaration of Independence. Governor of Virginia, 1779-81. Representative of the United States at the French court, 1784-89. First Secretary of State, 1789-93 (during Washington's administration). *Works,* 9 vols., 1853-4; *Memoirs and Correspondence,* 4 vols., 1829.
The selections are from his *Works.*

Eternal vigilance is the price of liberty.

Error of opinion may be tolerated where reason is left free to combat it.

I sincerely believe, with you, that banking establishments are more dangerous than standing armies; and that the principle of spending money to be paid by posterity, under the name of funding, is but swindling futurity on a large scale.

That government is best which governs least.

All eyes are opened or opening to the rights of man. The general spread of the light of science has already laid open to every view the palpable truth, that the mass of mankind has not been born with saddles on their backs, nor a favored few booted and spurred, ready to ride them legitimately, by the grace of God.

I am really mortified to be told that, in the United States of America, a fact like this can become a subject of inquiry, and of criminal inquiry too, as an offence against religion; that the question about the sale of a book can be carried before the civil magistrate. Is this then our freedom of religion? and are we to have a censor whose imprimatur shall say what books may be sold, and what we may buy? And who is thus to dogmatize religious opinions for our citizens? Whose foot is to be the measure to which ours are all to be cut or stretched? Is a priest to be our inquisitor, or shall a layman, simple as ourselves, set up his reason as the rule for what we are to read, and what we must believe? It is an insult to our citizens to question whether they are rational beings or not, and blasphemy against religion to suppose it cannot stand the test of truth and reason. If M. de Becourt's book be false in its facts, disprove them; if false in its reasoning, refute it. But, for God's sake, let us freely hear both sides, if we choose. I have been just reading the new constitution of Spain. One of its fundamental basis is expressed in these words: "The *Roman Catholic* religion, the only true one, is, and always shall be, that of the Spanish nation. The government protects it by wise and just laws, and prohibits the exercise of any other whatever." Now I wish this presented to those who question what you may sell, or we may buy, with a request to strike out the words, "Roman Catholic," and to insert the denomination of their own religion. This would ascertain the code of dogmas which each wishes should domineer over the opinions of all others, and be taken, like the Spanish religion, under the "protection of wise and just laws." It would shew to what they wish to reduce the liberty for which one generation has sacrificed life and happiness. It would present our boasted freedom of religion as a thing of theory only, and not of practice, as what would be a poor exchange for the theoretic thraldom, but practical freedom of Europe. But it is impossible that the laws of Pennsylvania, which set us the first example of the wholesome and happy effects of religious freedom, can permit the inquisitorial functions to be proposed to their courts. Under them you are surely safe.—*To M. Dufief, April* 19, 1814.

Government.—Societies exist under three forms, sufficiently distinguishable: (1) Without government, as among our Indians. (2) Under governments wherein the will of every one has a just influence; as is the case in England, in a slight degree, and in our States, in a great one. (3) Under governments of force; as is the case in all other monarchies, and in most of the other republics. To have an idea of the curse of existence under these last, they must be seen. It is a government of wolves over sheep. It is a problem, not clear in my mind, that the first condition is not the best. But I believe it to be inconsistent with any great degree of population. The second state has a great deal of good in it. The mass of mankind under that, enjoys a precious degree of liberty and happiness. It has its evils, too; the principal of which is the turbulence to which it is subject. But weight this against the oppressions of monarchy, and it becomes nothing. Even this evil is productive of good. It prevents the degeneracy of governments, and nourishes a general attention to the public affairs. I hold it, that a little rebellion, now and then, is a good thing, and as necessary in the political world as storms in the physical. Unsuccessful rebellions, indeed, generally establish the encroachments on the rights of the people, which have produced them. An observation of this truth should render honest republican governors so mild in their punishment of rebellions, as not to discourage them too much. It is a medicine necessary for the sound health of governments.—*To Madison.*

The people are the only censors of their governors; and even their errors will tend to keep these to the true principles of their institution. To punish these errors too severely would be to suppress the only safeguard of the public liberty. The way to prevent these irregular interpositions of the people, is to give them full information of their affairs through the channel of the public papers, and to contrive that those papers should penetrate the whole mass of the people. The basis of our governments being the opinion of the people, the very first object should be to keep that right; and were it left to me to decide whether we should have a government, without newspapers, or newspapers without government, I should not hesitate a moment to prefer the latter. But I should mean that every man should receive those papers, and be capable of reading them. I am convinced that those societies (as the Indians) which live without government, enjoy in their general mass an infinitely greater degree of happiness than those who live under the European governments. Among the former, public opinion is in the place of law, and restrains morals as powerfully as laws ever did anywhere. Among the latter, under pretense of governing, they have divided their nations into two classes, wolves and sheep. I do not exaggerate. This is a true picture of Europe. Cherish therefore, the spirit of our people and keep alive their attention. Do not be too severe upon their errors, but reclaim them by enlightening them. If once they become inattentive to the public affairs, you and I, and Congress and Assemblies, judges and governors, shall all become wolves. It seems to be the law of our general nature, in spite of individual exceptions; and experience declares that man is the only animal which devours his own kind; for I can apply no milder term to the governments of Europe, and to the general prey of the rich on the poor.—*To Carrington, Paris, Jan.* 16, 1787.

Law and Judges.—We have long enough suffered under the base prostitution of law to party passions in one judge, and the imbecility of another. In the hands of one the law is nothing more than an ambiguous text, to be explained by his sophistry into any meaning which may subserve his personal malice. Nor can any milk-and-water associate maintain his own dependence, and by a firm pursuance of what the law really is, extend its protection to the citizens or the public. I believe you will do it, and where you cannot induce your colleague to do what is right, you will be firm enough to hinder him from doing what is wrong, and by opposing sense to sophistry, leave the juries free to follow their own judgment.

I have long lamented with you the depreciation of law science. The opinion seems to be that Blackstone is to us what the Alcoran is to the Mahometans, that everything which is necessary is in him, and what is not in him is not necessary—*To Governor Tyler, May* 26, 1810.

War.—The two last Congresses have been the theme of the

most licentious reprobation for printers thirsting after war, some against France and some against England. But the people wish for peace with both. They feel no incumbency on them to become the reformers of the other hemisphere, and to inculcate, with fire and sword, a return to moral order. When, indeed, peace shall become more losing than war, they may owe to their interests what these Quixotes are clamoring for on false estimates of honor. The public are unmoved by these clamors, as the re-election of their legislators shows, and they are firm to their executive on the subject of the more recent clamors.—*To Colonel Monroe, May 5, 1811.*

Trial by Jury.—I will now tell you what I do not like. First, the omission of a bill of rights, providing clearly, and without the aid of sophism, for freedom of religion, freedom of the press, protection against standing armies, restriction of monopolies, the eternal and unremitting force of the habeas corpus laws, and trials by jury, in all matters of fact triable by the laws of the land, and not by the laws of nations. To say, as Mr. Wilson does, that a bill of rights was not necessary, because all is reserved in the case of the general governments which is not given, while in the particular ones, all is given which is not reserved, might do for the audience to which it was addressed; and it is opposed by strong inferences from the body of the instrument, as well as from the omission of the cause of our present confederation, which had made the reservation in express terms. It was hard to conclude, because there has been a want of uniformity among the States as to the cases triable by jury, because some have been so incautious as to dispense with this mode of trial in certain cases, therefore, the more prudent States shall be reduced to the same level of calamity. It would have been much more just and wise to have concluded the other way, that as most of the States had preserved with jealousy this sacred palladium of liberty, those who had wandered should be brought back to it; and to have established general right rather than general wrong. For I consider all the ill as established, which may be established. I have a right to nothing, which another has a right to take away; and Congress will have a right to take away trials by jury in all civil cases. Let me add, that a bill of rights is what the people are entitled to against every government on earth, general or particular; and what no just government should refuse, or rest on inference.—*From a letter to Madison, Paris, December 20, 1787.*

The operations which have taken place in America lately, fill me with pleasure. In the first place, they realize the confidence I had, that whenever our affairs go obviously wrong, the good sense of the people will interpose, and set them to rights. The example of changing a Constitution, by assembling the wise men of the State, instead of assembling armies, will be worth as much to the world as the former examples we had given them. . . . . A general concurrence of opinion seems to authorize us to say it (the Constitution) has some defects. I am one of those who think it a defect, that the important rights, not placed in security by the frame of the Constitution itself were not explicitly secured by a supplementary declaration. There are rights which it is useless to surrender to the governments, and which governments have yet always been found to invade. These are the rights of thinking, and publishing our thoughts by speaking or writing; the right of free commerce; the right of personal freedom. There are instruments for administering the government so peculiarly trustworthy, that we should never leave the legislature at liberty to change them. The new constitution has secured these in the executive and legislative departments; but not in the judiciary. It should have established trials by the people themselves; that is to say, by jury. There are instruments so dangerous to the rights of the nation, and which place them so totally at the mercy of their governors, that those governors, whether legislative or executive, should be restrained from keeping such instruments on foot, but in well defined cases. Such an instrument is a standing army.—*Letter to Colonel Humphrey*, 1789.

Capital Punishment.—The reformation of offenders, though an object worthy the attention of the laws, is not effected at all by capital punishment, which exterminates instead of reforming, and should be the last melancholy resource against those whose existence is become inconsistent with the safety of their fellow-citizens, which also weaken the State by cutting off so many, who, if reformed, might be restored sound members to society, who, even under a course of correction, might be rendered useful in various labors for the public, and would be living and long-continued spectacles to deter others from committing the like offenses. And for as much as the experience of all ages and countries hath shown, that cruel and sanguinary laws defeat their own purpose, by engaging the benevolence of mankind to withhold prosecutions, to smother testimony, or to listen to it with bias, when, if the punishment were only proportioned to the injury, men would feel it their inclination, as well as their duty, to see the laws observed.

Slavery.—Sir: I am very sensible of the honor you propose to me, of becoming a member of the Society for the Abolition of the Slave Trade. You know that nobody wishes more ardently to see an abolition, not only of the trade, but of the condition of slavery; and certainly nobody will be more willing to encounter every sacrifice for that object. But the influence and information of the friends to this proposition in France will be far above the need of my association. I am here as a public servant, and those whom I serve, having never yet been able to give their voice against the practice, it is decent for me to avoid too public a demonstration of my wishes to see it abolished. Without serving the cause here, it might render me less able to serve it beyond the water. I trust you will be sensible of the prudence of those motives, therefore, which govern my conduct on this occasion, and be assured of my wishes for the success of your undertaking, and the sentiments of esteem and respect with which I have the honor to be, sir, your most obedient, humble servant.—*To M. Warville, Paris, Feb. 12, 1788.*

Land.—I set out on this ground, which I suppose to be self-evident, that the earth belongs in usufruct to the living; that the dead have neither powers nor rights over it. The portion occupied by any individual ceases to be his when himself ceases to be, and reverts to the society. . . . .

No society can make a perpetual constitution, or even a perpetual law. The earth belongs always to the living generation: they may manage it, then, and what proceeds from it, as they please, during their usufruct. They are masters, too, of their own persons, and consequently may govern themselves as they please. But persons and property make the sum of the objects of government. The constitution and the laws of their predecessors are extinguished then, in their natural course, with those whose will gave them being. This could preserve that being till it ceased to be itself, and no longer. Every constitution, then, and every law, naturally expires at the end of thirty-four years (the average life). If it be enforced longer, it is an act of force, and not of right. It may be said, that the succeeding generation exercising, in fact, the power of repeal, this leaves them as free as if the constitution or law had been expressly limited to thirty-four years only. In the first place, this objection admits the right, in proposing an equivalent. But the power of repeal is not an equivalent. It might be, indeed, if every form of government were so perfectly contrived, that the will of the majority could always be obtained, fairly and without impediment. But this is true of no form. The people cannot assemble themselves; their representation is unequal and vicious. Various checks are opposed to every legislative proposition. Factions get possession of the public councils, bribery corrupts them, personal interests lead them astray from the general interests of their constituents; and other impediments arise, so as to prove to every practical man, that a law of limited duration is much more manageable than one which needs a repeal.—*To James Madison*, 1789.

Religious Freedom.—Had not the Roman Government permitted free enquiry Christianity could never have been introduced.

I know it will give great offense to the clergy, but the advocate of religious freedom is to expect neither peace nor forgiveness from them.

In every country and in every age the priest has been hostile to liberty; he is always in allegiance with the despot, abetting his abuses in return for protection for his own.

If anybody thinks that kings, nobles and priests are good conservators of the public happiness, send him here (Paris). It is the best school in the universe to cure him of that folly. He will see here with his own eyes that these descriptions of men are an abandoned confederacy against the happiness of the mass of the people.

Millions of innocent men, women, and children, since the introduction of Christianity, have been burnt, tortured, fined, and imprisoned; yet we have not advanced one inch toward uniformity. What has been the effect of coercion? To make one-half the world fools and the other half hypocrites.

We have most unwisely committed to the hierophants of our particular superstition the direction of public opinion—that lord of the universe. We have given them stated and privileged days to collect and catechise us, opportunities of delivering their oracles to the people in mass, and of molding their minds as wax in the hollow of their hands.

Fix Reason firmly in her seat, and call to her tribunal every fact, every opinion. Question with boldness even the existence of a God; because, if there be one, he must more approve the homage of reason than of blindfolded fear. . . . . Do not be frightened from this inquiry by any fear of its consequences. If it end in a belief that there is no God, you will find incitements to virtue in the comfort and pleasantness you feel in its exercise and in the love of others which it will procure for you.—*Works, Vol. II, p.* 217.

I doubt whether the people of this country would suffer an execution for heresy, or a three months' imprisonment for not comprehending the mysteries of the Trinity. But is the spirit of the people infallible—a permanent reliance? Is it government? Is this the kind of protection we receive in return for the rights we give up? Besides, the spirit of the times may alter—will alter. Our rulers will become corrupt, our people careless. A single zealot may become persecutor, and better men become his victims.—*Notes on Virginia.*

The Presbyterian clergy are the loudest, the most intolerant of all sects; the most tyrannical and ambitious, ready at the word of the law-giver, if such a word could now be obtained, to put their torch to the pile, and to rekindle in this virgin hemisphere the flame in which their oracle, Calvin, consumed the poor Servitus, because he could not subscribe to the proposition of Calvin, that magistrates have a right to exterminate all heretics to the Calvinistic creed! They pant to re-establish by law that holy inquisition which they can now only infuse into public opinion.

I consider the government of the United States as interdicted by the Constitution from meddling with religious institutions, their doctrines, discipline, or exercises. . . . . But it is only proposed that I should recommend, not prescribe a day of feasting and praying. That is, I should indirectly assume to the United States an authority over religious exercises, which the Constitution has directly precluded from them. . . . . Every one must act according to the dictates of his own reason and mine tells me that civil powers alone have been given to the President of the United States, and no authority to direct the religious exercises of his constituents.—*Letter to Rev. Millar.*

By our own act of Assembly of 1705, c. 30, if a person brought up in the Christian religion denies the being of God, or the

Trinity, or asserts there are more gods than one, or denies the Christian religion to be true, or the Scriptures to be of divine authority, he is punishable on the first offense by incapacity to hold any office or employment, ecclesiastical, civil, or military; on the second, by disability to sue, to take any gift or legacy, to be guardian, executor, or administrator, and by three years' imprisonment without bail. A father's right to the custody of his own children being founded in law on his right of guardianship, this being taken away, they may of course be severed from him, and put by the authority of the court, into more orthodox hands. This is a summary view of that religious slavery under which a people have been willing to remain, who have lavished their lives and fortunes for the establishment of civil freedom.

The legitimate powers of government extend to such acts only as are injurious to others. But it does me no injury for my neighbor to say there are twenty gods or no God. . . . . Constraint may make him worse by making him a hypocrite, but it will never make him a truer man.

Reason and persuasion are the only practicable instruments. To make way for these free inquiry must be indulged; how can we wish others to indulge it while we refuse it ourselves? But every State, says an inquisitor, has established some religion. No two, say I, have established the same. Is this a proof of the infallibility of establishments?

It is error alone which needs the support of government. Truth can stand by itself.—*Notes on Virginia.*

WILLIAM GODWIN

William Godwin, 1756-1836, novelist, historian, political and miscellaneous writer. Born in England, son of a dissenting minister; studied theology at Hoxton; preached from 1778 to 1782, but his faith in Christianity was shaken by the French philosophical writers and he left the ministry for literature. Sympathized with the French Revolution and became the representative of English radicalism; married Mary Wollstonecraft in 1797, though he objected to legal marriage on principle. The child of this marriage became the wife of the poet Shelly. Prof. Anton Menger in his *Right to the Whole Produce*, says: "The first scientific advocate of the right to the whole produce of labor known to me is William Godwin." Works include *Inquiry Concerning Political Justice*, etc., 1793; *History of the Commonwealth*, 1824-28; the novels *Caleb Williams*, 1794, *St. Leon*, 1799, *Mandeville*, 1817, etc.; histories of Rome, Greece, and England, a *Pantheon*, and *Fables*.

The following selections are from *An Inquiry Concerning Political Justice*.

Can we suppress truth? Can we arrest the progress of the inquiring mind? If we can, it will only be done by the most unmitigated despotism. Mind has a perpetual tendency to rise. It cannot be held down but by a power that counteracts its genuine tendency through every moment of its existence. Tyrannical and sanguinary must be the measures employed for this purpose. Miserable and disgustful must be the scene they produce. Their result will be thick darkness of the mind, timidity, servility, hypocrisy. This is the alternative, so far as there is any alternative in their power, between the opposite measures of which the princes and governments of the earth have now to choose: they must either suppress enquiry by the most arbitrary stretches of power, or preserve a clear and tranquil field in which every man shall be at liberty to discover and vindicate his opinion.

In this interesting period, in which mind shall arrive as it were at the true crisis of its story, there are high duties incumbent upon every branch of the community. First, upon those cultivated and powerful minds, that are fitted to be precursors to the rest in the discovery of truth. They are bound to be active, indefatigable and disinterested. It is incumbent upon them to abstain from inflammatory language, from all expressions of acrimony and resentment. It is absurd in any government to erect itself into a court of criticism in this respect, and to establish a criterion of liberality and decorum; but for that very reason it is doubly incumbent on those who communicate their thoughts to the public, to exercise a rigid censure over themselves. The tidings of liberty and equality are tidings of good will to all orders of men. They free the peasant from the iniquity that depresses his mind, and the privileged from the luxury and despotism by which he is corrupted.

Nor is it less necessary that they should be urged to tell the whole truth without disguise. No maxim can be more pernicious than that which would teach us to consult the temper of the times, and to tell only so much as we imagine our contemporaries will be able to bear. This practice is at present almost universal, and it is the mark of a very painful degree of depravity. We retail and mangle truth. We impart it to our fellows, not with the liberal measure with which we have received it, but with such parsimony as our own miserable prudence may chance to prescribe. We pretend that truths fit to be practised in one country, nay, truths which we confess to be eternally right, are not fit to be practised in another. That we may deceive others with a tranquil conscience, we begin with deceiving ourselves. We put shackles upon our minds, and dare not trust ourselves at large in the pursuit of truth. This practice took its commencement from the machinations of party, and the desire of one wise and adventurous leader to carry a troop of weak, timid and selfish supporters in his train. There is no reason why I should not declare in any assembly upon the face of the earth that I am a republican. There is no more reason why, being a republican under a monarchical government, I should enter into a desperate faction to invade the public tranquillity, than if I were monarchical under a republic. Every community of men, as well as every individual, must govern itself according to its ideas of justice. What I should desire is, not by violence to change its institutions, but by reason to change its ideas. I have no business with factions or intrigue, but simply to promulgate the truth, and to wait the tranquil progress of conviction. If there be any assembly that cannot bear this, of such an assembly I ought to be no member. It happens much oftener than we are willing to imagine, that "the post of honor," or, which is better, the post of utility, "is a private station."

Governments, no more than individual men, are infallible. The cabinets of princes and the parliaments of kingdoms are often less likely to be right in their conclusions than the theorist in his closet. What system of religion or government has not in its turn been patronized by national authority? The consequence therefore of admitting this authority is, not merely attributing to government a right to impose some, but any or all, opinions upon the community. Are Paganism and Christianity, the religions of Mahomet, Zoroaster, and Confucius, are monarchy and aristocracy in all their forms equally worthy to be perpetuated among mankind? Is it quite certain that the greatest of all calamities is change? Have no revolution in government and no reformation in religion been productive of more benefit than disadvantage? There is no species of reasoning in defense of the suppression of heresy which may not be brought back to this monstrous principle, that the knowledge of truth, and the introduction of right principles of policy, are circumstances altogether indifferent to the welfare of mankind.

Reason and good sense will not fail to augur ill of that system of things which is too sacred to be looked into; and to suspect that there must be something essentially weak that thus shrinks from the eye of inquiry.

Nothing can be more unreasonable than an attempt to retain men in one common opinion by the dictate of authority. The opinion thus obtruded upon the minds of the public is not their real opinion; it is only a project by which they are rendered incapable of forming an opinion. Whenever government assumes to deliver us from the trouble of thinking for ourselves, the only consequences it produces are those of torpor, imbecility. Wherever truth stands in the mind unaccompanied by the evidence upon which it depends, it cannot properly be said to be apprehended at all. The mind is in this case robbed of its essential character, and genuine employment, and along with them must be expected to lose all that is capable of rendering its operations salutary and admirable.

Either mankind will resist the assumptions of authority undertaking to superintend their opinions, and then these assumptions will produce no more than an ineffectual struggle; or they will submit, and then the effect will be injurious. He that in any degree consigns to another the task of dictating his opinions and his conduct, will cease to inquire for himself, or his inquiries will be languid and inanimate.

Regulations will originally be instituted in favor either of falsehood or truth. In the first case, no rational inquirer will pretend to allege anything in their defense; but, even should truth be their object, yet such is their nature, that they infallibly defeat the very purpose they were intended to serve. Truth, when originally presented to the mind, is powerful and invigorating; but, when attempted to be perpetuated by political institutions, becomes flaccid and lifeless. Truth in its unpatronized state improves the understanding; because in that state it is embraced only so far as it is perceived to be true. But truth when recommended by authority is weakly and irresolutely embraced. The opinions I entertain are no longer properly my own; I repeat them as a lesson appropriated by vote, but I do not, strictly speaking, understand them, and I am not able to assign the evidence upon which they rest. My mind is weakened while it is pretended to be improved. Instead of the firmness of independence, I am taught to bow to authority and know not why. Persons thus trammeled, are not, strictly speaking, capable of a single virtue. The first duty of man is, to take none of the principles of conduct upon trust; to do nothing without a clear and individual conviction that it is right to be done. He that resigns his understanding upon one particular topic, will not exercise it vigorously upon others. If he be right in any instance, it will be inadvertently and by chance. A consciousness of the degradation to which he is subjected will perpetually haunt him; or at least he will want the consciousness that accrued from independent consideration, and will therefore equally want that intrepid perseverance, that calm self-approbation that grows out of independence. Such beings are the mere dwarfs and mockery of men, their efforts comparatively pusillanimous, and the vigor with which they should execute their purposes, superficial and hollow.

Strangers to conviction, they will never be able to distinguish between prejudice and reason. Nor is this the worst. Even when the glimpses of inquiry suggest themselves, they will not dare to yield to the temptation. To what purpose inquire, when the law has told me what to believe, and what must be the termination of my inquiries? Even when opinion properly so called, suggest itself, I am compelled, if it differ in any degree from the established system, to shut my eyes, and loudly profess my adherence where I doubt the most.

A system like this does not content itself with habitually unnerving the mind of the great mass of mankind through all its ranks, but provides for its own continuance by debauching or terrifying the few individuals who, in the midst of the general emasculation, might retain their curiosity and love of enterprise. We may judge how pernicious it is in its operation in this respect, by the long reign of papal usurpation in the dark ages, and the many attacks upon it that were suppressed, previously to the successful one of Luther. Even yet how few are there that venture to examine into the foundation of Mahometanism and

Christianity, in those countries where those systems are established by law!

It is a mistake to suppose that speculative differences of opinion threaten materially to disturb the peace of society. It is only when they are enabled to arm themselves with authority of government, to form parties in the state, and to struggle for that political ascendency which is too frequently exerted in support of or in opposition to some particular creed, that they become dangerous. Wherever government is wise enough to maintain an inflexible neutrality, these jarring sects are always found to live together with sufficient harmony. The very means that have been employed for the preservation of order, have been the only means that have led to its disturbance. The moment government resolves to admit of no regulations oppressive to either party, controversy finds its level, and appeals to arguments and reason, instead of appealing to the sword or to the state. The moment government descends to wear the badge of a sect, religious war is commenced, the world is disgraced with inexpiable broils, and deluged with blood.

Once more let us be upon our guard against reducing men to the condition of brute machines. The objectors of the last chapter were partly in the right when they spoke of the endless variety of mind. It would be absurd to say that we are not capable of truth, of evidence and agreement. In these respects, so far as mind is in a state of progressive improvement, we are perpetually coming nearer to each other. But there are subjects about which we shall continually differ, and ought to differ. The ideas, the associations and the circumstances of each man are properly his own; and it is a pernicious system that would lead us to require all men, however different their circumstances, to act in many of the common affairs of life by a precise general rule. Add to this, that, by the doctrine of progressive improvement, we shall always be erroneous, though we shall every day become less erroneous. The proper method for hastening the decay of error, is not, by brute force, or by regulation which is one of the classes of force, to endeavor to reduce men to intellectual uniformity; but on the contrary by teaching every man to think for himself.

Wealth.—The spectacle of injustice which the established system of property exhibits, consists partly in caprice. If you would cherish in any man the love of rectitude, you must take care that its principles be impressed on him, not only by words, but actions. It sometimes happens during the period of education, that maxims of integrity and consistency are repeatedly enforced, and that the preceptor gives no quarter to the base suggestions of selfishness and cunning. But how is the lesson that has been read to the pupil confounded and reversed, when he enters upon the scene of the world? If he ask, "Why is this man honored?" the ready answer is, "Because he is rich." If he inquire further, "Why is he rich?" the answer in most cases is, "From the accident of birth, or from a minute and sordid attention to the cares of gain." The system of accumulated property is the offspring of civil policy; and civil policy, as we are taught to believe, is the production of accumulated wisdom. Thus the wisdom of legislators and senates has been employed to secure a distribution of property the most profligate and unprincipled, that bids defiance to the maxims of justice and the nature of man. Humanity weeps over the distresses of the peasantry of all civilized nations; and when she turns from this spectacle to behold the luxury of their lords, gross, imperious, and prodigal, her sensations certainly are not less acute. This spectacle is the school in which mankind have been educated. They have been accustomed to the sight of injustice, oppression, and iniquity, till their feelings are made callous, and their understandings incapable of apprehending the nature of true virtue.

In beginning to point out the evils of accumulated property, we compared the extent of those evils with the correspondent evils of monarchies and courts. No circumstances under the latter have excited a more pointed disapprobation than pensions and pecuniary corruption, by means of which hundreds of individuals are rewarded, not for serving, but betraying the public, and the hard earnings of industry are employed to fatten the servile adherents of despotism. But the rent-roll of the lands of England is a much more formidable pension list than that which is supposed to be employed in the purchase of ministerial majorities. All riches, and especially all hereditary riches, are to be considered as the salary of a sinecure office, where the laborer and the manufacturer perform the duties, and the principal spends the income in luxury and idleness. Hereditary wealth is in reality a premium paid to idleness, an immense annuity expended to retain mankind in brutality and ignorance. The poor are kept in ignorance by the want of leisure. The rich are furnished with the means of cultivation and literature, but they are paid for being dissipated and indolent. The most powerful means that malignity could have invented, are employed to prevent them from improving their talents, and becoming useful to the public.

Crime.—The fruitful source of crimes consists in this circumstance, one man's possessing in abundance that of which another man is destitute. We must change the nature of mind, before we can prevent it from being powerfully influenced by this circumstance, when brought strongly home to its perceptions by the nature of its situation. Man must cease to have senses, the pleasures of appetite and vanity must cease to gratify, before he can look on tamely at the monopoly of these pleasures. He must cease to have a sense of justice, before he can clearly and fully approve this mixed scene of superfluity and distress. It is true that the proper method of curing this inequality is by reason and not by violence. But the immediate tendency of the established system is to persuade men that reason is impotent. The injustice of which they complain is upheld by force, and they are too easily induced by force to attempt its correction. All they endeavor is the partial correction of an injustice, which education tells them is necessary, but more powerful reason affirms to be tyrannical.

Force grew out of monopoly. It might accidentally have occurred among savages whose appetites exceeded their supply, or whose passions were inflamed by the presence of the object of their desire; but it would gradually have died away, as reason and civilization advanced. Accumulated property has fixed its empire; and henceforth all is an open contention of the strength and cunning of one party against the strength and cunning of the other. In this case the violent and premature struggles of the necessitous are undoubtedly an evil. They tend to defeat the very cause in the success of which they are most deeply interested; they tend to procrastinate the triumph of truth. But the true crime is in the malevolent and partial propensities of men, thinking only of themselves, and despising the emolument of others; and of these the rich have their share.

War.—Our judgment will always suspect those weapons that can be used with equal prospect of success on both sides. Therefore we should regard all force with aversion. When we enter the lists of battle, we quit the sure domain of truth and leave the decision to the caprice of chance. The phalanx of reason is invulnerable; it moves forward with calm, sure step, and nothing can withstand it. But, when we lay aside arguments, and have recourse to the sword, the case is altered. Amidst the clamorous din of civil war, who shall tell whether the event will be prosperous or adverse? We must therefore distinguish carefully between instructing the people and exciting them. We must refuse indignation, rage, and passion, and desire only sober reflection, clear judgment, and fearless discussion.

The desire to gain a more extensive territory, to conquer or to hold in awe our neighboring States, to surpass them in arts or arms, is a desire founded in prejudice and error. Power is not happiness. Security and peace are more to be desired than a name at which nations tremble. Mankind are brethren. We associate in a particular district or under a particular climate, because association is necessary to our internal tranquillity, or to defend us against the wanton attacks of a common enemy. But the rivalship of nations is a creature of the imagination.

Government.—Since government, even in its best state is an evil, the object principally to be aimed at is that we should have as little of it as the general peace of human society will permit.

We cannot renounce our moral independence; it is a property that we can neither sell nor give away; and consequently no government can derive its authority from an original contract.

All government corresponds in a certain degree to what the Greeks denominated a tyranny. The difference is, that in despotic countries mind is depressed by a uniform usurpation; while in republics it preserves a greater portion of its activity, and the usurpation more easily conforms itself to the fluctuations of opinion. By its very nature positive institution has a tendency to suspend the elasticity and progress of mind. We should not forget that government is, abstractedly taken, an evil, a usurpation upon the private judgment and individual conscience of mankind.

A fundamental distinction exists between society and government. Men associated at first for the sake of mutual assistance.

Justice is the sum of all moral duty.

Society and government are different in themselves, and have different origins. Society is produced by our wants, and government by our wickedness. Society is in every state a blessing; government even in its best state but a necessary evil.

General justice and mutual interest are found more capable of binding men than signatures and seals.

Government can have no more than two legitimate purposes, the suppression of injustice against individuals within the community, and the common defence against external invasion.

The first of these purposes, which alone can have an uninterrupted claim upon us, is sufficiently answered by an association of such an extent as to afford room for the institution of a jury, to decide upon the offences of individuals within the community, and upon the questions and controversies respecting property which may chance to arise.

If juries might at length cease to decide and be contented to invite, if force might gradually be withdrawn and reason trusted alone, shall we not one day find that juries themselves, and every other species of public institution, may be laid aside as unnecessary? Will not the reasonings of one wise man be as effectual as those of twelve? Will not the competence of one individual to instruct his neighbors be a matter of sufficient notoriety, without the formality of an election? Will there be many vices to correct and much obstinacy to conquer? This is one of the most memorable stages of human improvement. With what delight must every well-informed friend of mankind look forward to the auspicious period, the dissolution of political government, of that brute engine, which has been the only perennial cause of the vices of mankind, and which has mischiefs of various sorts incorporated with its substance, and no otherwise to be removed than by its utter annihilation!

Law.—Law is an institution of the most pernicious tendency. The institution once begun, can never be brought to a close. No action of any man was ever the same as any other action, had ever the same degree of utility or injury. As new cases occur, the law is perpetually found deficient. It is therefore perpetually necessary to make new laws. The volume in which justice records her perscriptions is forever increasing, and the world would not contain the books that might be written. The consequence of the infinitude of law is its uncertainty. Law was made that a plain man might know what he had to expect, and yet the most skillful practitioners differ about the event of my suit.

Law we sometimes call the wisdom of our ancestors. But this is a strange imposition. It was as frequently the dictate of their passion, of timidity, jealousy, a monopolizing spirit, and a lust of power that knew no bounds. Are we not obliged perpetually to revise and remodel this misnamed wisdom of our ancestors? to correct it by a detection of their ignorance, and a censure of their intolerance?

As long as a man is held in the trammels of obedience, and habituated to look to some foreign guidance for the direction of his conduct, his understanding and the vigor of his mind will sleep. Do I desire to raise him to the energy of which he is capable? I must teach him to feel himself, to bow to no authority, to examine the principles he entertains, and render to his mind the reason of his conduct.

The juridical decisions that were made immediately after the abolition of law, would differ little from those during its empire. They would be the decisions of prejudice and habit. But habit, having lost the center about which it revolved, would diminish in the regularity of its operations. Those to whom the arbitration of any question was entrusted would frequently recollect that the whole case was committed to their deliberation, and they could not fail occasionally to examine themselves, respecting the reason of those principles which had hitherto passed uncontroverted. Their understandings would grow enlarged, in proportion as they felt the importance of their trust, and the unbounded freedom of their investigation. Here then would commence an auspicious order of things, of which no understanding man at present in existence can foretell the result, the dethronement of implicit faith, and the inauguration of unclouded justice.

V
WILHELM VON HUMBOLDT

Wilhelm von Humboldt, 1767-1835, German philologist and author, brother of Alexander von Humboldt. Born at Potsdam, Prussia. Studied jurisprudence at Frankfort-on-the-Oder and Goettingen; traveled extensively. Prussian minister resident in Rome, 1801-08; minister of public instruction, 1808, and instrumental in founding University of Berlin; afterward resident minister in Vienna; member of Vienna Congress; minister resident in London, and, finally, minister of the interior in Berlin. His principal work, *The Sphere and Duty of Government,* appeared posthumously, as did his *Letters to a Friend* and three philological volumes, *On the Kawi Language of the Island of Java.* The *Shpere and Duty of Government,* with its clear, free thinking, was even more fearless and distinctive than the volumes of critical philology.

The following selections are from *The Sphere and Duty of Government.*

The greater a man's freedom, the more does he become dependent on himself, and well-disposed towards others.

Men have now arrived at such a high pitch of civilization that all institutions which act in any way to obstruct or thwart the development of individuals, and compresses men together into vast uniform masses, are now far more hurtful than in earlier ages of the world.

All which concerns religion lies beyond the sphere of the State's activity; and that the choice of ministers, as well as all that relates to religious worship in general, should be left to the free judgment of the communities, without any special supervision on the part of the State.

Freedom exalts power; and, as is always the collateral effect of increasing strength, tends to induce a spirit of liberality. Coercion stifles power, and engenders all selfish desires, and all the mean artifices of weakness. Coercion may prevent many transgressions; but it robs even actions which are legal of a portion of their beauty. Freedom may lead to many transgressions, but it lends even to vices a less ignoble form.

It cannot surely be forgotten, that freedom of thought, and the enlightenment which never flourishes but beneath its shelter, are the most efficient of all means for promoting security. While all other methods are confined to the mere suppression of actual outbreaks, free inquiry acts immediately on the very dispositions and sentiments; and while those only serve to maintain due order and propriety in external actions, this creates an internal harmony between the will and the endeavor.

Freedom is the grand and indispensable condition which development presupposes; but there is besides another essential,—intimately connected with freedom, it is true,—a variety of situations. Even the most free and self-reliant of men is thwarted and hindered in his development by uniformity of position. But as it is evident on the one hand, that such a diversity is a constant result of freedom, and on the other, that there is a species of oppression, which, without imposing restrictions on man himself, gives a peculiar impress of its own to surrounding circumstances; these two conditions, of freedom and variety of situation, may be regarded, in a certain sense, as one and the same.

But, still, it cannot be doubted that freedom is the indispensable condition, without which even the pursuits most happily congenial to the individual nature, can never succeed in producing such fair and salutary influences. Whatever man is inclined to, without the free exercise of his own choice, or whatever only implies instruction and guidance, does not enter into his very being, but still remains alien to his true nature, and is, indeed, effected by him, not so much with human agency, as with the mere exactness of mechanical routine.

For by nothing is ripeness and capacity for freedom so much promoted as by freedom itself. This truth, perhaps, may not be acknowledged by those who have so often made use of this want of capacity as a plea for the continuance of repressive influences. But it seems to me to follow unquestionably from the very nature of man. The incapacity for freedom can only arise from a want of moral and intellectual power; to elevate this power is the only way to counteract this want; but to do this presupposes the exercise of that power, and this exercise presupposes the freedom which awakens spontaneous activity.

In estimating the advantages arising from increased freedom of thought and the consequent wide diffusion of enlightenment, we should moreover especially guard against presuming that they would be confined to a small proportion of the people only;—that to the majority, whose energies are exhausted by cares for the physical necessaries of life, such opportunities would be useless or even positively hurtful, and that the only way to influence the masses is to promulgate some definite points of belief—to restrict the freedom of thought. There is something degrading to human nature in the idea of refusing to any man, the right to be a man. There are none so hopelessly low on the scale of culture and refinement as to be incapable of rising higher; and even though the more pure and lofty views of philosophy and religion could not at once be entertained by a large portion of the community—though it should be necessary to array truth in some different garb before it could find admission to their convictions—should we have to appeal rather to their feeling and imagination than to the cold decision of reason, still, the diffusiveness imparted to all scientific knowledge by freedom and enlightenment spreads gradually downward even to them; and the happy results of perfect liberty of thought on the mind and character of the entire nation, extend their influence even to its humblest individuals.

I have in general aimed at discovering the most favorable position which man can occupy as member of a political community. And it has appeared to me to be, that in which the most manifold individuality and the most original independence subsisted, with the most various and intimate union of a number of men—a problem which nothing but the most absolute liberty can ever hope to solve. To point out the possibility of a political organization which should fall as little short of this end as possible, and bring man nearer to such a position, has been my strict design in these pages, and has for some time been the subject of all my thoughts and researches. I shall be satisfied to have shown that this principle should be, at least, the guiding one in all political constitutions, and the system which is based upon it the high ideal of the legislator.

And it is the mutual freedom of activity among all the members of the nation, which secures all those benefits for which men longed when they formed themselves into a society. The State constitution itself is strictly subordinate to this, as to the end for which it was chosen as a necessary means; and, since it is always attended with restrictions in freedom, as a necessary evil.

It has, therefore, been my secondary design in these pages to point out the fatal consequences which flow for human enjoyment, power, and character, from confounding the free activity of the nation with that which is enforced upon its members by the political constitution.

State.—The State must not make man an instrument to subserve its arbitrary designs, and induce him to neglect for these his proper individual ends.

A State, in which the citizens were compelled or actuated by such means to obey even the best of laws, might be a tranquil, peaceable, prosperous State; but it would always seem to me a multitude of well cared-for slaves, rather than a nation of free and independent men, with no restraint save such as was required to prevent any infringements on right. There are, doubtless, many methods of producing given actions and sentiments only; but none of these lead to true moral perfection. Sensual impulses, urging to the commission of certain actions, or the continuing necessity of refraining from these, gradually come to engender a habit; through the force of habit the satisfaction which was at first connected with these impulses alone, is transferred to the action itself; the inclination, which at first only slumbered under the pressure of necessity, becomes wholly stifled; and thus man may be led to keep his actions within the limits of virtue, and to a certain extent to entertain virtuous sentiments. But neither is his spiritual energy exalted by such a process, nor his views of his destination and his own worth made clearer, nor does his will gain greater power to conquer the dictates of his rebellious desires; and hence, he does not advance a single step towards true, actual perfection. They, therefore, who would pursue the task of developing man without any reference to external ends will never make use of such inadequate means. For, setting aside the fact that coercion and guidance can never succeed in producing virtue, they manifestly tend to weaken power; and what are tranquil order and outward morality without true moral strength and virtue? Moreover, however great an evil immorality may be, we must not forget that it is not without its beneficial consequences. It is only through extremes that men can arrive at the middle path of wisdom and virtue. Extremes, like large masses shining afar off, must operate at a distance. In order that blood be supplied to the most delicate ramifications of the arteries, there must be copious sources in the larger vessels. To wish to disturb the order of nature in these respects, is to acquiesce in a moral, in order to prevent a physical evil.

If it were possible to make an accurate calculation of the evils which police regulations occasion, and of those which they prevent, the number of the former would, in all cases, exceed that of the latter.

If now, in addition to this, we bring forward the principles before unfolded, which disapprove of all State agency directed to *positive* aims, and which apply here with especial force, since it is precisely the moral man who feels every restriction most deeply; reflecting further, that if there is one aspect of development more than any other which owes its highest beauty to freedom, this is precisely the culture of character and morals; then the justice of the following principle will be sufficiently manifest, viz. that the State must wholly refrain from every attempt to operate directly or indirectly on the morals and character of the nation, otherwise than as such a policy may become inevitable as a natural consequence of its other absolutely necessary measures; and that everything calculated to promote such a design, and particularly all special supervision of education, religion, sumptuary laws, etc., lies wholly outside the limits of its legitimate activity.

Freedom is but the *possibility* of a various and indefinite activity; while government, or the exercise of dominion, is a single, but yet real activity. The ardent desire for freedom, therefore, is at first only too frequently suggested by the deep-felt consciousness of its absence.

It may easily be foreseen, therefore, that the important inquiry into the due limits of State agency must conduct us to an ampler range of freedom for human forces, and a richer diversity of circumstances and situations. Now the possibility of any higher degree of freedom presupposes a proportionate advancement in civilization,—a decreasing necessity of acting in large, compacted masses,—a richer variety of resources in the individual agents. If, then, the present age in reality possesses this increased culture and this power and diversity of resources, the freedom of which these are the precious conditions should unquestionably be accorded it. And so its methods of reform would be happily correspondent with a progressive civilization—if we do not err in supposing this to be its favorable characteristic.

But if we examine into the origin of particular institutions and police-laws, we find that they frequently originate in the real or pretended necessity of imposing taxes on the subject, and in this we may trace the example, it is true, to the political characteristics of the ancient States, inasmuch as such institutions grow out of the same desire of securing the constitution which we noticed in them. With respect to those limitations of freedom, however, which do not so much affect the State as the individuals who compose it, we are led to notice a vast difference between ancient and modern governments.

And yet the peculiar nature of the limitations imposed on freedom in our States; the fact that they regard rather what man possesses than what he really is, and that with respect to the latter they do not cultivate, even to uniformity, the physical, intellectual, and moral faculties; and lastly and especially, the prevalence of certain determining ideas, more binding than laws, suppress those energies which are the source of every active virtue, and the indispensable condition of any higher and more various culture.

This individual vigor, then, and manifold diversity, combine themselves in *originality*; and hence, that on which the consummate grandeur of our nature ultimately depends,—that towards which every human being must ceaselessly direct his efforts, and on which especially those who design to influence their fellow men must ever keep their eyes, is the *Individuality of Power and Development*. Just as this individuality springs naturally from the perfect freedom of action, and the greatest diversity in the agents, it tends immediately to produce them in turn. Even inanimate nature, which, proceeding in accordance with unchangeable laws, advances by regular grades of progression, appears more individual to the man who has been developed in his individuality.

Still, it is certain that the sensuous element in our nature, as it is the earliest germ, is also the most vivid expression of the spiritual.

I therefore deduce, as the natural inference from what has been argued, that reason cannot desire for man any other condition than that in which each individual not only enjoys the freedom of developing himself by his own energies, in his perfect individuality, but in which external nature even is left unfashioned by any human agency, but only receives the impress given to it by each individual of himself and his own free will, according to the measure of his wants and instincts, and restricted only by the limits of his power and his rights.

We might embody in a general formula our idea of State agency when restricted to its just limits, and define its objects as all that a government could accomplish for the common weal, without departing from the principle just established; while, from this position, we could proceed to derive the still stricter limitation, that any State interference in private affairs, not directly implying violence done to individual rights, should be absolutely condemned.

Now, State measures always imply more or less positive control; and even where they are not chargeable with actual coercion, they accustom men to look for instruction, guidance, and assistance from without, rather than to rely upon their own expedients. The only method of instruction, perhaps, of which the State can avail itself, consists in its declaring the best course to be pursued as though it were the result of its investigations, and in enjoining this in some way on the citizen. But, however it may accomplish this, whether directly or indirectly by law, or by means of its authority, rewards, and other encouragements attractive to the citizen, or, lastly, by merely recommending its propositions to his attention by arguments—it will always deviate very far from the best system of instruction. For this unquestionably, consists in proposing, as it were, all possible solutions of the problem in question, so that the citizen may select, according to his own judgment, the course which seems to him to be the most appropriate; or, still better, so as to enable him to discover the happiest solution for himself, from a careful representation of all the contingent obstacles.

In proportion as each individual relies upon the helpful vigilance of the State, he learns to abandon to its responsibility the fate and well-being of his fellow-citizens. But the inevitable tendency of such abandonment is to deaden the living force of sympathy, and to render the natural impulse to mutual assistance inactive: or, at least, the reciprocal interchange of services and benefits will be most likely to flourish in its greatest activity and beauty, where the feeling is liveliest that such assistance is the only thing to rely upon; and experience teaches us that those classes of the community which suffer under oppression, and are, as it were, overlooked by the Government, are always cemented together by the closest ties. But wherever the citizen becomes insensible to the interests of his fellow-citizen, the husband will contract feelings of cold indifference to the wife, and the father of a family towards the members of his household.

The solicitude of a State for the positive welfare of its citizens, must further be hurtful, in that it has to operate upon a promiscous mass of individualities, and therefore does harm to these by measures which cannot meet individual cases.

It hinders the development of Individuality.

For every restrictive institution comes into collision with the free and natural development of power, and gives rise to an infinite multiplicity of new relations; and even if we suppose the most equable course of events, and set aside all serious and unlooked-for accidents, the number of these relations which it brings in its train is not to be foreseen. Any one who has an opportunity of occupying himself with the higher departments of State administration, must certainly feel conscious from experience how few political measures have really an immediate and absolute necessity, and how many, on the contrary, have only a relative and indirect importance, and are wholly dependent on foregone measures. Now, in this way a vast increase of means is rendered necessary, and even these very means are drawn away from the attainment of the true end. Not only does such a State require larger sources of revenue, but it needs in addition an increase of artificial regulations for the maintenance of mere political security; the separate parts cohere less intimately together—the supervision of the Government requires far more vigilance and activity. Hence comes the calculation, no less difficult, but unhappily too often neglected, whether the available resources of the State are adequate to provide the means which the maintenance of security demands; and should this calculation reveal a real misproportion, it only suggests the necessity of fresh artificial arrangements, which, in the end, overstrain the elasticity of the power—an evil from which (though not from this cause only) many of our modern States are suffering.

We must not overlook here one particular manifestation of this generally injurious agency, since it so closely affects human development; and this is, that the very administration of political affairs becomes in time so full of complications, that it requires an incredible number of persons to devote their time to its supervision, in order that it may not fall into utter confusion. Now, by far the greater portion of these have to deal with the mere symbols and formulas of things; and thus, not only men of first-rate capacity are withdrawn from anything which gives scope or stimulus to the thinking faculties, and men who would be usefully employed in some other way are diverted from their real course of action, but their intellectual powers are brought to suffer from this partly fruitless, partly one-sided employment. Wholly new sources of gain, moreover, are introduced and established by this necessity of despatching State affairs, and these render the servants of the State more dependent on the governing classes of the community than on the nation in general. Familiar as they have become to us in experience, we need not pause to describe the numerous evils which flow from such a dependence—what looking to the State for help, what a lack of self-reliance, what false vanity, what inaction even, and want. The very evils from which these hurtful consequences flow, are immediately produced by them in turn. When once thus accustomed to the transaction of State affairs, men gradually lose sight of the essential object, and limit their regard to the mere form; they are thus prompted to attempt new ameliorations, perhaps true in intention, but without sufficient adaptation to the required end; and the prejudicial operation of these necessitates new forms, new complications, and often new restrictions, and thereby creates new departments, which require for their efficient supervision a vast increase of functionaries. Hence it arises that in every decennial period the number of the public officials and the extent of registration increase, while the liberty of the subject proportionately declines.

I could here present an agreeable contrast of a people in the enjoyment of unfettered freedom, and of the richest diversity of individual and external relations; I could exhibit how, even in such a condition, fairer and loftier and more wonderful forms of diversity and originality must still be revealed, than even any in that antiquity which so unspeakably fascinates, despite the harsher features which must still characterize the individuality of a ruder civilization; a condition in which force would still keep pace with refinement, and even with the rich resources of revealed character, and in which, from the endlessly ramified interconnection between all nations and quarters of the globe, the very elements themselves would seem more numerous; I could then proceed to show what new force would bloom out and ripen into fruition, when every existing thing was organizing itself by its own unhindered agency; when even surrounded, as it would be, by the most exquisite forms, it transformed these present shapes of beauty into its own internal being with that unhampered spontaneity which is the cherished growth of freedom: I could point out with what delicacy and refinement the inner life of man would unfold its strength and beauty; how it would in time become the high, ultimate *object of his solicitude, and how everything physical and exter*nal would be transfused into the inner moral and intellectual being, and the bond which connects the two natures together would gain lasting strength, when nothing intervened to disturb the reaction of all human pursuits upon the mind and character: how no single agent would be sacrificed to the interest of another; but while each held fast the measure of power bestowed on him, he would for that very reason be inspired with a still lovelier eagerness to give it a direction conducive to the benefit of the others: how, when every one was progressing in his individuality, more varied and exquisite modifications of the beautiful human character would spring up, and one-sidedness would become more rare, as it is the result of feebleness and insufficiency; and as each, when nothing else would avail to make the other assimilate himself to him, would be more effectually constrained to modify his own being by the still continuing necessity of union with others: how, in such a people, no single energy or hand would be lost to the task of ennobling and enhancing human existence: and lastly, how through this focal concentration of energies, the views of all would be directed to this last end alone, and would be turned aside from every other object that was false or less worthy of humanity. I might then conclude, by showing how the beneficial consequences of such a constitution, diffused throughout the people of any nation whatever, would even remove an infinite share of the frightfulness of that human misery which is never wholly eradicable, of the destructive devastations of nature, of the fell ravages of hostile animosity, and of the wanton luxuriousness of excessive indulgence in pleasure. But I content myself with having limned out the more prominent features of the contrasting picture in a general outline; it is enough for me to throw out a few suggestive ideas, for riper judgments to sift and examine.

If we come now to the ultimate result of the whole argument we have been endeavoring to develop, the first principle we eliminate will be, that the State is to abstain from all solicitude for the positive welfare of the citizens, and not to proceed a step further than is necessary for their mutual security and protection against foreign enemies; for with no other object should it impose restrictions on freedom.

The more a man acts for himself, the more does he develop himself. In large associations he is too prone to become an instrument merely. A frequent effect of these unions moreover is to allow the symbol to be substituted for the thing, and this always impedes true development. The dead hieroglyphic does not inspire like living nature.

VI
JOHN STUART MILL

John Stuart Mill, 1806-1873, philosophical writer, logician and economist; eldest son of James Mill, the utilitarian English philosopher. Born in London, England; carefully educated by father, brought up an agnostic from infancy and never acquired any religious beliefs. Visited France in 1820; entered India House in 1823 as father's assistant; became chief examiner in 1856. In 1836 became superintendent of the *Westminster Review* after its amalgamation with the *London Review*; was proprietor 1837-40. Married Mrs. Taylor after a long and intimate friendship, in 1851; elected Member of Parliament for Westminster in 1865. Works, which were with one or two exceptions pre-eminently successful: *Essays on Unsettled Questions of Political Economy,* 1830; *Logic,* 1843; *Political Economy,* 1848; *Essay on Liberty,* 1859; *On the Subjection of Women,* 1869; *Autobiography,* 1873; *Thoughts on Parliamentary Reform,* 1859; *Dissertations and Discussions,* 1859-67; *Considerations on Representative Government,* 1861; *Utilitarianism,* 1863; *Examination of Sir William Hamilton's Philosophy,* 1865; *Auguste Comte and Positivism,* 1865; *England and Ireland,* 1868; *On the Irish Land Question,* 1870; *Nature, the Utility of Religion, and Theism,* 1874.

The selections are from the *Essay on Liberty,* Mill's most carefully written work.

Liberty of Thought, Speech and Press.—The time it is to be hoped, is gone by, when any defence would be necessary of the "Liberty of the press" as one of the securities against corrupt or tyrannical government. No argument, we may suppose, can now be needed, against permitting a legislature or an executive, not identified in interest with the people, to prescribe opinions to them, and determine what doctrines and what arguments they shall be allowed to hear. This aspect of the question, besides, has been so often and so triumphantly enforced by preceding writers, that it needs not be specially insisted on in this place. Though the law of England on the subject of the press, is as servile to this day as it was in the time of the Tudors, there is little danger of its being actually put in force against political discussion, except during some temporary panic, when fear of insurrection drives ministers and judges from their propriety; and, speaking generally, it is not, in constitutional countries, to be apprehended, that the government, whether completely

John Stuart Mill

responsible to the people or not, will often attempt to control the expression of opinion, except when in doing so it makes itself the organ of the general intolerance of the public. Let us suppose, therefore, that the government is entirely at one with the people, and never thinks of exerting any power of coercion unless in agreement with what it conceives to be their voice. But I deny the right of the people to exercise such coercion, either by themselves or by their government. The power itself is illegitimate. The best government has no more title to it than the worst. It is as noxious, or more noxious, when exerted in accordance with public opinion, than when in opposition to it. If all mankind minus one, were of one opinion, and only one person were of the contrary opinion, mankind would be no more justified in silencing that one person, than he, if he had the power, would be justified in silencing mankind. Were an opinion a personal possession of no value except to the owner; if to be obstructed in the enjoyment of it were simply a private injury, it would make some difference whether the injury was inflicted only on a few persons or on many. But the peculiar evil of silencing the expression of an opinion is, that it is robbing the human race, posterity as well as the existing generation; those who dissent from the opinion, still more than those who hold it. If the opinion is right, they are deprived of the opportunity of exchanging error for truth; if wrong, they lose, what is almost as great a benefit, the clearer perception and livelier impression of truth, produced by its collision with error.

It is necessary to consider separately these two hypotheses, each of which has a distinct branch of the argument corresponding to it. We can never be sure that the opinion we are endeavoring to stifle is a false opinion; and if we were sure, stifling it would be an evil still.

First: the opinion which it is attempted to suppress by authority may possibly be true. Those who desire to suppress it, of course deny its truth; but they are not infallible. They have no authority to decide the question for all mankind, and exclude every other person from the means of judging. To refuse a hearing to an opinion, because they are sure that it is false, is to assume that their certainty is the same thing as *absolute* certainty. All silencing of discussion is an assumption of infallibility. Its condemnation may be allowed to rest on this common argument, not the worse for being common.

Unfortunately for the good sense of mankind, the fact of their fallibility is far from carrying the weight in their practical judgment, which is always allowed to it in theory; for while everyone well knows himself to be fallible, few think it necessary to take any precautions against their own fallibility, or admit the supposition that any opinion, of which they feel very certain, may be one of the examples of the error to which they acknowledge themselves to be liable. Absolute princes, or others who are accustomed to unlimited deference, usually feel this complete confidence in their own opinions on nearly all subjects. People more happily situated, who sometimes hear their opinions disputed, and are not wholly unused to be set right when they are wrong, place the same unbounded reliance only on such of their opinions as are shared by all who surround them, or to whom they habitually defer; for in proportion to a man's want of confidence in his own solitary judgment, does he usually repose with implicit trust on the infallibility of "the world" in general. And the world, to each individual, means the part of it with which he comes in contact; his party, his sect, his church, his class of society; the man may be called, by comparison, almost liberal and large minded to whom it means anything so comprehensive as his own country or his own age. Nor is his faith in this collective authority at all shaken by his being aware that other ages, countries, sects, churches, classes, and parties have thought, and even now think, the exact reverse. He devolves upon his own world the responsibility of being in the right against the dissentient worlds of other people; and it never troubles him that mere accident has decided which of these numerous worlds is the object of his reliance, and that the same causes which make him a churchman in London, would have made him a Buddhist or a Confucian in Pekin. Yet it is as evident in itself, as any amount of argument can make it, that ages are no more infallible than individuals; every age having held many opinions which subsequent ages have deemed not only false but absurd; and it is as certain that many opinions, now general, will be rejected by future ages, as it is that many, once general, are rejected by the present.

When we consider either the history of opinion, or the ordinary conduct of human life, to what is to be ascribed that the one and the other are no worse than they are? Not certainly to the inherent force of the human understanding; for, on any matter not self-evident, there are ninety-nine persons totally incapable of judging of it, for one who is capable; and the capacity of the hundreth person is only comparative; for the majority of the eminent men of every past generation held many opinions now known to be erroneous, and did or approved numerous things which no one will now justify. Why is it, then, that there is on the whole a preponderance among mankind of rational opinions and rational conduct? If there really is this preponderance, which there must be unless human affairs are, and have always been, in an almost desperate state—it is owing to a quality of the human mind, the source of everything respectable in man either as an intellectual or as a moral being, namely, that his errors are corrigible. He is capable of rectifying his mistakes, by discussion and experience. Not by experience alone. There must be discussion, to show how experience is to be interpreted. Wrong opinions and practices gradually yield to fact and argument; but facts and arguments, to produce any effect on the mind, must be brought before it. Very few facts are able to tell their own story, without comments to bring out their meaning. The whole strength and value, then, of human judgment, depending on the one property, that it can be set right when it is wrong, reliance can be placed on it only when the means of setting it right are kept constantly at hand. In the case of any person whose judgment is really deserving of confidence, how has it become so? Because he has kept his mind open to criticism of his opinions and conduct. Because it has been his practice to listen to all that could be said against him; to profit by as much of it as was just, and expound to himself, and upon occasion to others, the fallacy of what was fallacious. Because he has felt, that the only way in which a human being can make some approach to knowing the whole of a subject, is by hearing what can be said about it by persons of every variety of opinion, and studying all modes in which it can be looked at by every character of mind. No wise man ever acquired his wisdom in any mode but this; nor is it in the nature of human intellect to become wise in any other manner. The steady habit of correcting and completing his own opinion by collating it with those of others, so far from causing doubt and hesitation in carrying it into practice, is the only stable foundation for a just reliance on it: for, being cognizant of all that can, at least obviously, be said against him, and having taken up his position against all gainsayers—knowing that he has sought for objections and difficulties, instead of avoiding them, and has shut out no light which can be thrown upon the subject from any quarter—he has a right to think his judgment better than that of any person, or any multitude, who have not gone through a similar process.

It is not too much to require that what the wisest of mankind, those who are best entitled to trust their own judgment, find necessary to warrant their relying on it, should be submitted to by that miscellaneous collection of a few wise and many foolish individuals, called the public. The most intolerant of churches, the Roman Catholic Church, even at the canonization of a saint, admits, and listens patiently to, a "devil's advocate." The holiest of men, it appears, cannot be admitted to posthumous honors, until all that the devil could say against him is known and weighed. If even the Newtonian philosophy were not permitted to be questioned, mankind could not feel as complete assurance of its truth as they now do. The beliefs which we have most warrant for, have no safeguard to rest on, but a standing invitation to the whole world to prove them unfounded. If the challenge is not accepted, or is accepted and the attempt fails, we are far enough from certainty still; but we have done the best that the existing state of human reason admits of; we have neglected nothing that would give the truth a chance of reaching us; if the lists are kept open, we may hope that if there be a better truth, it will be found when the human mind is capable of receiving it; and in the meantime, we may rely on having attained such approach to truth, as is possible in our own day. This is the amount of certainty attainable by a fallible being, and this the sole way of attaining it.

Strange it is, that men should admit the validity of the arguments for free discussion, but object to their being "pushed to an extreme;" not seeing that unless the reasons are good for an extreme case, they are not good for any case. Strange that they should imagine that they are not assuming infallibility when they acknowledge that there should be free discussion on all subjects which can possibly be doubtful, but think that some particular principle or doctrine should be forbidden to be questioned because it is so certain, that is, because they are certain that it is certain. To call any proposition certain, while there is anyone who would deny its certainty if permitted, but who is not permitted, is to assume that we ourselves, and those who agree with us, are the judges of certainty, and judges without hearing the other side.

In order more fully to illustrate the mischief of denying a hearing to opinions because we, in our own judgment, have condemned them, it will be desirable to fix down the discussion to a concrete case; and I choose by preference, the cases which are least favorable to me—in which the argument against freedom of opinion, both on the score of truth and on that of utility, is considered the strongest. Let the opinions impugned be the belief in a God and in a future state, or any of the commonly received doctrines of morality. To fight the battle on such ground, gives a great advantage to an unfair antagonist; since he will be sure to say (and many who have no desire to be unfair will say it internally), Are these the doctrines which you do not deem sufficiently certain to be taken under the protection of law? Is the belief in a God one of the opinions, to feel sure of which, you hold to be assuming infallibility? But I must be permitted to observe, that it is not the feeling sure of a doctrine (be it what it may) which I call an assumption of infallibility. It is the undertaking to decide that question for others, without allowing them to hear what can be said on the contrafy side. And I denounce and reprobate this pretension not the less, if put forth on the side of my most solemn convictions. However positive any one's persuasion may be, not only of the falsity but of the pernicious consequences, but (to adopt expressions which I altogether condemn) the immorality and impiety of an opinion; yet, if, in pursuance of that private judgment, though backed by the public judgment of his country or his cotemporaries, he prevents the opinion from being heard in its defence, he assumes infallibility. And so far from the assumption being less objectionable or less dangerous because the opinion is called immoral or impious, this is the case of all others in which it is most fatal. These are exactly the occasions on which the men of one generation commit those dreadful mistakes, which excite the astonishment and horror of posterity. It is among such that we find the instances memorable in history, when the arm of the law has been employed to root out the best men and the noblest doctrines; with deplorable success as to the men, though some of the doctrines have survived to be (as if in mockery) invoked, in defence of similar conduct towards those who dissent from them, or from their received interpretation.

Mankind can hardly be too often reminded, that there was once a man named Socrates, between whom and the legal authorities and public opinion of his time, there took place a memorable collision. Born in an age and country abounding in individual greatness, this man has been handed down to us by those who best knew both him and the age, as the most virtuous man in it; while *we* know him as the head and prototype of all subsequent teachers of virtue, the source equally of the lofty inspiration of Plato and the judicious utilitarianism of Aristotle, the two headsprings of ethical as of all other philosophy. This acknowledged master of all the eminent thinkers who have since lived—whose fame, still growing after more than two thousand years, all but outweighs the whole remainder of the names which make his native city illustrious—was put to death by his countrymen, after a judicial conviction, for impiety and immorality. Impiety, in denying the Gods recognized by the State; indeed his accusers asserted (see the "Apologia") that he believed in no gods at all. Immorality, in being, by his doctrines and instructions, a "corrupter of youth." Of these charges the tribunal, there is every ground for believing, honestly found him guilty, and condemned the man who probably of all then born had deserved best of mankind, to be put to death as a criminal.

The dictum that truth always triumphs over persecution, is one of those pleasant falsehoods which men repeat after one another till they pass into commonplaces, but which all experience refutes. History teems with instances of truth put down by persecution. If not suppressed forever, it may be thrown back for centuries. To speak only of religious opinions: the Reformation broke out at least twenty times before Luther, and was put down. Arnold of Brescia was put down. Fra Dolcino was put down. Savonarola was put down. The Albigeois were put down. The Vaudois were put down. The Lollards were put down. The Hussites were put down. Even after the era of Luther, wherever persecution was persisted in, it was successful. In Spain, Italy, Flanders, the Austrian empire, Protestantism was rooted out; and, most likely, would have been so in England, had Queen Mary lived, or Queen Elizabeth died. Persecution has always succeeded, save where the heretics were too strong a party to be effectually persecuted. No reasonable person can doubt that Christianity might have been extirpated in the Roman Empire. It spread, and became predominant because the persecutions were only occasional, lasting but a short time, and separated by long intervals of almost undisturbed propagandism. It is a piece of idle sentimentality that truth, merely as truth, has any inherent power denied to error, of prevailing against the dungeon and the stake. Men are not more zealous for truth than they often are for error, and a sufficient application of legal or even of social penalties will generally succeed in stopping the propagation of either. The real advantage which truth has consists in this, that when an opinion is true it may be extinguished once, twice, or many times, but in the course of ages there will generally be found persons to rediscover it, until some one of its reappearances falls on a time when from favorable circumstances it escapes persecution until it has made such head as to withstand all subsequent attempts to suppress it.

It will be said that we do not now put to death the introducers of new opinions: we are not like our fathers who slew the prophets, we even build sepulchres to them. It is true we no longer put heretics to death; and the amount of penal infliction which modern feeling would probably tolerate, even against the most obnoxious opinions, is not sufficient to extirpate them. But let us not flatter ourselves that we are yet free from the stain even of legal persecution. Penalties for opinion or at least for ts expression, still exist by law; and their enforcement is not, even in these times, so unexampled as to make it at all incredible that they may some day be revived in full force. In the year 1857, at the summer assizes of the County of Cornwall, an unfortunate man said to be of unexceptional conduct in all relations of life, was sentenced to twenty-one months' imprisonment, for uttering and writing on a gate, some offensive words concerning Christianity. Within a month of the same time, at the old Bailey, two persons, on two separate occasions, were rejected as jurymen, and one of them grossly insulted by the judge and by one of the counsel, because they honestly declared that they had no theological belief; and a third, a foreigner, for the same reason, was denied justice against a thief. This refusal of redress took place in virtue of the legal doctrine, that no person can be allowed to give evidence in a court of justice, who does not profess belief in a God (any god is sufficient) and in a future state; which is equivalent to declaring such persons to be outlaws, excluded from the protections of the tribunals; who may not only be robbed or assaulted with impunity, if no one but themselves, or persons of similar opinions be present, but anyone else may be robbed or assaulted with impunity, if the proof of the fact depends on their evidence. The assumption on which this is grounded, is that the oath is worthless, of a person who does not believe in a future state; a proposition which betokens much ignorance of history in those who assent to it (since it is historically true that a large proportion of infidels in all ages have been persons of distinguished integrity and honor); and would be maintained by no one who had the smallest conception how many of the persons in greatest repute with the world, both for virtues and attainments, are well known, at least to their intimates, to be unbelievers. The rule, besides, is suicidal, and cuts away its own foundation. Under pretence that atheists must be liars, it admits the testimony of all atheists who are willing to lie, and rejects only those who brave the obloquy of publicly confessing a detested creed rather than affirm a falsehood. A rule thus self-convicted of absurdity so far as regards its professed purpose, can be kept in force only as a badge of hatred, a relic of persecution; a persecution, too, having the peculiarity, that the qualification for undergoing it, is the being clearly proved not to deserve it. The rule, and the theory it implies, are hardly less insulting to believers than to infidels. For if he who does not believe in a future state necessarily lies, it follows that they who do believe are only prevented from lying, if prevented they are, by the fear of hell. We will not do the authors and abettors of the rule the injury of supposing, that the conception which they have formed of Christian virtue is drawn from their own consciousness.

Those in whose eyes this reticence on the part of heretics is no evil, should consider in the first place, that in consequence of it there is never any fair and thorough discussion of heretical opinions; and that such of them as could not stand such a discussion, though they may be prevented from spreading, do not disappear. But it is not the minds of heretics that are deteriorated most, by the ban placed on all inquiry which does not end in the orthodox conclusions. The greatest harm done is to those who are not heretics, and whose whole mental development is cramped, and their reason cowed, by the fear of heresy. Who can compute what the world loses in the multitude of promising intellects combined with timid characters, who dare not follow out any bold, vigorous, independent train of thought, lest it should land them in something which will admit of being considered irreligious or immoral? Among them we may occasionally see some man of deep conscientiousness, and subtle and refined understanding, who spends a life in sophisticating with an intellect which he cannot silence, and exhausts the resources of ingenuity in attempting to reconcile the promptings of his conscience and reason with orthodoxy, which yet, he does not, perhaps, to the end succeed in doing. No one can be a greater thinker, who does not recognize, that as a thinker it is his first duty to follow his intellect to whatever conclusions it may lead. Truth gains more even by the errors of one, who, with due study and preparation, thinks for himself, than by the true opinions of those who only hold them because they do not suffer themselves to think. Not that it is solely, or chiefly, to form great thinkers, that freedom of thinking is required. On the contrary, it is as much and even more indispensable, to enable average human beings to attain the mental stature which they are capable of. There have been, and may again be, great individual thinkers, in a general atmosphere of mental slavery. But there never has been, nor ever will be, in that atmosphere, an intellectually active people. Where any people has made a temporary approach to such a character, it has been because the dread of heterodox speculation was for a time suspended. Where there is a tacit convention that principles are not to be disputed; where the discussion of the greatest questions which can occupy humanity is considered to be closed, we cannot hope to find that generally high scale of mental activity which has made some periods of history so remarkable. Never when controversy avoided the subjects which are large and important enough to kindle enthusiasm, was the mind of a people stirred up from its foundations, and the impulse given which raised even persons of the most ordinary intellect to something of the dignity of thinking beings. Of such we have had an example in the condition of Europe during the times immediately following the Reformation; another, though limited to the Continent and to a more cultivated class, in the speculative movement of the latter half of the eighteenth century; and a third, of still briefer duration, in the intellectual fermentation of Germany during the Goethian and Fichtean period. These periods differ widely in the particular opinions which they developed; but were alike in this, that during all three the yoke of authority was broken. In each an old mental despotism had been thrown off, and no new one had yet taken its place. The impulse given at these three periods has made Europe what it now is. Every single improvement which has taken place either in the human mind or in institutions, may be traced distinctly to one or other of them. Appearances have for some time indicated that all three impulses are well nigh spent; and we can expect no fresh start, until we again assert our mental freedom.

The greatest orator, save one, of antiquity, has left it on record that he always studied his adversary's case with as great, if not still greater, intensity than even his own. What Cicero practiced as the means of forensic success, requires to be imitated by all who study any subject in order to arrive at the truth. He who knows only his own side of the case, knows little of that. His reasons may be good, and no one may have been able to refute them. But if he is equally unable to refute the reasons on the opposite side; if he does not so much as know what they are, he has no ground for preferring either opinion. The rational position for him would be suspension of judgment, and unless he contents himself with that, he is either led by authority, or adopts, like the generalty of the world, the side to which he feels most inclination. Nor is it enough that he should hear the arguments of adversaries from his own teachers, presented as they state them, and accompanied by what they offer as refutations. That is not the way to do justice to the arguments, or bring them into real contact with his own mind. He must be able to hear them from persons who actually believe them; who defend them in earnest, and do their very utmost for them. He must know them in their most plausible and persuasive form; he must feel the whole force of the difficulty which the true view of the subject has to encounter and dispose of; else he will never really possess himself of the portion of truth which meets and removes that difficulty. Ninety-nine in a hundred of what are called educated men are in this condition; even of those who can argue fluently for their opinions. Their conclusion may be true, but it might be false for anything they know; they have never thrown themselves into the mental position of those who think differently from them, and considered what such persons may have to say; and consequently they do not, in any proper sense of the word, know the doctrine which they themselves profess. They do not know those parts of it which explain and justify the remainder; the considerations which show that a fact which seemingly conflicts with another is reconcilable with it, or that, of two apparently strong reasons, one and not the other ought to be preferred. All that part of the truth which turns the scale, and decides the judgment of a completely informed mind, they are strangers to; nor is it ever really known, but to those who have attended equally and impartially to both sides, and endeavored to see the reasons for both in the strongest light. So essential is this discipline to a real understanding of moral and human subjects, that if opponents of all important truths do not exist, it is indispensable to imagine them, and supply them with the strongest arguments which the most skilful devil's advocate can conjure up.

If not the public, at least the philosophers and theologians who are to resolve the difficulties, must make themselves familiar with those difficulties in their most puzzling form; and this cannot be accomplished unless they are freely stated, and placed in the most advantageous light which they admit of. The Catholic Church has its own way of dealing with this embarrassing problem. It makes a broad separation between those who can be permitted to receive its doctrines on conviction, and those who must accept them on trust. Neither, indeed, are allowed any choice as to what they will accept; but the clergy, such at least as can be fully confided in, may admissibly and meritoriously make themselves acquainted with the arguments of opponents, in order to answer them, and may, therefore, read heretical books; the laity, not unless by special permission, hard to be obtained. This dicipline recognizes a knowledge of the enemy's case as beneficial to the teachers, but finds means, consistent with this, of denying it to the rest of the world; this giving the elite more mental culture, though not more mental freedom, than it allows to the mass. By this device it succeeds in obtaining the kind of mental superiority which its purposes require; for though culture without freedom never made a large and liberal mind, it can make a clever advocate of a cause. But in countries professing Protestantism, this resource is denied; since Protestants hold, at least in theory, that the responsibility for the choice of a religion must be borne by each for himself, and cannot be thrown off upon teachers. Besides, in the present state of the world, it is practically impossible that writings which are read by the instructed can be kept from the uninstructed. If the teachers of mankind are to be cognizant of all that they ought to know, everything must be free to be written and published without restraint.

A person who derives all his instruction from teachers or books, even if he escape the besetting temptation of contenting himself with cram, is under no compulsion to hear both sides; accordingly it is far from a frequent accomplishment, even among thinkers, to know both sides; and the weakest part of what everybody says in defence of his opinion, is what he intends as a reply to his antagonist. It is the fashion of the present time to disparage negative logic—that which points out weaknesses in theory or errors in practice, without establishing positive truths. Such negative criticism would indeed be poor enough as an ultimate result; but as a means to attaining any positive knowledge or conviction worthy the name, it cannot be valued too highly; and until people are again systematically trained to it, there will be few great thinkers, and a low general average of intellect, in any but the mathematical and physical departments of speculation. On any other subject no one's opinions deserves the name of knowledge, except so far as he has either had forced upon him by others, or gone through of himself, the same mental process which would have been required of him in carrying on an active controversy with opponents. That, therefore, which when absent, it is so indispensable, but so difficult, to create, how worse than absurd it is to forego, when spontaneously offering itself! If there are any persons who contest a received opinion, or who will do so if law or opinion will let them, let us thank them for it, open our minds to listen to them, and rejoice that there is someone to do for us what we otherwise ought, if we have any regard for either the certainty or the vitality of our convictions, to do with much greater labor for ourselves.

We have now recognized the necessity to the mental well-being of mankind (on which all their other well-being depends) of freedom of opinion, and freedom of the expression of opinion, on four distinct grounds; which we will now briefly recapitulate.

First, if any opinion is compelled to silence, that opinion may, for aught we can certainly know, be true. To deny this is to assume our own infallibility.

Secondly, though the silenced opinion be an error, it may, and very commonly does contain a portion of truth; and since the general or prevailing opinion on any subject is rarely or never the whole truth, it is only by the collision of adverse opinions that the remainder of the truth has any chance of being supplied.

Thirdly, even if the received opinion be not only true, but the whole truth; unless it is suffered to be, and actually is, vigorously and earnestly contested, it will, by most of those who receive it, be held in the manner of a prejudice, with little comprehension or feeling of its rational grounds. And not only this, but, fourthly, the meaning of the doctrine itself will be in danger of being lost, or enfeebled, and deprived of its vital effect on the character and conduct; the dogma becoming a mere formal profession, inefficacious for good, but cumbering the ground, and preventing the growth of any real and heartfelt conviction, from reason or personal experience.

Majority Rule.—The will of the people, moreover, practically means the will of the most numerous or the most active part of the people; the majority, or those who succeed in making themselves accepted as the majority; the people, consequently, may desire to oppress a part of their number; and precautions are as much needed against this as against any other abuse of power. The limitation, therefore, of the power of government over individuals loses none of its importance when the holders of power are regularly accountable to the community, that is, to the strongest party therein. This view of things, recommending itself equally to the intelligence of thinkers and to the inclination of those important classes in European society to whose real or supposed interests democracy is adverse, has had no difficulty in establishing itself; and in political speculations "the tyranny of the majority" is now generally included among the evils against which society requires to be on its guard.

Like other tyrannies, the tyranny of the majority was at first, and is still vulgarly held in dread, chiefly as operating through the acts of the public authorities. But reflecting persons perceived that when society is itself the tyrant—society collectively, over the separate individuals who compose it—its means of tyrannizing are not restricted to the acts which it may do by the hands of its political functionaries. Society can and does execute its own mandates; and if it issues wrong mandates instead of right, or any mandates at all in things with which it ought not to meddle, it practices a social tyranny more formidable than many kinds of political oppression since, though not usually upheld by such extreme penalties, it leaves fewer means of escape, penetrating much more deeply into the details of life, and enslaving the soul itself. Protection, therefore, against the tyranny of the magistrate is not enough; there needs protection also against the tyranny of the prevailing opinion and feeling; against the tendency of society to impose, by other means than civil penalties, its own ideas of practices as rules of conduct on those who dissent from them; to fetter the development, and, if possible, prevent the formation, of any individuality not in harmony with its ways, and compels all characters to fashion themselves upon the model of its own. There is a limit to the legitimate interference of collective opinion with individual independence; and to find that limit, and maintain it against encroachment, is as indispensable to a good condition of human affairs, as protection against political despotism.

Religious Intolerance.—Those who first broke the yoke of what called itself the Universal Church, were in general as little willing to permit difference or religious opinion as that church itself. But when the heat of the conflict was over, without giving a complete victory to any party, and each church or sect was reduced to limit its hopes to retaining possession of the ground it already occupied; minorities, seeing that they had no chance of becoming majorities, were under the necessity of pleading to those whom they could not convert, for permission to differ. It is accordingly on this battle field, almost solely, that the rights of the individual against society have been asserted on broad grounds of principle, and the claim of society to exercise authority over dissentients, openly controverted. The great writers to whom the world owes what religious liberty it possesses, have mostly asserted freedom of conscience as an indefeasible right, and denied absolutely that a human being is accountable to others for his religious belief. Yet so natural to mankind is intolerance in whatever they really care about, that religious freedom has hardly anywhere been practically realized, except where religious indifference, which dislikes to have its peace disturbed by theological quarrels, has added its weight to the scale. In the minds of almost all religious persons, even in the most tolerant countries, the duty of toleration is admitted with tacit reserves. One person will bear with dissent in matters of church government, but not of dogma; another can tolerate everybody, short of a Papist or an Unitarian; another, everyone who believes in revealed religion; a few extend their charity a little further, but stop at the belief in a God and in a future state. Wherever the sentiment of the majority is still genuine and intense, it is found to have abated little of its claim to be obeyed.

Sovereignty.—The object of this Essay is to assert one very simple principle as entitled to govern absolutely the dealings of society with the individual in the way of compulsion and control, whether the means used be physical force in the form of legal penalties, or the moral coercion of public opinion. That principle is that the sole end for which mankind are warranted, individually or collectively in interfering with the liberty of action of any of their number, is self-protection. That the only purpose for which power can be rightfully exercised over any member of a civilized community, against his will, is to prevent harm to others. His own good, either physical or moral, is not a sufficient warrant. He cannot rightfully be compelled to do or forbear because it will be better for him to do so, because it will make him happier, because, in the opinion of others, to do so would be wise or even right. These are good reasons for remonstrating with him, or reasoning with him, or persuading him, or entreating him, but not of compelling him, or visiting him with any evil in case he do otherwise. To justify that, the conduct from which it is desired to deter him, must be calculated to produce evil to someone else. The only part of the conduct of anyone for which he is amenable to society is that which concerns others. In the part which merely concerns himself, his independence is, of right, absolute. Over himself, over his own body and mind, the individual is sovereign.

Social Freedom.—But there is a sphere of action in which society, as distinguished from the individual, has, if any, only an indirect interest; comprehending all that portion of a person's life and conduct which affects only himself, or if it also affects others, only with their free, voluntary, and undeceived consent and participation. When I say only himself, I mean directly and in the first instance; for whatever affects himself, may affect others through himself; and the objection which may be grounded on this contingency, will receive consideration in the sequel. This, then, is the appropriate region of human liberty. It comprises, first, the inward domain of consciousness; demanding liberty of conscience, in the most comprehensive sense; liberty of thought and feeling; absolute freedom of opinion and sentiments on all subjects, practical or speculative, scientific, moral or theological. The liberty of expressing and publishing opinions may seem to fall under a different principle, since it belongs to that part of the conduct of an individual which concerns other people, but, being almost of as much importance as the liberty of thought itself, and resting in great part on the same reasons, is practically inseparable from it. Secondly, the principle requires liberty of tastes and pursuits; of framing the plan of our life to suit our own character; of doing as we like, subject to such consequences as may follow; without impediment from our fellow creatures, so long as what we do does not harm them, even though they should think our conduct foolish, perverse, or wrong. Thirdly, from this liberty of each individual, follows the liberty, within the same limits of combination among the individuals; freedom to unite, for any purpose not involving harm to others; the persons combining being supposed to be of full age, and not forced or deceived.

No society in which these liberties are not, on the whole, respected, is free, whatever may be its form of government; and none is completely free in which they do not exist absolutely and unqualified. The only freedom which deserves the name is that of pursuing our own good in our own way, so long as we do not attempt to deprive others of theirs, or impede their efforts to obtain it. Each is the proper guardian of his own health, whether bodily, or mental and spiritual. Mankind are greater gainers by suffering each other to live as seems good to themselves, than by compelling each to live as seems good to the rest.

Apart from the peculiar tenets of individual thinkers, there is also in the world at large an increasing inclination to stretch unduly the powers of society over the individual, both by the force of opinion and even by that of legislation; and as the tendency of all the changes taking place in the world is to strengthen society, and diminish the power of the individual, this encroachment is not one of the evils which tend spontaneously to disappear, but, on the contrary, to grow more and more formidable. The disposition of mankind, whether as rulers or fellow-citizens, to impose their own opinions and inclinations as a rule of conduct on others, is so energetically supported by some of the best and by some of the worst feelings incident to human nature, that it is hardly ever kept under restraint by anything but want of power; and as the power is not declining, but growing, unless a strong barrier of moral conviction can be raised against the mischief, we must expect, in the present circumstances of the world, to see it increase.

Originality.—It will not be denied by anybody, that originality is a valuable element in human affairs. There is always need of persons not only to discover new truths and point out when what were once truths are true no longer, but also to commence new practices, and set the example of more enlightened conduct, and better taste and sense in human life. This cannot well be gainsayed by anybody who does not believe that the world has already attained perfection in all its ways and practices. It is true that this benefit is not capable of being rendered by everybody alike; there are but few persons, in comparison with the whole of mankind, whose experiments, if adopted by others, would be likey to be any improvement on established practice. But these few are the salt of the earth; without them human life would become a stagnant pool. Not only is it they who introduce good things which did not before exist; it is they who keep the life in those which already exist. If there were nothing new to be done, would human intellect cease to be necessary? Would it be a reason why those who do the old things should forget why they are done, and do them like cattle, not like human beings? There is only too great a tendency in the best beliefs and practices to degenerate into the mechanical; and unless there were a succession of persons whose ever-recurring originality prevents the grounds of those beliefs and practices from becoming merely traditional, such dead matter would not resist the smallest shock from anything really alive, and there would be no reason why civilization should not die out, as in the Byzantine Empire. Persons of genius, it is true, are, and are always likely to be, a small minority; but in order to have them, it is necessary to preserve the soil in which they grow. Genius can only breathe freely in the atmosphere of freedom. Persons of genius are, *ex vi termini*, more individual than any other people—less capable, consequently, of fitting themselves, without hurtful compression, into any of the small number of moulds which society provides in order to save its members the trouble of forming their own character. If from timidity they consent to be forced into one of these moulds and to let all that part of themselves which cannot expand under the pressure remain unexpanded, society will be little the better for their genius. If they are of a strong character, and break their fetters they become a mark for the society which has not succeeded in reducing them to commonplace, to point out with solemn warning as "wild," "erratic," and the like; much as if one should complain of the Niagara River for not flowing smoothly between its banks like a Dutch Canal.

I insist thus emphatically on the importance of genius, and the necessity of allowing it to unfold itself freely both in thought and practice, being well aware that no one will deny the position in theory, but knowing also that almost everyone, in reality, is totally indifferent to it. People think genius a fine thing if it enables a man to write an exciting poem or paint a picture. But in its true sense, that of originality in thought and action, though no one says that it is not a thing to be admired, nearly all, at heart, think that they can do very well without it. Unhappily this is too natural to be wondered at. Originality is the one thing which unoriginal minds cannot feel the use of. They cannot see what it is to do for them: how should they? If they could see what it would do for them, it would not be originality. The first service which originality has to render them, is that of opening their eyes: which being once fully done, they would have a chance of being themselves original.

Meanwhile, recollecting that nothing was ever yet done which someone was not the first to do, and that all good things which exist are the fruits of originality, let them be modest enough to believe that there is something still left for it to accomplish, and assure themselves that they are more in need of originality, the less they are conscious of the want.

The initiation of all wise or noble things comes and must come from individuals; generally at first from some one individual. The honor and glory of the average man is that he is capable of following the initiative; that he can respond internally to wise and noble things, and be led to them with his eyes open. I am not countenancing the sort of "hero-worship" which applauds the strong man of genius for forcibly seizing on the government of the world and making it do his bidding in spite of itself. All he can claim is, freedom to point out the way. The power of compelling others into it is not only inconsistent with the freedom and development of all the rest, but corrupting to the strong man himself. It does seem, however, that when the opinions of masses of merely average men are everywhere become or becoming the dominant power, the counterpoise and corrective to that tendency would be, the more and more pronounced individuality of those who stand on the higher eminences of thought. It is in these circumstances most especially, that exceptional individuals, instead of being deterred, should be encouraged in acting differently from the mass. In other times there was no advantage in their doing so, unless they acted not only differently, but better. In this age, the mere example of non-conformity, the mere refusal to bend the knee to custom, is itself a service. Precisely because the tyranny of opinion is such as to make eccentricity a reproach, it is desirable, in order to break through that tyranny, that people should be eccentric. Eccentricity has always abounded when and where strength of character has abounded; and the amount of eccentricity in a society has been proportional to the amount of genius, mental vigor, and moral courage it contained. That so few now dare to be eccentric, marks the chief danger of the time.

VII
RALPH WALDO EMERSON

Ralph Waldo Emerson, 1803-1882, celebrated American essayist, lecturer and poet. Educated at Harvard; Unitarian clergyman in Boston, 1829-32; lectured extensively (1833-73) on such subjects as *Human Culture, Human Life, The Philosophy of History, The Times, The Present Age*, etc., the philosophical and libertarian attitude of which have profoundly influenced modern thought; edited *The Dial*, 1842-44; author of *Nature*, 1886; *Essays*, 1841-44; *Poems*, 1846; *Representative Men*, 1850; *Memoirs of Margaret Fuller*, 1852; *English Traits*, 1856; *Conduct of Life*, 1860; *May Day and other Pieces*, 1867; *Society and Solitude*, 1870; *Letters and Social Aims*, 1876; *Poems*, 1876. The selections for this chapter are from many of his books, but mostly from his essays on *Self-Reliance* and on *Politics*.

Every man is a consumer and ought to be a producer.

Beware when the great God lets loose a thinker on this planet.

It will never make any difference to a hero what the laws are.

That country is the fairest which is inhabited by the noblest.

The law of self-preservation is surer policy than any legislation can be.

No picture of life can have any veracity which does not admit the odious facts.

For what avail the plough or sail
Or land or life, if freedom fail?

The wise know that foolish legislation is a rope of sand which perishes in the twisting.

Goodness dies in wishes; as Voltaire said, " 'Tis the misfortune of worthy people that they are cowards."

It is only as a man puts off all foreign support and stands alone that I see him to be strong and to prevail.

If you put a chain around the neck of a slave, the other end fastens itself around your own.

He that feeds men serveth few;
He serves all who dares be true.

Our distrust is very expensive. The money we spend for courts and prisons is very ill laid out.

Literary history and all history is a record of the power of minorities of one.

As men's prayers are a disease of the will, so are their creeds a disease of the intellect.

The history of the State sketches in coarse outline the progress of thought, and follows at a distance the delicacy of culture and of aspiration.

The one serious and formidable thing in nature is will. Society is servile from want of will, and therefore the world wants saviours and religions.

What forests of laurel we bring, and the tears of mankind, to those who stand firm against the opinions of their contemporaries! The measure of a master is his success in bringing all men 'round to his opinion twenty years later.

> Be just at home; then write your scroll
> Of honor o'er the sea,
> And bid the broad Atlantic roll
> A ferry of the free.
> And, henceforth, there shall be no chain,
> Save underneath the sea
> The wires shall murmur through the main
> Sweet songs of Liberty.

Every actual State is corrupt. Good men must not obey the laws too well. What satire on government can equal the severity of censure conveyed in the word *politics* which now for ages has signified *cunning*, intimating that the State is a trick?

The boundaries of personal influence it is impossible to fix, as persons are organs of moral or supernatural force. Under the dominion of an idea, which possesses the minds of multitudes, as civil freedom, or the religious sentiment, the powers of persons are no longer subjects of calculation. A nation of men unanimously bent on freedom, or conquest, can easily confound the arithmetic of statists, and achieve extravagant actions, out of all proportion to their means; as the Greeks, the Saracens, the Swiss, the Americans, and the French have done.

When a quarter of the human race assume to tell me what I must do, I may be too much disheartened by the circumstance to see clearly the absurdity of this command. This is the condition of women, for whom I have the same compassion that I would have for a prisoner so long cramped in a narrow cage that he could not use his limbs. While many women are thinking their own thoughts there are others without so potent a brain, who have as yet failed to see the absurdity of allowing others to think for them. For this condition of mental and moral blunders the church is responsible.

A man should learn to detect and watch that gleam of light which flashes across his mind from within, more than the lustre of the firmanent of bards and sages. Yet he dismisses without notice his thought, because it is his. In every work of genius we recognize our own rejected thoughts: they come back to us with a certain alienated majesty. Great works of art have no more affecting lesson for us than this. They teach us to abide by our spontaneous impression with good humored inflexibility the most when the whole cry of voices is on the other side. Else, tomorrow a stranger will say with masterly good sense precisely what we have thought and felt all the time, and we shall be forced to take with shame our own opinion from another.

Society everywhere is in conspiracy against the manhood of every one of its members. Society is a joint-stock company, in which the members agree, for the better securing of his bread to each shareholder, to surrender the liberty and culture of the eater. The virtue in most request is conformity. Self-reliance is its aversion. It loves not realities and creators, but names and customs.

Who would be a man must be a non-conformist. He who would gather immortal palms must not be hindered by the name of goodness, but must explore if it be goodness. Nothing is at last sacred but the integrity of your own mind. Absolve you to yourself, and you shall have the suffrage of the world. I remember an answer which when quite young I was prompted to make to a valued adviser, who was wont to importune me with the dear old doctrines of the church. On my saying, What have I to do with the sacredness of traditions, if I live wholly from within? my friend suggested: "But these impulses may be from below, not from above." I replied: "They do not seem to me to be such; but if I am the Devil's Child, I will live then from the Devil." No law can be sacred to me but that of my nature. Good and bad are but names very readily transferable to that or this; the only right is what is after my constitution, the only wrong what is against it. A man is to carry himself in the presence of all opposition, as if everything were titular and ephemeral but him. I am ashamed to think how easily we capitulate to badges and names, to large societies and dead institutions.

What I must do is all that concerns me, not what the people think. This rule, equally arduous in actual and in intellectual life, may serve for the whole distinction between greatness and meanness. It is the harder, because you will always find those who think they know what is your duty better than you know it. It is easy in the world to live after the world's opinion; it is easy in solitude to live after our own; but the great man is he who in the midst of the crowd keeps with perfect sweetness the independence of solitude.

I hear a preacher announce for his text and topic the expediency of one of the institutions of his church. Do I not know beforehand that not possibly can he say a new and spontaneous word? Do I not know that, with all this ostentation of examining the grounds of the institution, he will do no such thing? Do I not know that he is pledged to himself not to look but at one side,—the permitted side, not as a man, but as a parish minister? He is a retained attorney, and these airs of the bench are the emptiest affectation. Well, most men have bound their eyes with one or another handkerchief, and attached themselves to some one of these communities of opinion. This conformity makes them not false in a few particulars, authors of a few lies, but false in all particulars. Their every truth is not quite true. Their two is not the real two, their four not the real four; so that every word they say chagrins us, and we know not where to begin to set them right. Meantime nature is not slow to equip us in the prison-uniform of the party to which we adhere. We come to wear one cut of face and figure, and acquire by degrees the gentlest asinine expression.

There will be an agreement in whatever variety of actions, so they be each honest and natural in their hour. For of one will, the actions will be harmonious, however unlike they seem. These varieties are lost sight of at a little distance, at a little height of thought. One tendency unites them all. The voyage of the best ship is a zigzag line of a hundred tacks. See the line from a sufficient distance, and it straightens itself to the average tendency. Your geniune action will explain itself, and will explain your other geniune actions. Your conformity explains nothing. Act singly, and what you have already done singly will justify you now. Greatness appeals to the future. If I can be firm enough today to do right, and scorn eyes, I must have done so much right before as to defend me now. Be it how it will, do right now. Always scorn appearances, and you always may. The force of character is cumulative.

Whenever a mind is simple, and receives a divine wisdom, old things pass away,—means, teachers, texts, temples, fall; it lives now, and absorbs past and future into the present hour. All things are made sacred by relation to it,—one as much as another. All things are dissolved to their center by their cause, and, in the universal miracle, petty and particular miracles disappear. If, therefore, man claims to know and speak of God, and carries you backward to the phraseology of some old mouldered nation in another country, in another world, believe him not. Is the acorn better than the oak which is its fulness and completion? Is the parent better than the child into whom he has cast his ripened being? Whence, then, this worship of the past? The centuries are conspirators against the sanity and authority of the soul.

Check this lying hospitality and lying affection. Live no longer to the expectation of these deceived and deceiving people with whom we converse. Say to them, O father, O mother, O wife, O brother, O friend, I have lived with you after appearances hitherto. Henceforward I am the truth's. Be it known unto you that henceforward I obey no law less than the eternal law. I will have no covenants but proximities. I shall endeavor to nourish my parents, to support my family, to be the chaste husband of one wife,—but these relations I must fill after a new and unprecedented way. I appeal from your customs. I must be myself. I cannot break myself any longer for you, or you. If you can love me for what I am, we shall be the happier. If you cannot, I will seek to deserve that you should. I will not hide my tastes or aversions. I will so trust that what is deep is holy, that I will do strongly before the sun and moon whatever inly rejoices me, and the heart appoints. If you are noble, I will love you; if you are not, I will not hurt you and myself by hypocritical attentions. If you are true, but not in the same truth with me, cleave to your companions; I will seek my own. It is alike your interest, and mine, and all men's, however long we have dealt in lies, to live in truth. Does this sound harsh today? You will soon love what is dictated by your nature as well as mine, and, if we follow the truth, it will bring us out safe at last. But so you may give these friends pain. Yes, but I cannot sell my liberty and my power, to save their sensibility. Besides, all persons have their moments of reason, when they look out into the region of truth; then will they justify me, and do the same thing.

The sinew and heart of man seem to be drawn out, and we

are become timorous, desponding whimperers. We are afraid of truth, afraid of fortune, afraid of death, and afraid of each other. Our age yields no great and perfect persons. We want men and women who shall renovate life and our social state, but we see that most natures are insolvent, cannot satisfy their own wants, have an ambition out of all proportion to their practical force, and do lean and beg day and night continually. Our housekeeping is mendicant, our arts, our occupations, our marriages, our religion, we have not chosen, but society has chosen for us. We are parlour soldiers. We shun the rugged battle of fate, where strength is born.

Insist on yourself; never imitate. Your own gift you can present every moment with the cumulative force of a whole life's cultivation; but of the adopted talent of another, you have only an extemporaneous, half possession. That which each can do best, none but his Maker can teach him. No man yet knows what it is, nor can, till that person has exhibited it. Where is the master that could have taught Shakespeare? Where is the master who could have instructed Franklin, or Washington, or Bacon, or Newton? Every great man is a unique. The Scipionism of Scipio is precisely that part he could not borrow. Shakespeare will never be made by the study of Shakespeare. Do that which is assigned you, and you cannot hope too much or dare too much. There is at this moment for you an utterance brave and grand as that of the colossal chisel of Phidias, or trowel of the Egyptians, or the pen of Moses, or Dante, but different from all these. Not possibly will the soul all rich, all eloquent, with thousand-cloven tongue, deign to repeat itself; but if you can hear what these patriarchs say, surely you can reply to them in the same pitch of voice; for the ear and the tongue are two organs of one nature. Abide in the simple and noble regions of thy life, obey thy heart, and thou shalt reproduce the Foreworld again.

Society always consists, in greatest part, of young and foolish persons. The old, who have seen through the hypocrisy

of courts and statesmen, die, and leave no wisdom to their
sons. They believe their own newspaper, as their fathers
did at their age. With such an ignorant and deceivable majority, States would soon run to ruin, but that there are limitations, beyond which the folly and ambition of governors cannot
go. Things have their laws, as well as men; and things refuse
to be trifled with. Property will be protected. Corn will not
grow, unless it is planted and manured; but the farmer will not
plant or hoe it, unless the chances are a hundred to one that he
will cut and harvest it. Under any forms, persons and property
must and will have their just sway. They exert their power, as
steadily as matter its attraction. Cover up a pound of earth
never so cunningly, divide and subdivide it; melt it to liquid,
convert it to gas; it will always weigh a pound; it will always
attract and resist other matter, by the full virtue of one pound
weight;—and the attributes of a person, his wit and his moral
energy, will exercise, under any law or extinguishing tyranny,
their proper force,—if not overtly, then covertly; if not for the
law, then against it; with right, or by might.

Every man's nature is a sufficient advertisement to him of
the character of his fellows. My right and my wrong, is their
right and their wrong. Whilst I do what is fit for me, and
abstain from what is unfit, my neighbor and I shall often agree
in our means, and work together for a time to one end. But
whenever I find my dominion over myself not sufficient for me,
and undertake the direction of him also, I overstep the truth,
and come into false relations to him. I may have so much
more skill or strength than he, that he cannot express adequately
his sense of wrong, but it is a lie, and hurts like a lie both him
and me. Love and nature cannot maintain the assumption:
it must be executed by a practical lie, namely, by force. This
undertaking for another is the blunder which stands in colossal
ugliness in the governments of the world. It is the same thing
in numbers as in a pair, only not quite so intelligible. I can
see well enough a great difference between myself setting my-

self down to a self-control, and my going to make somebody else act after my views: but when a quarter of the human race assume to tell me what I must do, I may be too much disturbed by the circumstances to see so clearly the absurdity of their command. Therefore, all public ends look vague and quixotic beside private ones. For, any laws but those which men make for themselves, are laughable. If I put myself in the place of my child, and we stand in one thought, and see that things are thus or thus, that perception is law for him and me. We are both there, both act. But if, without carrying him into the thought, I look over into his plot, and guessing how it is with him, ordain this or that, he will never obey me. This is the history of governments,—one man does something which is to bind another. A man who cannot be acquainted with me, taxes me; looking from afar at me, ordains that a part of my labors shall go to this or that whimsical end, not as I, but as he happens to fancy. Behold the consequence. Of all debts, men are least willing to pay the taxes. What a satire is this on Government! Everywhere they think they get their money's worth, except for these.

Hence, the less government we have, the better—the fewer laws, the less confided power. The antidote to this abuse of formal Government is the influence of private character, the growth of the Individual; the appearance of the principal to supersede the proxy; the appearance of the wise man, of whom the existing government is, it must be owned, a shabby imitation. That which all things tend to educe, which freedom, cultivation, intercourse, revolutions, go to form and deliver, is character; that is the end of nature, to reach unto this coronation of her king. To educate the wise man, the State exists; and with the appearance of the wise man, the State expires. The appearnace of character makes the State unnecessary. The wise man needs no army, fort, or navy,— he loves men too well.

Senators and presidents have climbed so high with pain

enough, not because they think the place specially agreeable, but as an apology for real worth and to vindicate their manhood in our eyes. This conspicuous chair is their compensation to themselves for being of a poor, cold, hard nature. They must do what they can. Like one class of forest animals, they have nothing but a prehensile tail: climb they must, or crawl. If a man found himself so rich-natured that he could enter into strict relations with the best persons, and make life serene around him by the dignity and sweetness of his behavior, could he afford to circumvent the favor of the caucus and the press, and covet relations so hollow and pompous as those of a politician? Surely nobody would be a charlatan, who could afford to be sincere.

The tendencies of the times favor the idea of self-government, and leave the individual, for all code, to the rewards and penalties of his own constitution, which work with more energy than we believe, whilst we depend on artificial restraints. The movement in this direction has been very marked in modern history. Much has been blind and discreditable, but the nature of the revolution is not affected by the vices of the revolters; for this is a purely moral force. It was never adopted by any party in history, neither can be. It separates the individual from all party, and unites him, at the same time, to the race. It promises a recognition of higher rights than those of personal freedom, or the security of property. A man has the right to be employed, to be trusted, to be loved, to be revered. The power of love, as the basis of a state, has never been tried. We must not imagine that all things are lapsing into confusion, if every tender protestant be not compelled to bear his part in certain social conventions; nor doubt that roads can be built, letters carried, and the fruit of labor secured, when the government of force is at an end. Are our methods now so excellent that all competition is hopeless? Could not a nation of friends even devise better ways? On the other hand, let not the most conservative and timid fear anything from a premature surrender of the bayonet, and the system of force. For, according to the order of nature, which is quite superior to our will, it stands thus; there will always be a government of force, where men are invasive; and when they are pure enough to abjure the code of force, they will be wise enough to see how these public ends of the postoffice, of the highway, of commerce, and the exchange of property, of museums, and libraries, of institutions for art and science, can be answered.

We live in a very low state of the world, and pay unwilling tribute to governments founded on force. There is not, among the most religious and instructed men of the most religious and civil nations, a reliance on the moral sentiment, and a sufficient belief in the unity of things to persuade them that society can be maintained without artificial restraints, as well as the solar system, or that the private citizen might be reasonable, and a good neighbor, without the hint of a jail or a confiscation. What is strange, too, there never was in any man sufficient faith in the power of rectitude, to inspire him with the broad design of renovating the State on the principle of right and love. All those who have pretended this design have been partial reformers, and have admitted in some manner the supremacy of the bad State. I do not call to mind a single human being who has steadily denied the authority of the laws, on the simple ground of his own moral nature. Such designs, full of genius and full of fate as they are, are not entertained except avowedly as air-pictures. If the individual who exhibits them dare to think them practicable, he disgusts scholars and churchmen; and men of talent, and women of superior sentiments, cannot hide their contempt. Not the less does nature continue to fill the heart of youth with suggestions in this enthusiasm, and there are now men—if indeed I can speak in the plural number— more exactly, I will say, I have just been conversing with one man, to whom no weight of adverse experience will make it for a moment appear impossible, that thousands of human beings might exercise toward each other the grandest and simplest sentiments, as well as a knot of friends, or a pair of lovers.

VIII
WILLIAM LLOYD GARRISON

William Lloyd Garrison, 1805-1879, noted American abolitionist. Learned printer's trade, became journalist. In 1831, in Boston, began publishing *The Liberator*, a journal advocating the abolition of slavery at the South, and conducted it until its discontinuance in 1865; founded an abolition society at Boston, 1832, which became the model for similar societies all over the world. President of American Anti-Slavery Society, 1843-65; apostle of freedom, lover of humanity, defender of the oppressed. His *Life and Letters*, 4 vols., have been published by his sons.

Liberty for each, for all, and forever.

No person will rule over me with my consent. I will rule over no man.

Enslave the liberty of but one human being and the liberties of the world are put in peril.

When I look at these crowded thousands, and see them trample on their consciences and the rights of their fellowmen at the bidding of a piece of parchment, I say, my curse be on the Constitution of the United States.

Why, sir, no freedom of speech or inquiry is conceded to me in this land. Am I not vehemently told both at the North and the South that I have no right to meddle with the question of slavery? And my right to speak on any other subject, in opposition to public opinion, is equally denied to me.

I am aware that many object to the severity of my language; but is there not cause for severity? I will be as harsh as Truth, and as uncompromising as Justice. On this subject I do not wish to think, or speak, or write, with moderation. No! No! Tell a man whose house is on fire to give a moderate alarm; tell him to moderately rescue his wife from the hands of the ravisher; tell the mother to gradually extricate her babe from the fire into which it has fallen—but urge me not to use moderation in a cause like the present. I am in earnest—I will not equivocate—I will not excuse—I will not retreat a single inch—and I will be heard. The apathy of the people is enough to make every statue leap from its pedestal and hasten the resurrection of the dead.—*In first issue of the Liberator, January 1, 1831.*

They may not talk of faith in God, or of standing on the eternal rock, who turn pale with fear or are flushed with anger when their cherished convictions are called in question, or who cry out: "If we let him thus alone, all men will believe on him, and the Romans shall come and take away both our place and nation." They know not what spirit they are of; the light that is in them is darkness, and how great that darkness! It was not Jesus that was filled with consternation, but his enemies, on account of the heresy of untrammelled thought and free utterance: "Then the high priest rent his clothes saying, He hath spoken blasphemy; what further need have we of witnesses? Behold now ye have heard his blasphemy. What think ye? They answered and said: He is guilty of death. Then did they spit in his face, and buffeted him, and others smote him with the palms of their hands." So have ever behaved the pious advocates of error, such has ever been the treatment of the "blasphemous" defender of truth.—*Essay on "Free Speech and Free Inquiry."*

War.—In the course of the fearful developments of Slave Power, and its continued aggressions on the rights of the people of the North, in my judgment a sad change has come over the spirit of anti-slavery men, generally speaking. We are growing more and more warlike, more and more disposed to repudiate the principles of peace, more and more disposed to talk about "finding a joint in the neck of the tyrant," and breaking that neck, "cleaving tyrants down from the crown to the groin," with the sword which is carnal, and so inflaming one another with the spirit of violence and for a bloody work. Just in proportion as this spirit prevails, I feel that our moral power is departing and will depart. I say this not so much as an Abolitionist as a man. I believe in the spirit of peace, and in sole and absolute reliance on truth and the application of it to the hearts and consciences of the people. I do not believe that the weapons of liberty ever have been, or ever can be, the weapons of despotism. I know that those of despotism are the sword, the revolver, the cannon, the bomb-shell; and, therefore, the weapons to which tyrants cling, and upon which they depend, are not the weapons for me, as a friend of liberty. I will not trust the war spirit anywhere in the universe of God, because the experience of six thousand years proves it not to be at all reliable in such a struggle as ours. . . . .

I pray you, abolitionists, still to adhere to that truth. Do not get impatient; do not become exasperated; do not attempt any new political organization; do not make yourselves familiar with the idea that blood must flow. Perhaps blood will flow— God knows, I do not; but it shall not flow through any counsel of mine. Much as I detest the oppression exercised by the Southern slaveholder, he is a man, sacred before me. He is a man, not to be harmed by my hand nor with my consent. He is a man, who is grievously and wickedly trampling upon the rights of his fellow-man; but all I have to do with him is to rebuke his sin, to call him to repentance, to leave him without excuse for his tyranny.—*Liberator*, 1858.

Non-resistance.—We say that he who votes to empower Congress to declare war, and to provide the necessary instruments of war, and to constitute the President commander-in-chief of the army and navy, has no right, when war actually comes, to plead conscientious scruples as a peace man; but is bound to stand by his vote, or else to make confession of wrong-doing and take his position outside of the government. He cannot be allowed to strain at a gnat, and swallow a camel; to play fast and loose with his conscience; to make the amplest provisions for war, and then beg to be excused from its dangers and hardships in deference to his peace sentiments. The Government has a right to apply this test, and the voter has no right to complain when it is rigidly enforced in his own case.

But we submit to all the people, that such as wholly abstain from voting to uphold the Constitution because of its war provisions, and thus religiously exclude themselves from all share in what are deemed official honors and emoluments, ought not to be drafted in time of war, or compelled to pay an equivalent, or go to prison for disobedience. If conscience is to be respected and provided for in any case, it is in theirs.

We know of no law, however, for their exemption; and, therefore, some of them may be drafted and put to a trial of their faith. In that case, let them possess their souls in patience and serenity, and meet without any outcry, "as though some strange thing had happened unto them," whatever penalty may follow their non-compliance with the draft. There is no loss, but great gain, in suffering for righteousness' sake. They surely knew the liabilities to which they subjected themselves, when they gave in their adhesion to the principles of Non-resistance; and they will not try to shirk the cross when it is presented, but rejoice that they are counted worthy to bear it. One thing they can and should do, in order to prevent any misconception as to their feelings and views in relation to the conduct of those who have risen up in rebellion; and that is, denounce it as horribly perfidious, and as having for its object the overthrow of every safeguard of popular liberty, and register their testimony that the Government has exercised no injustice towards the South, nor given any occasion for such a treasonable outbreak. Thus defining their position, it will be seen by the nation that they are acting in a manner as just and discriminating toward the Government as it is upright and conscientious on their part.

It can hardly be asked by any Non-Resistant, "How, if drafted, about hiring a substitute?" because what we do by another as our agent or representative we do ourselves. To hire a substitute is, as a matter of principle, precisely the same as to go to the battlefield in person.

"But if the alternative be, to pay a stipulated sum to the Government, or else be imprisoned or shot, may we pay the fine?"

That is a matter for the individual conscience to decide. Speaking personally, we see no violation of Non-Resistance principles in paying the money; because it is a choice presented between different forms of suffering, and, "other things being equal," it will be natural to wish to avoid as much of it as the case will admit. Thus, a highwayman placing his pistol to our head demands in our helplessness, "Your money, or your life!" To part with the money is certainly more reasonable than to part with life; nor, in yielding it, do we give any sanction to the demand. But if the highwaymen should say, "Your money, and an acknowledgment of my right to extort it, or your life," then there would be no alternative but to die, or else prove recreant to truth and honesty.

"But," it may be said, "though I should refuse to hire a substitute, yet, if I pay the price demanded, will not the Government take the money and apply it for that purpose? And is there any essential moral difference here?" We think there is. In hiring a substitute yourself, you actively sustain the war, and become an armed participant in it, and so violate the principles which you profess to revere. In paying a tax, you passively submit to the exaction, which, in itself, commits no violence upon others, but is only a transfer of so much property to other hands. If, then, the Government shall proceed to apply it to war purposes, the responsibility will rest with the Government, not with you. This is the light in which we regard it; still, we offer no other suggestion than this, "Let every one be fully persuaded in his own mind." We shall honor none the less him who may feel it his duty to take the most afflicting alternative, as the most effectual method to meet the issue before the community. Of that he must be the judge; and especially must he be sure to count the cost and act intelligently.—*Liberator* 1862.

> Spirit of freedom, on!—
> Oh! pause not in thy flight
> Till every clime is won

William Lloyd Garrison

Who worship in thy light;
Speed on thy glorious way,
  And wake the sleeping lands!
Millions are watching for thy ray,
  And lift to thee their hands.
Still "Onward!" be thy cry—
  Thy banner on the blast;
And, like a tempest, as thou rushest by,
  Despots shall shrink aghast.
On! till thy name is known
  Throughout the peopled earth;
On! till thou reign'st alone,
  Man's heritage by birth;
On! till from every vale, and where the mountains rise,
The beacon lights of Liberty shall kindle to the skies!

(Quoted by William Lloyd Garrison)

IX
WENDELL PHILLIPS

Wendell Phillips, 1811-1884, American orator and abolitionist; educated at Harvard; admitted to bar in 1834; leading orator of the abolitionists, 1837-61; president of the Anti-Slavery Society, 1865-70; prominent advocate of woman suffrage, penal and labor reforms, etc. Candidate of the labor reformers and prohibitionists for governor of Massachusetts, 1870. *Speeches* were published in 1863. The selections are from his speeches.

If there is anything that cannot bear free thought, let it crack.

Nothing but Freedom, Justice, and Truth is of any permanent advantage to the mass of mankind. To these society, left to itself, is always tending.

"The right to think, to know, and to utter," as John Milton said, is the dearest of all liberties. Without this right, there can be no liberty to any people; with it, there can be no slavery.

When you have convinced thinking men that it is right, and humane men that it is just, you will gain your cause. Men always lose half of what is gained by violence. What is gained by argument, is gained forever.

The manna of liberty must be gathered each day, or it is rotten.

Only by unintermitted agitation can a people be kept sufficiently awake to principle not to let liberty be smothered in material prosperity.

Let us believe that the whole of truth can never do harm to the whole of virtue; and remember that in order to get the whole of truth, you must allow every man, right or wrong, freely to utter his conscience, and protect him in so doing. Entire unshackled freedom for every man's life, no matter what his doctrine—the safety of free discussion, no matter how wide its range. The community which dares not protect its humblest and most hated member in the free utterance of his opinions, no matter how false or hateful, is only a gang of slaves.

I have used strong words. But I was born in Boston, and

the good name of the old town is bound up with every fibre of my heart. I dare not trust myself to describe the insolence of men who undertake to dictate to you and me what we shall say on these grand old streets. But who can adequately tell the sacredness and the value of free speech? Who can fitly describe the enormity of the crime of its violation? Free speech, at once the instrument and the guaranty and the bright consummate flower of all liberty. Free speech in these streets, once trod by Henry Vane, its apostle and champion. Free speech, in that language which holds the dying words of Algernon Sidney, its martyr.

South Carolina said to Massachusetts in 1835, when Edward Everett was Governor, "Abolish free speech,—it is a nuisance." She is right,—from her standpoint it is. That is, it is not possible to preserve the quiet of South Carolina consistently with free speech; but you know the story Sir Walter Scott told of the Scotch laird, who said to his old butler, "Jock, you and I can't live under this roof." "And where does your honor think of going?" So free speech says to South Carolina today.

How shall we ever learn toleration for what we do not believe? The last lesson a man ever learns is, that liberty of thought and speech is the right for all mankind; that the man who denies every article of our creed is to be allowed to preach just as often and just as loud as we ourselves. We have learned this,—been taught it by persecution on the question of slavery. No matter whose the lips that would speak, they must be free and ungagged. Let us always remember that he does not really believe his own opinions, who dares not give free scope to his opponent. Persecution *is really want of faith in our creed.* Let us see to it, my friends, Abolitionists, that we learn the lesson the whole circle round. Let us believe that the whole of truth can not do harm to the whole of virtue. Trust it. And remember, that, in order to get the whole of truth, you must allow every man, right or wrong, freely to utter his conscience, and protect him in so doing.

I know what reform needs, and all it needs, in a land where discussion is free, the press untrammelled, and where public halls protect debate. There, as Emerson says, "What the tender and poetic youth dreams today, and conjures up with inarticulate speech, is to-morrow the vociferated result of public opinion, and the day after is the charter of nations." Lieber said, in 1870, "Bismarck proclaims to-day in the Diet the very principles for which we were hunted and exiled fifty years ago." Submit to risk your daily bread, accept social ostracism, count on a mob now and then, "be in earnest, don't equivocate, don't excuse, don't retreat a single inch," and you will finally be heard.

Church.—I would never join one of those petty despotisms which usurp in our day the name of a Christian Church. I would never put my neck in that yoke of ignorance and superstition led by a Yankee Pope, and give my good name as a football for their spleen and bigotry. That lesson I learned of my father long before boyhood ceased.

Our enterprise is pledged to nothing but the abolition of slavery. When we set out, we said we would do our work under the government and under the Church. We tried it. We found that we could not work in either way; we found it necessary to denounce the Church and withdraw from the government. We did what we could to work through both. We saw that it was expedient to work through them both, if we could. Finding it impossible, we let experience dictate our measures.

I am willing to confess my faith. It is this: that the Christianity of this country is worth nothing, except it is or can be made capable of dealing with the question of slavery. I am willing to confess another article of my faith: that the Constitution and government of this country is worth nothing, except it is or can be made capable of grappling with the great question of slavery. I agree with Burke: "I have no idea of a liberty unconnected with honesty and justice. Nor do I believe that any good constitutions of government or of freedom can find it necessary for their security to doom any part of the people to a permanent slavery. Such a constitution of freedom, if such can be, is in effect no more than another name for the tyranny of the strongest faction; and factions in republics have been and are full as capable as monarchs of the most cruel oppression and injustice." That is the language of Edmund Burke to the electors of Bristol; I agree with it. The greatest praise government can win is, that its citizens know their rights, and dare to maintain them. The best use of good laws is to teach men to trample bad laws under their feet.

Harriet Martineau, instead of lingering in the camps of the Philistines, could, with courage, declare, "I will go among the Abolitionists, and see for myself." Shortly after the time of the State-street mob she came to Cambridge; and her hosts there begged her not to put her hand into their quarrels. The Abolitionists held a meeting there. The only hall of that day open to them was owned by infidels. Think of that, ye friends of Christianity! And yet the infidelity of that day is the Christianity of today. To this meeting in this hall Miss Martineau went, to express her entire sympathy with the occasion. As a result of her words and deeds, such was the lawlessness of that time that she had to turn back from her intended journey to the West, and was assured that she would be lynched if she dared set foot in Ohio. She gave up her journey, but not her principles.

Government.—Law has always been wrong. Government is the fundamental ism of the soldier, bigot, and priest.

It is easy to be independent when all behind you agree with you, but the difficulty comes when nine hundred and ninety-nine of your friends think you wrong.

I think little of the direct influence of governments. I think, with Guizot, that "it is a gross delusion to believe in the sovereign power of political machinery." To hear some men talk of the government, you would suppose that Congress was the law of gravitation, and kept the planets in their places.

Let History close the record. Let her allow that "on the side of the oppressor there was power,"—power "to frame mischief by a law;" that on that side were all the *forms* of law, and behind those forms, most of the elements of control: wealth, greedy of increase, and anxious for order, at any sacrifice of principle,—priests prophesying smooth things, and arrogating to themselves the name of Christianity,—ambition, baptizing itself statesmanship,—and that unthinking patriotism, child of habit and not of reason, which mistakes government for liberty and law for justice.

Did you ever read the fable of the wolf and the house-dog? The one was fat, the other gaunt and famine-struck. The wolf said to the dog, "You are very fat." "Yes," replied the dog, "I get along very well at home." "Well," said the wolf, "could you take me home?" "O, certainly." So they trotted along together; but as they neared the house, the wolf caught sight of several ugly scars on the neck of the dog, and stopping, cried, "Where did you get those scars on your neck? they look very sore and bloody." "O," said the dog, "they tie me up at night, and I have rather an inconvenient iron collar on my neck. But that's a small matter; they feed me well." "On the whole," said the wolf, "taking the food and the collar together, I prefer to remain in the woods."

The time has been when it was the duty of the reformer to show cause why he appeared to disturb the quiet of the world. But during the discussion of the many reforms that have been advocated, and which have more or less succeeded, one after another,—freedom of the lower classes, freedom of food, freedom of the press, freedom of thought, reform in penal legislation, and a thousand other matters,—it seems to me to have proved conclusively, that government commenced in usurpation and oppression; that liberty and civilization, at present, are nothing else than the fragments of rights which the scaffold and the stake have wrung from the strong hands of the usurpers.

Every step of progress the world has made has been from scaffold to scaffold, and from stake to stake. It would hardly be exaggeration to say, that all the great truths relating to society and government have been first heard in the solemn protests of martyred patriotism, or the loud cries of crushed and starving labor. The law has been always wrong. Government began in tyranny and force, began in the feudalism of the soldier and bigotry of the priest; and the ideas of justice and humanity have been fighting their way, like a thunder storm, against the organized selfishness of human nature. And this is the last great protest against the wrong of ages. It is no argument to my mind, therefore, that the old social fabric of the past is against us.

Labor.—I rejoice at every effort working-men make to organize; I do not care on what basis they do it. Men sometimes say to me, "Are you an Internationalist?" I say, "I do not know what an Internationalist is;" but they tell me it is a system by which the working men from London to Gibraltar, from Moscow to Paris, can clasp hands. Then I say, God speed to that or any similar movement.

So I welcome organization. I do not care whether it calls itself Trades-union, Crispin, International, or Commune, anything that masses up the units in order that they may put in a united force to face the organization of capital, anything that does that, I say *amen* to it. One hundred thousand men! It is an immense army. I do not care whether it considers chiefly the industrial or the political questions; it can control the nation if it is in earnest. The reason why the Abolitionists brought the nation down to fighting their battle is that they were really in earnest, knew what they wanted, and were determined to have it. Therefore they got it. The leading statesmen and orators of the day said they would never urge abolition; but a determined man in a printing office said that they should, and they did it.

Only organize, and stand together. Claim something together, and at once; let the nation hear a united demand from the laboring voice, and then, when you have got that, go on after another; but get something.

If there is any one feature which we can distinguish in all Christendom, under different names—trades unions, co-operation, and internationals—under all flags, there is one great movement. It is for the people peaceably to take possession of their own.

No reform, moral or intellectual, ever came from the upper class of society. Each and all came from the protest of martyr and victim. The emancipation of the working people must be achieved by the working people themselves.

We affirm, as a fundamental principle, that labor, the creator of wealth, is entitled to all it creates.

Affirming this, we avow ourselves willing to accept the final results of the operation of a principle so radical—such as the overthrow of the whole profit-making system, the extinction of all monopolies, the abolition of privileged classes, universal education and fraternity, perfect freedom of exchange, and, best and grandest of all, the final obliteration of that foul stigma upon our so-called Christian civilization—the poverty of the masses. . . . Therefore,

Resolved, That we declare war with the wages system, which demoralizes the life of the hirer and the hired, cheats both, and enslaves the workingman; war with the present system of finance, which robs labor, and gorges capital, makes the rich richer and the poor poorer, and turns a republic into an aristocracy of capital; war with these lavish grants of the public lands to speculating companies, and whenever in power we pledge ourselves to use every just and legal means to resume all such grants heretofore made; war with the system of enriching capitalists by the creation and increase of public interest-bearing debts.

We demand that every facility, and all encouragement, shall be given by law to co-operation in all branches of industry and trade, and that the same aid be given to co-operative efforts that has heretofore been given to railroads and other enterprises.—*At the Labor-Reform Convention, at Worcester, Mass., Sept. 4, 1870.*

Address to Boys.—Now, boys, this is my lesson to you today. You cannot be as good as your fathers, unless you are better. You have your fathers' example,—the opportunities and advantages they have accumulated,—and to be only as good is not enough. You must be better, You must copy only the spirit of your fathers, and not their imperfections. There was an old Boston merchant, years ago, who wanted a set of china made in Pekin. You know that Boston men sixty years ago looked at both sides of a cent before they spent it, and if they earned twelve cents they would save eleven. He could not spare a whole plate, so he sent a cracked one, and when he received the set, there was a crack in every piece. The Chinese had imitated the pattern exactly.

Now, boys, do not imitate us, or there will be a great many cracks. Be better than we. We have invented a telegraph, but what of that? I expect, if I live forty years, to see a telegraph that will send messages without wire, both ways at the same time. If you do not invent it, you are not so good as we are. You are bound to go ahead of us.

X
JOSIAH WARREN

Josiah Warren, 1798-1874, American inventive genius, social philosopher, peaceful revolutionist, descendant of General Joseph Warren of Bunker Hill fame. Given musical education, became bandmaster; through influence of Robert [Owen became advocate of principles of Equitable Commerce; founder and leader of the famous "Time Stores." Bought and sold land according to ideas of equity; founder and inspiration of the "Boston House of Equity" and of the "New Harmony" communistic community, and the equitable village "Modern Times." Has numerous inventions to his credit, including the "Speed press" and various typographical inventions designed to extend methods of stereotyping to all branches of printing, illustration and artistic reproduction; life spent in alternating periods of invention and participation in social experiments. Published *The Peaceful Revolutionist,* 1833; *Periodical Letters,* 1854-6; *Reflections upon the Civil War,* 1863; *True Civilization,* 1873. Had many English disciples; William Parr of Dublin read part of *Equitable Commerce,* before British Association for the Advancement of Science in 1855. This book is quite rare; the following selections are from it.

Liberty.—What is liberty? Who will allow me to define it for him, and agree beforehand to square his life by my definition? Who does not wish to see it first, and sit in judgment on it, and decide for himself as to its propriety? and who does not see that it is his own individual interpretation of the word that he adopts? And who will agree to square his whole life by a rule, according to his own interpretation of it, and which, although good at present, may not prove applicable to all cases? Who does not wish to preserve his liberty to act according to the peculiarities or individualities of future cases, and to sit in judgment on the merits of each, and to change or vary from time to time with new developments and increasing knowledge? Each individual being thus at liberty at all times, would be sovereign of himself. No greater amount of liberty can be conceived—any less would not be liberty! Liberty, then, is the sovereignty of the individual, and never shall man know liberty until each and every individual is acknowledged to be the only legitimate sovereign of his or her person, time and property, each living and acting at his own cost; and not until we live in society where each can exercise his right of sovereignty at all times without clashing with or violating that of others.

Individuality.—Nothing is more common than the remark, that "no two persons are alike"—that "circumstances alter cases"—"that we must agree to disagree," etc.; and yet we are constantly forming institutions which require us to be alike —which make no allowance for the individuality of persons or of circumstances, and which render it necessary for us to agree, and leave us no liberty to differ from each other, nor to modify our conduct according to circumstances.

There is an individuality of countenance, stature, gait, voice, which characterizes every one, and each of these peculiarities is inseparable from the person; he has no power to divest himself of these—they constitute his physical individuality, and were it not so, the most immeasurable confusion would derange all our social intercourse. Every one would be liable to the same name! One man would be mistaken for another! Our relations and friends would be strangers to us, and vice versa! A piece of business begun with one would end with another, or never be finished! Indeed, there would be an end to all business, all order, all society—one universal chaos would pervade all human affairs, and defeat all human designs. The fact that these peculiarities of each are inseparable from each— not to be conquered—not to be divided or "alienated" from each, is, apparently, the only element of social order that man in his mad career of "policy" and "expediency," has not overthrown or smothered; and this, therefore, is selected as the first stepping-stone in his ascent towards order and harmony.

I have spoken only of four of the elements constituting the physical Individuality of each person, and yet these are so differently combined in each, that no two are found with the same. What, then, shall we conclude from the myriads on myriads of various combinations of impressions, thoughts, and feelings, that make up the mental part of each individual? Every thought, every feeling, every impulse, being at the moment of its existence, just as much a constituent part of the individual as the countenance or the stature! and yet, all human institutions call on us to be alike, in thought, motive, and action! Not only are no two minds alike each other, but no one remains the same from one hour to another! Old impressions are becoming obliterated—new ones are being made; new combinations of old thoughts constantly being formed, and old ones exploded. The surrounding atmosphere, the contact of various persons and circumstances, the food we subsist on, the condition of the vital organs, the circulation of the blood, and various other influences, are all combining and acting variously on every one's different constitution, and, like the changes of the kaleidoscope, seldom or never twice alike, even upon the same individual! On what, then, rest all custom and institutions which demand conformity? They are all directly opposed to this individuality and are therefore false. Every one is by nature constituted to be his or her own government, his own law, his own church—each individual is a system within himself; and the great problem must be solved with the broadest admission of the right of individuality which forbids any attempt to *govern* each other, and confines all our legislation to the adjustment and regulation of our intercourse or commerce with each other.

To require conformity in the appreciation of sentiments or the interpretation of language, or uniformity of thought, feeling, or action, is a fundamental error in human legislation—a madness which would be only equalled by requiring all to possess the same countenance, the same voice, or the same stature. It would be just as reasonable to expect a number of looking-glasses in different parts of the town to reflect images alike, as to expect any two individuals to be alike; and just as much so, to expect one glass to reflect always one image while multitudes were constantly passing before it, as to expect any individual to remain the same person, through the different scenes and varying circumstances, and internal differences that continually surround and act upon him. We are intrinsically Individual—we must differ from each other—we must differ from ourselves;—this is nature's own mandate, and who shall say nay?

When one finds his different papers, bills, receipts, orders, letters, etc., all in one confused heap, and wishes to restore them to order, what does he do but separate, disconnect, divide, and disunite them—putting each Individual kind in an Individual place, until all are Individualized? If a mechanic goes to his tool chest and finds all in confusion, what does he do to restore them to order but disconnect, divide, separate, individualize them?

It is within every one's experience that when many things of any kind are heterogeniously mixed together separation, disconnection, division, Individuality restores them to order, but no other process will do it.

If a multitude of ideas crowd at once upon the mind of a speaker or a writer, what can he do to prevent confusion but divide his subject, disconnect, disunite its parts, giving to each an Individual time and place?

Phonography, a gigantic improvement in letters, which is probably to work a total revolution in literature and book education, consists in Individualizing the elements of speech and the signs which represent them; giving to every Individual element an Individual sign or representative.

Musical harmony is produced by those sounds only which differ from each other. A continuous reiteration of one note, in all respects the same, has no charms for anyone. The beats of a drum, although the same as to "tune," are not so as to stress or accent; in this respect they differ, and this difference occurring at regular intervals, the strong contrasted with the weak, enables the attention to dwell upon them with more or less satisfaction; but the unremitted repition of one dull unvarying sound would either not command attention or make us run mad. It is when the voice or an instrument sounds different notes, one after the other, that we obtain melody; and it is only when different notes are sounded together that we produce harmony. The keynote, its fifth, its octave, and its tenth, when sounded together produce a delightful chord; but these are all different from each other, and they retain their separate Individualities, even while thus associated in the closest possible manner; so that while all are sounding together, the practiced ear can distinguish either from the others. They never become combined. They never unite into one sound, even in the most complicated nor in the most enchanting harmonious associations! If such were the result, if they were to lose their individualities in association and to unite into one sound, all musical harmony would be unknown or be suddenly swept from the earth. It is to the indestructible Individuality of each note of the scale that we are indebted for all that we enjoy from this most humanizing element of our social condition.

The disconnection of Church and State was a master stroke for freedom and harmony. The great moving power, the very soul of the Protestant Reformation, was that it left every one free to interpret the Scriptures according to his own Individual views.

Children.—If we would have children respect the rights of property in others, we must respect their rights of property. If we would have them respect the individual peculiarities and the proper liberty of others, then we must respect their individual peculiarities and their personal liberty. If we would have them know and claim for themselves, and award to others the proper reward of labor in adult age, we must give them the proper reward of their labor in childhood. If we would qualify them to sustain and preserve themselves in after life, they must be permitted to sustain and preserve themselves in childhood and in youth. If we would have them capable of self-government in adult age, they should be allowed the right of self-government in childhood. If we would have them learn to govern themselves rationally, with a view to the consequences of their acts, they must be allowed to govern themselves by these consequences in childhood. Children are principally the creatures of example—whatever surrounding adults do, they will do. If we strike them, they will strike each other. If they see us attempting to govern each other they will imitate the same barbarism. If we habitually admit the right of sovereignty in each other and in them, then they will become equally respectful of our rights and of each other's. All these propositions are probably self-evident, yet not one of them is practicable under the present mixture of the interests and responsibilities between adults and between parents and children. To solve the problem of education, children must be surrounded with equity and must be equitably treated, and each and every one, parent or child, must be understood to be an individual, and must have his or her individual rights equitably respected.

XI
MAX STIRNER

Max Stirner, pseud. of Johann Kaspar Schmidt, 1806-1856, individualist philosopher, writer, apostle of Egoism. Born at Bayreuth in Bavaria. Studied philosophy and theology at Berlin and at Erlangen; traveled; taught in young ladies' seminary in Berlin, 1839-44. His remarkable book, *The Ego and His Own* (*Der Einzige und sein Eigentum*), translated by Stephen T. Byington and published by Benj. R. Tucker, but now out of print, was known only to a few academicians until its recent revival through the investigations of his biographer, John Henry Mackay, the German poet, and through the sudden fame of the writings of Friedrich Nietzsche, who shows an intellectual kinship to Stirner. A great lover of freedom, both for himself and others, Stirner in his writings lays the philosophical foundation for political liberty and encourages the practical development of egoism to the dissolution of the State and the union of free men.

If it be right to me, it is right.

Freedom cannot be granted. It must be taken.

Individually free is he who is responsible to no *man*.

The great are great only because we are on our knees. Let us rise!

The men of future generations will yet win many a liberty of which we do not even feel the want.

One is free in proportion as one is strong; there is no real liberty save that which one takes for one's self.

Fool, you who are an unique humanity, that you make a merit of wanting to live for another than you are.

A race of altruists is necessarily a race of slaves. A race of free men is necessarily a race of egoists.

"Give God the glory" corresponds with the modern "Give Man the glory." But I mean to keep it for myself.

There is to come into existence a true "society of men," in which every "man" finds room. Liberalism means to realize "Man," i. e. create a world for him.

The freedom of man is, in political liberalism, freedom from *persons*, from personal dominion, from the *master*; the securing of each individual person against other persons, personal freedom.

The egoist, you know, never takes trouble about a thing for the sake of the thing, but for his sake: the thing must serve him. It is egoistic to ascribe to no thing a value of its own, an "absolute" value, but to seek its value in me.

Now, in the first place, the discoverer of a great truth doubtless knows that it can be useful to the rest of men, and, as a jealous withholding furnishes him no enjoyment, he communicates it; but, even though he has the consciousness that his communication is highly valuable to the rest, yet he has in no wise sought and found his truth for the sake of the rest, but for his own sake, because he himself desired it, because darkness and fancies left him no rest till he had procured for himself light and enlightenment to the best of his powers.

He labors, therefore, for his own sake and for the satisfaction of his want. That along with this he was also useful to others, yes, to posterity, does not take from his labor the egoistic character.

Doubtless I have similarity with others; yet that holds good only for comparison or reflection; in fact I am incomparable, unique. My flesh is not their flesh, my mind is not their mind. If you bring them under the generalities "flesh, mind," those are your *thoughts*, which have nothing to do with *my* flesh, *my* mind, and can least of all issue a "call" to mine.

I do not want to recognize or respect in you anything, neither the proprietor nor the ragamuffin, nor even the man, but to *use you*. In salt I find that it makes food palatable to me, therefore I dissolve it; in the fish I recognize an aliment, therefore I eat it; in you I discover the gift of making my life agreeable, therefore I choose you as a companion.

What is to happen, though? Is social life to have an end, and all companionableness, all fraternization, everything that is created by the love or society principle, to disappear?

As if one will not always seek the other because he *needs* him; as if one must not accommodate himself to the other when he *needs* him. But the difference is this, that then the individual really *unites* with the individual, while formerly they were bound together by a tie; son and father are bound together before majority, after it they can come together independently; before it they *belonged* together as members of the Family, after it they unite as egoists; sonship and fatherhood remain, but son and father no longer pin themselves down to these.

When one is anxious only to live, he easily, in this solicitude, forgets the enjoyment of life. If his only concern is for life, and he thinks "if I only have my dear life," he does not apply his full strength to using, i. e. enjoying, life. But how does one use life? In using it up, like the candle, which one uses in burning it up. One uses life, and consequently himself the living one, in consuming it and himself. Enjoyment of life is using life up.

Not till I am certain of myself, and no longer seeking for myself, am I really my property; I have myself, therefore I use and enjoy myself. On the other hand, I can never take comfort in myself so long as I think that I have still to find my true self.

In the old I go toward myself, in the new I start from myself; in the former I long for myself, in the latter I have myself and do with myself as one does with any other property,—I enjoy myself at my pleasure. I am no longer afraid for my life, but "squander" it.

Henceforth the question runs, not how one can acquire life, but how one can squander, enjoy it; or, not how one is to produce the true self in himself, but how one is to dissolve himself, to live himself out.

What else should the ideal be but the sought-for, ever-distant self? One seeks for himself, consequently one does not yet have himself; one aspires toward what one ought to be, consequently one is not it. One lives in longing and has lived thousands of years in it, in hope. Living is quite another thing in—enjoyment!

You poor beings who could live so happily if you might skip

according to your mind, you are to dance to the pipe of schoolmasters and bear-leaders, in order to perform tricks that you yourselves would never use yourselves for. And you do not even kick out of the traces at last against being always taken otherwise than you want to give yourselves. No, you mechanically recite to yourselves the question that is recited to you: "What am I called to? What ought I to do?" You need only ask thus, to have yourselves *told* what you ought to do and *ordered* to do it, to have your *calling* marked out for you, or else to order yourselves and impose it on yourselves according to the spirit's prescription. Then in reference to the will the word is, I will to do what I ought.

A man is "called" to nothing, and has no "calling," no "destiny," as little as a plant or a beast has a "calling." The flower does not follow the calling to complete itself, but it spends all its forces to enjoy and consume the world as well as it can,— i. e. it sucks in as much of the juices of the earth, as much air of the ether, as much light of the sun, as it can get and lodge. The bird lives up to no calling, but it uses its forces as much as is practicable; it catches beetles and sings to its heart's delight. But the forces of the flower and the bird are slight in comparison to those of a man, and a man who applies his forces will affect the world much more powerfully than flower and beast. A calling he has not, but he has forces that manifest themselves where they are because their being consists solely in their manifestation, and are as little able to abide inactive as life, which, if it "stood still" only a second, would no longer be life.

Now, as this rose is a true rose to begin with, this nightingale always a true nightingale, so I am not for the first time a true man when I fulfil my calling, live up to my destiny, but I am a "true man" from the start. My first babble is the token of the life of a "true man," the struggles of my life are the outpourings of his force, my last breath is the last exhalation of the force of the "man."

The true man does not lie in the future, an object of longing, but lies, existent and real, in the present. Whatever and whoever I may be, joyous and suffering, a child or a greybeard, in confidence or doubt, in sleep or in waking, I am it, I am the true man.

But, if I am Man, and have really found in myself him whom religious humanity designated as the distant goal, then everything "truly human" is also my own. What was ascribed to the idea of humanity belongs to me. That freedom of trade, e. g., which humanity has yet to attain,—and which, like an enchanting dream, people remove to humanity's golden future, —I take by anticipation as my property and carry it on for the time in the form of smuggling. There may indeed be but few smugglers who have sufficient understanding to thus account to themselves for their doings, but the instinct of egoism replaces their consciousness. Above I have shown the same thing about freedom of the press.

Everything is my own, therefore I bring back to myself what wants to withdraw from me; but above all I always bring myself back when I have slipped away from myself to my tributariness. But this too is not my calling, but my natural act.

Without doubt culture has made me powerful. It has given me power over all motives, over the impulses of my nature as well as over the exactions and violences of the world. I know, and have gained the force for it by culture, that I need not let myself be coerced by any of my appetites, pleasures, emotions, etc.; I am their—master; in like manner I become, through the sciences and arts, the master of the refractory world, whom sea and earth obey, and to whom even the stars must give an account of themselves.

I receive with thanks what the centuries of culture have acquired for me; I am not willing to throw away and give up anything of it: I have not lived in vain. The experience that I have power over my nature, and need not be the slave of my appetites, shall not be lost to me; the experience that I can subdue the world by culture's means is too dear-bought for me to be able to forget it.

People think again that society gives what we need, and we are under obligations to it on that account, owe it everything. They are still at the point of wanting to serve a "supreme giver of all good." That society is no ego at all, which could give, bestow, or grant, but an instrument or means, from which we may derive benefit; that we have no social duties, but solely interests for the pursuance of which society must serve us; that we owe society no sacrifice, but, if we sacrifice anything, sacrifice it to ourselves,—of this the Socialists do not think, because they—as liberals—are imprisoned in the religious principle, and zealously aspire after—a sacred society, such as the State was hitherto.

Society, from which we have everything, is a new master, a new spook, a new "supreme being," which "takes us into its service and allegiance!"

But now those people go on and ask: For whose sake do you care about God's and the other commandments? You surely do not suppose that this is done merely out of complaisance toward God? No, you are doing it—for your sake again.— Here too, therefore, you are the main thing, and each must say to himself, I am everything to myself and I do everything on my account. If it ever became clear to you that God, the commandments, etc., only harm you, that they reduce and ruin you, to a certainty you would throw them from you just as the Christians once condemned Apollo or Minerva or heathen morality. They did indeed put in the place of these Christ and afterward Mary, as well as a Christian morality; but they did this for the sake of their souls' welfare too, therefore out of egoism or ownness.

And it was by this egoism, this ownness, that they got rid of the old world of gods and became free from it. Ownness created a new freedom; for ownness is the creator of everything, as genius (a definite ownness), which is always originality, has for a long time already been looked upon as the creator of new productions that have a place in the history of the world.

If your efforts are ever to make "freedom" the issue, then exhaust freedom's demands. Who is it that is to become free? You, I, we. Free from what? From everything that is not you, not I, not we. I, therefore, am the kernel that is to be delivered from all wrappings and—free from all cramping shells. Selfishness, in the Christian sense, means something like this: I look only to see whether anything is of use to me as a sensual man. But is sensuality then the whole of my ownness? Am I in my own senses when I am given up to sensuality? Do I follow myself, my own determination, when I follow that? I am my own only when I am master of myself, instead of being mastered either by sensuality or by anything else (God, man, authority, law, State, Church, etc.); what is of use to me, this self-owned or self-appertaining one, my selfishness pursues.

Now then, I and the egoistic are the really general, since everyone is an egoist and of paramount importance to himself. The Jewish is not the purely egoistic, because the Jew still devotes himself to Jehovah; the Christian is not, because the Christian lives on the grace of God and subjects himself to him. As Jew and as Christian alike a man satisfies only certain of his wants, only a certain need, not himself: a half-egoism, because the egoism of a half-man, who is half he, half Jew, or half his own proprietor, half a slave. Therefore, too, Jew and Christian always halfway exclude each other; i. e., as men they recognize each other, as slaves they exclude each other, because they are servants of two different masters. If they could be complete egoists, they would exclude each other wholly and hold together so much the more firmly. Now it is clear, God cares only for what is his, busies himself only with himself, thinks only of himself, and has only himself before his eyes; woe to all that is not well-pleasing to him! He serves no higher person, and satisfies only himself. His cause is—a purely egoistic cause.

Let me then likewise concern myself for myself, who am equally with God the nothing of all others, who am my all, who am the only one.

Nothing is more to me than myself!

Now, let one imagine a French revolutionist in the year 1778, who among friends let fall the now well-known phrase, "the world will have no rest till the last king is hanged with the guts of the last priest." The king then still had all power, and, when the utterance is betrayed by an accident, yet without its being possible to produce witnesses, confession is demanded from the accused. Is he to confess or not? If he denies, he lies and—remains unpunished; if he confesses, he is candid and—is beheaded. If truth is more than everything else to him, all right, let him die. Only a paltry poet could try to make a tragedy out of the end of his life; for what interest is there in seeing how a man succumbs from cowardice? But, if he had the courage not to be a slave of truth and sincerity, he would ask somewhat thus: Why need the judges know what I have spoken among friends? If I had wished them to know, I should have said it to them as I said it to my friends. I will not have them know it. They force themselves into my confidence without my having called them to it and made them my confidants; they will learn what I will keep secret. Come on then, you who wish to break my will by your will, and try your arts. You can torture me by the rack, you can threaten me with hell and eternal damnation, you can make me so nerveless that I swear a false oath, but the truth you shall not press out of me, for I will lie to you because I have given you no claim and no right to my sincerity. Let God, "who is truth," look down ever so threateningly on me, let lying come ever so hard to me, I have nevertheless the courage of a lie; and, even if I were weary of my life, even if nothing appeared to me more welcome than your executioner's sword, you nevertheless should not have the joy of finding in me a slave of truth, whom by your priestly arts you make a traitor to his will. When I spoke those treasonable words, I would not have had you know anything of them; I now retain the same will, and do not let myself be frightened by the curse of the lie.

Sigismund is not a miserable caitiff because he broke his princely word because he was a caitiff; he might have kept his word and would still have been a caitiff, a priest-ridden man. Luther, driven by a higher power, became unfaithful to his monastic vow: he became so for God's sake. Both broke their oath as possessed persons: Sigismund, because he wanted to appear as a sincere professor of the divine truth, i. e. of the true, genuinely Catholic faith; Luther, in order to give testimony for the gospel sincerely and with entire truth, with body and soul; both became prejured in order to be sincere toward the "higher truth." Only, the priests absolved the one, the other absolved himself. What else did both observe than what is contained in those apostolic words, "Thou hast not lied to men, but to God"? They lied to men, broke their oath before the world's eyes, in order not to lie to God, but to serve him. Thus they show us a way to deal with truth before men. For God's glory, and for God's sake, a—breach of oath, a lie, a prince's word broken!

How would it be, now, if we changed the thing a little and wrote, A perjury and lie for—my sake? Would not that be pleading for every baseness? It seems so assuredly, only in this it is altogether like the "for God's sake." For was not every baseness committed for God's sake, were not all the scaffolds filled for his sake and all the auto-da-fes held for his sake? and do they not today still for God's sake fetter the mind in tender children by religious education? Were not sacred vows broken for his sake, and do not missionaries and priests still go around every day to bring Jews, heathen, Protestants or Catholics, etc., to treason against the faith of their fathers,—for his sake?

It is despicable to deceive a confidence that we voluntarily call forth; but it is no shame to egoism to let every one who wants to get us into his power by an oath bleed to death by the unsuccessfulness of his untrustful craft. If you have wanted to bind me, then learn that I know how to burst your bonds.

The point is whether I give the confider the right to confidence. If the pursuer of my friend asks me where he has fled to, I shall surely put him on a false trail. Why does he ask precisely me, the pursued man's friend? In order not to be a false friend, I prefer to be false to the enemy. I might certainly, in courageous conscientiousness, answer "I will not tell" (so Fichte decides the case); by that I should salve my love of truth and do for my friend as much as—nothing, for, if I do not mislead the enemy, he may accidentally take the right street, and my love of truth would have given up my friend as a prey, because it hindered me from the—courage for a lie. He who has in the truth an idol, a sacred thing, must humble himself before it, must not defy its demands, not resist courageously; in short, he must renounce the heroism of the lie. For to the lie belongs not less courage than to the truth: a courage that young men are most apt to be defective in, who would rather confess the truth and mount the scaffold for it than confound the enemy's power by the impudence of a lie. To them the truth is "sacred," and the sacred at all times demands blind reverence, submission, and self-sacrifice. If you are not impudent, not mockers of the sacred, you are tame and its servants. Let one but lay a grain of truth in the trap for you, you peck at it to a certainty, and the fool is caught. You will not lie? Well, then, fall as sacrifices to the truth and become—martyr! Martyrs!—for what? For yourselves, for self-ownership? No, for your goddess,—the truth. You know only two services, only two kinds of servants: servants of the truth and servants of the lie.

The State.—The State always has the sole purpose to limit, tame, subordinate, the individual—to make him subject to some generality or other; it lasts only so long as the individual is not all in all, and it is only the clearly-marked restriction of me, my limitation, my slavery. Never does a State aim to bring in the free activity of individuals, but always that which is bound to the purpose of the State. Through the State nothing in common comes to pass either, as little as one can call a piece of cloth the common work of all the individual parts of a machine; it is rather the work of the whole machine as a unit, machine work. In the same style everything is done by the State machine too; for it moves the clockwork of the individual minds, none of which follow their own impulse. The State seeks to hinder every free activity by its censorship, its supervision, its police, and holds this hindering to be its duty, because it is in truth a duty of self-preservation. The State wants to make something out of man, therefore there live in it only made men; everyone who wants to be his own self is its opponent.

Society leaves it to the individual's decision whether he will draw upon himself evil consequences and inconveniences by his mode of action, and hereby recognizes his free decision; the State behaves in exactly the reverse way, denying all right to the individual's decision, and, instead, ascribing the sole right to its own decision, the law of the State, so that he who transgresses the State's commandment is looked upon as if he were acting against God's commandment,—a view which likewise was once maintained by the Church. Here God is the Holy in and of himself, and the commandments of the Church, as of the State, are the commandments of this Holy One, which he transmits to the world through his anointed and Lords-by-the-Grace-of-God. If the Church had deadly sins, the State has capital crimes; if the one had heretics, the other has traitors; the one ecclesiastical penalties, the other criminal penalties; the one inquisitorial processes, the other fiscal; in short, there sins, here crimes, there sinners, here criminals, there inquisition and here—inquisition. Will the sanctity of the State not fall like the Church's? The awe of its laws, the reverence for its highness, the humility of its "subjects", will this remain? Will the "saint's" face not be stripped of its adornment?

The State has no anxiety about me and mine, but about itself and its: I count for something to it only as its child, as "a son of the country;" as ego I am nothing at all for it. For the State's understanding, what befalls me as ego is something accidental, my wealth as well as my impoverishment. But, if I with all that is mine am an accident in the State's eyes, this proves that it cannot comprehend me: I go beyond its concepts, or, its understanding is too limited to comprehend me. Therefore it cannot do anything for me either.

Labor and the State.—The State does not let me come to my value, and continues in existence only through my valuelessness: it is forever intent on getting benefit from me, i. e. exploiting me, turning me to account, using me up, even if the use it gets from me consists only in my supplying a proles (proletariat); it wants me to be "its creature."

Pauperism can be removed only when I as ego realize value from myself, when I give my own self value, and make my price myself. I must rise in revolt to rise in the world.

What I produce, flour, linen, or iron and coal, which I toilsomely win from the earth, etc., is my work that I want to realize value from. But then I may long complain that I am not paid for my work according to its value: the payer will not listen to me, and the State likewise will maintain an apathetic attitude so long as it does not think it must "appease" me that I may not break out with my dreaded might. But this "appeasing" will be all, and, if it comes into my head to ask for more, the State turns against me with all the force of its lion-paws and eagle-claws: for it is the king of beasts, it is lion and eagle. If I refuse to be content with the price that it fixes for my ware and labor, if I rather aspire to determine the price of my ware myself, i. e. "to pay myself," in the first place I come into conflict with the buyers of the ware. If this were stilled by a mutual understanding, the State would not readily make objections; for how individuals get along with each other troubles it little, so long as therein they do not get in its way. Its damage and its danger begin only when they do not agree, but, in the absence of a settlement, take each other by the hair. The State cannot endure that man stand in a direct relation to man; it must step between as—mediator, must—intervene. What Christ was, what the saints, the Church were, the State has become,—to-wit, "mediator." It tears man from man to put itself between them as a "spirit". The laborers who ask for higher pay are treated as criminals as soon as they want to compel it. What are they to do? Without compulsion they don't get it, and in compulsion the State sees a self-help, a determination of price by the ego, a genuine, free realization of value from his property, which it cannot admit of. What then are the laborers to do? Look to themselves and ask nothing about the State?——

But, as is the situation with regard to my material work, so it is with my intellectual too. The State allows me to realize value from all my thoughts and to find customers for them (I do not realize value from them, e. g., in the very fact that they bring me honor from the listeners, and the like); but only so long as my thoughts are—its thoughts. If, on the other hand, I harbor thoughts that it cannot approve (i. e. make its own), then it does not allow me at all to realize value from them, to bring them into exchange, into commerce. My thoughts are free only if they are granted to me by the State's grace, i. e. if they are the State's thoughts. It lets me philosophize, freely only so far as I prove myself "philosopher of State"; against the State I must not philosophize, gladly as it tolerates my helping it out of its "deficiencies," "furthering" it.—Therefore, as I may behave only as an ego most graciously permitted by the State, provided with its testimonial of legitimacy and police pass, so too it is not granted me to realize value from what is mine, unless this proves to be its, which I hold as fief from it. My ways must be its ways, else it distrains me; my thoughts its thoughts, else it stops my mouth.

The State has nothing to be more afraid of than the value of me, and nothing must it more carefully guard against than every occasion that offers itself to me for realizing value from myself.

I am the deadly enemy of the State, which always hovers between the alternatives, it or I.

If an age is imbued with an error, some always derive advantage from the error, while the rest have to suffer from it. In the Middle Ages the error was general among Christians that the church must have all power, or the supreme lordship on earth; the heirarchs believed in this "truth" not less than the laymen, and both were spell-bound in the like error. But by it the heirarchs had the advantage of power, the laymen had to suffer subjection. However, as the saying goes, "one learns wisdom by suffering"; and so the laymen at last learned wisdom and no longer believed in the mediavel "truth."—A like relation exists between the commonalty and the laboring class. Commoner and laborer believe in the "truth" of money; they who do not possess it believe in it no less than those who possess it: the laymen, therefore, as well as the priests.

"Money governs the world" is the keynote of the civic epoch. A destitute aristocrat and a destitute laborer, as "starvelings," amount to nothing so far as political consideration is concerned; birth and labor do not do it, but money brings consideration. The possessors rule, but the State trains up from the destitute its "servants," to whom, in proportion as they are to rule (govern) in its name, it gives money (a salary).

I receive everything from the State. Have I anything without the State's assent? What I have without this it takes from me as soon as it discovers the lack of a "legal title." Do not I, therefore, have everything through its grace, its assent?

On this alone, on the legal title, the commonalty rests. The commoner is what he is through the protection of the State, through the State's grace. He would necessarily be afraid of losing everything if the State's power were broken.

But how is it with him who has nothing to lose, how with the proletarian? As he has nothing to lose, he does not need the protection of the State for his "nothing." He may gain, on the contrary, if that protection of the State is withdrawn from the protege.

Therefore the non-possessor will regard the State as a power protecting the possessor, which privileges the latter, but does nothing for him, the non-possessor, but to—suck his blood. The State is a—commoner's State, is the estate of the commonalty. It protects man not according to his labor, but according to his tractableness ("loyalty"),—to wit, according to whether the rights entrusted to him by the State are enjoyed and managed in accordance with the will, i. e. laws, of the State.

Under the regime of the commonalty the laborers always fall into the hands of the possessors—i. e. of those who have at their disposal some bit of the State domains (and everything possessible is State domain, belongs to the State, and is only a fief of the individual), especially money and land; of the capitalists, therefore. The laborer cannot realize on his labor to the extent of the value that it has for the consumer. "Labor is badly paid!" The capitalist has the greatest profit from it.— Well paid, and more than well paid, are only the labors of those who heighten the splendor and dominion of the State, the labors of high State servants. The State pays well that its "good citizens," the possessors, may be able to pay badly without danger; it secures to itself by good payment its servants, out of whom it forms a protecting power, a "police" (to the police belong soldiers, officials of all kinds, e. g. those of justice, education, etc.,—in short, the whole "machinery of the State") for the "good citizens," and the "good citizens" gladly pay high tax-rates to it in order to pay so much lower rates to their laborers. To be a good Christian one needs only to believe, and that can be done under the most oppressive circumstances. Hence the Christian-minded take care only of the oppressed laborers' piety, their patience, submission, etc. Only so long as the down-trodden classes were Christians could they bear all their misery: for Christianity does not let their murmurings and exasperation rise. Now the hushing of desires is no longer enough, but their sating is demanded. The bourgeoisie has proclaimed the gospel of the enjoyment of the world, of material enjoyment, and now wonders that this doctrine finds adherents among us poor; it has shown that not faith and poverty, but culture and possessions, make a man blessed; we proletarians understand that too.

You bring into a union your whole power, your competence, and make yourself count; in a society you are employed, with your working power; in the former you live egoistically, in the latter humanly, i. e. religiously, as a "member in the body of this Lord", to a society you owe what you have, and are in duty bound to it, are—possessed by "social duties"; a union you utilize, and give it up undutifully and unfaithfully when you see no way to use it further. If a society is more than you, then it is more to you than yourself; a union is only your instrument, or the sword with which you sharpen and increase your natural force; the union exists for you and through you, the society conversely lays claim to you for itself and exists even without you; in short, the society is sacred, the union your own; the society consumes you, you consume the union.

Nevertheless people will not be backward with the objection that the agreement which has been concluded may again become burdensome to us and limit our freedom; they will say, we too would at last come to this, that "every one must sacrifice a part of his freedom for the sake of the generality." But the sacrifice would not be made for the "generality's" sake a bit, as little as I concluded the agreement for the "generality's" or even for any other man's sake; rather I came into it only for the sake of my own benefit, from selfishness. But, as regards the sacrificing, surely I "sacrifice" only that which does not stand in my power, i. e. I "sacrifice" nothing at all.

The laborers have the most enormous power in their hands, and, if they once became thoroughly conscious of it and used it, nothing would withstand them; they would only have to stop labor, regard the product of labor as theirs, and enjoy it. This is the sense of the labor disturbances which show themselves here and there.

The State rests on the—slavery of labor. If labor becomes free, the State is lost.

XII
HENRY DAVID THOREAU

Henry David Thoreau, 1817-1860, American writer, educated at Harvard; taught school, became land-surveyor. Lived alone on shore of Walden Pond, Concord, 1845-7; Transcendentalist, thinker, idealist, friend of Emerson, Alcott, and group of writers who formed the "Brook Farm." Great lover of nature; stood out for the rights of the individual; was at one time imprisoned for his refusal to pay taxes; wrote for leading periodicals and was author of several poems. Among his works are: *A Week on the Concord and Merrimac Ribers*, 1849; *Walden, or Life in the Woods*, 1854; *Excursions in Field and Forest*, 1863, with a memoir by Emerson; *The Main Woods*, 1864; *Cape Cod*, 1865; *Letters to Various Persons*, 1865—with a notice by Emerson; *A Yankee in Canada*, 1866.

This chapter is his famous essay *On the Duty of Civil Disobedience*, slightly abridged. The short selections are from *Walden*.

If a man does not keep pace with his companions, perhaps it is because he hears a different drummer.

If there is an experiment you would like to try, try it. Do not entertain doubts if they are not agreeable to you.

Do not be too moral. You may cheat yourself out of much life so. Aim above morality. Be not simply good; be good for something.

It is impossible to give the soldier a good education without making him a deserter. His natural foe is the government that drills him.

In my short experience of human life, the outward obstacles, if there were any such, have not been living men, but the institutions of the dead.

The man who goes alone can start today; but he who travels with another must wait till that other is ready, and it may be a long time before they get off.

All men are partially buried in the grave of custom, and of some we see only the crown of their head above ground. Better are they physically dead, for they more lively rot.

When I have not paid the tax which the state demanded for that protection which I did not want, itself has robbed me;

when I have asserted the liberty it presumed to declare, itself has imprisoned me.

There is something servile in the habit of seeking after a law which we may obey. We may study the laws of matter at and for our convenience, but a successful life knows no law.

He for whom the law is made, who does not obey the law, but whom the law obeys, reclines on pillows of down, and is wafted at will whither he pleases; for man is superior to all laws, both of heaven and earth, when he takes his liberty.

I have not surely so foreseen that any Cossack or Chippeway would come to disturb the honest and simple commonwealth as that some monster institution would at length embrace and crush its free members in its scaly folds; for it is not to be forgotten, that while the law holds fast the thief and murderer, it lets itself go loose.

I love mankind, but I hate the institutions of the dead unkind. Men execute nothing so faithfully as the wills of the dead, to the last codicil and letter. They rule this world, and the living are but their executors. Such foundation, too, have our lectures and our sermons commonly. They are all Dudelian; and piety derives its origin still from that exploit of pious Aeneas, who bore his father, Anchises, on his shoulder from the ruins of Troy. Or rather, like some Indian tribes, we bear about with us the mouldering relics of our ancestors on our shoulders. If, for instance, a man asserts the value of individual liberty over the merely political commonweal, his neighbor still tolerates him, that is he who is living near him, sometimes even sustains him, but never the State.

The Duty of Civil Disobedience.—I heartily accept the motto—"That government is best which governs least;" and I should like to see it acted up to more rapidly and systematically. Carried out, it finally amounts to this, which also I believe—"That government is best which governs not at all;" and when men are prepared for it, that will be the kind of government which they will have. Government is at best but an expedient; but most governments are usually, and all governments are sometimes, inexpedient.

The objections which have been brought against a standing army, and they are many and weighty, and deserve to prevail, may also at last be brought against a standing government. The standing army is only an arm of the standing government. The government itself, which is only the mode which the people have chosen to execute their will, is equally liable to be abused and perverted before the people can act through it. Witness the present Mexican war (1849), the work of comparatively a few individuals using the standing government as their tool; for, in the outset, the people would not have consented to this measure.

This American government—what is it but a tradition, though a recent one, endeavoring to transmit itself unimpaired to posterity, but each instant losing some of its integrity? It has not the vitality and force of a single living man; for a single man can bend it to his will. It is a sort of wooden gun to the people themselves. But it is not the less necessary for this; for the people must have some kind of complicated machinery or other, and hear its din, to satisfy that idea of government which they have.

Governments show thus how successfully men can be imposed on, even impose on themselves, for their own advantage. It is excellent, we must all allow. Yet this government never of itself furthered any enterprise, but by the alacrity with which it got out of its way.

After all, the practical reason why, when the power is once in the hands of the people, a majority are permitted, and for a long period continue, to rule, is not because they are most likely to be in the right, nor because this seems fairest to the minority, but because they are physically the strongest. But a government in which the majority rule in all cases cannot be based on justice, even as far as men understand it.

Can there not be a government in which majorities do not

virtually decide right and wrong, but conscience?—in which majorities decide only those questions to which the rule of expediency is applicable? Must the citizen ever for a moment, or in the least degree, resign his conscience to the legislator? Why has every man a conscience, then? I think that we should be men first, and subjects afterwards. It is not desirable to cultivate a respect for the law, so much as for the right. The only obligation which I have a right to assume, is to do at any time what I think right. It is truly enough said, that a corporation has no conscience; but a corporation of conscientious men is a corporation *with* a conscience.

Law never made men a whit more just; and, by means of their respect for it, even the well-disposed are daily made the agents of injustice. A common and natural result of an undue respect for law is that you may see a file of soldiers, colonel, captain, corporal, privates, powder-monkeys, and all, marching in admirable order over hill and dale to the wars, against their wills, ay, against their common sense and consciences, which makes it very steep marching indeed, and produces a palpitation of the heart. They have no doubt that it is a damnable business in which they are concerned; they are all peaceably inclined. Now, what are they? Men at all? or small movable forts and magazines, at the service of some unscrupulous man in power?

The mass of men serve the State thus, not as men mainly, but as machines, with their bodies. They are the standing army, and the militia, gaolers, constables, posse comitatus, etc. In most cases there is no free exercise whatever of the judgment or of the moral sense; but they put themselves on a level with wood and earth and stones; and wooden men can perhaps be manufactured that will serve the purpose as well. Such command no more respect than men of straw or a lump of dirt. They have the same sort of worth only as horses and dogs. Yet such as these even are commonly esteemed good citizens.

Others—as most legislators, politicians, lawyers, ministers, and office-holders—serve the State chiefly with their heads; and, as they rarely make any moral distinctions, they are as likely to serve the devil, without *intending* it, as God.

How does it become a man to behave toward this American government today? I answer, that he cannot without disgrace be associated with it. I cannot for an instant recognize that political organization as *my* government which is the *slave's* government also.

All men recognize the right of revolution; that is, the right to refuse allegiance to, and to resist, the government, when its tyranny or its inefficiency are great and unendurable. But almost all say that such is not the case now. But such was the case, they think, in the Revolution of '75.

If one were to tell me that this was a bad government because it taxed certain foreign commodities brought to its ports, it is most probable that I should not make an ado about it, for I can do without them. All machines have their friction, and possibly this does enough good to counter-balance the evil. At any rate, it is a great evil to make a stir about it. But when the friction comes to have its machine, and oppression and robbery are organized, I say, let us not have such a machine any longer. In other words, when a sixth of the population of a nation which has undertaken to be the refuge of liberty are slaves, and a whole country is unjustly overrun and conquered by a foreign army, and subjected to military law, I think that it is not too soon for honest men to rebel and revolutionize. What makes this duty the more urgent is the fact that the country so overrun is not our own, but ours is the invading army.

Paley, a common authority with many on moral questions, in his chapter on "Duty of Submission to Civil Government," resolves all civil obligation into expediency; and he proceeds to say, "that so long as the interest of the whole society requires it, that is, so long as the established government cannot be resisted or changed without public inconvenience, it is the will of God that the established government be obeyed, and no longer. . . . This principle being admitted, the justice of every particular case of resistance is reduced to a computation of the quality of the danger and grievance on the one side, and of the probability and expense of redressing it on the other." Of this, he says, every man shall judge for himself.

But Paley appears never to have contemplated those cases to which the rule of expediency does not apply, in which a people, as well as an individual, must do justice, cost what it may. If I have unjustly wrested a plank from a drowning man, I must restore it to him though I drown myself. This, according to Paley, would be inconvenient. But he that would save his life in such a case, shall lose it. This people must cease to hold slaves, and to make war on Mexico, though it cost them their existence as a people.

In their practice, nations agree with Paley; but does any one think that Massachusetts does exactly what is right at the present crisis?

A drab of state, a cloth-o'-silver slut,

To have her train borne up, and her soul trail in the dirt.
Practically speaking, the opponents to a reform in Massachusetts are not a hundred thousand politicians at the South, but a hundred thousand merchants and farmers here, who are more interested in commerce and agriculture than they are in humanity, and are not prepared to do justice to the slave and to Mexico, *cost what it may*. I quarrel not with far-off foes, but with those who, near at home, co-operate with, and do the bidding of, those far away, and without whom the latter would be harmless.

We are accustomed to say that the mass of men are unprepared; but improvement is slow, because the few are not materially wiser or better than the many. It is not so important that many should be as good as you, as that there be some absolute goodness somewhere, for that will leaven the whole lump.

There are thousands who are in opinion opposed to slavery

and to the war, who yet in effect do nothing to put an end to them; who, esteeming themselves children of Washington and Franklin (Cromwell and Gladstone?) sit down with their hands in their pockets, and say that they know not what to do, and do nothing; who even postpone the question of freedom to the question of free-trade, and quietly read the prices-current along with the latest advices from Mexico, after dinner, and, it may be, fall asleep over them both.

What is the price-current of an honest man and patriot today? They hesitate, and they regret, and sometimes they petition; but they do nothing in earnest and with effect. They will wait, well disposed, for others to remedy the evil, that they may no longer have it to regret. At most, they give only a cheap vote, and a feeble countenance and God-speed, to the right, as it goes by them.

There are nine hundred and ninety-nine patrons of virtue to one virtuous man. But it is easier to deal with the real possessor of a thing than with the temporary guardian of it.

All voting is a sort of gaming, like checkers or backgammon with a slight moral tinge to it, a playing with right and wrong, with moral questions; and betting naturally accompanies it. The character of the voters is not staked. I cast my vote, perchance, as I think right; but I am not vitally concerned that that right should prevail. I am willing to leave it to the majority. Its obligation, therefore, never exceeds that of expediency.

Even voting for the right is doing nothing for it. It is only expressing to men feebly your desire that it should prevail. A wise man will not leave the right to the mercy of chance, nor wish it to prevail through the power of the majority. There is but little virtue in the action of masses of men. When the majority shall at length vote for the abolition of slavery, it will be because they are indifferent to slavery, or because there is but little slavery left to be abolished by their vote. They will then be the only slaves. Only his vote can hasten the abolition of slavery who asserts his own freedom by his vote.

I hear of a convention to be held at Baltimore, or elsewhere, for the selection of a candidate for the Presidency, made up chiefly of editors, and men who are politicians by profession; but I think, what is it to any independent, intelligent, and respectable man what decision they may come to? Shall we not have the advantage of his wisdom and honesty, nevertheless? Can we not count upon some independent votes? Are there not many individuals in the country who do not attend conventions?

But no: I find that the respectable man, so-called, has immediately drifted from his position, and despairs of his country, when his country has more reason to despair of him. He forthwith adopts one of the candidates thus selected as the only available one, thus proving that he is himself available for any purposes of the demagogue. His vote is of no more worth than that of any unprincipled foreigner or hireling native, who may have been bought.

Oh for a man who is a *man*, and, as my neighbor says, has a bone in his back which you cannot pass your hands through! Our statistics are at fault; the population has been returned too large. How many *men* are there to a square thousand miles in this country? Hardly one. Does not America offer any inducement for men to settle here?

The American has dwindled into an Odd Fellow,—one who may be known by the development of his organ of gregariousness, and a manifest lack of intellect and cheerful self-reliance; whose first and chief concern, on coming into the world, is to see the Almshouses are in good repair; and, before he has lawfully donned the virile garb, to collect a fund for the support of the widows and orphans that may be; who, in short, ventures to live only by the aid of the Mutual Insurance Company, which has promised to bury him decently.

It is not a man's duty, as a matter of course, to devote himself to the eradication of any, even the most enormous wrong;

he may still properly have other concerns to engage him; but it is his duty, at least, to wash his hands of it, and, if he gives it no thought longer, not to give it practically his support. If I devote myself to other pursuits and contemplations, I must first see, at least, that I do not pursue them, sitting upon another man's shoulders. I must get off him first, that he may pursue his contemplations too.

See what gross inconsistency is tolerated. I have heard some of my townsmen say, "I should like to have them order me out to help put down an insurrection of the slaves, or to march to Mexico—see if I would go"; and yet these very men have each, directly by their allegiance, and so indirectly, at least, by their money, furnished a substitute.

The soldier is applauded who refuses to serve in an unjust war by those who do not refuse to sustain the unjust government which makes the war; is applauded by those whose own act and authority he disregards and sets at naught; as if the State were penitent to that degree that it hired one to scourge it while it sinned, but not to that degree that it left off sinning for a moment. Thus, under the name of Order and Civil Government, we are all made at last to pay homage to and support our own meanness.

After the first blush of sin comes its indifference; and from immoral it becomes, as it were, unmoral, and not quite unnecessary to that life which we have made.

The broadest and most prevalent error requires the most disinterested virtue to sustain it. The slight reproach to which the virtue of patriotism is commonly liable, the noble are most likely to incur. Those who, while they dissapprove of the character and measures of a government, yield to it their allegiance and support, are undoubtedly its most conscientious supporters, and so frequently the most serious obstacles to reform.

Some are petitioning the State to dissolve the Union, to disregard the requisitions of the President. Why do they not dissolve it themselves,—the union between themselves and the State,—and refuse to pay their quota into its treasury? Do not they stand in the same relation to the State, that the State does to the Union? And have not the same reasons prevented the State from resisting the Union, which have prevented them from resisting the State?

How can a man be satisfied to entertain an opinion merely and enjoy *it*? Is there any enjoyment in it, if his opinion is that he is aggrieved? If you are cheated out of a single dollar by your neighbor, you do not rest satisfied with knowing that you are cheated, or with saying that you are cheated, or even with petitioning him to pay you your due; but you take effectual steps at once to obtain the full amount, and see that you are never cheated again.

Action from principle, the perception and the performance of right, changes things and relations; it is essentially revolutionary, and does not consist wholly with anything which was. It not only divides states and churches, it divides families; ay, it divides the individual, separating the diabolical in him from the divine.

Unjust laws exist: shall we be content to obey them, or shall we endeavor to amend them, and obey them until we have succeeded, or shall we transgress them at once?

Men generally, under such a government as this, think that they ought to wait until they have persuaded the majority to alter them. They think that, if they should resist, the remedy would be worse than the evil. But it is the fault of the government itself that the remedy is worse than the evil. *It* makes it worse. Why is it not more apt to anticipate and provide for reform? Why does it not cherish its wise minority? Why does it cry and resist before it is hurt? Why does it not encourage its citizens to be on the alert to point out its faults and *do* better than it would have them? Why does it always crucify Christ, and excommunicate Copernicus and Luther, and pronounce Washington and Franklin rebels?

One would think that a deliberate and practical denial of its authority was the only offence never contemplated by government; else, why has it not assigned its definite, its suitable and proportionate penalty? If a man who has no property refuses but once to earn nine shillings for the State, he is put in prison for a period unlimited by any law that I know, and determined only by the discretion of those who placed him there; but if he should steal ninety times nine shillings from the State, he is soon permitted to go at large again.

If the injustice is a part of the necessary friction of the machine of government, let it go; perchance it will wear smooth —certainly the machine will wear out. If the injustice has a spring, or a pulley, or a rope, or a crank, exclusively for itself, then perhaps you may consider whether the remedy will not be worse than the evil; but if it is of such a nature that it requires you to be the agent of injustice to another, then, I say, break the law. Let your life be a counterfriction to stop the machine. What I have to do is to see, at any rate, that I do not lend myself to the wrong which I condemn.

As for adopting the ways which the State has provided for remedying the evil, I know not of such ways. They take too much time, and a man's life will be gone. I have other affairs to attend to. I came into this world, not chiefly to make this a good place to live in, but to live in it, be it good or bad. A man has not everything to do, but something; and because he cannot do *everything*, it is not necessary that he should do *something* wrong.

It is not my business to be petitioning the Governor or the Legislature any more than it is theirs to petition me; and if they should not hear my petition, what should I do then? But in this case the State has provided no way; its very Constitution is the evil. This may seem to be harsh and stubborn and unconciliatory; but it is to treat with the utmost kindness and consideration the only spirit that can appreciate or deserves it. So is all change for the better, like birth and death, which convulse the body.

I do not hesitate to say that those who call themselves Abolitionists should at once effectually withdraw their support both in person and property, from the government of Massachusetts, and not wait until they constitute a majority of one, before they suffer the right to prevail through them. I think that it is enough if they have God on their side, without waiting for that other one. Moreover, any man more right than his neighbors constitutes a majority of one already.

I meet this American government, or its representative, the State government, directly, and face to face, once a year—no more—in the person of its tax-gatherer; this is the only mode in which a man situated as I am necessarily meets it; and it then says distinctly, Recognize me; and the simplest, the most effectual, and, in the present posture of affairs, the indispensable mode of treating with it on this head, of expressing your little satisfaction with and love for it, is to deny it then.

My civil neighbor, the tax-gatherer, is the very man I have to deal with,—for it is, after all, with men and not with parchment that I quarrel,—and he has voluntarily chosen to be an agent of the government. How shall he ever know well what he is and does as an officer of the government, or as a man, until he is obliged to consider whether he shall treat me, his neighbor, for whom he has respect, as a neighbor and well-disposed man, or as a maniac and disturber of the peace, and see if he can get over this obstruction to his neighborliness without a ruder and more impetuous thought or speech corresponding with his action?

I know this well, that if one thousand, if one hundred, if ten men whom I could name—if ten honest men only—ay, if *one* honest man, in this State of Massachusetts, ceasing to hold slaves, were actually to withdraw from this co-partnership, and be locked up in the county jail therefor, it would be the abolition of slavery in America. For it matters not how small the beginning may seem to be; what is once well done is done forever. But we love better to talk about it: that we say is our mission.

Reforms keep many scores of newspapers in its service, but not one man. If my esteemed neighbor, the State's ambassador, who will devote his days to the settlement of the question of human rights in the Council Chamber, instead of being threatened with the prisons of Carolina, were to sit down the prisoner of Massachusetts, that State which is so anxious to foist the sin of slavery upon her sister—though at present she can discover only an act of inhospitality to be the ground of a quarrel with her—the Legislature would not wholly waive the subject the following winter.

Under a government which imprisons any unjustly, the true place for a just man is also a prison. The proper place today, the only place which Massachusetts has provided for her freer and less desponding spirits, is in her prisons, to be put out and locked out of the State by her own act, as they have already put themselves out by their principles. It is there that the fugitive slave, and the Mexican prisoner on parole, and the Indian come to plead the wrongs of his race, should find them; on that separate but more free and honorable ground, where the State places those who are not with her but against her—the only house in a slave State in which a free man can abide with honor.

If any think that their influence would be lost there, and their voices no longer afflict the ear of the State, that they would not be as an enemy within its walls, they do not know by how much truth is stronger than error, nor how much more eloquently and effectively he can combat injustice who has experienced a little in his own person.

Cast your whole vote, not a strip of paper merely, but your whole influence. A minority is powerless while it conforms to the majority; it is not even a minority then; but it is irresistible when it clogs by its whole weight.

If the alternative is to keep all just men in prison, or give up war and slavery, the State will not hesitate which to choose. If a thousand men were not to pay their tax-bills this year, that would not be a violent and bloody measure, as it would be to pay them, and enable the State to commit violence and shed innocent blood.

This is, in fact, the definition of a peaceful revolution, if any such is possible. If the tax-gatherer or any other public officer asks me, as one has done, "But what shall I do?" my answer is, "If you really wish to do anything, resign your office." When the subject has refused allegiance, and the officer has resigned his office, then the revolution is accomplished.

But even if blood should flow. Is there not a sort of blood shed when the conscience is wounded? Through this wound a man's real manhood and immortality flow out, and he bleeds to an everlasting death. I see this blood flowing now.

I have contemplated the imprisonment of the offender rather than the seizure of his goods—though both will serve the same purpose—because they who assert the purest right, and consequently are most dangerous to a corrupt State, commonly have not spent much time in accumulating property. To such the State renders comparatively small service, and a slight tax is wont to appear exorbitant, particularly if they are obliged to earn it by special labor with their hands.

If there were one who lived wholly without the use of money, the State itself would hesitate to demand it of him. But the rich man—not to make any invidious comparison—is always sold to the institution which makes him rich. Absolutely speaking, the more money the less virtue; for money comes between a man and his objects, and obtains them for him; and it was certainly no great virtue to obtain it. It puts to rest many questions which he would otherwise be taxed to answer; while the only new question which it puts is the hard but superfluous one, how to spend it. Thus his moral ground is taken from under his feet. The opportunities of living are diminished in proportion as what are called the "means" are increased.

The best thing a man can do for his culture when he is rich is to endeavor to carry out those schemes which he entertained when he was poor. Christ answered the Herodians according to their condition. "Show Me the tribute-money," said He—and one took a penny out of his pocket—if you use money which has the image of Caesar on it, and which he has made current and valuable—that is, *if you are men of the State*, and gladly enjoy the advantages of Caesar's government, then pay him back some of his own when he demands it; "Render therefore to Caesar that which is Caesar's, and to God those things which are God's"—leaving them no wiser than before as to which was which; for they did not wish to know.

When I converse with the freest of my neighbors, I perceive that, whatever they may say about the magnitude and seriousness of the question, and their regard for the public tranquillity, the long and the short of the matter is, that they cannot spare the protection of the existing government, and they dread the consequences to their property and families of disobedience to it. For my own part, I should not like to think that I ever rely on the protection of the State.

But, if I deny the authority of the State when it presents its tax-bill, it will soon take and waste all my property, and so harass me and my children without end. This is hard. This makes it impossible for a man to live honestly, and at the same time comfortably, in outward respects. It will not be worth the while to accumulate property; that would be sure to go again. You must hire or squat somewhere, and raise but a small crop, and eat that soon. You must live within yourself, always tucked up and ready for a start, and not have many affairs.

A man may grow rich in Turkey even, if he will be in all respects a good subject of the Turkish government. Confucius said: "If a state is governed by the principles of reason, poverty and misery are subjects of shame; if a state is not governed by the principles of reason, riches and honors are the subjects of shame." No: until I want the protection of Massachusetts to be extended to me in some distant Southern port, where my liberty is endangered, or until I am bent solely on building up an estate at home by peaceful enterprise, I can afford to refuse allegiance to Massachusetts, and her right to my property and life.

It costs me less in every sense to incur the penalty of disobedience to the State than it would to obey. I should feel as if I were worth less in that case.

Some years ago the State met me in behalf of the Church, and commanded me to pay a certain sum towards the support of a clergyman whose preaching my father attended, but never I myself. "Pay," it said, "or be locked up in the jail." I declined to pay. But, unfortunately, another man saw fit to pay it. I did not see why the schoolmaster should be taxed to support the priest, and not the priest the schoolmaster; for I was not the State's schoolmaster, but I supported myself by voluntary subscription. I did not see why the lyceum should not present its tax-bill, and have the State to back its demand, as well as the Church.

However, at the request of the selectmen, I condescended to make some such statement as this in writing: "Know all men by these presents, that I, Henry Thoreau, do not wish to be regarded as a member of any incorporated society which I have not joined." This I gave to the town clerk; and he has it.

The State, having thus learned that I did not wish to be regarded as a member of that Church, has never made a like demand on me since; though it said it must adhere to its original presumption that time. If I had known how to name them, I should then have signed off in detail from all the societies which I never signed onto; but I did not know where to find a complete list.

I have paid no poll-tax for six years. I was put into a jail once on this account for one night; and as I stood considering the walls of solid stone, two or three feet thick, the door of wood and iron, a foot thick, and the iron grating which strained the light, I could not help being struck with the foolishness of that institution which treated me as if I were mere flesh and blood and bones, to be locked up.

I wondered that it should have concluded at length that this was the best use it could put me to, and had never thought to avail itself of my services in some way.

I saw that, if there was a wall of stone between me and my townsmen, there was a still more difficult one to climb or break through before they could get to be as free as I was. I did not for a moment feel confined, and the walls seemed a great waste of stone and mortar. I felt as if I alone of all my townsmen had paid my tax. They plainly did not know how to treat me, but behaved like persons who are underbred. In every threat and in every compliment there was a blunder; for they thought that my chief desire was to stand the other side of that stone wall. I could not but smile to see how industriously they locked the door on my meditations, which followed them out again without let or hindrance, and they were really all that was dangerous. As they could not reach me they had resolved to punish my body; just as boys, if they cannot come at some person against whom they have a spite, will abuse his dog.

I saw that the State was half-witted, that it was timid as a lone woman with her silver spoons, and that it did not know its friends from its foes, and I lost all my remaining respect for it, and pitied it.

Thus the State never intentionally confronts a man's senses, intellectual or moral, but only his body, his senses. It is not armed with superior wit or honesty, but with superior physical strength. I was not born to be forced. I will breathe after my own fashion. Let us see who is the strongest. What orce has a multitude? They only can force me who obey a higher law than I. They force me to become like themselves. I do not hear of men being forced to live this way or that by masses of men. What sort of life were that to live?

When I meet a government which says to me, "Your money or your life," why should I be in haste to give it my money? It may be in a great strait, and not know what to do; I cannot help that. It must help itself; do as I do. It is not worth the while to snivel about it. I am not responsible for the successful working of the machinery of society. I am not the son of the engineer.

I perceive that, when an acorn and a chestnut fall side by side, the one does not remain inert to make way for the other, but both obey their own laws, and spring and grow and flourish as best they can, till one, perchance, overshadows and destroys the other. If a plant cannot live according to its nature, it dies; and so a man.

I have never declined paying the highway tax, because I am as desirous of being a good neighbor as I am of being a bad subject; and as for supporting schools, I am doing my part to educate my fellow-countrymen now. It is for no particular item in the tax-bill that I refuse to pay it. I simply wish to refuse allegiance to the State, to withdraw and stand aloof from it effectually. I do not care to trace the course of my dollar, if I could, till it buys a man or a musket to shoot one with; the dollar is innocent, but I am concerned to trace the effects of my allegiance.

In fact, I quietly declare war with the State, after my fashion, though I will still make what use and get what advantage of her I can, as is usual in such cases.

If others pay the tax which is demanded of me from a sympathy with the State, they do but what they have already done in their own case, or rather they abet injustice to a greater extent than the State requires. If they pay the tax from a mistaken interest in the individual taxed, to save his property, or prevent his going to jail, it is because they have not considered wisely how far they let their private feelings interfere with the public good.

However, the government does not concern me much, and I shall bestow the fewest possible thoughts on it. It is not many moments that I live under a government, even in this world. If a man is thought-free, fancy-free, imagination-free, that which *is not* never for a long time appearing *to be* to him, unwise rulers or reformers cannot fatally interrupt him.

. . . There will never be a really free and enlightened State until the State comes to recognize the individual as a higher and independent power, from which all its own power and authority are derived, and treats him accordingly. I please myself with imagining a State at last which can afford to be just to all men, and to treat the individual with respect as a neighbor; which would even not think it inconsistent with its own repose if a few were to live aloof from it, not meddling with it, nor embraced by it, who fulfilled all the duties of neighbors and fellow-men. A State which bore this kind of fruit, and suffered it to drop off as fast as it ripened, would prepare the way for a still more perfect and glorious State, which also I have imagined, but not yet anywhere seen.

XIII
HERBERT SPENCER

Herbert Spencer, 1820-1903, celebrated English philosopher, founder of the system named by himself the synthetic philosophy. Educated by father, a schoolmaster at Derby, and uncle, rector of Hinton; articled to a civil engineer in 1837; abandoned engineering in 1845 and devoted himself to literature; assistant editor of *Economist*, 1848-53; lectured in United States, 1882. Published *The Proper Sphere of Government*, 1843; *Principles of Psychology*, which is based on the principle of evolution, 1855, four years before the appearance of Darwin's *Origin of Species*. His works, published in the United States by D. Appleton & Co., are prolific and include his *System of Synthetic Philosophy*, 1862-96, in which he traces the progress of evolution in life, mind, society, and morality; *Over-Legislation*, 1854; *Essays*, 1857-74; *Education*, 1861; *Classification of the Sciences*, 1864; *Illustrations of Universal Progress*, 1864; *The Study of Sociology*, 1873; *Progress, its Law and Course*, 1881; *Descriptive Sociology*, 1874-82; *The Man vs. the State*, 1884; and some forty books covering the entire range of human happiness, ethics and morality, justice, political and ecclesiastical institutions, law, man and his relation to all forms of government, organic evolution.

Social Statics, 1850, contained a chapter on *The Right to Ignore the State*, which Libertarians consider unanswerable, but which was omitted from later editions, with no attempt to answer its arguments. *The Right to Ignore the State* is here printed in its entirety, together with his Law of Equal Freedom and selections from his writings on ethics.

Answering to each of the actions which it is requisite for us to perform, we find in ourselves some prompter called a desire; and the more essential the action, the more powerful is the impulse to its performance, and the more intense the gratification derived therefrom. Thus, the longing for food, for sleep, for warmth, are irresistible; and quite independent of foreseen advantages. The continuance of the race is secured by others equally strong, whose dictates are followed, not in obedience to reason, but often in defiance of it. That men are not impelled to accumulate the means of subsistence solely by a view to consequences, is proved by the existence of misers, in whom the love of acquirement is gratified to the neglect of the ends to be subserved.

Of self-evident truths so dealt with, the one which here concerns us is that a creature must live before it can act. From this it is a corollary that the acts by which each maintains his own life must, speaking generally, precede in imperativeness all other acts of which he is capable. For if it be asserted that these other acts must precede in imperativeness the acts which maintain life, and if this, accepted as a general law of conduct, is conformed to by all, then by postponing the acts which maintain life to the other acts which make life possible, all must lose their lives. That is to say, ethics has to recognize the truth, recognized in unethical thought, that egoism comes before altruism. The acts required for continued self-preservation, including the enjoyment of benefits achieved by such acts, are the first requisites to universal welfare. Unless each duly cares for himself, his care for all others is ended by death; and if each thus dies, there remain no others to be cared for.

This permanent supremacy of egoism over altruism, made manifest by contemplating existing life, is further made manifest by contemplating life in course of evolution.

Those who have followed with assent the recent course of thought do not need telling that throughout past eras, the life, vast in amount, and varied in kind, which has overspread the earth has progressed in subordination to the law that every individual shall gain by whatever aptitude it has for fulfilling the conditions to its existence. The uniform principle has been that better adaptation shall bring greater benefit, which greater benefit, while increasing the prosperity of the better adapted, shall increase also its ability to leave offspring inheriting more or less its better adaptation. And, by implication, the uniform principle has been that the ill-adapted, disadvantaged in the struggle for existence shall bear the consequent evils, either disappearing when its imperfections are extreme, or else rearing fewer offspring, which, inheriting its imperfections, tend to dwindle away in posterity.

It has been thus with innate superiorities; it has been thus also with acquired ones. All along the law has been that increased function brings increased power, and that therefore such extra activities as aid welfare in any member of a race produce in its structures greater ability to carry on such extra activities—the derived advantages being enjoyed by it to the heightening and lengthening of its life. Conversely, as lessened function ends in lessened structure, the dwindling of unused faculties has ever entailed loss of power to achieve the correlative ends—the result of inadequate fulfilment of the ends being diminished ability to maintain life. And by inheritance, such functionally produced modifications have respectfully furthered or hindered survival in posterity.

As already said, the law that each creature shall take the benefits and the evils of its own nature, be they those derived from ancestry or those due to self-produced modifications, has been the law under which life has evolved thus far, and it must continue to be the law, however much further life may evolve. Whatever qualifications this natural course of action may now or hereafter undergo are qualifications that cannot, without fatal results, essentially change it. Any arrangements which in a considerable degree prevent superiority from profiting by the rewards of superiority, or shield inferiority from the evils it entails—any arrangements which tend to make it as well to be inferior as to be superior, are arrangements diametrically opposed to the progress of organization and the reaching of a higher life.

But to say that each individual shall reap the benefits brought to him by his own powers, inherited and acquired, is to enunciate egoism as an ultimate principle of conduct. It is to say that egoistic claims must take precedence of altruistic claims.

Under its biological aspect this proposition cannot be contested by those who agree in the doctrine of evolution; but probably they will not at once allow that admission of it under its ethical aspect is equally unavoidable. While, as respects development of life, the well-working of the universal principle described is sufficiently manifest, the well-working of it as respects increase of happiness may not be seen at once. But the two cannot be disjoined.

Incapacity of every kind and of whatever degree causes unhappiness directly and indirectly—directly by the pain consequent on the overtaxing of inadequate faculty, and indirectly by the non-fulfilment, or imperfect fulfilment, of certain conditions to welfare. Conversely, capacity of every kind sufficient for the requirement conduces to happiness immediately and remotely—immediately by the pleasure accompanying the normal exercise of each power that is up to its work, and remotely by the pleasures which are furthered by the ends achieved. A creature that is weak or slow of foot, and so gets food only by exhausting efforts or escapes enemies with difficulty, suffers the pains of overstrained powers, of unsatisfied appetites, of distressed emotions; while the strong and swift creature of the same species delights in its efficient activities, gains more fully the satisfactions yielded by food as well as the renewed vivacity this gives, and has to bear fewer and smaller pains in defending itself against foes or escaping from them. Similarly with duller and keener senses, or higher and lower degrees of sagacity. The mentally inferior individual of any race suffers negative and positive miseries, while the mentally superior individual receives negative and positive gratifications. Inevitably, then, this law, in conformity with which each member of a species takes the consequences of its own nature, and in virtue of which the progeny of each member, participating in its nature, also takes such consequences, is one that tends ever to raise the aggregate of happiness of the species, by furthering the multiplication of the happier and hindering that of the less happy.

All this is true of human beings as of other beings. The conclusion forced on us is that the pursuit of individual happiness within those limits prescribed by social conditions is the first requisite to the attainment of the greatest general happiness. To see this it needs but to contrast one whose self-regard has maintained bodily well-being with one whose regardlessness of self has brought its natural results, and then to ask what must be the contrast between two societies formed of two such kinds of individuals.

Equal Freedom (*First Principles*).—If men have like claims to that freedom which is needful for the exercise of their faculties, then must the freedom of each be bounded by the similar freedoms of all. When, in the pursuit of their respective ends, two individuals clash, the movements of the one remain free only in so far as they do not interfere with the like movements of the other. This sphere of existence into which we are thrown, not affording room for the unrestrained activity of all, and yet all possessing in virtue of their constitutions similar claims to such unrestrained activity, there is no course but to apportion the unavoidable restraint equally. Wherefore we arrive at the general proposition, that every man may claim the fullest liberty to exercise his faculties compatible with the possession of like liberty by every other man.

Upon a partial consideration this statement of the law will perhaps seem open to criticism. It may be thought better to limit the right of each to exercise his faculties; by the proviso that he shall not *hurt* anyone else—shall not inflict *pain* on any one else. But although at first sight satisfactory, this expression of the law allows of erroneous deductions. It is true that men, who fulfil those conditions to greatest happiness set forth in the foregoing chapter, cannot exercise their faculties to the aggrieving of one another. It is not, however, that each avoids giving pain by refraining from the full exercise of his faculties; but it is that the faculties of each are such that the full exercise of them offends no one. And herein lies the difference. The giving of pain may have two causes. Either the abnormally-constituted man may do something displeasing to the normal feelings of his neighbors, in which case he acts wrongly; or the behavior of the normally-constituted man may irritate the abnormal feelings of his neighbors, in which case it is not his behavior that is wrong, but their characters are so. Under such circumstances the due exercise of his faculties is right, although it gives pain; and the remedy for the evil lies in the modification of those abnormal feelings to which pain is given.

To elucidate this distinction let us take a few illustrations. An honest man discovers some friend, of whom he had previously thought well, to be a rogue. He has certain high instincts to which roguery is repugnant; and, allowing free play to these, he drops the acquaintanceship of this unworthy one. Now, though in doing so he gives pain, it does not follow that he transgresses the law. The evil must be ascribed, not to an undue exercise of faculties by him, but to the immorality of the man who suffers. Again, a Protestant in a Roman Catholic country refuses to uncover his head on the passing of the host. In so obeying the promptings of certain sentiments, he annoys the spectators; and were the above modified expression of the law correct, would be blameable. The fault, however, is not with him, but with those who are offended. It is not that he is culpable in thus testifying to his belief, but it is that they ought not to have so tyrannical an intolerance of other opinions than their own. Or again, a son, to the great displeasure of his father and family, marries one who, though in all respects admirable, is dowerless. In thus obeying the dictates of his nature, he may entail considerable distress of mind on his relatives; but it does not follow that his conduct is bad; it follows, rather, that the feelings which his conduct has wounded are bad.

Hence we see that in hourly-occurring cases like these, to limit the exercise of faculties by the necessity of not giving pain to others, would be to stop the proper exercise of faculties in some persons, for the purpose of allowing the improper exercise of faculties in the rest. Moreover, the observance of such a rule does not, in reality, prevent pain. For though he who is restrained by it avoids inflicting suffering on his fellows, he does so at the expense of suffering to himself. The evil must be borne by some one, and the question is by whom. Shall the Protestant, by showing reverence for what he does not revere, tell a virtual lie, and thus do violence to his conscientious feeling that he may avoid vexing the intolerant spirit of his Catholic neighbors? or shall he give the rein to his own healthy sincerity and independence, and offend their unhealthy bigotry? Shall the honest man repress those sentiments that make him honest, lest the exhibition of them should give pain to a rogue? or shall he respect his own nobler feelings, and hurt the other's baser ones? Between these alternatives no one can well pause. And here indeed we get down to the root of the matter. For be it remembered the universal law of life is, that the exercise or gratification of faculties strengthens them; while, contrariwise, the curbing or inflicting pain on them, entails a diminution of their power. And hence it follows that when the action of a normal faculty is checked, to prevent pain being given to the abnormal faculties of others, those abnormal faculties remain as active as they were, and the normal one becomes weaker or abnormal. Whereas under converse circumstances the normal one remains strong, and the abnormal ones are weakened, or made more normal. In the one case the pain is detrimental, because it retards the approximation to that form of human nature under which the faculties of each may be fully exercised without displeasure to the like faculties of all. In the other case the pain is beneficial, because it aids the approximation to that form. Thus, that first expression of the law which arises immediately from the conditions to social existence, turns out to be the true one: any such modification of it as the above, necessitating conduct that is in many cases mischievous.

Whether we reason our way from those fixed conditions under which alone greatest happiness can be realized—whether we draw our inferences from man's constitution, considering him as a congeries of faculties—or whether we listen to the moni-

Herbert Spencer 217

tions of a certain mental agency, which seems to have the function of guiding us in this matter; we are alike taught, as the law of right social relationships, that—Every man has freedom to do all that he wills, provided he infringes not the equal freedom of any other man. Though further qualifications of the liberty of action thus asserted are necessary, yet we have seen that in the just regulation of a community no further qualifications of it can be recognized. Such further qualifications must remain for private and individual application. We must therefore adopt this law of equal freedom in its entirety, as the law on which a correct system of equity is to be based.

Some will, perhaps, object to this first principle, that being in the nature of an axiomatic truth—standing towards the inferences to be drawn from it in the position of one, it ought to be recognized by all; which it is not.

Respecting the fact thus alleged, that there have been, and are, men impervious to this first principle, there can be no question. Probably it would have been dissented from by Aristotle, who considered it a "self-evident maxim that nature intended barbarians to be slaves." Cardinal Julian, who "abhorred the impiety of keeping faith with infidels," might possibly have disputed it. It is a doctrine which would scarcely have suited the abbot Guibert, who, in his sermons, called the free cities of France "those execrable communities, where serfs, against law and justice, withdraw themselves from the power of their lords." And perhaps the Highlanders, who in 1748 were reluctant to receive their freedom on the abolition of the heritable jurisdictions, would not have admitted it. But the confession that the truth of this principle is not self-evident to all, by no means invalidates it. The Bushmen can count only as high as three; yet arithmetic is a fact, and we have a Calculus of Functions by the aid of which we find new planets. As, then, the disability of the savage to perceive the elementary truths of number is no argument against their existence, and no obstacle to their discovery and development; so, the circumstance that some do not see the law of equal freedom to be an elementary truth of ethics, does not disprove the statement that it is one.

So far indeed is this difference in men's moral perceptions from being a difficulty in our way, that it serves to illustrate a doctrine already set forth. As already explained, a man's original circumstances "required that he should sacrifice the welfare of other beings to his own;" whereas his present circumstances require that "each individual shall have such desires only as may be fully satisfied without trenching upon the ability of other individuals to obtain like satisfactions." And it was pointed out that, in virtue of the law of adaptation, the human constitution is changing from the form which fitted it to the first set of conditions to a form fitting it for the last. Now it is by the growth of those two faculties which together originate what we term a Moral Sense, that fitness for these last conditions is secured. In proportion to the strength of sympathy and the instinct of personal rights, will be the impulse to conform to the law of equal freedom. And in the mode elsewhere shown, the impulse to conform to this law will generate a correlative belief in it. Only therefore, after the process of adaptation has made considerable advance, can there arise either subordination to this law or a perception of its truth. And hence any general recognition of it during the earlier stages of social development must not be looked for.

The process by which we may develop this first principle into a system of equity is sufficiently obvious .We shall have to consider of every deed, whether in committing it, a man does, or does not, trespass on the freedom of his neighbor—whether, when placed side by side, the shares of liberty the two respectively assume are equal. And by thus separating that which can be done by each without trenching on the liberties of others, from that which cannot be so done, we may classify actions into lawful and unlawful.

Difficulties may now and then occur in the performance of

this process. We shall occasionally find ourselves unable to decide whether a given action does or does not trespass against the law of equal freedom. But such an admission by no means implies any defect in that law. It merely implies human incapacity—an incapacity which puts a limit to our discovery of physical truth as well as of moral truth. It is, for instance, beyond the power of any mathematician to state in degrees and minutes, the angle at which a man may lean without falling. Not being able to find accurately the center of gravity of a man's body, he cannot say with certainty whether, at a given inclination, the line of direction will or will not fall outside the base. But we do not, therefore, take exception to the first principles of mechanics. In spite of our inability to follow out those first principles to all their consequences, we know that the stability or instability of a man's attitude might be accurately determined by them, were our perceptions competent to take in all the data of such a problem. Similarly, it is argued that, although there may arise out of the more complex social relationships, questions which are apparently not soluble by comparing the respective amounts of freedom the concerned persons assume, it must nevertheless be granted that, whether we see it or not, the claims they make *are* either equal or unequal, and the dependent actions right or wrong accordingly.

Liberty of action being the first essential to the exercise of faculties, and therefore the first essential to happiness; and the liberty of each limited by the like liberties of all, being the form which this first essential assumes when applied to many instead of one; it follows that this liberty of each, limited by the like liberties of all, is the rule in conformity with which society must be organized. Freedom being the pre-requisite to normal life in the individual, equal freedom becomes the pre-requisite to normal life in society. And if this law of equal freedom is the primary law of right relationship between man and man, then no desire to get fulfilled a secondary law can warrant us in breaking it.

Conversely, we find that those who have not a strong sense of what is just to themselves, are likewise deficient in a sense of what is just to their fellow-men. This has long been a common remark. As one of our living writers puts it—the tyrant is nothing but a slave turned inside out. In earlier days, when feudal lords were vassals to the king, they were also despots to their retainers. In our own time, the Russian noble is alike a serf to his autocrat and an autocrat to his serf. It is remarked, even by school-boys, that the bully is the most ready of all to knock under to a bigger bully. We constantly observe that those who fawn upon the great are overbearing to their inferiors. That "emancipated slaves exceed all other owners (of slaves) in cruelty and oppression," is a truth established by numerous authorities.

The Right to Ignore the State

1. As a corollary to the proposition that all institutions must be subordinated to the law of equal freedom, we cannot choose but admit the right of the citizen to adopt a condition of voluntary outlawry. If every man has freedom to do all that he wills, provided he infringes not the equal freedom of any other man, then he is free to drop connection with the State,—to relinquish its protection and to refuse paying toward its support. It is self-evident that in so behaving he in no way trenches upon the liberty of others; for his position is a passive one, and, whilst passive, he cannot become an aggressor. It is equally self-evident that he cannot be compelled to continue one of a political corporation without a breach of the moral law, seeing that citizenship involves payment of taxes; and the taking away of a man's property against his will is an infringement of his rights. Government being simply an agent employed in common by a number of individuals to secure to them certain advantages, the very nature of the connection implies that it is for each to say whether he will employ such an agent or not. If any one of them determines to ignore this mutual-safety confederation, nothing can be said, except

that he loses all claim to its good offices, and exposes himself to the danger of maltreatment,—a thing he is quite at liberty to do if he likes. He cannot be coerced into political combination without a breach of the law of equal freedom; he *can* withdraw from it without committing any such breach; and he has therefore a right so to withdraw.

2. "No human laws are of any validity if contrary to the law of nature; and such of them as are valid derive all their force and all their authority mediately or immediately from this original." Thus writes Blackstone, to whom let all honor be given for having so far outseen the ideas of his time,—and, indeed, we may say of our time. A good antidote, this, for those political superstitions which so widely prevail. A good check upon that sentiment of power-worship which still misleads us by magnifying the prerogatives of constitutional governments as it did those of monarchs. Let men learn that a legislature is *not* "our God upon earth," though, by the authority they ascribe to it and the things they expect from it, they would seem to think it is. Let them learn rather that it is an institution serving a purely temporary purpose, whose power, when not stolen, is, at the best, borrowed.

Nay, indeed, have we not seen that government is essentially immoral? Is it not the offspring of evil, bearing about it all the marks of its parentage? Does it not exist because crime exists? Is is not strong, or, as we say, despotic, when crime is great? Is there not more liberty—that is, less government—as crime diminishes? And must not government cease when crime ceases, for very lack of objects on which to perform *its functions*? Not only does magisterial power exist *because* of evil, but it exists *by* evil. Violence is employed to maintain it; and all violence involves criminality. Soldiers, policemen, and jailers; swords, batons, and fetters,—are instruments for inflicting pain; and all infliction of pain is, in the abstract, wrong. The state employs evil weapons to subjugate evil, and is alike contaminated by the objects with which it deals and the means by which it works. Morality cannot recognize it; for morality, being simply a statement of the perfect law, can give no countenance to anything growing out of, and living by, breaches of that law. Wherefore legislative authority can never be ethical—must always be conventional merely.

Hence there is a certain inconsistency in the attempt to determine the right position, structure, and conduct of a government by appeal to the first principles of rectitude. For, as just pointed out, the acts of an institution which is, in both nature and origin, imperfect cannot be made to square with the perfect law. All that we can do is to ascertain, firstly, in what attitude a legislature must stand to the community to avoid being by its mere existence an embodied wrong; secondly, in what manner it must be constituted so as to exhibit the least incongruity with the moral law; and, thirdly, to what sphere its actions must be limited to prevent it from multiplying those breaches of equity it is set up to prevent.

The first condition to be conformed to before a legislature can be established without violating the law of equal freedom is the acknowledgment of the right now under discussion—the right to ignore the State.

3. Upholders of pure despotism may fitly believe State-control to be unlimited and unconditional. They who assert that men are made for governments and not governments for men may consistently hold that no one can remove himself beyond the pale of political organization. But they who maintain that the people are the only legitimate source of power—that legislative authority is not original, but deputed—cannot deny the right to ignore the State without entangling themselves in an absurdity.

For, if legislative authority is deputed, it follows that those from whom it proceeds are the masters of those on whom it is conferred: it follows further that as masters they confer the said authority voluntarily: and this implies that they may give or withhold it as they please. To call that deputed which is wrenched from men whether they will or not is nonsense. But what is here true of all collectively is equally true of each separately. As a government can rightly act for the people only when empowered by them, so also can it rightly act for the individual only when empowered by him. If A, B, and C debate whether they shall employ an agent to perform for them a certain service, and if, whilst A and B agree to do so, C dissents, C cannot equitably be made a party to the agreement in spite of himself. And this must be equally true of thirty as of three: and, if of thirty, why not of three hundred, or three thousand, or three millions?

4. Of the political superstitions lately alluded to, none is so universally diffused as the notion that majorities are omnipotent. Under the impression that the preservation of order will ever require power to be wielded by some party, the moral sense of our time feels that such power cannot rightly be conferred on any but the largest moiety of society. In interprets literally the saying that "the voice of the people is the voice of God," and, transferring to the one the sacredness attached to the other, it concludes that from the will of the people—that is, of the majority—there can be no appeal. Yet is this belief entirely erroneous.

Suppose, for the sake of argument, that, struck by some Malthusian panic, a legislature duly representing public opinion were to enact that all children born during the next ten years should be drowned. Does any one think such an enactment would be warrantable? If not, there is evidently a limit to the power of a majority. Suppose, again, that of two races living together—Celts and Saxons, for example—the most numerous determined to make the others their slaves. Would the authority of the greatest number be in such case valid? If not, there is something to which its authority must be subordinate. Suppose, once more, that all men having incomes under £50 a year were to resolve upon reducing every income above that amount to their own standard, and appropriating the excess for public purposes. Could their resolution be justified? If not, it must be a third time confessed that there is a law to which the popular voice must defer. What, then, is that law, if not the law of pure equity—the law of equal freedom? These restraints, which all would put to the will of the majority, are exactly the restraints set up by that law. We deny the right of a majority to murder, to enslave, or to rob, simply because murder, enslaving, and robbery are violations of that law—violations too gross to be overlooked. But, if great violations of it are wrong, so also are smaller ones. If the will of the many cannot supersede the first principle of morality in these cases, neither can it in any. So that, however insignificant the minority, and however trifling the proposed trespass against their rights, no such trespass is permissible.

When we have made our constitution purely democratic, thinks to himself the earnest reformer, we shall have brought government into harmony with absolute justice. Such a faith, though perhaps needful for the age, is a very erroneous one. By no process can coercion be made equitable. The freest form of government is only the least objectionable form. The rule of the many by the few we call tyranny: the rule of the few by the many is tyranny also, only of a less intense kind. "You shall do as we will, and not as you will," is in either case the declaration; and, if the hundred make it to ninety-nine, instead of the ninety-nine to the hundred, it is only a fraction less immoral. Of two such parties, whichever fulfills this declaration, necessarily breaks the law of equal freedom: the only difference being that by the one it is broken in the persons of ninety-nine, whilst by the other it is broken in the persons of a hundred. And the merit of the democratic form of government consists solely in this,—that it trespasses against the smallest number.

The very existence of majorities and minorities is indicative of an immoral state. The man whose character harmonizes with the moral law, we found to be one who can obtain complete happiness without diminishing the happiness of his fellows. But the enactment of public arrangements by vote implies a society consisting of men otherwise constituted—implies that the desires of some cannot be satisfied without sacrificing the desires of others—implies that in the pursuit of their happiness the majority inflict a certain amount of *un*happiness on the minority—implies, therefore, organic immorality. Thus, from another point of view, we again perceive that even in its most equitable form it is impossible for government to dissociate itself from evil; and further, that, unless the right to ignore the State is recognized, its acts must be essentially criminal.

5. That a man is free to abandon the benefits and throw off the burdens of citizenship, may indeed be inferred from the admissions of existing authorities and of current opinion. Unprepared as they probably are for so extreme a doctrine as the one here maintained, the radicals of our day yet unwittingly profess their belief in a maxim which obviously embodies this doctrine. Do we not continually hear them quote Blackstone's assertion that "no subject of England can be constrained to pay any aids or taxes even for the defence of the realm or the support of government, but such as are imposed by his own consent, or that of his representative in parliament?" And what does this mean? It means, say they, that every man should have a vote. True: but it means much more. If there is any sense in words, it is a distinct enunciation of the very right now contended for. In affirming that a man may not be taxed unless he has directly or indirectly given his consent, it affirms that he may refuse to be so taxed; and to refuse to be taxed is to cut all connection with the State. Perhaps it will be said that this consent is not a specific, but a general one, and that the citizen is understood to have assented to everything his representative may do, when he voted for him. But suppose he did not vote for him; and on the contrary did all in his power to get elected some one holding opposite views—what then? The reply will probably be that, by taking part in such an

election, he tacitly agreed to abide by the decision of the majority. And how if he did not vote at all? Why then he cannot justly complain of any tax, seeing that he made no protest against its imposition. So, curiously enough, it seems that he gave his consent in whatever way he acted—whether he said yes, whether he said no, or whether he remained neuter! A rather awkward doctrine, this. Here stands an unfortunate citizen who is asked if he will pay money for a certain proffered advantage; and, whether he employs the only means of expressing his refusal or does not employ it, we are told that he practically agrees, if only the number of others who agree is greater than the number of those who dissent. And thus we are introducted to the novel principle that A's consent to a thing is not determined by what A says, but by what B may happen to say!

It is for those who quote Blackstone to choose between this absurdity and the doctrine above set forth. Either his maxim implies the right to ignore the State, or it is sheer nonsense.

6. There is a strange heterogeneity in our political faiths. Systems that have had their day, and are beginning here and there to let the daylight through, are patched with modern notions utterly unlike in quality and color; and men gravely display these systems, wear them, and walk about in them, quite unconscious of their grotesqueness. This transition state of ours, partaking as it does equally of the past and the future, breeds hybrid theories exhibiting the oddest union of bygone despotism and coming freedom. Here are types of the old organization curiously disguised by the germs of the new—peculiarities showing adaptation to a preceding state modified by rudiments that prophesy of something to come—making altogether so chaotic a mixture of relationships that there is no saying to what class these births of the age should be referred.

As ideas must of necessity bear the stamp of the time, it is useless to lament the contentment with which these incongruous beliefs are held. Otherwise it would seem unfortunate that men do not pursue to the end the trains of reasoning which have led to these partial modifications. In the present case, for example, consistency would force them to admit that, on other points besides the one just noticed, they hold opinions and use arguments in which the right to ignore the State is involved.

For what is the meaning of Dissent? The time was when a man's faith and his mode of worship were as much determinable by law as his secular acts; and, according to provisions extant in our statute-book, are so still. Thanks to the growth of a Protestant spirit, however, we have ignored the State in this matter—wholly in theory, and partly in practice. But how have we done so? By assuming an attitude which, if consisttently maintained, implies a right to ignore the State entirely. Observe the positions of the two parties. "This is your creed," says the legislator, "you must believe and openly profess what is here set down for you." "I shall not do anything of the kind," answers the non-conformist; "I will go to prison rather."

"Your religious ordinances," pursues the legislator, "shall be such as we have prescribed. You shall attend the churches we have endowed, and adopt the ceremonies used in them." "Nothing shall induce me to do so," is the reply; "I altogether deny your power to dictate to me in such matters, and mean to resist to the uttermost." "Lastly," adds the legislator, "we shall require you to pay such sums of money toward the support of these religious institutions as we may see fit to ask." "Not a farthing will you have from me," exclaims our sturdy Independent: "even did I believe in the doctrines of your church (which I do not), I should still rebel against your intereference; and, if you take my property, it shall be by force and under protest."

What now does this proceeding amount to when regarded in the abstract? It amounts to an assertion by the individual of the right to exercise one of his faculties—the religious sentiment—without let or hindrance, and with no limit save that set up by the equal claims of others. And what is meant by ignoring the State? Simply an assertion of the right similarly to exercise *all* the faculties. The one is just an expansion of the other—rests on the same footing with the other—must stand or fall with the other. Men do indeed speak of civil and religious liberty as different things: but the distinction is quite arbitrary. They are parts of the same whole, and cannot philosophically be separated.

"Yes they can," interposes an objector; "assertion of the one is imperative as being a religious duty. The liberty to worship God in the way that seems to him right, is a liberty without which a man cannot fulfill what he believes to be divine commands, and therefore conscience requires him to maintain it." "True enough; but how if the same can be asserted of all other liberty? How if maintenance of this also turns out to be a matter of conscience? Have we not seen that human happiness is the divine will—that only by exercising our faculties is this happiness obtainable—and that it is impossible to exercise them without freedom? And, if this freedom for the exercise of faculties is a condition without which the divine will cannot be fulfilled, the preservation of it is, by our objector's own showing, a duty. Or, in other words, it appears not only that the maintenance of liberty of action *may* be a point of conscience, but that it ought to be one. And thus we are clearly shown that the claims to ignore the State in religious and in secular matters are in essence identical. The other reason commonly assigned for nonconformity admits of similar treatment. Besides resisting State dictation in the abstract, the dissenter resists it from disapprobation of the doctrines taught. No legislative injunction will make him adopt what he considers an erroneous belief; and, bearing in mind his duty toward his fellowmen, he refuses to help through the medium of his purse in disseminating this erroneous belief. The position is perfectly intelligible. But it is one which either commits its adherents to civil nonconformity also, or leaves them in a dilemma. For why do they refuse to be instrumental in spreading error? Because error is adverse to human happiness. And on what ground is any piece of secular legislation disapproved? For the same reason—because thought adverse to human happiness. How then can it be shown that the State ought to be resisted in the one case and not in the other? Will any one deliberately assert that, if a government demands money from us to aid in *teaching* what we think will produce evil, we ought to refuse it, but that, if the money is for the purpose of doing what we think will produce evil, we ought not to refuse it? Yet such is the hopeful proposition which those have to maintain who recognize the right to ignore the State in religious matters, but deny it in civil matters.

7. The substance of the chapter once more reminds us of the incongruity between a perfect law and an imperfect state. The practicability of the principle here laid down varies directly as social morality. In a thoroughly vicious community its admission would be productive of anarchy. In a completely virtuous one its admission will be both innocuous and inevitable. Progress toward a condition of social health—a condition, that is, in which the remedial measures of legislation will no longer be needed—is progress toward a condition in which those remedial measures will be cast aside, and the authority prescribing them disregarded. The two changes are of necessity coordinate. That moral sense whose supremacy will make society harmonious and government unnecessary is the same moral sense which will then make each man assert his freedom even to the extent of ignoring the State is the same moral sense which, by deterring the majority from coercing the minority, will eventually render government impossible. And, as what are merely different manifestations of the same sentiment must bear a constant ratio to each other, the tendency to repudiate governments will increase only at the same rate that governments become needless.

Let not any be alarmed, therefore, at the promulgation of the foregoing doctrine. There are many changes yet to be passed through before it can begin to exercise much influence. Probably a long time will elapse before the right to ignore the State will be generally admitted, even in theory. It will be still longer before it receives legislative recognition. And even then there will be plenty of checks upon the premature exercise of it. A sharp experience will sufficiently instruct those who may too soon abandon legal protection. Whilst, in the majority of men, there is such a love of tried arrangements, and so great a dread of experiments, that they will probably not act upon this right until long after it is safe to do so.

It is a mistake to assume that government must necessarily last forever. The institution marks a certain stage of civilization—is natural to a particular phase of human development. It is not essential, but incidental. As amongst the Bushmen we find a state antecedent to government, so may there be one in which it shall have become extinct. Already has it lost something of its importance. The time was when the history of a people was but the history of its government. It is otherwise now. The once universal despotism was but a manifestation of the extreme necessity of restraint. Feudalism, serfdom, slavery, all tyrannical institutions, are merely the most vigorous kinds of rule, springing out of, and necessary to, a bad state of man. The progress from these is in all cases the same—less government. Constitutional forms mean this. Political freedom means this. Democracy means this. In societies, associations, joint-stock companies, we have new agencies occupying big fields filled in less advanced times and countries by the State. With us the legislature is dwarfed by newer and greater powers—is no longer master, but slave. "Pressure from without" has come to be acknowledged as ultimate ruler. The triumph of the Anti-Corn Law League is simply the most marked instance yet of the new style of government, that of opinion, overcoming the old style, that of force. It bids fair to become a trite remark that the law-maker is but the servant of the thinker. Daily is Statecraft held in less repute. Even the "Times" can see that "the social changes thickening around us establish a truth sufficiently humiliating to legislative bodies," and that "the great stages of our progress are determined rather by the spontaneous workings of society, connected as they are with the progress of art and science, the operations of nature, and other such unpolitical causes, than by the proposition of a bill, the passing of an act, or any other event of politics or of State." Thus, as civilization advances, does government decay. To the bad it is essential; to the good, not. It is the check which national wickedness makes to itself, and exists only to the same degree. Its continuance is proof of still-existing barbarism. What a cage is to the wild beast, law is to the selfish man. Restraint is for the savage, the rapacious, the violent; not for the just, the gentle, the benevolent. All necessity for external force implies a morbid state. Dungeons for the felon; a strait jacket for the maniac; crutches for the lame; stays for the weak-backed; for the infirm of purpose a master; for the foolish a guide; but for the sound mind in a sound body none of these. Were there no thieves and murderers, prisons would be unnecessary. It is only because tyranny is yet rife in the world that we have armies. Barristers, judges, juries, all the instruments of law, exist simply because knavery exists. Magisterial force is the sequence of social vice, and the policeman is but the complement of the criminal. Therefore it is that we call government "a necessary evil."

What then must be thought of a morality which chooses this probationary institution for its basis, builds a vast fabric of conclusions upon its assumed permanence, selects acts of parliament for its materials, and employs the statesman for its architect? The expediency-philosophy does this. It takes government into partnership, assigns to it entire control of its affairs, enjoins all to defer to its judgment, makes it, in short, the vital principle, the very soul, of its system. When Paley teaches that "the interest of the whole society is binding upon every part of it," he implies the existence of some supreme power by which "that interest of the whole society" is to be determined. And elsewhere he more explicitly tells us that for the attainment of a national advantage the private will of the subject is to give way, and that "the proof of this advantage lies with the legislature." Still more decisive is Bentham when he says that "the happiness of the individuals of whom a community is composed—that is, their pleasures and their security—is the sole end which the legislator ought to have in view, the sole standard in conformity with which each individual ought, as far as depends upon the legislature, to be made to fashion his behavior." These positions, be it remembered, are not voluntarily assumed; they are necessitated by the premises. If, as its propounder tells us, "expediency" means the benefit of the mass, not of the individual,—of the future as much as of the present,—it presupposes some one to judge of what will most conduce to that benefit. Upon the "utility" of this or that measure the views are so various as to render an umpire essential. Whether protective duties, or established religions, or capital punishments, or poor-laws, do or do not minister to the "general good" are questions concerning which there is such difference of opinion that, were nothing to be done till all agreed upon them, we might stand still to the end of time. If each man carried out, independently of a State power, his own notions of what would best secure "the greatest happiness of the greatest number," society would quickly lapse into confusion. Clearly, therefore, a morality established upon a maxim of which the practical interpretation is questionable involves the existence of some authority whose decisions respecting it shall be final,—that is, a legislature. And without that authority such a morality must ever remain inoperative.

See here, then, the predicament, a system of moral philosophy professes to be a code of correct rules for the control of human beings—fitted for the regulation of the best as well as the worst members of the race—applicable, if true, to the guidance of humanity in its highest conceivable perfection. Government, however, is an institution originating in man's imperfection; an institution confessedly begotten by necessity out of evil; one which might be dispensed with were the world peopled with the unselfish, the conscientious, the philanthropic; one, in short, inconsistent with this same "highest conceivable perfection." How, then, can that be a true system of morality which adopts government as one of its premises?

Militarism.—Change in the ideas and feelings which thus become characteristic of the militant form of organization, can take place only where circumstances favor development of the industrial form of organization. Being carried on by voluntary co-operation instead of by compulsory co-operation, industrial life as we know it, habituates men to independent activities, leads them to enforce their own claims while respecting the claims of others, strengthens the consciousness of personal rights, and prompts them to resist excesses of governmental control. But since the circumstances which render war less frequent arise but slowly, and since the modifications of nature caused by the transition from a life predominantly militant to a life predominantly industrial can therefore go on but slowly, it happens that the old sentiments and ideas give place to new ones by small degrees only. We have at present but partially emerged from the militant regime and have but partially entered on that industrial regime to which this doctrine is proper.

Whatever fosters militarism makes for barbarism; whatever fosters peace makes for civilization. There are two fundamentally opposed principles on which social life may be organized—compulsory co-operation and voluntary co-operation, the one implying coercive institutions, the other free institutions. Just in proportion as military activity is great does the coercive regime more pervade the whole society. Hence, to oppose militancy is to oppose return toward despotism.

Taxation.—If justice asserts the liberty of each limited only by the like liberties of all, then the imposing of any further limit is unjust; no matter whether the power imposing it be one man or a million of men. . . . . In our time the tying of men to the lands they were born on, and the forbidding any other occupations than the prescribed ones, would be considered as intolerable aggressions on their liberties. But if these larger inroads on their rights are wrong, then also are smaller inroads. As we hold that a theft is a theft whether the amount stolen be a pound or a penny, so we must hold that an aggression is an aggression whether it be great or small. . . . We do not commonly see in a tax a diminution of freedom, and yet it clearly is one. The money taken represents so much labor gone through, and the product of that labor being taken away, either leaves the individual to go without such benefit as was achieved by it or else to go through more labor. In feudal days, when the subject classes had, under the name of corvees, to render services to their lords, specified in time or work, the partial slavery was manifest enough; and when the services were commuted for money, the relation remained the same in substance though changed in form. So is it now. Tax-payers are subject to a state corvee, which is none the less decided because, instead of giving their special kinds of work, they give equivalent sums; and if the corvee in the original undisguised form was a deprivation of freedom, so is it in its modern disguised form. "Thus much of your work shall be devoted, not to your own purposes, but to our purposes," say the authorities to the citizens; and to whatever extent this is carried, to that extent the citizens become slaves of the government.

"But they are slaves for their own advantage," will be the reply—"and the things to be done with the money taken from them are things which will in one way or other conduce to their welfare." Yes, that is the theory—a theory not quite in harmony with the vast mass of mischievous legislation filling the statute books. But this reply is not to the purpose. The question is a question of justice; and even supposing that the benefits to be obtained by these extra public expenditures were fairly distributed among all who furnish funds, which they are not, it would still remain true that they are at variance with the fundamental principle of an equitable social order. A man's liberties are none the less aggressed upon because those who coerce him do so in the belief that he will be benefited. In thus imposing by force their wills upon his will, they are breaking the law of equal freedom in his person; and what the motive may be matters not. Aggression which is flagitious when committed by one, is not sanctioned when committed by a host.

Land Titles.—It can never be pretended that the existing titles to landed property are legitimate. The original deeds were written with the sword, soldiers were the conveyancers, blows were the current coin given in exchange, and for seals, blood. Those who say that "time is a great legaliser" must find satisfactory answers to such questions as—How long does it take for what was originally wrong to become right? At what rate per annum do invalid claims become valid?

XIV
STEPHEN PEARL ANDREWS

Stephen Pearl Andrews, 1812-1886, an American writer and orator, author of works on language, law, phonography, and philosophy. Educated at Amherst; practiced law in Texas, where he agitated in favor of making it a free state; was so ardent an abolitionist that he was mobbed and driven from home in the middle of the night, 1843; became a leader in anti-slavery movement in Boston. Founded present system of phonographic reporting, edited two journals in the interest of phonography and spelling reform; had intimate knowledge of thirty-two languages; author of a system of teaching languages and of Universology, a universal science of language to replace the two or three thousand languages of the earth; contributed to periodicals. Works include *Comparison of the Common Law with the Roman, French or Spanish Civil Law*, 1839; *The Constitution of Government in the Sovereignty of the Individual*, 1851; *Love, Marriage and Divorce*, 1853; *Discoveries in Chinese*, a contribution to philology and ethnology, 1854; *Constitution or Organic Basis of the New Catholic Church*, 1860; *The Great American Crisis*, 1864; *A Universal Language*, 1864; *Basis of Universology*, 1881; *The Labor Dollar*, 1881; *Ideological Etymology*, 1881; *Transactions of the Colloquium, with Documents and Exhibits*, 1883; *The Church and Religion of the Future*, 1886.

These selections are from *The Sovereignty of the Individual.*

I will first endeavor to set before you a clearer view of the doctrine of the Sovereignty of the Individual, as based upon the principle of the infinite individuality of things. I will then show that this sovereignty of the individual furnishes the law of the development of human society, as illustrated in the progressive movements of modern times. Finally, I shall endeavor to trace the development which is hereafter to result from the further operation of this principle, and to fix, so nearly as may be, the condition of human affairs toward which it conducts, especially in that particular department of human affairs which constitutes the subject of investigation, namely, the government of mankind.

The doctrine of the Sovereignty of the individual—in one sense itself a principle—grows out of the still more fundamental principle of "Individuality," which pervades universal nature. Individuality is positively the most fundamental and universal principle which the finite mind seems capable of discovering, and the best image of the infinite. There are no two objects in the universe which are precisely alike. Each has its own constitution and peculiarities, which distinguish it from every other. Infinite diversity is the universal law. In the multitude of human countenances, for example, there are no two alike, and in the multitude of human characters there is the same variety. It applies equally to persons, to things, and to events. There have been no two occurrences which were precisely alike during all the cycling periods of time. No action, transaction, or set of circumstances whatsoever ever corresponded precisely to any other action, transaction, or set of circumstances. Had I a precise knowledge of all the occurrences which have ever taken place up to this hour, it would not suffice to enable me to make a law which would be applicable in all respects to the very next occurrence which shall take place, nor to any one of the infinite millions of events which shall hereafter occur. This diversity reigns throughout every kingdom of nature, and mocks at all human attempts to make law, or constitutions, or regulations, or governmental institutions of any sort which shall work justly and harmoniously amidst the unforseen contingencies of the future.

The individualities of objects are least, or, at all events, they are less apparent when the objects are inorganic or of a low grade of organization. The indivualities of the grains of sand which compose the beach, for example, are less marked than those of vegetables, and those of vegetables are less than those of animals, and, finally, those of animals are less than those of man. In proportion as an object is more complex, it embodies a greater number of elements, and each element has its own individualities, or diversities, in every new combination into which it enters. Consequently these diversities are multiplied into each other, in the infinite augmentation of geometrical progression. Hence the individualities of such a being are utterly immeasurable, and every attempt to adjust the capacities, the adaptations, the wants, or the responsibilities of one human being by the capacities, the adaptations, the wants, or the responsibilities of another human being, except in the very broadest generalities, is unqualifiedly futile and hopeless. Hence every ecclesiastical, governmental, or social institution which is based in the idea of demanding conformity or likeness in any thing, has ever been, and ever will be, frustrated by the operation of this subtle, all-pervading principle of individuality.

In the next place this individuality is inherent and unconquerable, except, as I have just said, by extinguishing the man himself. The man himself has no power over it. He cannot divest himself of his organic peculiarties of character, any more than he can divest himself of his features. It attends him even in the effort he makes, if he makes any, to divest himself of it. He may as well attempt to flee his own shadow as to rid himself of the indefeasible, God-given inheritance of his own individuality.

Finally, this indestructible and all-pervading individuality furnishes, itself, the law, and the only true law, of order and harmony.

Governments have hitherto been established, and have apologized for the unseemly fact of their existence, from the necessity of establishing and maintaining order; but order has never yet been maintained, revolutions and violent outbreaks have never yet been ended, public peace and harmony have never yet been secured, for the precise reason that the organic, essential, and indestructible natures of the objects which it was attempted to reduce to order have always been constricted and infringed by every such attempt. Just in proportion as the effort is less and less made to reduce men to order, just in that proportion they become more orderly, as witness the difference in the state of society in Austria and the United States. Plant an army of one hundred thousand soldiers in New York, as at Paris, to preserve the peace, and we should have a bloody revolution in a week; and be assured that the only remedy for what little of turbulence remains among us, as compared with European societies, will be found to be more liberty. When there remain positively no external restrictions, there will be positively no disturbance, provided always certain regulating principles of justice, to which I shall advert presently, are accepted and enter into the public mind, serving as substitutes for every species of repressive laws.

I was saying that individuality is the essential law of order. This is true throughout the universe. When every individual particle of matter obeys the law of its own attraction, and comes into that precise position, and moves in that precise direction, which its own inherent individualities demand, the harmony of the spheres is evolved. By that means only natural classification, natural order, natural organization, natural harmony and agreement are attained. Every scheme or arrangement which is based upon the principle of thwarting the inherent affinities of the individual monads which compose any system or organism is essentially vicious, and the organization is false,— a mere bundle of revolutionary and antagonistic atoms. It is time that human system builders should begin to discover this universal truth. The principle is self-evident. Objects bound together contrary to their nature must and will seek to rectify themselves by breaking the bonds which confine them, whilst those which come together by their own affinities remain quiescent and content. Let human system makers of all sorts, then, admit the principle of an infinite individuality among men, which cannot be suppressed, and which must be indulged and fostered, at all events, as one element in the solution of the problem they have before them. If they are unable to see clearly how all external restrictions can be removed with safety to the well-being of society, let them, nevertheless, not abandon a principle which is self-evident, but let them modestly suspect that there may be some other elements in the solution of the same problem, which their sagacity has not yet enabled them to discover. In all events, and at all hazards, this individuality of every member of the human family must be recognized and indulged, because first, as we have seen, it is infinite, and cannot be measured or prescribed for; then, because it is inherent, and cannot be conquered; and, finally, because it is the essential element of order, and can not, consequently, be infringed without engendering infinite confusion, such as has hitherto universally reigned, in the administration of human affairs.

If now, individuality is a universal law which must be obeyed if we would have order and harmony in any sphere, and, consequently, if we would have a true constitution of human government, then the absolute Sovereignity of the Individual necessarily results. The monads or atoms of which human society is composed are the individual men and women in it. They must be so disposed of, as we have seen, in order that society may be harmonic, that the destiny of each shall be controlled by his or her own individualities of taste, conscience, intellect, capacities, and will. But man is a being endowed with consciousness. He, and no one else, knows the determining force of his own attractions. No one else can therefore decide for him, and hence Individuality can only become the law of human action by securing to each individual the sovereign determination of his own judgment and of his own conduct, in all things, with no right reserved either of punishment or censure on the part of anybody else whomsoever; and this is what is meant by the Soviergnity of the Individual, limited only by the ever accompanying condition, resulting from the equal Sovereignty of all others, that the onerous consequences of his actions be assumed by himself.

The highest type of human society in the existing social order is found in the parlor. In the elegant and refined reunions of the aristocratic classes there is none of the impertinent intereference of legislation. The individuality of each is fully admitted. Intercourse, therefore, is perfectly free. Conversation is continuous, brilliant, and varied. Groups are formed according to attraction. They are continuously broken up, and re-formed through the operation of the same subtle and all-pervading influence. Mutual deference pervades all classes, and the most perfect harmony ever yet attained in complex human relations prevails under precisely those circumstances which legislators and statesmen dread as the conditions of inevitable anarchy and confusion. If there are laws of etiquette at all, they are mere suggestions of principles admitted into and judged of for himself or herself by each individual mind.

Is it conceivable that in all the future progress of humanity, with all the innumerable elements of development which the present age is unfolding, society generally, and in all its relations, will not attain as high a grade of perfection as certain portions of society, in certain special relations, have already attained?

Suppose the intercourse of the parlor to be regulated by specific legislation. Let the time which each gentleman shall be allowed to speak to each lady be fixed by law; the position in which they should sit or stand be precisely regulated; the subjects which they shall be allowed to speak of, and the tone of voice and accompanying gestures with which each may be treated, carefully defined, all under pretext of preventing disorder and encroachment upon each other's privileges and rights, and can anything be conceived better calculated or more certain to convert social intercourse into intolerable slavery and hopeless confusion?

It would, perhaps, be injudicious to conclude this exhibit of the doctrine of the indivudal soveriegnity, without a more formal statement of the scientific limit upon the exercise of that sovereignty which the principle itself supplies. If the principle were predicated of one individual alone, the assertion of his sovereignty, or, in other words, of his absolute right to do as he pleases, or to pursue his own happiness in his own way, would be confessedly to invest him with the attributes of despotism over others. But the doctrine which I have endeavored to set forth is not that. It is the assertion of the concurrent sovereignty of all men, and of all women, and, within the limits I am about to state, of all children. This concurrence of sovereignty necessarily and appropriately limits the sovereignty of each. Each is sovereign only within his own dominions, because he cannot extend the exercise of his sovereignty beyond those limits without trenching upon, and interferring with, the prerogatives of others, whose sovereignty the doctrine equally affirms. What, then, constitutes the boundaries of one's own dominions? This is a pregnant question for the happiness of mankind, and one which has never, until now, been specifically and scientifically asked and answered. The answer if correctly given, will fix the precise point at which sovereignty ceases and encroachment begins; and that knowledge as I have said, accepted into the public mind, will do more than laws, and the sanctions of laws, to regulate individual conduct and intercourse. The limitation is this: every individual is the rightful sovereign over his own conduct in all things, whenever, and just so far as, the consequences of his conduct can be assumed by himself; or, rather, inasmuch as no one objects to assuming agreeable consequences, whenever, and as far as, this is true of the disagreeable consequences. For disagreeable consequences, endurance, or burden of all sorts, the term "cost" is elected as a scientific technicality. Hence the exact formula of the doctrine, with its inherent limitation, may be stated thus; "the soveriegnty of the individual, to be exercised at his own cost."

This limitation of the doctrine, being inherent, and necessarily involved in the idea of the sovereignty of all, may possibly be left with safety, after the limitation is understood, to implication, and the simple sovereignty of the individual be asserted as the inclusive formula. The limitation has never been distinctly and clearly set forth in the announcements which have been made either of the Protestant or the Democratic creed. Protestantism promulgates the one single, bald, unmodified proposition that in all matters of conscience the individual judgment is the sole tribunal, from which there is no appeal. As against this there is merely the implied right in others to resist when the conscience of the individual leads *him to attack* or encroach upon them. It is the same with the Democratic prerogative of the "pursuit of happiness;" the limitation has been felt rather than distinctly and scientifically propounded.

It results from this analysis that, wherever such circumstances exist that a person cannot exercise his own individuality and sovereignty without throwing the "cost," or burden, of his actions upon others, the principle has so far to be compromised. Such circumstances arise out of connected or amalgamated interests, and the sole remedy is disconnection. The exercise of sovereignty is the exercise of the deciding power. Whoever has to bear the cost should have the deciding power in every case. If one has to bear the cost of another's conduct, and just so far as he has to do so, he should have the deciding power over the conduct of the other. Hence dependence and close connection of interest demand continual concessions and compromises. Hence, too, close connection and mutual dependence is the legitimate and scientific root of despotism, as disconnection or individualization of interests is the root of freedom and emancipation.

If the close combination, which demands the surrender of our will to another, is one instituted by nature, as in the case of the mother and the infant, then the relation is a true one, notwithstanding. The surrender is based upon the fact that the child is not yet strictly an individual. The unfolding of its individuality is gradual, and its growing development is precisely marked, by the increase of its ability to assume the consequences of its own acts. If the close combination of interests is artificial or forced, then the parties exist toward each other in false relations, and to false relations no true principle can apply. Consequently in such relations, the sovereignty of the individual must be abandoned. The law of such relations is collision and conflict, to escape which, while remaining in the relations, there is no other means but mutual concessions and surrenders of the selfhood.

Hence, inasmuch as the interests of mankind have never yet been scientifically individualized by the operations of an equitable commerce, and the limits of encroachment never scientifically defined, the axioms of morality, and even the provisions of positive legislation, have been doubtless appropriate adaptations to the ages of false social relations to which they have been applied, as the cataplasm or the sinapism may be for disordered conditions of the human system. We must not, however, reason, in either case, from that temporary adaptation in a state of disease to the healthy condition of society or the individual. Much that is relatively good is only good as a necessity growing out of evil. The greater good is the removal of the evil altogether. The almshouse and the foundling hospital may be neccessary and laudable charities, but they can only be regarded by the enlightened philanthropist as the stinking apothecary's salve, or the dead flies, applied to the bruises and sores of the body politic. Admitted temporary necessities, they are offensive to the nostrils of good taste. The same reflection is applicable to every species of charity. The oppressed classes do not want charity, but justice, amd with simple justice the necessity for charity will disappear or be reduced to a minimum. So in the matter before us. The disposition to forego one's own pleasures to secure the happiness of others is a positive virtue in all those close connections of interest which render such a sacrifice necessary, and inasmuch as such have hitherto always been the circumstances of the individual in society, this abnegation of selfhood is the highest virtue which the world has hitherto conceived. But these close connections of interest are themselves wrong, for the very reason that they demand this sacrifice and surrender of what ought to be enjoyed and developed to the highest extent. The truest and the highest virtue, in the true relations of men, will be the fullest unfolding of all the individualities of each, and the truest relations of men are those which permit that unfolding of the individualities of each, not only without collision or injury to any, but with mutual advantage to all,— the reconciliation of the individual and the interests of the individual with society and the interests of society,—that composite harmony, or, if you will, unity, of the whole, which results from the discreet unity and distinctive individuality of each particular monad in the complex natural organization of society.

I will conclude by warning you against one other misconception, which is very liable to be entertained by those to whom individuality is for the first time presented as the great remedy for the prevalent evils of the social state. I mean the conception that individuality has something in common with isolation, or the severance of all personal relations with one's fellow-men. Those who entertain this idea will object to it, because they desire, as they will say, co-operation and brotherhood. That objection is conclusive proof that they have not rightly comprehended the nature of individuality, or else they would have seen that it is through the individualization of interests alone that harmonic co-operation and universal brotherhood can be attained. It is not the disruption of relationships, but the creation of distinct and independent personalities, between whom relations can exist. The more distinct the personalities, and the more cautiously they are guarded and preserved, the more intimate the relations may be, without collision or disturbance. Persons may be completely individualized in their interests who are in the most immediate personal contact, as in the case of the lodgers at an hotel, or they may have combined or amalgamated interests, and be remote from each other, as in the case of partners residing in different countries. The players at shuttlecock co-operate in friendly competition with each other, while facing and opposing each other, each fully directing his own movements, which they could not do if their arms and legs were tied together, nor even if they stood side by side. The game of life is one which demands the same freedom of movement on the part of every player, and every attempt to procure harmonious cooperation by fastening different individuals in the same position will defeat its own object.

Internationalism.—The universal extension of commerce and intercommunication, by means of steam navigation, railroads, and the magnetic telegraph, together with the general progress of enlightenment, are rapidly oblitering natural boundaries, and blending the human family into one. The cessation of war is becoming a familiar idea, and with the cessation of war armies and navies will cease, of course, to be required. It is probable that even the existing languages of the earth will melt, within another century or two, into one common and universal tongue, from the same causes operating upon a more extended scale, as those which have blended the dialects of the different counties of England, of the different departments of France, and of the kingdoms of Spain into the English, the French, and the Spanish languages respectively. We have premonitions of the final disbanding of the armies and navies of the world in the substitution of a citizen militia, in the growing unpopularity of even that ridiculous shadow of an army, the militia itself, and in the substitution of the merchant steamship with merely an incidental warlike equipment instead of the regular man-of-war. The navy and war departments of government will thus be dispensed with. The state department now takes charge of the intercourse of the nation with foreign nations. But with the cessation of war there will be no foreign nations, and consequently the state or foreign department may in turn take itself away. Patriotism will expand into philanthropy. Nations, like sects, will dissolve into the individuals who compose them. Every man will be his own nation, and, preserving his own sovereignty and respecting the sovereignty of others, he will be a nation at peace with all others. The term, "a man of the world," reveals the fact that it is the cosmopolite in manners and sentiments whom the world already recognizes as the true gentleman,—the type and leader of civilization. The home department of government is a common receptacle of odds and ends, every one of whose functions would be better managed by individual enterprise, and might take itself away with advantage any day. The treasury department is merely a kind of secretory gland, to provide the means of carrying on the machinery of the other departments. When they are removed, it will of course have no apology left for continuing to exist. Finances for administering government will no longer be wanted when there is no longer any government to administer. The judiciary is, in fact, a branch of the executive, and falls of course, as we have seen, with the introduction of principles which will put an end to aggression and crime. The legislature enacts what the executive and judiciary execute. If the execution itself is unnecessary, the enactment, of course, is no less so. Thus, piece by piece, we dispose of the whole complicated fabric of government, which looms up in such gloomy grandeur, overshadowing the freedom of the individual, impressing the minds of men with a false conviction of its necessity, as if it were, like the blessed light of day, indispensible to life and happiness.

Government.—Is it within the bounds of possibility, and, if so, is it within the limits of rational anticipation, that all human governments, in the sense in which government is now spoken of, shall pass away, and be reckoned among the useless lumber of an experimental age,—that forcible government of all sorts shall, at some future day, perhaps not far distant, be looked back upon by the whole world, as we in America now look back upon the maintenance of a religious establishment, supposed in other times, and in many countries still, to be essential to the existence of religion among men; and as we look back upon the ten thousand other impertinent interferences of government, as government is practiced in those countries where it is an institution of far more validity and consistency than it has among us? Is it possible, and, if so, is it rationally probable, that the time shall ever come when every man shall be, in fine, his own nation as well as his own sect? Will this tendency to universal enfranchisement—indications of which present themselves, as we have seen, in exuberant abundance on all hands in this age—ultimate itself, by placing the individual above all political institutions,—the man above all subordination to municipal law?

I assert that it is not only possible and rationally probable, but that it is rigidly consequential upon the right understanding of the constitution of man, that all government, in the sense of involuntary restraint upon the individual, or substantially all, must finally cease, and along with it the whole complicated paraphernalia and trumpery of kings, emperors, presidents, legislatures, and judiciary. I assert that the indicia of this result abound in existing society, and that it is the instinctive or intelligent perception of that fact by those who have not bargained for so much which gives origin and vital energy to the reaction in Church and State and social life. I assert that the distance is less today forward from the theory and practice of government as it is in these United States, to the total abrogation of all government above that of the individual, than it is backward to the theory and practice of government as government now is in the despotic countries of the old world.

In the high condition of society toward which mankind is unconsciously advancing, men will shun all responsibility for and arbitrary control over the conduct of others as sedulously as during past ages they have sought them as the chief good. Washington declined to be made king, and the whole world has not ceased to make the welkin ring with laudations of the disinterested act. The time will come yet when the declinature, on all hands of every species of governmental authority over others will not even be deemed a virtue, but simply the plain dictate of enlightened self-interest.

It is certain that in such a state of society as that which we are now contemplating no influence will be tolerated, in the place of government, which is maintained or exerted by force in any, even the subtlest forms of involuntary compulsion. But there is still a sense in which men are said to exert power,— a sense in which the wills of the governor and the governed concur, and blend, and harmoize with each other. It is in such a sense as this that the great orator is said to control the minds of his auditory, or that some matchless queen of song sways an irresistible influence over the hearts of men. When mankind graduates out of the period of brute force, that man will be the greatest hero and conqueror who levies the heaviest tribute of homage by excellence of achievement in any depart ment of human performance. The avenues to distinction will not be then, as now, open only to the few. Each individual will truly govern the mind, and hearts, and conduct of others. Those who have the most power to impress themselves upon the community in which they live will govern in larger, and those who have less will govern in smaller spheres. All will be priests and kings, serving at the innumerable altars and sitting upon the thrones of that manifold hierarchy, the foundations of which God himself has laid in the constitution of man. Genius, talent, industry, discovery, the power to please, every development of individuality, in fine, which meets the approbation of another, will be freely recognized as the divine anointing which constitutes him a sovereign over others,—a sovereign having sovereigns for his subjects,—subjects whose loyalty is proved and known, because they are ever free to transfer their fealty to other lords. With the growing development of individuality even in this age, new spheres of honorable distinction are continually evolved. The accredited heroes of our times are neither politicians nor warriors. It is the discoverers of great principles, the projectors of beneficent designs, and the executors of magnificent undertakings of all sorts who, even now, command the homage of mankind. While politics are falling into desuetude and contempt, while war, from being the admiration of the world, is rapidly becoming its abhorrence, the artist and the artisan are rising into relative importance and estimation.

As an instance of the superiority of administration in the private enterprise over the national combination, I was myself at Washington during the last winter, when the mails were interrupted by the breaking up of a railroad bridge between Baltimore and Philadelphia, and when, for nearly two weeks, the newspapers of the Commercial metropolis were regularly delayed one whole day, on their way to the political metropolis of the country, while the same papers came regularly and promptly through every day by the private expresses. The President, members of Congress, and cabinet ministers, even the postmaster-general himself, was regularly served with the news by the enterprise of a private individual, who performed one of the functions of the government, in opposition to the government, and better than the government, levying tribute upon the very functionary of the government who was elected, consecrated, and anointed for the performance of that identical function.

It is the actual performance of the function which is all that there is good in the idea of government. All that there is besides that is mere restriction, and consequent annoyance and oppression of the public, as when our government undertook to suppress those private expresses, which serve the public better than it. The point, then, is this: I affirm that every useful function, or nearly every one, which is now performed by government, and the use of which will remain in the more advanced conditions of mankind, toward which the present tendencies of society converge, can be better performed by the individual, self-elected and self-authorized, than by any constituted government whatsoever.

Products of Labor.—In order to this consummation two conditions are indispensably necessary: the first is the cordial and universal acceptance of this very principle of the sovereignty of the individual—each claiming his own sovereignty, and each religiously respecting that of all others. The second is the equitable interchange of the products of labor, measured by the scientific law relating to that subject to which I have referred, and the consequent security to each of the full enjoyment and unlimited control of just that portion of wealth which he or she produces, the effect of which will be the introduction of general comfort and security, the moderation of avarice, and the supply of a definite knowledge of the limits of rights and encroachments.

Land.—The very foundation principles of the ownership of land, as vested in individuals and protected by law, cannot escape much longer from a searching and radical investigation; and when that comes, the arbitrary legislation of Government will have to give place to such natural and scientific principles regulating the subject as may be evolved. Land reform, in its present aspect, is merely the prologue to a thorough and unsparing, but philosophical and equitable agrarianism, by means of which either the land itself, or an equal participation in the benefits of the land, shall be secured to the whole people. Science, not human legislation, must finally govern the distribution of the soil.

Prisons.—Government still deals with criminals by the old-fashioned process of punishment, but both science and philanthropy concur in pronouncing that the grand remedial agency for crime is prevention, and not cure. The whole theory of vindictive punishment is rapidly becoming obsolescent. That theory once dead, all that remains of punishment is simply defensive. Imprisonment melts into the euphemism, detention; and, while detained, the prisoner is treated tenderly, as a diseased or unfortunate person.

Statesmen and jurists have hitherto dealt with effects instead of causes. They have looked upon crime and encroachment of all sorts as a fact to be remedied, but never as a phenomenon to be accounted for. They have never gone back to inquire what conditions of existence manufactured the criminal, or provoked or induced the encroachment. A change in this respect is beginning to be observed, for the first time, in the present generation. The superiority of prevention over cure is barely beginning to be admitted,—a reform in the methods of thought which is an incipient stage of the revolution in question.

XV
ABRAHAM LINCOLN

Abraham Lincoln, 1809-1865, sixteenth President of the United States. Admitted to the bar in 1835; served in the Black Hawk War, 1832; Whig member of Illinois State Legislature, 1834-42; Whig member of Congress, 1847-49. In 1858 he held a series of joint discussions with Stephen A. Douglas, in which he took a pronounced stand against the institution of slavery. A staunch defender of liberty, lover of humanity and an avowed abolitionist, his election as President, 1860, was the signal for the secession of the Southern States. Issued the famous emancipation proclamation, 1863; re-elected President, 1864; assassinated, 1865, at the close of the Civil War, when occupied with plans for the reconstruction of the South. The selections which follow are from his speeches and public documents.

The man who will not investigate both sides of a question is dishonest.

The cause of civil liberty must not be surrendered at the end of one or even one hundred defeats.

In giving freedom to the slave we assure freedom to the free—honorable alike in what we give and what we preserve.

When the conduct of men is designed to be influenced, persuasion, kind, unassuming persuasion, should ever be adopted.

Though I now sink out of view, I believe I have made some mark which will tell for the cause of liberty long after I am gone.

It is not much in the nature of man to be driven to anything; still less to be driven about that which is exclusively his own business.

The authors of the Declaration of Independence meant it to be a stumbling block to those who in after times might seek to turn a free people back into the paths of despotism.

I have always thought that all men should be free, but if any should be slaves, it should be first those who desire it for themselves, and secondly those who desire it for others.

If there is anything that it is the duty of the whole people never to intrust to any hands but their own, that thing is the preservation and perpetuity of their own liberties and institutions.

I fear you do not fully comprehend the danger of abridging the liberties of the people. A government had better go to the very extreme of toleration than to do aught that could be construed into an interference with or to jeopardize in any degree the common rights of the citizen.

A house divided against itself cannot stand. I believe this government cannot endure permanently half slave and half free. I do not expect the Union to be dissolved—I do not expect the house to fall—but I do expect it will cease to be divided. It will become all one thing or all the other.

Friends, this thing (abolition) has been retarded long enough. The time has come when these sentiments should be uttered; and if it is decreed that I should go down because of this speech, then let me go down linked to truth—let me die in the advocacy of what is just and right.

There is no reason in the world why the Negro is not entitled to all the rights enumerated in the Declaration of Independence, the right to life, liberty, and the pursuit of happiness. I hold that he is as much entitled to these as the white man. I agree with Judge Douglas, he is not my equal in any respect, certainly not in color, perhaps not in moral or intellectual endowments, but in the right to eat the bread, without the leave of anybody else, which his own hand earns, he is my equal and the equal of Judge Douglas, and the equal of any living man.

All the political sentiments I entertain have drawn from the sentiments which originated in and were given to the world from this hall (Independence Hall). I have never had a feeling politically, that did not spring from the sentiments embodied in the Declaration of Independence. The great principle of the Declaration was that sentiment which gave liberty not alone to the people of this country, but, I hope, to all the world for all future time. It was that which gave promise that in due time the weights would be lifted from the shoulders of all men, and that all should have an equal chance.

That is the real issue which will continue in this country when these poor tongues of Judge Douglas and myself shall be silent. It is the eternal struggle between these two principles, right and wrong, throughout the world. They are the two principles that have stood face to face from the beginning of time. The one is the common right of humanity, the other the divine right of kings. It is the same principle in whatever shape it develops itself. It is the same spirit that says "you toil and work and earn bread and I'll eat it."

Church and Ministers.—The United States Government must not undertake to run the churches. When an individual in a church, or out of it, becomes dangerous to the public interest he must be checked.

I am approached with the most opposite opinions and advice, and by religous men who are certain they represent the Divine will . . . . I hope it will not be irreverent in me to say, that if it be probable that God would reveal his will to others, on a point so connected with my duty, it might be supposed he would reveal it directly to me.

Here are twenty-three ministers of different denominations, and all of them are against me but three; and here are a great many prominent members of the churches, a very large majority of whom are against me.

All the powers of the earth seem rapidly combining against him. (the Negro). Mammon is after him, . . . and the theology of the day is fast joining in the cry.

Both read the same Bible and pray to the same God, and each invokes his aid against the other. It may seem strange that any man should dare to ask a just God's assistance in wringing their bread from the sweat of other men's faces; but let us judge not, that we be not judged. The prayers of both could not be answered. That of neither has been answered fully.

Politicians are a set of men who have interests aside from the interests of the people and who, to say the most of them, are, taken as a mass, at least one long step removed from honest men.

If the policy of the government, upon vital questions affecting the whole people, is to be irrevocably fixed by decisions of the supreme court, the people will have ceased to be their own rulers.

When a white man governs himself, that is self government. But when he governs himself and also governs some other man, that is worse than self government—that is despotism. What I do mean to say is that no man is good enough to govern another man without that other's consent.

This country, with its institutions, belongs to the people who inhabit it. Whenever they shall grow weary of the existing government, they can exercise their constitutional right of amending it, or their revolutionary right to dismember or overthrow it. . . . . Why should there not be a patient confidence in the ultimate justice of the people? Is there any better or equal hope in the world?

Labor and Capital.—Inasmuch as most good things are produced by labor, it follows that all such things ought to belong to those whose labor has produced them. But it has happened in all ages of the world that some have labored, and others, without labor, have enjoyed a large proportion of the fruits. This is wrong, and should not continue. To secure to each laborer the whole product of his labor as nearly as possible is a worthy object of any good government.

It continues to develop that the insurrection is largely, if not exclusively, a war upon the first principles of popular government—the rights of the people. . . . . Monarchy itself is sometimes hinted at as a possible refuge from the power of the people.

In my present position I could scarcely be justified were I to omit raising a warning voice against this approach of returning despotism.

It is not needed nor fitting here that a general argument

should be made in favor of popular institutions, but there is one point, with its connections, not so hackneyed as most others, to which I ask a brief attention. It is the effort to place capital on an equal footing with, if not above, labor in the structure of government. It is assumed that labor is available only in connection with capital; that nobody labors unless somebody else, owning capital, somehow by the use of it, induces him to labor. This assumed, it is next considered whether it is best that capital shall hire laborers, and thus induce them to work by their own consent, or buy them and drive them to do it without their consent. Having proceeded so far, it is naturally concluded that all laborers are either hired laborers or what we call slaves.

Now, there is no such relation between capital and labor as assumed. . . . Labor is prior to and independent of capital. Capital is only the fruit of labor, could never have existed if labor had not first existed. Labor is the superior of capital and deserves much the higher consideration.

These capitalists generally act harmoniously and in concert to fleece the people.

XVI
LYSANDER SPOONER

Lysander Spooner, 1808-1887. American jurist. Born on a farm in Athol, Mass. At the age of 26 he began the study of law in the office of John Davis, a celebrated member of the Worcester bar, and finished his studies in the office of Charles Allen, who was counted among the foremost of Massachusetts lawyers. Probably these men of talent little imagined what a giant intellect was developing under their eyes. Mr. Spooner opened a law-office in Worcester, Mass., but only practiced law a short time, but was a student of it all his life, writing on all phases of the subject, mostly in opposition to the accepted theories. The titles of some of his books are *The Unconstitutionality of Slavery; A Defence of Fugitive Slaves; Address to the Free Constitutionalists; No Treason—The Constitution of No Authority.* The selections are from his great legal work, *Trial by Jury.*

Trial by Jury as a Palladium of Liberty

No man can delegate, or give to another, any right of arbitrary dominion.

Juries, and not congresses and judges, are the palladium of our liberties.

The law does not require a man to cease to be a man, and act without regard to consequences, when he becomes a juror.

There can be no such thing as freedom of industry where there is no freedom to lend and hire capital for such industry.

All restraints upon men's natural liberty, not necessary for the simple maintenance of justice, are of the nature of slavery, and differ from each other only in degree.

All governments, the worst on earth and the most tyrannical on earth, are free governments to that portion of the people who voluntarily support them.

Any law which compels a man to pay a certain sum of money to the government for the privilege of speaking to a distant individual, or which debars him of the right of employing such a messenger as he prefers to intrust with his communications, "abridges" his "freedom of speech."

If the jury have no right to judge of the justice of a law

of the government, they plainly can do nothing to protect the people against the oppressions of the government; for there are no oppressions which the government may not authorize by law.

Such being the principles on which the government is formed, the question arises, how shall this government, when formed, be kept within the limits of the contract by which it was established? How shall this government, instituted by the whole people, agreed to by the whole people, supported by the contributions of the whole people, be confined to the accomplishment of those purposes alone which the whole people desire? How shall it be preserved from degenerating into a mere government for the benefit of a part only of those who established it and who support it? How shall it be prevented from even injuring a part of its own members for the aggrandizement of the rest? Its laws must be (or, at least, now are) passed, and most of its other acts performed, by mere agents,—agents chosen by a part of the people, and not by the whole. How can these agents be restrained from seeking their own interests, and the interests of those who elected them, at the expense of the rights of the remainder of the people, by the passage and enforcement of laws partial, unequal, and unjust in their operation?

That is the great question. And the trial by jury answers it.

"The trial by jury" is a trial by the country—that is, by the people—as distinguished from a trial by the government.

It was anciently called trial per pais,—that is, trial by the country. And now in every criminal trial the jury are told that the accused "has, for trial, put himself upon the country, which country you (the jury) are."

The object of this trial by the country, or by the people, in preference to a trial by the government, is to guard against every species of oppression by the government. In order to effect this end, it is indispensable that the people, or the country, judge of and determine their own liberties against the government, instead of the government's judging of and determining its own powers over the people. How is it possible that juries can do anything to protect the liberties of the people against the government, if they are not allowed to determine what those liberties are?

Any government that is its own judge of, and determines authoritatively for the people, what are its own powers over the people, is an absolute government. It has all the powers that it chooses to exercise. There is no other, or, at least, no more accurate, definition of a despotism than this.

On the other hand, any people that judge of, and determine authoritatively for the government, what are their own liberties against the government, of course retain all the liberties they wish to enjoy. And this is freedom. At least, it is freedom to them; because, although it may be theoretically imperfect, it nevertheless corresponds to their highest notions of freedom.

To secure this right of the people to judge of their own liberties against the government, the jurors must be taken from the body of the people, by lot, or by some process that precludes any previous knowledge, choice, or selection of them, on the part of the government. This is done to prevent the government's constituting a jury of its own partisans or friends; in other words, to prevent the government's packing a jury with a view to maintain its own laws and accomplish its own purposes.

It is supposed that, if twelve men be taken by lot from the mass of the people, without the possibility of any previous knowledge, choice, or selection of them on the part of the government, the jury will be a fair epitome of the country at large, and not merely of the party or faction that sustain the measures of the government; that substantially all classes of opinions prevailing among the people will be represented in the jury; and especially that the opponents of the government (if the government have any opponents) will be represented there as well as its friends; that the classes who are oppressed by the laws of the government (if any are thus oppressed) will have their representatives in the jury as well as those who take side with the oppressor—that is, with the government.

It is fairly presumable that such a tribunal will agree to no conviction except such as substantially the whole country would agree to, if they were present taking part in the trial. A trial by such a tribunal is therefore in effect a trial by the country. In its result it probably comes as near to a trial by the whole country as any trial that it is practicable to have without too great inconvenience and expense. And as unanimity is required for a conviction, it follows that no one can be convicted except for the violation of such laws as substantially the whole country wish to have maintained. The government can enforce none of its laws (by punishing offenders through the verdict of juries) except such as substantially the whole people wish to have enforced. The government, therefore, consistently with the trial by jury, can exercise no powers over the people (or—what is the same thing—over the accused person, who represents the rights of the people) except such as substantially the whole people of the country consent that it may exercise. In such a trial, the country, or the people, judge of and determine their own liberties against the government, instead of the government's judging of and determining its own powers over the people.

But all this "trial by the country" would be no trial at all by the country, but only a trial by the government, if the government could either declare who may and who may not be jurors, or could dictate to the jury anything whatever, either of law or evidence, that is of the essence of the trial.

If the government may decide who may and who may not be jurors, it will of course select only its partisans and those friendly to its measures. It may not only prescribe who may and who may not be eligible to be drawn as jurors, but it may also question each person drawn as a juror as to his sentiments in regard to the particular law involved in each trial before suffering him to be sworn on the panel, and exclude him if he be found unfavorable to the maintenance of such a law.

So, also, if the government may dictate to the jury what laws they are to enforce, it is no longer a trial by the country, but a trial by the government; because the jury then try the accused, not by any standard of their own, but by a standard dictated to them by the government. And the standard thus dictated by the government becomes the measure of the people's liberties If the government dictate the standard of trial, it of course dictates the results of the trial. And such a trial is a trial by the government. In short, if the jury have no right to judge of the justice of a law of the government, they plainly can do nothing to protect the people against the oppressions of the government; for there are no oppressions which the government may not authorize by law.

The jury are also to judge whether the laws are rightly expounded to them by the court. Unless they judge on this point, they do nothing to protect their liberties against the oppressions that are capable of being practiced under cover of a corrupt exposition of the laws. If the judiciary can authoritatively dictate to the jury any exposition of the law, they can dictate to them the law itself, and such laws as they please; because laws are in practice one thing or another according as they are expounded.

The jury must also judge whether there really be any such law as the accused is charged with having transgressed.

The jury must also judge of ths laws of evidence. If the government can dictate to a jury the laws of evidence, it can not only shut out any evidence it pleases, tending to vindicate the accused, but it can require that any evidence whatever that it chooses to offer be held as conclusive proof of any offence whatever which the government chooses to allege.

It is manifest, therefore, that the jury must judge of and try the whole case, and every part and parcel of the case, free of any dictation or authority on the part of the government. They must judge of the existence of the law; of the true exposition of the law; of the justice of the law; and of the admissibility and weight of all the evidence offered: otherwise the government will have everything its own way, the jury will be mere puppets in its hands, and the trial will be in reality a trial by the Government. And not a trial by the country. By such trials the government will determine its own powers over the people, instead of the people's determining their liberties against the government; and it will be an entire delusion to talk, as for centuries we have done, of the trial by jury as a "palladium of liberty," or as any protection to the people against the oppression and tyranny of the government.

Unless such be the right and duty of jurors, it is plain that instead of juries being a palladium of liberty, a barrier against the tyranny of the government, they are really mere tools in its hands for carrying into execution any injustice and oppression it may desire to have executed.

But for their right to judge of the law, and the justice of the law, juries would be no protection to an accused person, even as to matters of fact; for, if the government can dictate to a jury any law whatever in a criminal case, it can certainly dictate to them the laws of evidence. That is, it can dictate what evidence is admissible and what inadmissible, and also what force or weight is to be given to the evidence admitted. And if the government can thus dictate to a jury the laws of evidence, it can not only make it necessary for them to convict on a partial exhibition of the evidence rightfully pertaining to the case, but it can even require them to convict on any evidence that it pleases to offer them.

The question, then, between trial by jury as thus described, and trial by the government, is simply a question between liberty and despotism. The authority to judge what are the powers of the government and what the liberties of the people must necessarily be vested in one or the other of the parties themselves, because there is no third party to whom it can be entrusted. If the authority be vested in the government, the government is absolute, and the people have no liberties except such as the government sees fit to indulge them with. If, on the other hand, that authority be vested in the people, then the people have all liberties except such as the whole people choose to disclaim; and the government can exercise no power except such as the whole people consent that it may exercise.

The force and justice of the preceding argument cannot be evaded by saying that the government is chosen by the people; that, in theory, it represents the people; that it is designed to do the will of the people; that its members are all sworn to observe the fundamental or constitutional law instituted by the people; that its acts are therefore entitled to be considered the acts of the people; and that to allow a jury repsenting the people to invalidate the acts of the government would therefore be arraying the people against themselves.

There are two answers to such an argument.

One answer is that in a representative government there is no absurdity or contradiction, nor any arraying of the people against themselves, in requiring that the statutes or enactments of the government shall pass the ordeal of any number of separate tribunals before it shall be determined that they are to have the force of laws. Our American institutions have provided five of these separate tribunals, to wit, representatives, senate, executive, jury, and judges; and have made it necessary that each enactment shall pass the ordeal of any number of separate tribunals before its authority can be established by the punishment of those who transgress it. And there is no more absurdity or inconsistency in making a jury one of these several tribunals and giving it a veto upon the laws than there is in giving a veto to each of these other tribunals. The people are no more arrayed against themselves when a jury puts its veto upon a statute which the other tribunals have sanctioned than they are when the same veto is exercised by the executives or the judges.

But another answer is that the government, and all the departments of the government, are merely the servants and agents of the people, not invested with arbitrary or absolute authority to bind the people, but required to submit their enactments to the judgment of a tribunal more fairly representing the whole people before they carry them into execution. If the government were not thus required to submit their enactments to the judgment of the country; if, in other words, the people had reserved to themselves no veto upon the acts of the government, then the government, instead of being a mere servant and agent of the people, would be an absolute despot over the people. It would have all power in its own hands, because the power to punish carries all other powers with it. A power that can of itself, and by its own authority, punish disobedience, can compel obedience and submission, and is above all responsibility for the character of its laws. In short, it is a despotism.

And it is of no consequence to inquire how a government came by this power to punish, whether by prescription, by inheritance, by usurpation, or by delegation from the people. If it have now but got it, the government is absolute.

It is plain, therefore, that, if the people have invested the government with power to make laws that are absolutely binding, and to punish transgressors, they have surrendered their liberties unreservedly into the hands of the government.

It is of no avail to say in answer to this view of the case that in thus surrendering their liberties the people took an oath from the government that it would exercise its power within certain constitutional limits; for when did oaths ever restrain a government that was otherwise unrestrained? Or when did a government fail to determine that all its acts were within the constitutional and authorized limits of its power, if it were permitted to determine that question for itself?

Neither is it of any avail to say that, if the government abuse its power and enact unjust and oppressive laws, the government may be changed by the influence of discussion and the exercise of the right of suffrage. Discussion can do nothing to prevent the enactment, or procure the repeal, of unjust laws, unless it be understood that the discussion is to be followed by resistance. Tyrants care nothing for discussions that are to end only in discussion. Such discussion as does not interfere with the enforcement of their laws is but idle wind to them. Suffrage is equally powerless and unreliable. It can be exercised only periodically, and the tyranny must at least be borne until the time for suffrage comes. Besides, when the suffrage is exercised, it gives no guaranty for the repeal of existing laws that are oppressive and no security against the enactment of new ones that are equally so. The second body of legislators are likely and liable to be just as tyrannical as the first. If it be said that the second body may be chosen for their integrity, the answer is that the first were chosen for that very reason and yet proved tyrants. The second will be exposed to the same temptations as the first and will be just as likely to prove tyrannical. Who ever heard that succeeding legislatures were, on the whole, more honest than those that precede them? What is there in the nature of men or things to make them so? If it be said that the first body were chosen from motives of injustice, that fact proves that there is a portion of society who desire to establish injustice; and if they were powerful or artful enough to procure the election of their instruments to compose the first legislature, they will be likely to succeed equally well with the second. The right of suffrage, therefore, and even a change of legislators, guarantees no change of legislation,—certainly no change for the better. Even if a change for the better actually comes, it comes too late, because it comes only after more or less injustice has been irreparably done.

But at best the right of suffrage can be exercised only periodically, and between the periods the legislators are wholly irresponsible. No despot was ever more entirely irresponsible than are republican legislators during the period for which they are chosen. They can neither be removed from their office, nor called to account while in their office, nor punished after they leave their office, be their tyranny what it may. Moreover, the judicial and executive departments of the government are equally irresponsible to the people, and are only responsible (by impeachment, and dependence for their salaries) to these irresponsible legislators. This dependence of the judiciary and executive upon the legislature is a guaranty that they will always sanction and execute its laws, whether just or unjust. Thus the legislators hold the whole power of the government in their hands, and are at the same time utterly irresponsible for the manner in which they use it.

If, now, this government (the three branches thus really united into one) can determine the validity of, and enforce, its own laws, it is, for the time being, entirely absolute and wholly irresponsible to the people.

But this is not all. These legislators and this government, so irresponsible while in power, can perpetuate their power at pleasure, if they can determine what legislation is authoritative upon the people and enforce obedience to it; for they can not only declare their power perpetual, but they can enforce submission to all legislation that is necessary to secure its perpetuity. They can, for example, prohibit all discussion of the rightfulness of their authority; forbid the use of the suffrage; prevent the election of any successors; disarm, plunder, imprison, and even kill all who refuse submission. If, therefore, the government be absolute for a day—that is, if it can, for a day enforce obedience to its own laws—it can, in that day, secure its power for all time, like the queen who wished to reign for a day, but in that day caused the king, her husband, to be slain, and usurped his throne.

Nor will it avail to say that such acts would be unconstitutional, and that unconstitutional acts may be lawfully resisted; for everything a government pleases to do will of course be determined to be constitutional, if the government itself be permitted to determine the question of the constitutionality of its own acts. Those who are capable of tyranny are capable of perjury to sustain it.

The conclusion, therefore, is that any government that can, for a day, enforce its own laws, without appealing to the people (or to a tribunal fairly representing the people) for their consent is, in theory, an absolute government, irresponsible to the people, and can perpetuate its power at pleasure.

The trial by jury is based upon a recognition of this principle, and therefore forbids the government to execute any of its laws by punishing violators, in any case whatever, without first getting the consent of "the country," or the people, through a jury. In this way the people, at all times, hold their liberties in their own hands and never surrender them, even for a moment, into the hands of the government.

The trial by jury, then, gives to any and every individual the liberty, at any time, to disregard or resist any law whatever of the government, if he be willing to submit to the decision of a jury the questions whether the law be intrinsically just and obligatory, and whether his conduct in disregarding or resisting it were right in itself. And any law which does not in such trial obtain the unanimous sanction of twelve men, taken at random from the people, and judging according to the standard of justice in their own minds, free from all dictation and authority of the government, may be transgressed and resisted with impunity by whomsoever it pleases to transgress or resist it.

The trial by jury authorizes all this, or it is a sham and a hoax, utterly worthless for protecting the people against oppression. If it do not authorize an individual to resist the first and least act of injustice or tyranny on the part of the government, it does not authorize him to resist the last and the greatest. If it do not authorize individuals to nip tyranny in the bud, it does not authorize them to cut it down when its branches are filled with the ripe fruits of plunder and oppression.

Those who deny the right of a jury to protect an individual in resisting an unjust law of the government, deny him all legal defence whatsoever against oppression. The right of revolution which tyrants in mockery accord to mankind is no *legal* right *under* a government; it is only a right to overturn a government. The government iself never acknowledges this right. And the right is practically established only when and because the government no longer exists to call it in question. The right therefore can be exercised with impunity only when it is exercised victoriously. All unsuccessful attempts at revolution, however justifiable in themselves, are punished as treason. The government itself never admits the injustice of its laws as a legal defence for those who have attempted a revolution and failed. The right of revolution therefore is a right of no practical value except for those who are stronger than the government. So long, therefore, as the oppressions of a government are kept within such limits as simply not to exasperate against it a power greater than its own, the right of revolution cannot be appealed to and is inapplicable to the case. This affords a wide field for tyranny; and if a jury cannot intervene here, the oppressed are utterly defenseless.

It is manifest that the only security against the tyranny of the government is in forcible resistance to the execution of the injustice; because the injustice will certainly be executed unless forcibly resisted. And if it be but suffered to be executed, it must then be borne; for the government never makes compensation for its own wrongs.

Since, then, this forcible resistance to the injustice of the government is the only possible means of preserving liberty, it is indispensable to all legal liberty that this resistance should be legalized. It is perfectly self-evident that, where there is no legal right to resist the oppression of government, there can be no legal liberty. And here it is all-important to notice that, practically speaking, there can be no legal right to resist the oppressions of the government unless there be some legal tribunal other than the government, and wholly independent of and above the government, to judge between the government and those who resist its oppression; in other words, to judge what laws of the government are to be obeyed and what held for naught. The only tribunal known to our laws for this purpose is a jury. If a jury have not the right to judge between the government and those who disobey its laws, the government is absolute, and the people, legally speaking, are slaves. Like other slaves, they may have sufficient courage and strength to keep their masters somewhat in check; but they are nevertheless known to the law as slaves.

That this right of resistance was recognized as a common law right when the ancient and genuine trial by jury was enforced is not only proved by the nature of the trial itself, but is acknowledged by history.

This right of resistance is recognized by the constitution of the United States as a strictly legal right. It is so recognized, first, by the provisions that "the trial of all crimes, except in cases of impeachment, shall be by jury"—that is, by the country, and not by the government; secondly, by the provision that "the right of the people to keep and bear arms shall not be infringed." This constitutional security for the right to keep and bear arms implies the right to use them,—as much as a constitutional security for the right to buy and keep food would have implied the right to eat it. The constitution, therefore, takes it for granted that the people will judge of the conduct of the government and that, as they have the right, they will also have the sense to use arms whenever the necessity of the case justifies it. And it is a sufficient and legal defence for a person accused of using arms against the government, if he can show, to the satisfaction of a jury, or even any one of a jury, that the law he resisted was an unjust one.

But for the right of resistance on the part of the people, all governments would become tyrannical to a degree of which few people are aware. Constitutions are utterly worthless to restrain the tyranny of governments, unless it be understood that the people will by force compel the government to keep within constitutional limits. Practically speaking, no government knows any limits to its power except the endurance of the people. But that the people are stronger than the government and will resist in extreme cases, our governments would be little or nothing else than organized systems of plunder and oppression. All, or nearly all, the advantage there is in fixing any constitutional limits to the power of a government is simply to give notice to the government of the point at which it will meet with resistance. If the people are then as good as their word, they may keep the government within the bounds they have set for it; otherwise it will disregard them, as is proved by the example of all our American governments, in which the constitutions have all become obsolete for nearly all purposes except the appointment of officers who at once become practically absolute.

The bounds set to the power of the government by the trial by jury are these,—that the government shall never touch the person, property, or civil rights of an individual against his consent, except for the purpose of bringing him before a jury for trial, unless in pursuance and execution of a judgment or decree rendered by a jury upon such evidence, and such law, as are satisfactory to their own understandings and consciences, irrespective of all legislation of government.

XVII
ROBERT G. INGERSOLL

Robert Green Ingersoll, born Dresden, N. Y., 1833; died Dobbs Ferry, 1899. American lawyer, lecturer, orator, critic, philosopher. Settled in Peoria, Ill., 1857; became colonel of the Eleventh Illinois Cavalry, 1862, and attorney general for Illinois, 1866; the most powerful pioneer of religious freedom in America; in spite of his atheistical beliefs, won tremendous popularity with all classes by his brilliant oratory, keen humor, and sympathetic grasp of human problems; had more friends and more enemies than any other man in America. Published *The Gods, and Other Lectures*, 1876; *Some Mistakes of Moses*, 1879; *Great Speeches*, 1887; *Liberty in Literature; Ghosts and Other Lectures*. His *Complete Works*, 12 volumes, were published by his brother-in-law, C. P. Farrall of Dresden Pub. Co., New York, with a *Biographical Appreciation* by Dr. Herman E. Kittridge, in 1912.

These selections are from his lectures, *Liberty of Man, Woman and Child; How to Reform Mankind; Crimes Against Criminals; Individuality*, and *Voltaire*.

I believe in liberty, always and everywhere.

A believer is a bird in a cage, a freethinker is an eagle parting the clouds with tireless wing.

In all ages, hypocrites called priests, have put crowns upon the heads of thieves, called kings.

Our fathers reasoned with instruments of torture. They believed in the logic of fire and sword. They hated reason. They despised thought. They abhorred liberty.

Civilization is the child of free thought. The new world has drifted away from the rotten wharf of superstition. The politics of this country are being settled by the new ideas of individual liberty, and parties and churches that cannot accept the new truths must perish.

As man develops, he places a greater value upon his own rights. Liberty becomes a grander and diviner thing. As he values his own rights, he begins to value the rights of others. And when all men give to all others all the rights they claim for themselves, this world will be civilized.

Away, forever away with the creeds and books and forms and laws and religions that take from the soul liberty and reason. Down with the idea that thought is dangerous! Perish the infamous doctrine that man can have property in man. Let us resent with indignation every effort to put a chain upon our minds.

Liberty is a word hated by kings—loathed by popes. It is a word that shatters thrones and altars—that leaves the crowned without subjects, and the outstretched hand of superstition without alms. Liberty is the blossom and fruit of justice—the perfume of mercy. Liberty is the seed and soil, the air and light, the dew and rain of progress, love and joy.

Liberty cannot be sacrificed for the sake of anything. It is of more value than anything else. . . . Liberty sustains the same relation to all our virtues that the sun does to life. The world had better go back to barbarism, to the dens, to the caves and lairs of savagery; better lose all art, all invention, than to lose liberty.

A government founded upon anything except liberty and justice cannot and ought not to stand. All the wrecks on either side of the stream of time, all the wrecks of the great cities, and all the nations that have passed away—all are a warning that no nation founded upon injustice can stand. From the sand-enshrouded Egypt, from the marble wilderness of Athens, and from every fallen, crumbling stone of the once mighty Rome, comes a wail as it were, the cry that no nation founded upon injustice can permanently stand.

I have a dream that this world is growing better and better every day and every year; that there is more charity, more justice, more love every day. I have a dream that prisons will not always curse the earth; that the shadow of the gallows will not always fall on the land; that finally wisdom will sit in the legislature, justice in the courts, charity will occupy all the pulpits, and that finally the world will be controlled by liberty and love, by justice and charity. That is my dream, and if it does not come true, it shall not be my fault.

O Liberty, thou art the god of my idolatry! Thou art the

only deity that hateth bended knees. In thy vast and unwalled temple, beneath the roofless dome, star-gemmed and luminous with suns, thy worshippers stand erect! They do not cringe, or crawl, or bend their foreheads to the earth. The dust has never borne the impress of their lips. Upon thy altars mothers do not sacrifice their babes, nor men their rights. Thou askest naught from man except the things that good men hate—the whip, the chain, the dungeon key. Thou hast no popes, no priests, who stand between their fellow-men and thee. Thou carest not for foolish forms or selfish prayers. At thy sacred shrine hypocrisy does not bow, virtue does not tremble, superstition's feeble tapers do not burn, but Reason holds aloft her inextinguishable torch whose holy light will one day flood the world.

I am going to say what little I can to make the American people brave enough and generous enough and kind enough to give everybody else the rights they have themselves. Can there ever be any progress in this world to amount to anything until we have liberty? The thoughts of a man who is not free are not worth much—not much. A man who thinks with the club of a creed over his head—a man who thinks casting his eye askance at the flames of hell, is not apt to have very good thoughts. And for my part, I would not care to have any status or social position even in heaven if I had to admit that I never would have been there only I got scared. When we are frightened we do not think very well. If you want to get at the honest thoughts of a man he must be free. If he is not free you will not get his honest thought.

There is no slavery but ignorance. Liberty is the child of intelligence.

The history of man is simply the history of slavery, of injustice and brutality, together with the means by which he has, through the dead and desolate years, slowly and painfully advanced. He has been the sport and prey of priest and king, the food of superstition and cruel might. Crowned force has governed ignorance through fear. Hypocrisy and tyranny—two vultures—have fed upon the liberties of man. From all these there has been, and is, but one means of escape—intellectual development.

Individuality.—It is a blessed thing that in every age some one has had individuality enough and courage enough to stand by his own convictions,—some one who had the grandeur to say his say. I believe it was Magellan who said, "the church says the earth is flat; but I have seen its shadow on the moon, and I have more confidence even in a shadow than in the Church." On the prow of his ship were disobedience, defiance, scorn, and success.

Nearly all people stand in great horror of annihilation, and yet to give up your individuality is to annihilate yourself. Mental slavery is mental death, and every man who has given up his intellectual freedom is the living coffin of his dead soul. In this sense, every church is a cemetery and every creed an epitaph.

We should all remember that to be like other people is to be unlike ourselves, and that nothing can be more detestable in character than servile imitation. The great trouble with imitation is, that we are apt to ape those who are in reality far below us. After all, the poorest bargain that a human being can make, is to give his individuality for what is called respectability.

I tell you there is something splendid in man that will not always mind. Why, if we had done as the kings told us five hundred years ago, we would all have been slaves. If we had done as the priests told us, we would all have been idiots. If we had done as the doctors told us, we would all have been dead. We have been saved by disobedience. We have been saved by that spendid thing called independence, and I want to see more of it day after day, and I want to see children raised so they will have it. That is my doctrine.

Nothing can be more infamous than intellectual tyranny.

276   Liberty and the Great Libertarians

To put chains upon the body is as nothing compared with putting shackles on the brain. No god is entitled to the worship or the respect of man who does not give, even to the meanest of his children, every right that he claims for himself.

I do not believe that the tendency is to make men and women brave and glorious when you tell them that there are certain ideas upon certain subjects that they must never express; that they must go through life with a pretense as a shield; that their neighbors will think much more of them if they will only keep still; and that above all is a God who despises one who honestly expresses what he believes. For my part, I believe men will be nearer honest in business, in politics, grander in art—in everything that is good and grand and beautiful, if they are taught from the cradle to the coffin to tell their honest opinions.

Is it possible that an infinite God created this world simply to be the dwelling-place of slaves and serfs? simply for the purpose of raising orthodox Christians? That he did a few miracles to astonish them; that all the evils of life are simply his punishments, and that he is finally going to turn heaven into a kind of religious museum filled with Baptist barnacles, petrified Presbyterians and Methodist mummies? I want no heaven for which I must give my reason; no happiness in exchange for my liberty, and no immortality that demands the surrender of my individuality. Better rot in the windowless tomb, to which there is no door but the red mouth of the pallid worm, than wear the jewelled collar even of a god.

There can be nothing more utterly subversive of all that is really valuable than the suppression of honest thought. No man, worthy of the form he bears, will at the command of Church and State solemnly repeat a creed his reason scorns. It is the duty of each and every one to maintain his individuality. "This above all, to thine own self be true, and it must follow as the night the day, thou canst not then be false to any man." It is a magnificent thing to be the sole proprietor of yourself. It is a terrible thing to wake up at night and say, "There is nobody in this bed." It is humiliating to know that your ideas are all borrowed; that you are indebted to your memory for your principles; that your religion is simply one of your habits, and that you would have convictions if they were only contagious. It is mortifying to feel that you belong to a mental mob and cry "crucify him," because the others do; that you reap what the great and brave have sown, and that you can benefit the world only by leaving it.

Surely every human being ought to attain to the dignity of the *unit*. Surely it is worth something to be *one*, and to feel that the census of the universe would be incomplete without counting you. Surely there is grandeur in knowing that in the realm of thought, at least, you are without a chain; that you have the right to explore all heights and all depths; that there are no walls nor fences, nor prohibited places, nor sacred corners in all the vast expanse of thought; that your intellect owes no allegiance to any being, human or divine; that you hold all in fee and upon no condition and by no tenure whatever; that in the world of mind you are relieved from all personal dictation, and from the ignorant tyranny of majorities. Surely it is worth something to feel that there are no priests, no popes, no parties, no governments, no kings, no gods, to whom your intellect can be compelled to pay a reluctant homage. Surely it is a joy to know that all the cruel ingenuity of bigotry can devise no prison, no dungeon, no cell in which for one instant to confine a thought; that ideas cannot be dislocated by racks, nor crushed in iron boots, nor burned with fire. Surely it is sublime to think that the brain is a castle, and that within its curious bastions and winding halls the soul, in spite of all worlds and all beings, is the supreme sovereign of itself.

Egoism.—I have heard all my life about self-denial. There never was anything more idiotic than that. No man who does right practices self-denial. To do right is the bud and blossom and fruit of wisdom. To do right should always be dictated by the highest possible selfishness and the most perfect generosity. No man practices self-denial unless he does wrong. To inflict an injury upon yourself is an act of self-denial. He who denies justice to another denies it to himself. To plant seeds that will forever bear the fruit of joy, is not an act of self-denial. So this idea of doing good to others only for their sake is absurd. You want to do it, not simply for their sake, but for your own; because a perfectly civilized man can never be perfectly happy while there is one unhappy being in this universe.

Let us take another step. The barbaric world was to be rewarded in some other world for acting sensibly in this. They were promised rewards in another world, if they would only have self-denial enough to be virtuous in this. If they would forego the pleasures of larceny and murder; if they would forego the thrill and bliss of meanness here, they would be rewarded hereafter for that self-denial. I have exactly the opposite idea. Do right, not to deny yourself, but because you love yourself and because you love others. Be generous, because it is better for you. Be just, because any other course is the suicide of the soul. Whoever does wrong plagues himself, and when he reaps that harvest, he will find that he was not practicing self-denial when he did right.

If you want to be happy yourself, if you are truly civilized, you want others to be happy. Every man ought, to the extent of his ability, to increase the happiness of mankind, for the reason that that will increase his own. No one can be really prosperous unless those with whom he lives share the sunshine and the joy.

Upon the back of industry has been the whip. Upon the brain have been the fetters of superstition. Nothing has been left undone by the enemies of freedom. Every art and artifice, every cruelty and outrage has been practiced and perpetrated to destroy the rights of man. In this great struggle every crime has been rewarded and every virtue has been punished. Reading, writing, thinking and investigating have all been crimes.

Every science has been an outcast.

All the alters and all the thrones united to arrest the forward march of the human race. The king said that mankind must not work for themselves. The priest said that mankind must not think for themselves. One forged chains for the hands, the other for the soul. Under this infamous *regime* the eagle of the human intellect was for ages a slimy serpent of hypocrisy.

The human race was imprisoned. Through some of the prison bars came a few struggling rays of light. Against these bars Science pressed its pale and thoughtful face, wooed by the holy dawn of human advancement. Bar after bar was broken away. A few grand men escaped and devoted their lives to the liberation of their fellows.

Only a few years ago there was a great awakening of the human mind. Men began to inquire by what right a crowned robber made them work for him. The man who asked this question was called a traitor. Others asked by what right does a robed hypocrite rule my thought? Such men were called infidels. The priest said, and the king said, where is this spirit of investigation to stop? They said then and they say now, that it is dangerous for man to be free. I deny it. Out on the intellectual sea there is room enough for every sail. In the intellectual air there is space enough for every wing.

The man who does not do his own thinking is a slave, and is a traitor to himself and to his fellow-men.

Every man should stand under the blue and stars, under the infinite flag of nature, the peer of every other man.

Standing in the presence of the Unknown, all have the same right to think, and all are equally interested in the great questions of origin and destiny. All I claim, all I plead for, is liberty of thought and expression. That is all. I do not pretend to tell what is absolutely true, but what I think is true. I do not pretend to tell all the truth.

I do not claim that I have floated level with the heights of thought, or that I have descended to the very depths of things. I simply claim that what ideas I have, I have a right to express; and that any man who denies that right to me is an intellectual thief and robber. That is all.

Take those chains from the human soul. Break those fetters. If I have no right to think, why have I a brain? If I have no such right, have three or four men, or any number, who may get together, and sign a creed, and build a house, and put a steeple upon it, and a bell in it—have they the right to think? The good men, the good women are tired of the whip and lash in the realm of thought. They remember the chain and fagot with a shudder. They are free and they give liberty to others. Whoever claims any right that he is unwilling to accord to his fellow-men is dishonest and infamous.

In the good old times, our fathers had the idea that they could make people believe to suit them. Our ancestors, in the ages that are gone, really believed that by force you could convince a man. You cannot change the conclusion of the brain by torture; nor by social ostracism. But I will tell you what you can do by these, and what you have done. You can make hypocrites by the million. You can make a man say that he has changed his mind; but he remains of the same opinion still.

In the old times of which I have spoken, they desired to make all men think exactly alike. All the mechanical ingenuity of the world cannot make two clocks run exactly alike, and how are you going to make hundreds of millions of people, differing in brain and disposition, in education and aspiration, in conditions and surroundings, each clad in a living robe of passionate flesh—how are you going to make them think and feel alike? If there is an infinite god, one who made us, and wishes us to think alike, why did he give a spoonful of brains to one, and a magnificent intellectual development to another? Why is it that we have all degrees of intelligence, from orthodoxy to genius, if it was intended that all should think and feel alike?

Is it nothing to free the mind? Is it nothing to civilize mankind? Is it nothing to fill the world with light, with discovery, with science? Is it nothing to dignify man and exalt the intellect? Is it nothing to grope your way into the dreary prisons, the damp and dropping dungeons, and dark and silent cells of superstition, where the souls of men are chained to floors of stone? Is it nothing to conduct these souls gradually into the blessed light of day,—to let them see again the happy fields, the sweet green earth, and hear the everlasting music of the waves? Is it nothing to make men wipe the dust from their swollen knees, the tears from their blanched and furrowed cheeks? Is it nothing to relieve the heavens of an insatiate monster, and write upon the eternal dome, glittering with stars, the grand word—Liberty?

What do I mean by liberty? By physical liberty I mean the right to do anything which does not interfere with the happiness of another. By intellectual liberty I mean the right to think right and the right to think wrong. Thought is the means by which we endeavor to arrive at truth. If we know the truth already, we need not think. All that can be required is honesty of purpose. You ask my opinion about anything; I examine it honestly, and when my mind is made up, what should I tell you? Should I tell you my real thought? What should I do? There is a book put in my hands. I am told this is the Koran; it was written by inspiration. I read it, and when I get through, suppose that I think in my heart and in my brain, that it is utterly untrue, and you then ask me, what do you think? Now, admitting that I live in Turkey, and have no chance to get any office unless I am on the side of the Koran, what should I say? Should I make a clean breast and say, that upon my honor I do not believe it? What would you think then of my fellow-citizens if they said: "That man is dangerous, he is dishonest."

Suppose I read the book called the bible, and when I get through I make up my mind that it was written by men. A minister asks me, "Did you read the bible?" I answer that I did. "Do you think it divinely inspired?" What should I reply? Should I say to myself, "If I deny the inspiration of the scriptures, the people will never clothe me with power." What ought I to answer? Ought I not to say like a man: "I have read it; I do not believe it." Should I not give the real transcript of my mind? Or should I turn hypocrite and pretend what I do not feel, and hate myself forever after for being a cringing coward. For my part I would rather a man would tell me what he honestly thinks. I would rather he would preserve his manhood. I had a thousand times rather be a manly unbeliever than an unmanly believer. And if there is a judgment day, a time when all will stand before some supreme being, I believe I will stand higher, and stand a better chance of getting my case decided in my favor, than any man sneaking through life pretending to believe what he does not.

I have made up my mind to say my say. I shall do it kindly, distinctly; but I am going to do it. I know there are thousands of men who substantially agree with me, but who are not in a condition to express their thoughts. They are poor; they are in business; and they know that should they tell their honest thought, persons will refuse to patronize them—to trade with them, they wish to get bread for their little children; they wish to take care of their wives; they wish to have homes and the comforts of life. Every such person is a certificate of the meanness of the community in which he resides. And yet I do not blame these people for not expressing their thought. I say to them: "Keep your ideas to yourselves; feed and clothe the ones you love; I will do your talking for you. The church cannot touch, cannot crush, cannot starve, cannot stop or stay me; I will express your thoughts."

Oh Liberty, float not forever in the far horizon—remain not forever in the dream of the enthusiast, the philanthropist and poet, but come and make thy home among the children of men!

My Religion'—To love justice, to long for the right, to love mercy, to pity the suffering, to assist the weak, to forget wrongs and remember benefits, to love the truth, to be sincere, to utter honest words, to love liberty, to wage relentless war against slavery in all its forms, to love wife and child and friend, to make a happy home, to love the beautiful in art, in nature, to cultivate the mind, to be familiar with the mighty thoughts that genius has expressed, the noble deeds of all the world; to cultivate courage and cheerfulness, to make others happy, to fill life with the splendor of generous acts, the warmth of loving words; to discard error, to destroy prejudice, to receive new truths with gladness, to cultivate hope, to see the calm beyond the storm, the dawn beyond the night, to do the best that can be done and then be resigned. This is the religion of reason, the creed of science. This satisfies the brain and heart.

Church and State.—The infidels of one age have often been the aureoled saints of the next.

The destroyers of the old are the creators of the new.

As time sweeps on the old passes away and the new in its turn becomes old.

There is in the intellectual world, as in the physical, decay and growth, and ever by the grave of buried age stand youth and joy.

The history of intellectual progress is written in the lives of infidels.

Political rights have been preserved by traitors; the liberty of mind by heretics.

To attack the king was treason; to dispute the priest was blasphemy.

For many centuries the sword and cross were allies. Together they attacked the rights of man. They defended each other.

The throne and altar were twins—two vultures from the same egg.

James I said "No bishop, no king." He might have added:

No cross, no crown. The king owned the bodies of men; the priests, the souls. One lived on taxes collected by force, the other on alms collected by fear—both robbers, both beggars.

These robbers and these beggars controlled two worlds. The king made laws, the priest made creeds. Both obtained their authority from God, both were the agents of the Infinite.

With bowed backs the people carried the burdens of one, and with wonder's open mouth received the dogmas of the other.

If the people aspired to be free, they were crushed by the king, and every priest was a Herod, who slaughtered the children of the brain.

The king ruled by force, the priest by fear, and both by both.

The king said to the people: "God made you peasants, and He made me king; He made you to labor and me to enjoy; He made rags and hovels for you, robes and palaces for me. He made you to obey and me to command. Such is the justice of God."

And the priest said: "God made you ignorant and vile; He made me holy and wise; you are the sheep, I am the shepherd; your fleeces belong to me. If you do not obey me here, God will punish you now and torment you forever in another world. Such is the mercy of God."

"You must not reason. Reason is a rebel. You must not contradict—contradiction is born of egotism; you must believe. He that hath ears to hear let him hear." Heaven was a question of ears.

Fortunately for us, there have been traitors and there have been heretics, blasphemers, thinkers, investigators, lovers of liberty, men of genius who have given their lives to better the condition of their fellowmen.

I love any man who gave me, or helped to give me, the liberty I enjoy tonight. I love every man who helped put our flag in heaven. I love every man who has lifted his voice in all the ages for liberty, for a chainless body and a fetterless brain. I love every man who has given to every other human being every right that he claimed for himself. I love every man who thought more of principle than he did of position. I love the men who have trampled crowns beneath their feet that they might do something for mankind.

Law.—It has been contended for many years that the ten commandments are the foundation of all ideas of justice and of law. Eminent jurists have bowed to popular prejudice, and deformed their works by statements to the effect that the Mosaic laws are the fountains from which sprang all ideas of right and wrong. Nothing can be more stupidly false than such assertions. Thousands of years before Moses was born, the Egyptians had a code of laws. They had laws against blasphemy, murder, adultery, larceny, perjury, laws for the collection of debts and the enforcement of contracts.

Laws spring from the instinct of self-preservation. Industry objected to supporting idleness, and laws were made against theft. Laws were made against murder, because a very large majority of the people have always objected to being murdered. All fundamental laws were born simply of the instinct of self-defense. Long before the Jewish savages assembled at the foot of Sinai, laws had been made and enforced, not only in Egypt and India, but by every tribe that ever existed. A very curious thing about these commandments is that their supposed author violated nearly every one. From Sinai, according to the account, He said: "Thou shalt not kill," and yet He ordered the murder of millions; "Thou shalt not commit adultery," and He gave captured maidens to gratify the lust of captors; "Thou shalt not steal," and yet He gave to Jewish marauders the flocks and herds of others; "Thou shalt not covet thy neighbor's house, nor his wife," and yet He allowed His chosen people to destroy the homes of neighbors and to steal their wives; "Honor thy father and mother," and yet this same God had thousands of fathers butchered, and with the sword of war killed children yet unborn; "Thou shalt not bear false witness against thy neighbor," and yet He sent abroad "lying spirits" to deceive his own prophets, and in a hundred ways paid tribute to deceit. So far as we know, Jehovah kept only one of these commandments—he worshiped no other god.

War.—As long as nations meet on the fields of war—as long as they sustain the relations of savages to each other—as long as they put the laurel and the oak on the brows of those who kill—just so long will citizens resort to violence, and the quarrels of individuals be settled by dagger and revolver.

No man has imagination enough to paint the agonies, the horrors, the cruelties, of war. Think of sending shot and shell crashing through the bodies of men! Think of the widows and orphans! Think of the maimed, the mutilated, the mangled!

Every good man, every good woman, should try to do away with war, to stop the appeal to savage force.

Vision of the Future.—A vision of the future rises; . . . . I see a world where thrones have crumbled and where kings are dust. The aristocracy of idleness has perished from earth.

I see a world without a slave. Man at last is free. Nature's forces have by science been enslaved. Lightning and light, wind and wave, frost and flame, and all the secret subtle powers of the earth and air are the tireless toilers for the human race.

I see a world at peace, adorned with every form of art, with music's myriad voices thrilled, while lips are rich with words of love and truth; a world in which no exile sighs, no prisoner mourns; a world on which the gibbet's shadow does not fall; a world where labor reaps its full reward, where work and worth go hand in hand, where the poor girl, trying to win bread with a needle—the needle that has been called "the asp for the breast of the poor,"—is not driven to the desperate choice of crime or death, of suicide or shame.

I see a world without the beggar's outstretched palm, the

miser's heartless, stony stare, the piteous wail of want, the livid lips of lies, the cruel eyes of scorn.

I see a race without disease of flesh or brain—shapely and fair, married harmony of form and function, and, as I look, life lengthens, joy deepens, love canopies the earth; and over all in the great dome shines the eternal star of human hope.

Criminals.—Now, we have in this country another class. We call them "criminals." Let me take another step:

" 'Tis not enough to help the feeble up,
But to support him after."

Recollect what I said in the first place—that every man is as he must be. Every crime is a necessary product. The seeds were all sown, the land thoroughly plowed, the crop well attended to, and carefully harvested. Every crime is born of necessity. If you want less crime, you must change the conditions. Poverty makes crime. Want, rags, crusts, misfortune—all these awake the wild beast in man, and finally he takes, and takes contrary to law, and becomes a criminal. And what do you do with him? You punish him. Why not punish a man for having consumption? The time will come when you will see that that is just as logical. What do you do with the criminal? You send him to the penitentiary. Is he made better? Worse. The first thing you do is to try to trample out his manhood, by putting an indignity upon him. You mark him. You put him in stripes. At night you put him in darkness. His feeling for revenge grows. You make a wild beast of him, and he comes out of that place branded in body and soul, and then you won't let him reform if he wants to. You put on airs above him, because he has been in the penitentiary. The next time you look with scorn upon a convict, let me beg of you to do one thing. Maybe you are not as bad as I am, but do one thing: think of all the crimes you have wanted to commit; think of all the crimes you would have committed if you had had the opportunity; think of all the temptations to which you would have yielded had nobody been looking; and then put your hand on your heart and say whether you can justly look with contempt even upon a convict.

Is it not possible that the tyranny of governments, the injustice of nations, the fierceness of what is called the law, produce in the individual a tendency in the same direction? Is it not true that the citizen is apt to imitate his nation? Society degrades its enemies—the individual seeks to degrade his. Society plunders its enemies, and now and then the citizen has the desire to plunder his. Society kills its enemies, and possibly sows in the heart of some citizen the seeds of murder.

Only a few years ago there were more than two hundred offences in Great Britain punishable by death. The gallows-tree bore fruit through all the year, and the hangman was the busiest official in the kingdom—but the criminals increased.

Crimes were committed to punish crimes, and crimes were committed to prevent crimes. The world has been filled with prisons and dungeons, with chains and whips, with crosses and gibbets, with thumb-screws and racks, with hangmen and headsmen—and yet these frightful means and instrumentalities and crimes have accomplished little for the preservation of property or life. It is safe to say that governments have committed far more crimes than they have prevented. As long as society bows and cringes before the great thieves, there will be little ones enough to fill the jails.

There is but one hope. Ignorance, poverty, and vice must stop populating the world. This cannot be done by moral suasion. This cannot be done by talk or example. This cannot be done by religion or by law, by priest or by hangman. This cannot be done by force, physical or moral.

To accomplish this there is but one way. Science must make woman the owner, the mistress of herself. Science, the only possible savior of mankind, must put it in the power of woman to decide for herself whether she will or will not become a mother.

This is the solution of the whole question. This frees woman. The babes that are then born will be welcome. They will be clasped with glad hands to happy breasts. They will fill homes with light and joy.

When that time comes the prison walls will fall, the dungeons will be flooded with light, and the shadow of the scaffold will cease to curse the earth. Poverty and crime will be childless.

Labor.—Give to every man the fruit of his own labor—the labor of his hand and of his brain.

I propose to say a few words upon subjects that are near to us all, and in which every human being ought to be interested—and if he is not, it may be that his wife will be, it may be that his orphans will be; and I would like to see this world, at last, so that a man could die and not feel that he left his wife and children a prey to the greed, the avarice, or the cruelties of mankind. There is something wrong in a government where they who do the most have the least. There is something wrong when honesty wears a rag, and rascality a robe; when the loving, the tender, eat a crust, while the infamous sit at banquets.

The struggle is so hard. And just exactly as we have risen in the scale of being, the per cent. of failures has increased. It is so that all men are not capable of getting a living. They are not cunning enough, have not intelligence enough, muscle enough—they are not strong enough. They are too generous, or they are too negligent; and then some people seem to have what is called "bad luck"—that is to say, when anything falls, they are under it; when anything bad happens, it happens to them.

And now there is another trouble. Just as life becomes complex and as every one is trying to accomplish certain objects, all the ingenuity of the brain is at work to get there by a shorter way, and, in consequence, this has been an age of invention. Myriads of machines have been invented—every one of them to save labor. If these machines helped the laborer, what a blessing they would be! But the laborer does not own the machine; the machine owns him. That is the trouble.

. . . . We have got into that contest between machines

and men, and if extravagance does not keep pace with ingenuity, it is going to be the most terrible question that man has ever settled.

Land.—No man should be allowed to own any land that he does not use. Everybody knows that—I do not care whether he has thousands or millions. I have owned a great deal of land, but I know just as well as I know I am living that I should not be allowed to have it unless I use it. And why? Don't you know that if people could bottle the air, they would? Don't you know that there would be an American Air-bottling Association? And don't you know that they would allow thousands and millions to die for want of breath, if they could not pay for air? I am not blaming anybody. I am just telling how it is. Now, the land belongs to the children of nature. Nature invites into this world every babe that is born. And what would you think of me, for instance, tonight, if I had invited you here—nobody had charged you anything, but you had been invited—and when you got here you had found one man pretending to occupy a hundred seats, another fifty, and another seventy-five, and thereupon you were compelled to stand up—what would you think of the invitation? It seems to me that every child of nature is entitled to his share of the land, and that he should not be compelled to beg the privilege to work the soil, of a babe that happened to be born before him. And why do I say this? Because it is not to our interest to have a few landlords and millions of tenants.

The tenement house is the enemy of modesty, the enemy of virtue, the enemy of patriotism. Home is where the virtues grow. I would like to see the law so that every home, to a small amount, should be free, not only from sale for debts, but should be absolutely free from taxation, so that every man could have a home.

XVIII
HENRY GEORGE

Henry George, born at Philadelphia, 1839; died at New York, 1897. American writer on political economy and sociology. Went to sea at an early age, and in 1858 settled in California, where he became a journalist. In 1879 he published his chief work, *Progress and Poverty,* expounding the principles of the Single Tax. It has been more universally read than any other work on the subject. He went to New York in 1880; was an unsuccessful candidate of the United Labor Party for the mayoralty in 1886; afterwards founded a weekly paper, *The Standard.* Other works include *The Land Question,* 1883; *Social Problems,* 1884; *Protection or Free Trade,* 1886; *The Science of Political Economy,* 1897; *A Perplexed Philosopher,* 1892. His biography has been published by his son, Henry George Jr.

The selections are from *Progress and Poverty, Social Problems,* and *Protection or Free Trade.*

Liberty.—We honor Liberty in name and in form. We set up her statues and sound her praises. But we have not fully trusted her. And with our growth so grow her demands. She will have no half service!

Liberty! it is a word to conjure with, not to vex the ear in empty boastings. For Liberty means Justice, and Justice is the natural law—the law of health and symmetry and strength, of fraternity and co-operation.

They who look upon Liberty as having accomplished her mission when she has abolished hereditary privileges and given men the ballot, who think of her as having no further relations to the everyday affairs of life, have not seen her real grandeur,—to them the poets who have sung of her must seem rhapsodists, and her martyrs fools! As the sun is the lord of life, as well as of light; as his beams not merely pierce the clouds, but support all growth, supply all motion, and call forth from what would otherwise be a cold and inert mass all the infinite diversities of being and beauty, so is liberty to mankind. It is not for an abstraction that men have toiled and died; that in every age the witnesses of Liberty have stood forth, and the martyrs of Liberty have suffered.

We speak of Liberty as one thing, and of virtue, wealth, knowledge, invention, national strength and national independence as other things. But, of all these, Liberty is the source, the mother, the necessary condition. She is to virtue what light is to color.; to wealth what sunshine is to grain; to knowledge what eyes are to sight. She is the genius of invention, the brawn of national strength, the spirit of national independence. Where Liberty rises, there virtue grows, wealth increases, knowledge expands, invention multiplies human powers, and in strength and spirit the freer nation rises among her neighbors as Saul amid his brethren—taller and fairer. Where Liberty sinks, there virtue fades, wealth diminishes, knowledge is forgotten, invention ceases, and empires once mighty in arms and arts become a helpless prey to freer barbarians!

Only in broken gleams and partial light has the sun of Liberty yet beamed upon men, but all progress hath she called forth.

Liberty came to a race of slaves crouching under Egyptian whips, and led them forth from the House of Bondage. She hardened them in the desert and made of them a race of conquerors. The free spirit of the Mosaic law took their thinkers up to heights where they beheld the unity of God, and inspired their poets with strains that yet phrase the highest exaltations of thought. Liberty dawned on the Phoenician coast, and ships passed the Pillars of Hercules to plow the unknown sea. She shed a partial light on Greece, and marble grew to shapes of ideal beauty, words became the instruments of subtlest thought, and against the scanty militia of free cities the countless hosts of the Great King broke like surges against a rock. She cast her beams on the four-acre farms of Italian husbandmen, and born of her strength a power came forth that conquered the world. They glinted from shields of German warriors, and Augustus wept his legions. Out of the night that followed her eclipse, her slanting rays fell again on free cities, and a lost learning revived, modern civilization began, a new world was unveiled; and as Liberty grew, so grew art, wealth, power, knowledge, and refinement. In the history of every nation we may read the same truth. It was the strength born of Magna Charta that won Crecy and Agincourt. It was the revival of Liberty from the despotism of the Tudors that glorified the Elizabethan age. It was the spirit that brought a crowned tyrant to the block that planted here the seed of a mighty tree. It was the energy of ancient freedom, that, the moment it had gained unity, made Spain the mightiest power of the world, only to fall to the lowest depths of weakness when tyranny succeeded liberty. See, in France, all intellectual vigor dying under the tyranny of the Seventeenth century to revive in splendor as Liberty awoke in the Eighteenth, and on the enfranchisement of French peasants in the Great Revolution, basing the wonderful strength that has in our time defied defeat.

Shall we not trust her?

In our time, as in times before, creep on the insidious forces that, producing inequality, destroy Liberty. On the horizon the clouds begin to lower. Liberty calls to us again. We must follow her further; we must trust her fully. Either we must wholly accept her or she will not stay. It is not enough that men should vote; it is not enough that they should be theoretically equal before the law. They must have liberty to avail themselves of the opportunities and means of life; they must stand on equal terms with reference to the bounty of nature. Either this, or Liberty withdraws her light! Either this, or darkness comes on, and the very forces that progress has evolved turn to powers that work destruction. This is the universal law. This is the lesson of the centuries. Unless its foundations be laid in justice the social structure cannot stand.

Let us not disguise it. Over and over again has the standard of Truth and Justice been raised in this world. Over and over again has it been trampled down—oftentimes in blood. If they are weak forces that are opposed to Truth, how should

Error so long prevail? If Justice has but to raise her head to have Injustice flee before her, how should the wail of the oppressed so long go up?

But for those who see Truth and would follow her; for those who recognize Justice and would stand for her, success is not the only thing. Success! Why, Falsehood has often that to give; and Injustice often has that to give. Must not Truth and Justice have something to give that is their own by proper right—theirs in essence, and not by accident?

Land.—The equal right of all men to the use of land is as clear as their equal right to breathe the air—it is a right proclaimed by the fact of their existence. For we cannot suppose that some men have a right to be in this world and others no right.

The recognition of individual proprietorship of land is the denial of the natural rights of other individuals—it is a wrong which must show itself in the inequitable division of wealth. For as labor cannot produce without the use of land, the denial of the equal right to the use of land is necessarily the denial of the right of labor to its own produce. If one man can command the land upon which others must labor, he can appropriate the produce of their labor as the price of his permission to labor. The fundamental law of nature, that her enjoyment by man shall be consequent upon his exertion, is thus violated. The one receives without producing; the others produce without receiving. The one is unjustly enriched; the others are robbed. To this fundamental wrong we have traced the unjust distribution of wealth which is separating modern society into the very rich and the very poor. It is the continuous increase of rent—the price that labor is compelled to pay for the use of land, which strips the many of the wealth they justly earn, to pile it up in the hands of the few, who do nothing to earn it.

Why should they who suffer from this injustice hesitate for one moment to sweep it away? Who are the land holders that they should thus be permitted to reap where they have not sown?

Consider for a moment the utter absurdity of the titles by which we permit to be gravely passed from John Doe to Richard Roe the right exclusively to possess the earth, giving absolute dominion as against all others. In California our land titles go back to the Supreme Government of Mexico, who took from the Spanish King, who took from the Pope, when by a stroke of the pen he divided lands yet to be discovered between the Spanish or Portugese—or if you please they rest upon conquest. In the Eastern States they go back to treaties with the Indians and grants from the English Kings; in Louisiana to the Government of France; in Florida to the Government of Spain; while in England they go back to the Norman conquerors. Everywhere, not to a right which obliges, but to a force which compels. And when a title rests but on force, no complaint can be made when force annuls it. Whenever the people, having the power, choose to annul those titles, no objection can be made in the name of justice. There have existed men who had the power to hold or to give exclusive possession of portions of the earth's surface, but when and where did there exist the human being who had the right?

The right to exclusive ownership of anything of human production is clear. No matter how many the hands through which it has passed, there was, at the beginning of the line, human labor—some one who, having procured or produced by his exertions, had to it a clear title as against all the rest of mankind, and which could justly pass from one to another by sale or gift. But at the end of what string of conveyances or grants can be shown or supposed a like title to any part of the material universe? To improvements such an original title can be shown; but it is a title only to the improvements and not to the land itself. If I clear a forest, drain a swamp, or fill a morass, all I can justly claim is the value given by these exertions. They give me no right to the land itself, no claim other than to my equal share with every other member of the community in the value which is added to it by the growth of the community.

But it will be said: There are improvements which in time become indistinguishable from the land itself! Very well; then the titles to the improvements become blended with the title to the land; the individual right is lost in the common right. It is the greater that swallows up the less, not the less that swallows up the greater. Nature does not proceed from man, but man from nature, and it is into the bosom of nature that he and all his works must return again.

Yet, it will be said: As every man has a right to the use and enjoyment of nature, the man who is using land must be permitted the exclusive right to its use in order that he may get the full benefit of his labor. But there is no difficulty in determining where the individual right ends and the common right begins. A delicate and exact test is supplied by value, and with its aid there is no difficulty, no matter how dense population may become, in determining and securing the exact rights of each, the equal rights of all. The value of land, as we have seen, is the price of monopoly. It is not the absolute, but the relative, capability of land that determines its value. No matter what may be its intrinsic qualities, land that is no better than other land which may be had for the using can have no value. And the value of land always measures the difference between it and the best land that may be had for the using. Thus, the value of land expresses in exact and tangible form the right of the community in land held by an individual; and rent expresses the exact amount which the individual should pay to the community to satisfy the equal rights of all other members of the community. Thus, if we concede to priority of possession the undisturbed use of land, confiscating rent for the benefit of the community, we reconcile the fixity of tenure which is necessary for improvement with a full and complete recognition of the equal rights of all to the use of land.

As for the deduction of a complete and exclusive individual right to land from priority of occupation, that is, if possible, the most absurd ground on which land ownership can be defended. Priority of occupation give exclusive and perpetual title to the surface of a globe on which, in the order of nature, countless generations succeed each other! Had the men of the last generation any better right to the use of this world than we of this? or the men of a hundred years ago? or of a thousand years ago? Had the mound-builders, or the cave-dwellers, the contemporaries of the mastodon and the three-toed horse, or the generations still further back, who, in dim aeons that we can think of only as geologic periods, followed each other on the earth we now tenant for our little day?

Has the first comer at a banquet the right to turn back all the chairs and claim that none of the other guests shall partake of the food provided, except as they make terms with him? Does the first man who presents a ticket at the door of a theater, and passes in, acquire by his priority the right to shut the doors and have the performance go on for him alone? Does the first passenger who enters a railroad car obtain the right to scatter his baggage over all the seats and compel the passengers who come in after him to stand up?

The cases are perfectly analogous. We arrive and we depart, guests at a banquet continually spread, spectators and participants in an entertainment where there is room for all who come; passengers from station to station, on an orb that whirls through space—our rights to take and possess cannot be exclusive; they must be bounded everywhere by the equal rights of others. Just as the passenger in a railroad car may spread himself and his baggage over as many seats as he pleases, until other passengers come in, so may a settler take and use as much land as he chooses, until it is needed by others—a fact which is shown by the land acquiring a value—when his right must be curtailed by the equal rights of the others, and no priority of appropriation can have a right which will bar these equal rights of others. If this were not the case, then by priority of appropriation one man could acquire and could transmit to whom he pleased, not merely the exclusive right to 160 acres, or to 640 acres, but to a whole township, a whole State, a whole continent.

And to this manifest absurdity does the recognition of individual right to land come when carried to its ultimate—that any one human being, could he concentrate in himself the individual rights to the land of any country, could expel therefrom all the rest of its inhabitants; and could he thus concentrate the individual rights to the whole surface of the globe, he alone of all the teeming population of the earth would have the right to live.

Single Tax.—But a question of method remains. How shall we do it?

We should satisfy the law of justice, we should meet all economic requirements, by at one stroke abolishing all private titles, declaring all land public property, and letting it out to the highest bidders in lots to suit, under such conditions as would sacredly guard the private right to improvements.

Thus we would secure, in a more complex state of society, the same equality of rights which in a ruder state were secured by equal partitions of the soil, and by giving the use of the land to whoever could procure the most from it we should secure the greatest production.

I do not propose either to purchase or to confiscate private property in land. The first would be unjust; the second, needless. Let the individuals who now hold it still retain, if they want to, possession of what they are pleased to call their land. Let them continue to call it their land. Let them buy and sell, and bequeath and devise it. We may safely leave them the shell, if we take the kernel. It is not necessary to confiscate land; it is only necessary to confiscate rent.

Nor to take rent for public uses it is necessary that the State should bother with the letting of lands, and assume the chances of the favoritism, collusion, and corruption this might involve. It is not necessary that any new machinery should be created. The machinery already exists. Instead of extending it, all we have to do is to simplify and reduce it. By leaving to land owners a percentage of rent which would probably be much less than the cost and less involved in attempting to rent lands through State agency, and by making use of this existing machinery, we may, without jar or shock, assert the common right to land by taking rent for public uses.

We already take some rent in taxation. We have only to make some changes in our modes of taxation to take it all.

What I, therefore, propose, as the simple yet sovereign remedy, which will raise wages, increase the earnings of capital, extirpate pauperism, abolish poverty, give remunerative employment to whoever wishes it, afford free scope to human powers, lessen crime, elevate morals, and taste, and intelligence, purify government and carry civilization to yet nobler heights, is—to appropriate rent by taxation.

In this way the State may become the universal landlord without calling herself so, and without assuming a single new function. In form, the ownership of land need not be dispossessed, and no restriction need be placed upon the amount of land anyone could hold. For, rent being taken by the State in taxes, land, no matter in whose name it stood, or in what parcels it was held, would be really common property, and every member of the community would participate in the advantages of its ownership.

Now, insomuch as the taxation of rent, or land values, must necessarily be increased just as we abolish other taxes, we may put the proposition into practical form by proposing—

To abolish all taxation save that upon land values.

As we have seen, the value of land is at the beginning of society nothing, but as society develops by the increase of population and the advance of the arts, it becomes greater and greater. In every civilized country, even the newest, the value of the land taken as a whole is sufficient to bear the entire expenses of government. In the better developed countries it is much more than sufficient. Hence it will not be enough merely to place all taxes upon the value of land. It will be necessary, where rent exceeds the present governmental revenues, commensurately to increase the amount demanded in taxation, and to continue this increase as society progresses and rent advances. But this is so natural and easy a matter, that it may be considered as involved, or at least understood, in the proposition to put all taxes on the value of land. That is the first step, upon which the practical struggle must be made. When the hare is once caught and killed, cooking him will follow as a matter of course. When the common right to land is so far appreciated that all taxes are abolished save those which fall upon rent, there is no danger of much more than is necessary to induce them to collect the public revenues being left to individual land holders.

Experience has taught me (for I have been for some years endeavoring to popularize this proposition) that wherever the idea of concentrating all taxation upon land values finds lodgment sufficient to induce consideration, it invariably makes way, but that there are few of the classes most to be benefited by it, who at first, or even for a long time afterward, see its full significance and power. It is difficult for workingmen to get over the idea that there is a real antagonism between capital and labor. It is difficult for small farmers and homestead owners to get over the idea that to put all taxes on the value of land would be unduly to tax them. It is difficult for both classes to get over the idea that to exempt capital from taxation would be to make the rich richer, and the poor poorer. These ideas spring from confused thought. But behind ignorance and prejudice there is a powerful interest, which has hitherto dominated literature, education, and opinion. A great wrong always dies hard, and the great wrong which in every civilized country condemns the masses of men to poverty and want will not die without a bitter struggle.

But all other monopolies are trivial in extent as compared with the monopoly of land. And the value of land expressing a monopoly, pure and simple, is in every respect fitted for taxation. That is to say, while the value of a railroad or telegraph line, the price of gas or of a patent medicine, may express the price of monopoly, it also expresses the exertion of labor and capital; but the value of land, or economic rent, as we have seen, is in no part made up from these factors, and expresses nothing but the advantage of appropriation. Taxes levied upon the value of land cannot check production in the slightest degree, until they exceed rent, or the value of land taken annually, for unlike taxes upon commodities, or exchange, or capital, or any of the tools or processes of production, they do not bear upon production. The value of land does not express reward of production, as does the value of crops, of cattle, of buildings, or any of the things which are styled personal property and improvements. It expresses the exchange value of monopoly. It is not in any case the creation of the individual who owns the land; it is created by the growth of the community. Hence the community can take it all without in any way lessening the incentive to improvement or in the slightest degree lessening the production of wealth. Taxes may be imposed upon the value of land until all rent is taken by the State, without reducing the wages of labor or the reward of capital one iota; without increasing the price of a single commodity, or making production in any way more difficult.

Patent Rights.—No man can justly claim ownership in natural laws, nor in any of the relations which may be perceived by the human mind, nor in any of the potentialities which nature holds for it. . . . Ownership comes from production. It cannot come from discovery. Discovery can give no right of ownership. . . . . No man can discover anything which, so to speak, was not put there to be discovered, and which someone else might not in time have discovered. If he finds it, it was not lost. It, or its potentiality, existed before he came. It was there to be found. . . . In the production of any material thing—a machine, for instance—there are two separable parts,—the abstract idea or principle, which may be usually expressed by drawing, by writing, or by word of mouth; and the concrete form of the particular machine itself, which is produced by bringing together in certain relations certain quantities and qualities of matter, such as wood, steel, brass, brick, rubber, cloth, etc. There are two modes in which labor goes to the making of the machine,—the one in ascertaining the principle on which such machines can be made to work; the other in obtaining from their natural reservoirs and bringing together and fashioning into shape the quantities and qualities of matter which in their combination constitute the concrete machine. In the first mode labor is expended in discovery. In the second mode it is expended in production. The work of discovery may be done once for all, as in the case of the discovery in prehistoric time of the principle or idea of the wheelbarrow. But the work of production is required afresh in the case of each particular thing. No matter how many thousand millions of wheelbarrows have been produced, it requires fresh labor of production to make another one. . . . The natural reward of labor expended in discovery is in the use that can be made of the discovery without interference with the right of any one else to use it. But to this natural reward our patent laws endeavor to add an artificial reward. Although the effect of giving to the discoverers of useful devices or processes an absolute right to their exclusive use would be to burden all industry with most grievous monopolies, and to greatly retard, if not put a stop to, further inventions, yet the theory of our patent laws is that we can stimulate discoveries by giving a modified right of ownership in their use for a term of years. In this we seek by special laws to give a special reward to labor expended in discovery, which does not belong to it of natural right, and is of the nature of a bounty. But as for labor expended in the second of these modes,—in the production of the machine by the bringing together in certain relations of certain quantities and qualities of matter,—we need no special laws to reward that. Absolute ownership attaches to the results of such labor, not by special law, but by common law. And if all human laws were abolished, men would still hold that, whether it were a wheelbarrow or a phonograph, the concrete thing belonged to the man who produced it. And this, not for a term of years, but in perpetuity. It would pass at his death to his heirs or to those to whom he devised it.

Freedom in Trade.—Near the window by which I write a great bull is tethered by a ring in his nose. Grazing round and round he has wound his rope about the stake until now he stands a close prisoner, tantalized by rich grass he cannot reach, unable even to toss his head to rid him of the flies that cluster on his shoulders. Now and again he struggles vainly, and then, after pitiful bellowings, relapses into silent misery.

This bull, a very type of massive strength, who, because he has not wit enough to see how he might be free, suffers want in sight of plenty, and is helplessly preyed upon by weaker creatures, seems to me no unfit emblem of the working masses.

In all lands, men whose toil creates abounding wealth are pinched with poverty, and, while advancing civilization opens wider vistas and awakens new desires, are held down to brute levels by animal needs. Bitterly conscious of injustice, feeling in their inmost souls that they were made for more than so narrow a life, they, too, spasmodically struggle and cry out. But until they trace effect to cause, until they see how they are fettered and how they may be freed, their struggles and outcries are as vain as those of the bull. Nay, they are vainer. I shall go out and drive the bull in the way that will untwist his rope. But who shall drive men into freedom? Till they use the reason with which they have been gifted, nothing can avail.

Protection implies prevention. To protect is to preserve or defend.

What is it that protection by tariff prevents? It is trade. To speak more exactly, it is that part of trade which consists in bringing in from other countries commodities that might be produced at home.

But trade, from which "protection" essays to preserve and defend us, is not, like flood, earthquake, or tornado, something that comes without human agency. Trade implies human action. There can be no need of preserving from or defending against trade, unless there are men who want to trade and try to trade. Who, then, are the men against whose efforts to trade "protection" preserves and defends us?

If I had been asked this question before I had come to think over the matter for myself, I should have said that the men against whom "protection" defends us are foreign producers who wish to sell their goods in our home markets. This is the assumption that runs through all protectionist arguments—the assumption that foreigners are constantly trying to force their products upon us, and that a protective tariff is a means for defending ourselves against what they want to do.

Yet a moment's thought will show that no effort of foreigners to sell us their products could of itself make a tariff necessary. For the desire of one party, however strong it may be, cannot of itself bring about trade. To every trade there must be two parties who mutually desire to trade, and whose actions are reciprocal. No one can buy unless he can find some one willing to sell; and no one can sell unless there is some other one willing to buy. If Americans did not want to buy foreign goods, foreign goods could not be sold here even if there were no tariff. The efficient cause of the trade which our tariff aims to prevent is the desire of Americans to buy foreign goods, not the desire of foreign producers to sell them. Thus protection really prevents what the "protected" themselves want to do. It is not from foreigners that protection preserves and defends us; it is from ourselves.

Trade is not invasion. It does not involve aggression on one side and resistance on the other, but mutual consent and gratification. There cannot be a trade unless the parties to it agree, any more than there can be a quarrel unless the parties to it differ. England, we say, forced trade with the outside world upon China, and the United States upon Japan. But, in both cases, what was done was not to force the people to trade, but to force their governments to let them. If the people had not wanted to trade, the opening of the ports would have been useless. . . .

Looking further, we see in every direction that it is not the fact that low-priced labor gives advantage in production. If this is the fact, how was it that the development of industry in the slave states of the American Union was not more rapid than in the free states? How is it that Mexico, where peon labor can be had for from four to six dollars a month, does not undersell the products of our more highly paid labor? How is it that China and India and Japan are not "flooding the world" with the products of their cheap labor? How is it that England, where labor is better paid than on the Continent, leads the whole of Europe in commerce and manufactures? The truth is, that a low rate of wages does not mean a low cost of production, but the reverse. The universal and obvious truth is, that the country where wages are highest can produce with the greatest economy, because workmen have there the most intelligence, the most spirit, and the most ability; because invention and discovery are there most quickly made and most readily utilized. The great inventions and discoveries which so enormously increase the power of human labor to produce wealth have all been made in countries where wages are comparatively high.

That low wages mean inefficient labor may be seen whatever we look. Half a dozen Bengalese carpenters are needed to do a job that one American carpenter can do in less time. American residents in China get servants for almost nothing, but find that so many are required that servants cost more than in the United States; yet the Chinese who are largely employed in domestic service in California, and get wages that they would not have dreamed of in China, are efficient workers. Go to High Bridge, and you will see a great engine attended by a few men, exerting the power of thousands of horses in pumping up a small river for the supply of New York City, while on the Nile you may see Egyptian fellahs raising water by buckets and tread-wheels. In Mexico, with labor at four or five dollars a month, silver ore has for centuries been carried to the surface on the backs of men who climbed rude ladders, but when silver mining began in Nevada, where labor could not be had for less than five or six dollars a day, steam power was employed. In Russia, where wages are very low, grain is still reaped by the sickle and threshed with the flail or by the hoofs of horses, while in our Western States, where labor is very high as compared with the Russian standard, grain is reaped, threshed and sacked by machinery.

If it were true that equal amounts of labor always produced equal results, then cheap labor might mean cheap production. But this is obviously untrue. The power of human muscle is, indeed, much the same everywhere, and if his wages be sufficient to keep him in good bodily health the poorly paid laborer can, perhaps, exert as much physical force as the highly paid laborer. But the power of human muscles, though necessary to all production, is not the primary and efficient force in production. That force is human intelligence, and human muscles are merely the agency by which that intelligence makes connection with and takes hold of external things, so as to utilize natural forces and mould matter to conformity with its desires. A race of intelligent pygmies with muscles no stronger than those of the grasshopper could produce far more wealth than a race of stupid giants with muscles as strong as those of the elephant. Now, intelligence varies with the standard of comfort, and the standard of comfort varies with wages. Wherever men are condemned to a poor, hard and precarious living their mental qualities sink toward the level of the brute. Wherever easier conditions prevail, the qualities that raise man above the brute and give him power to master and compel external nature develop and expand. And so it is that the efficiency of labor is greatest where laborers get the best living and have the most leisure—that is to say, where wages are highest.

The free trade principle is, as we have seen, the principle of free production—it requires not merely the abolition of protective tariffs, but the removal of all restrictions upon production.

Within recent years a class of restrictions on production, imposed by concentrations and combinations which have for their purpose the limiting of production and the increase of prices, have begun to make themselves felt and to assume greater and greater importance.

This power of combinations to restrict production arises in some cases from temporary monopolies granted by our patent laws, which (being the premium that society holds out to invention) have a compensatory principle, however faulty they may be in method.

Such cases aside, this power of restricting production is derived, in part, from tariff restrictions. Thus the American steel makers who have recently limited their production, and put up the price of rails 40 per cent. at one stroke, are enabled to do this only by the heavy duty on imported rails. They are able, by a combination, to put up the price of steel rails to the point at which they could be imported plus the duty, but no further. Hence, with the abolition of the duty this power would be gone. To prevent the play of competition, a combination of the steel workers of the whole world would then be necessary, and this is practically impossible.

In other part, this restrictive power arises from ability to monopolize natural advantages. This would be destroyed if the taxation of land values made it unprofitable to hold land without using it. In still other part, it arises from the control of businesses which in their nature do not admit of competition, such as those of railway, telegraph, gas, and other similar companies.

I read in the daily papers that half a dozen representatives of the "anthracite coal interest" met last evening (March 24, 1886) in an office in New York. Their conference, interrupted only by a collation, lasted till three o'clock in the morning. When they separated they had come to "an understanding among gentlemen" to restrict the production of anthracite coal and advance its price.

Now how comes it that half a dozen men, sitting around some bottles of champagne and a box of cigars in a New York office, can by an "understanding among gentlemen" compel Pennsylvania miners to stand idle, and advance the price of coal along the whole eastern seaboard? The power thus exercised is derived in various parts from three sources.

1. From the protective duty on coal. Free trade would abolish that.

2. From the power to monopolize land, which enables them to prevent others from using coal desposits which they will not use themselves. True free trade, as we have seen, would abolish that.

3. From the control of railways, and the consequent power of fixing rates and making discriminations in transportation.

The power of fixing rates of transportation, and in this way of discriminating against persons and places, is a power essentially of the same nature as that exercised by governments in levying import duties. And the principle of free trade as clearly requires the removal of such restrictions as it requires the removal of import duties.

In throwing open our ports to the commerce of the world we

shall far better secure their safety than by fortifying them with all the "protected" plates that our steel ring could make. For not merely would free trade give us again that mastery of the ocean which protection has deprived us of, and stimulate the productive power in which real fighting strength lies; but while steel-clad forts could afford no defence against the dynamite-dropping balloons and death-dealing airships which will be the next product of destructive invention, free trade would prevent their ever being sent against us. The spirit of protectionism, which is the real thing that it is sought to defend by steel-plating, is that of national enmity and strife. The spirit of free trade is that of fraternity and peace.

A nobler career is open to the American Republic than the servile imitation of European follies and vices. Instead of following in what is mean and low, she may lead toward what is grand and high.

This league of sovereign states, settling their differences by a common tribunal and opposing no impediments to trade and travel, has in it possibilities of giving to the world a more than Roman peace.

What are the real substantial advantages of this Union of ours? Are they not summed up in the absolute freedom of trade which it secures, and the community of interests that grows out of this freedom? If our states were fighting each other with hostile tariffs, and a citizen could not cross a state boundary line without having his baggage searched, or a book printed in New York could not be sent across the river to Jersey City without being held in the postoffice until duty was paid, how long would our Union last, or what would it be worth? The true benefits of our Union, the true basis of the interstate peace it secures, is that it has prevented the establishment of state tariffs and given us free trade over the better part of a continent.

We may "extend the area of freedom" whenever we choose to—whenever we apply to our intercourse with other nations the same principle that we apply to intercourse between our states. We may annex Canada to all intents and purposes whenever we throw down the tariff wall we have built around ourselves. We need not ask for any reciprocity; if we abolish our custom-houses and call off our baggage searchers and Bible confiscators, Canada would not and could not maintain hers. This would make the two countries practically one. Whether the Canadians chose to maintain a separate Parliament and pay a British lordling for keeping up a mock court at Rideau Hall need not in the slightest concern us. The intimate relations that would come of unrestricted commerce would soon obliterate the boundary line; and mutual interest and mutual convenience would speedily induce the extension over both countries of the same general laws and institutions.

And so would it be with our kindred over the sea. With the abolition of our custom-houses and the opening of our ports to the free entry of all good things, the trade between the British Islands and the United States would become so immense, the intercourse so intimate, that we should become one people, and would inevitably so conform currency and postal system and general laws that Englishman and American would feel themselves as much citizens of a common country as do New Yorker and Californian. Three thousand miles of water are no more of an impediment to this than are three thousand miles of land. And with relations so close, ties of blood and language would assert their power, and mutual interest, general convenience and fraternal feeling might soon lead to a pact which, in the words of our own Constitution, would unite all the English speaking peoples in a league "to establish justice, insure domestic tranquillity, for the common defence, promote the general welfare and secure the blessings of liberty."

Thus would free trade unite what a century ago protectionism severed, and in a federation of the nations of English speech—the world-tongue of the future—take the first step to a federation of mankind.

And upon our relations with all other nations our repudiation of protection would have a similar tendency. The sending of delegations to ask the trade of our sister republics of Spanish America avails nothing so long as we maintain a tariff which repels their trade. We have but to open our ports to draw their trade to us and avail ourselves of all their natural advantages.

And more potent than anything else would be the moral influence of our action. The spectacle of a continental republic such as ours really putting her faith in the principle of freedom would revolutionize the civilized world.

The dangers to the Republic come not from without but from within. What menaces her safety is no armada launched from European shores, but the gathering cloud of tramps in her own highways.

That Krupp is casting monstrous cannon and that in Cherbourg and Woolwich projectiles of unheard-of destructiveness are being stored, need not alarm her, but there is black omen in the fact that Pennsylvania miners are working for 65 cents a day. No triumphant invader can tread our soil till the blight of "great estates" has brought "failure of the crop of men"; if there be danger that our cities blaze, it is from torches lit in faction fight, not from foreign shells.

Against such dangers forts will not guard us, iron-clads protect us, or standing armies prove of any avail. They are not to be avoided by any aping of European protectionism; they come from our failure to be true to that spirit of liberty which was invoked at the formation of the Republic. They are only to be avoided by conforming our institutions to the principle of freedom.

For it is true, as was declared by the first National Assembly of France, that "ignorance, neglect, or contempt of human rights are the sole causes of public misfortunes and corruptions of government."

Here is the conclusion of the whole matter: That we should

do unto others as we would have them do to us. That we should respect the rights of others as scrupulously as we would have our own rights respected is not a mere counsel of perfection to individuals, but it is the law to which we must conform social institutions and national policy, if we would secure the blessings of abundance and peace.

XIX
LYOFF N. TOLSTOY

Lyoff N. Tolstoy, 1828-1911, novelist, social and religious reformer, political non-resistant. Born in the government of Tula, Russia. Educated at University of Kazan; appointed commander of a battery in the Army of the Caucasus in Crimean war, 1855; fought in the battle of the Tchernaya, was in the storming of Sebastopol, and sent as a special courier to St. Petersburg. After liberation of serfs, lived on his estates, working with and relieving the peasants and devoting himself to study and literature. He became a pronounced recluse, living the life of the peasant, and his last years were spent in rigid self-denial, altruism and loneliness. In his attitude toward government Tolstoy was an Anarchist, and his later works reflect his Anarchistic philosophy. His works include *War and Peace* (1865-68) and *Anna Karenina* (1875-78), novels; *Sevastopol*, 1853-55; *The Cossacks, Ivan Ilyitch*, 1886; *Two Pilgrims; Childhood, Boyhood, and Youth; My Religion*, 1885; *My Confession; A Commentary on the Gospel; Life; The Kreutzer Sonata*, 1890; *Church and State, and Other Essays*, including *Money*, 1891 (Benj. R. Tucker); *The Slavery of Our Times*, 1900; *War*, 1892.

Selections are from *Money, The Slavery of our Times,* and *War.*

War.—When kings are tried and executed like Charles I, Louis XVI, Maximilian of Mexico, or killed in a palace conspiracy like Peter III, Paul, and all kinds of sultans, shahs, and khans, the event is generally passed over in silence. But when one of them is killed without a trial, and not by a palace conspiracy, like Henry IV, Alexander II, Carnot, the Empress of Austria, the Shah of Persia, and just now King Humbert, then such murder causes great surprise and indignation among kings and emperors, and those attached to them, as if these persons were the great enemies of murder, as if they never profited by murder, never took part in it, and never gave orders to commit it. And yet the kindest of these murdered kings, such as Alexander II or Humbert, were guilty of the murder of tens of thousands of persons killed on the battlefield, not to mention those executed at home; while hundreds of thousands, even millions of people have been killed, hanged, beaten to death or shot, by the more cruel kings and emperors. Kings and emperors should not be indignant when such murders as that of Alexander II or Humbert occur, but should, on the contrary, be surprised that such murders are rare, considering the continual and universal example of committing murders they themselves set the people. Kings and emperors are surprised and horrified when one of themselves is murdered, and yet the whole of their activity consists in managing murder and preparing for murder. The keeping up, the teaching and exercising of armies with which kings and emperors are always so much occupied, and of which they are the organizers, what is it but preparation for murder?

The masses are so hypnotized that, though they see what is continually going on around them, they do not understand what it means. They see the unceasing care kings, emperors, and presidents bestow on disciplined armies, see the parades, reviews, and maneuvers they hold, and of which they boast to one another, and the people eagerly crowd to see how their own brothers, dressed up in bright-colored, glittering clothes, are turned into machines to the sound of drums and trumpets, and who, obedient to the shouting of one man, all make the same movements; and they do not understand the meaning of it all. Yet the meaning of such drilling is very clear and simple. It is preparing for murder. It means the stupefying of men in order to convert them into instruments for murdering. And it is just kings and emperors and presidents who do it, and organize it and pride themselves on it. And it is these same people whose special employment is murder-organizing, who have made murder their profession, who dress in military uniforms, carry weapons (swords at their side), who are horror-struck and indignant when one of themselves is killed.

It is not because such murders as the recent murder of Humbert are exceptionally cruel that they are so terrible. Things done by the order of kings and emperors, not only in the days of old, such as the massacre of St. Bartholomew, persecutions for faith, terrible ways of putting down peasant riots, but also the present executions, the torture of solitary confine-ments and disciplinary battalions, hanging, decapitation, shooting and slaughter at the wars, are incomparably more cruel than the murders committed by Anarchists. It is not on account of their injustice that these murders are terrible. If Alexander and Humbert did not deserve death, the thousands of Russians who perished at Plevna, and Italians who perished in Abyssinia, deserved it even less. No, it is not because of their cruelty and injustice these murders are terrible, but because of the want of reason in those who perpetrate them. If the regicides commit murder under the influence of their feeling of indignation evoked by witnessing the sufferings of the enslaved people, for which sufferings they hold Alexander II, Carnot, or Humbert responsible, or by the personal feeling of desire for revenge, however immoral such person's conduct may be, still it is comprehensible; but how can an organized body of Anarchists by whom, as it is now reported, Bressi was sent out, and by whom another emperor was threatened, how can it, quietly considering means of improvement of the condition of the people, find nothing better to do than to murder people, the killing of whom is as useful as cutting off one of the Hydra's heads?

Kings and emperors have long established a system resembling the arrangement of the magazine rifle, i. e., as soon as one bullet flies out another takes its place. "The king is dead—long live the king!" Then what is the use of killing them? It is only from a most superficial point of view that the murder of such persons can seem a means of saving the people from oppression and wars, which destroy their lives. We need only remember that the same kind of oppression and war went on quite independent of those who stood at the head of the government, whether it was Nicholas or Alexander, Louis or Napoleon, Frederic or William, Palmerston or Gladstone, McKinley or anyone else, to see that it is not some definite person who causes the oppression and the wars from which the people suffer.

The misery of the people is not caused by individuals, but by an order of society by which they are bound together in a way that puts them in the power of a few, or more often one man: a man so depraved by his unnatural position of having the fate and lives of millions of people in his power that he is always in an unhealthy state, and suffering more or less from a mania of self-aggrandizement, which is not noticed in him only because of his exceptional position. Apart from the fact that such men are surrounded from the cradle to the grave by the most insane luxury and its usual accompaniment of flattery and servility, the whole of their education, all their occupations, are centered on the one object of murder, the study of murder in the past, the best means of murdering in the present, the best ways of preparing for murder. From their earliest years they learn the art of murder in all possible forms, always carry about with them instruments of murder, dress in different uniforms, attend parades, maneuvers, and reviews, visit each other, present orders and commands of regiments to each other. And yet not only does nobody tell them the real name of their actions, not only does nobody tell them that preparing for murder is revolting and criminal, but they hear nothing except praise and words of admiration from all around them for these actions. That part of the press which alone reaches them, and which seems to them to be the expression of the feelings of the best of the people or their best representatives, exalts all their words and deeds, however silly and wicked they may be, in the most servile manner. All who surround them, men and women, whether cleric or laymen, all these people who do not value human dignity, vie with each other in flattering them in the most refined manner, agree with them in everything, and deceive them continually, making it impossible for them to know life as it is. These men might live to be a hundred and never see a real, free man, and never hear the truth.

We are sometimes appalled by the words and deeds of these men, but if we only consider their state we cannot but see that any man would act in the same way in such a position. A reasonable man can do but one thing in such a position, i. e., leave it. Everyone who remains in such a position will act in the same manner. What must indeed be going on in the head of some William of Germany, a man of limited understanding, little education, and with a great deal of ambition, whose ideals are like those of a German "yunker," when any silly or horrid thing he may say is always met with an enthusiastic "Hoch!" and commented on as if it were something very important by the press of the whole world? He says that the soldiers should be prepared to kill their own fathers in obedience to his command. The answer is "Hurrah!" He says the Gospel must be introduced with a fist of iron. "Hurrah!" He says that the army must not take any prisoners in China, but kill all, and he is not placed in a lunatic asylum, but they cry, "Hurrah!" and set sail for China to execute his orders. Or Nicholas who, though naturally modest, begins his reign by declaring to venerable old men, in answer to the desire they express of being allow'd to discuss their own affairs, that their hope for self-government is a senseless dream. And the organs of the press that reach him, and the people whom he meets, praise him for it. He proposes a childish, silly, and untruthful project of universal peace at the same time that he is ordering an increase of the army, and even then there are no limits to the laudations of his wisdom and his virtue. Without any reason, he senselessly and pitilessly offends the whole of the Finnish nation, and again hears nothing but praise. At last he starts the Chinese slaughter, terrible by its injustice, cruelty, and its contrast with his project of peace; and he gets simultaneously applauded from all sides, both for his own conquests and for his adherence to his father's policy of peace. What must indeed be going on in the heads and hearts of such men? So that it is not Alexanders and Humberts, Williams, Nicholases and Chamberlains who are the cause of oppression and war, even though they do organize them, but those who have placed them and support them in a position in which they have power over the life and death of men. Therefore it is not necessary to kill Alexanders and Nicholases, Williams and Humberts, but only to leave off supporting the social condition of which they are the product.

It is the selfishness and stupefied state of the people who sell their freedom and their honor for insignificant material advantages, which supports the present state of society. Those who stand on the lowest rung of the ladder, partly as a consequence of being stupefied by a patriotic and falsely religious education, partly for the sake of personal advantages, give up their freedom and their feeling of human dignity to those who stand higher, and who offer them material advantages. In a like position are those standing a little higher. They, too, through being stupefied, and especially for material advantages, give up their freedom and sense of human dignity. The same is true of those standing still higher; and so it continues up to the highest rungs, up to the person or persons who, standing on the very summit of the social cone, have no one to submit to, nor anywhere to rise to, and have no motive for action except ambition and love of power. These are generally so depraved and stupefied by their insane power over life and death, and by the flattery and servility from those around them, which is connected with such power, that while doing evil they feel convinced they are the benefactors of the human race. It is the people themselves who, by sacrificing their human dignity for material profits, produce these men, and are afterwards angry with them for their stupid and cruel acts; murdering such people is like spoiling children and then whipping them.

Very little seems needed to stop oppression and useless war, and to prevent any one from being indignant with those who seem to be the cause of such oppression and war. Only that things should be called by their right names and seen as they are; that it should be understood that an army is an instrument of murder, that the recruiting and drilling of armies which kings, emperors, and presidents carry on with so much self-assurance are preparations for murder. If only every king, emperor, and president would understand that his work of organizing armies is not an honorable and important duty, as his flatterers persuade him it is, but a most abominable business, i. e., the preparing for and the managing of murder. If only every private individual understood that the payment of taxes which helps equip soldiers, and above all military service, are not immaterial but highly immoral actions, by which he not only permits murder, but takes part in it himself—then this power of the kings and emperors which arouses an indignation, and for which they now get killed, would of itself come to an end. And so the Alexanders, Carnots, Humberts, and others must not be killed, but it ought to be proved to them that they are murderers; and above all, they should not be allowed to kill men: their orders to murder should not be obeyed. If men do not yet act in this manner, it is only because of the hypnotic influence governments for self-preservation so diligently exercised on them. Therefore we can contribute toward stopping people killing kings and each other, not by murder,—murders only strengthen this hypnotic state,—but by awakening men from it. And when the soldiers are enrolled, and hired, and armed, they are subjected to a special training called discipline, introduced in recent times, since soldiers have ceased to share the plunder. Discipline consists in this, that by complex and artful methods, which have been perfected in the course of ages, people who are subjected to this training and remain under it for some time are completely deprived of man's chief attribute, rational freedom, and become submissive, machine-like instruments of murder in the hands of their organized hierarchical stratocracy. And it is in this disciplined army that the essence of the fraud dwells which gives to modern governments dominion over the peoples. As soon as the government has the money and the soldiers, instead of fulfilling their promises to defend their subjects from foreign enemies, and to arrange things for their benefit, they do all they can to provoke the neighboring nations and to produce war; and they not only do not promote the internal well-being of their poeple, but they ruin and corrupt them.

Slavery.—Every kind of oppression of man by man rests on the possibility which a man has of taking another's life and, by keeping a threatening attitude, compelling his obedience. One may assert without fear of being in error that, wherever there is subjection of man,—that is, the doing by one, against his will, in accordance with another's wishes, certain personally undesired acts,—the cause of it is force having for its basis the threat of taking life. Where a man surrenders the whole of his labor to another, goes without sufficient nourishment, consigns his little children to hard labor, and devotes his whole life to repugnant and (to him) useless labor,—as is done before our own eyes in our own world (called civilized by us because we live in it),—it may with certainty be said that he does all this because, for nonfulfilment, he is threatened with the loss of life. Therefore, in our cultured world, where the majority of men, under terrible privations, perform hateful and (to them) useless labor,—the majority of men are in a state of slavery, founded on the threat of loss of life.

In what, then, does this slavery manifest itself, and how is the threat expressed? In ancient times the method of enslavement and the threat of taking life were plain enough; the primitive method of enslaving men consisted of the direct threat of death by the sword. The armed said to the unarmed: "I can kill you, as you saw I did with your brother; but I do not wish to do it; I will spare you, primarily because both for me and for you it will be more profitable if you will consent to work instead of being killed. So do everything I command you; if you refuse, I will kill you." And the unarmed surrendered to the armed and did all that he commanded. The unarmed worked, the armed threatened.

This was that personal slavery which early appears among

all nations and which is now still to be met with among savage nations. This method of enslaving men is the first to come into vogue, but as life grows complex, this method is modified. Under complex conditions of life this method presents great inconveniences for the oppressor. In order to profit by the labor of the weak, the oppressor must feed and clothe them,— that is, take such care of them as might make them fit for work, —and this limits the number of the enslaved; moreover, this method forces the oppressor to perpetually guard the enslaved in a threatening attitude. And so a new form of subjection is evolved.

Land.—The second form of the enslavement of men is by means of taking away their land; that is, their food. This method of enslavement has also always existed wherever men have been held in subjection; and no matter what changes of form it undergoes, it exists everywhere. In some cases the land all belongs to the emperor, as in Turkey, while the tenth part of the crops is appropriated by the crown; in some cases only a portion of the land is thus owned and the taxes are collected from its products; in some cases, all the land belongs to a small number of persons and taxes are paid for its use, as in England; in some cases, a larger or smaller part belongs to large proprietors, as in Russia, Germany, and France. But where slavery exists there goes with it the appropriation of the land by the enslaver. The screw of this form of slavery is tightened or loosened according to the degree of tightness in which the other screws are held. Thus, in Russia, when the personal slavery was extended over the majority of laborers, the slavery by land monopoly was a superfluity; and the screw of personal slavery was loosened in Russia, only when the land and taxation screws had been tightened. They had arbitrarily made all members of respective communities, made emigration difficult, and had appropriated the land or divided it among private individuals, and then they—gave the peasants freedom! In England, for example, enslavement through land monopoly is the predominating form, and the issue of the naturalization of land means simply that the screw of taxation is to be tightened and the land slavery screw loosened.

Money.—The third method of enslavement by means of taxes, tribute, has also always existed; and in our time, with the extension of similar money-tokens in different governments and the strengthening of governmental authority, it has become peculiarly strong; it has in fact so developed that it ever tends to supplant the second method, that of land slavery.

Money in the proper sense comes in vogue among people only when they are all forcibly made to pay money. Then only does money become indispensable to each as the means to secure immunity from violence; then only does money receive a constant exchange value. And not that which is convenient for exchange receives exchange value, but that which is demanded by government; if the government demands gold, gold will receive the exchange value; if colored stones are demanded, colored stones will have that value. If this is not true, then why has it always been a government prerogative to issue this medium of exchange? A people, say the Fijians, have determined upon a new medium of exchange. Well, leave them in peace to exchange in any manner they choose, and do not interfere with their exchanges, you who have the power. But you coin the tokens, prohibiting others from coining similar ones; or else, as in Russia, you print pieces of paper, put upon them the images of czars, add peculiar signatures, and provide severe punishments for counterfeiters; then you distribute them among your assistants, and demand, under the name of taxes and duties, from the laborers, so many of such coins or papers that the laborer is obliged to sell his labor in order to obtain these coins or papers. And you assure us that this money is necessary as a medium of exchange. Here are all men free; no one oppresses anybody else or keeps him in subjection; no sooner does money appear in the society than there is an Iron Law, thanks to which rent rises while wages decrease to the minimum. The fact that half, or more than half of the Russian peasants sell themselves to landed proprietors and manufacturers, to get means to pay the direct and indirect taxes of all kinds, by no means signifies (as seems obvious) that the compulsory levying of money taxes for the benefit of the government and its landlord-accomplices, compels the laborers to become the slaves of those who levy the taxes; it signifies that these are: money, a means of exchange, and an iron law.

Slaves.—We have in Russia, within our own recollection, passed through two changes in the form of slavery. When the serfs were liberated and the proprietors left in possession of a large part of the land, the latter feared that their power over the former would vanish; but, as experience has now shown, they simply had to let go the old chain of personal slavery, and take hold of another,—the land-monopoly chain. The peasant lacked bread to feed himself, while the proprietor had the land and the stores of products; hence the peasant remained the same slave. The next transformation was when the government tightened the screw of taxation and the majority of laborers were compelled to sell themselves to the proprietors and manufacturers. This new form is holding the people still tighter, so that nine-tenths of the Russian laboring population work for the landed proprietors and manufacturers because they are driven to it by the demand of the government for land and other taxes. This is so obvious that, were the government to refrain for one year from demanding direct, indirect and land taxes, all the work on the landlords' fields and in the factories would stop entirely. Nine-tenths of the Russian people hire themselves out at the time taxes are wanted and solely on account of the taxes.

The three methods of enslaving men have always existed and exist today; but people are apt to overlook them the moment a new excuse for them is provided; and, the strangest thing of all is that just that method upon which today everything is rested, which sustains all,—is not noticed at all. When in the ancient world the entire economic fabric rested on personal slavery, the greatest minds could not see it. To Xenophon and Plato, and Aristotle, and the Romans it seemed that things could not be different, and that slavery was the inevitable and natural result of wars, without which, in turn, humanity was inconceivable. Similarly, in the Middle Ages, and until very recently, people could not perceive the significance of landed property and the slavery consequent upon it, which upheld the entire economic structure of the Middle Ages. . . And even so, today, nobody sees, or wishes to see, that in our time the enslavement of the majority of men is based on the money-taxes, levied upon land and otherwise, which are collected by government from the subjects,—taxes collected by the administration and the army, the very administration and army which subsist upon these taxes. There has long existed and still exists a terrible superstition, which has done men more harm, perhaps, than the most awful religious superstitions, and it is this superstition, which with all its might and perseverance the so-called political science upholds. The superstition is similar in every respect to religious superstitions. It consists in the affirmation that, besides the duties of man to man, there are still more important obligations to an imaginary being. In theology the imaginary being is God, and in political sciences the imaginary being is Government.

The religious superstition consists in the belief that the sacrifices, often of human lives, made to the imaginary being are essential, and that men may and should be brought to that state of mind by all methods, not excluding violence. The political superstition consists in the belief that, besides the duties of man to man, there are more important duties to the imaginary being, Government, and that the sacrifices—often of human lives—made to the imaginary being are also essential, and that men may and should be brought to that state of mind by all possible means, not excluding violence. This superstition it is, formerly maintained by the priests of various religions, which the so-called political science now maintains. Men are subjected to the most terrible and worst kinds of slavery; but political science endeavors to assure them that it is all necessary and cannot be different. Government must exist for the good of the people and to execute its affairs,—to rule the people and defend it from enemies. To do this, government needs money and an army. Money should be provided by all the citizens of the government, and hence all the relations of men must be considered in their relation to the necessary conditions of governmentalism. Government,—that is, armed and aggressive men, determine how much they want from those whom they invade (as the English in their relation to the Fijians); they determine how much labor they want of the slaves; determine how many assistants they need to collect the products; organize these assistants as soldiers, as landed proprietors, and as tax-collectors. And the slaves surrender their labor and at the same time think that they surrender it, not because their masters want it so, but because for their own liberty and welfare are needed services and sacrifices to the diety called Government; and that, aside from their services to the deity, they are free. This they believe because they have been told so, formerly by religion, priests, and latterly by political science, learned people.

But one needs only to cease to believe blindly what other people who call themselves priests or political scientists say, to have the senselessness of these assertions made evident. Men, oppressing others, assure them that the compulsion is necessary in the interest of the government, while the government is indispensable to the liberty and welfare of men:—according to this, the oppressors force men for their own freedom and do them wrong for their own good. But men are rational beings and hence ought to understand wherein is their good, and to have liberty to do that. Things, therefore, the beneficence of which is not clear to men and to the performance of which they have to be driven by force, cannot be for their good. That can alone be a good to a rational being which his intelligence perceives as such. If men, in consequence of passion or unwisdom, show preference for evil, then all that men who are wiser than their fellows may do is to try to persuade these to do that which is for their good. It is possible to persuade men that their welfare will be greater if they will serve as soldiers, if they will be deprived of land, if they will give away their labor in the shape of taxes; but until all men consider this their good and do it voluntarily, it cannot be called men's welfare. The sole indication of the beneficence of a thing is that men freely perform it. And of such things the life of men is full.

Ten laborers organize an association to work together, and in doing this they undoubtedly do something that is for their common benefit; but it is impossible to imagine that these laborers, compelling another laborer to join them and work with them against his will, should assert that the eleventh member's interests are identical with their own. The same applies to gentlemen giving a dinner to some friend of theirs; it cannot be affirmed that the dinner will be a good to the man forced to pay ten roubles for it. The same with peasants who might think the existence of a pond a greater good than the labor expended on it; for them the digging would be a common benefit. But for him who should think the existence of a pond a lesser good than the getting in of his crops, in which he was tardy, the digging of the pond could not be a benefit. The same with roads built by men, with a church, with a museum, and with all the different social and governmental affairs. All these affairs can be beneficial for those only who think them so and freely and voluntarily perform them, as the purchase of tools for the co-operative workshop, the dinner given by the masters, the pond dug by the peasants.

But things to which men must be driven by force, cease to be, thanks to the force, for the common good. All this is so clear and simple that, if men had not been deceived so long, it would not be necessary to make them plain. The abolition of slavery has gone on for a long time. Rome abolished slavery, America abolished it, and we did, but only the words were abolished, not the thing.

Slavery means the freeing themselves, by some, of the necessity of labor for the satisfaction of their needs and the throwing of this labor upon others by means of physical force; and where there is a man who does not labor because another is compelled to work for him, there slavery is. And where, as in all European societies, men by force exploit the labor of thousands of men and regard it as their prerogative, while the latter submit to force and regard it as their duty, there we have slavery in terrible proportions. Slavery exists. Where, then, do we find it? Where it has always been and without which it cannot be: in the compulsion exercised by the strong and armed upon the weak and unarmed. Slavery has three fundamental methods: direct personal violence, militarism, land-taxes, upheld by the military power, and direct and indirect taxes upon citizens, also upheld by the military power. The three methods exist today as much as formerly. Only, we do not see it, because each of these three forms of slavery has received a new excuse which veils its real significance. The personal violence of the armed upon the unarmed is justified on the ground of defence of fatherland against imaginary enemies; in reality, it has the same old function—the subjection of the conquered to the invaders. The indirect force of the appropriation of the lands of those who work on them is justified as compensation for services to the alleged common welfare and sanctioned by the right of inheritance; in reality, it is the same land-robbery and enslavement which was once carried out by the military power. The last, the money-taxation species of force, the most powerful and popular at the present time, has received the most wonderful justification,—namely, that the denial of liberty, property, and every good to men is in the interest of the common liberty and welfare. In reality it is nothing else than slavery, only impersonal.

Where force is set up as law, there will slavery be. Whether it is princes and their warlike bands who invade, kill wives and children, and burn down the village; whether slaveholders demand money or labor from the slaves for the land, and in case of non-compliance call the armed bands to their aid; or whether the Ministry of Internal Affairs is collecting money through the governors and police officials, and, in case of non-success, sending armed regiments,—as long as there shall be tyranny supported by the bayonet there will be no distribution of wealth among men, but all the wealth will go to the tyrants. A striking illustration of the truth of this position is afforded by Henry George's project of nationalizing land. George proposes to declare all land government property, and to substitute a rent-tax for all direct and indirect taxes. That is, every one using land should pay the government its rental value. What would be the outcome? Land would belong to the government: to the English, the land of England, to the Americans the land of that country, and so forth; that is, there would be slavery, determined by the quantity of land in use. Perhaps the condition of some laborers (such as agricultural) would be improved; but since there would remain the forcible collection of the tax of the rental values, there would also remain slavery. The land cultivator, in a bad year, not being able to pay the rent exacted from him by force, would have to enslave himself to the man with money in order to keep his land and not lose everything.

The German Socialists have termed the combination of conditions which puts the worker in subjection to the capitalists the iron law of wages, implying by the word "iron" that this law is immutable. But in these conditions there is nothing immutable. These conditions merely result from human laws concerning taxes, land, and, above all, concerning things which satisfy our requirements—that is, concerning property. Laws are framed and repealed by human beings. So that it is not some sociological "iron law," but ordinary, man-made law that produces slavery. In the case in hand the slavery of our times is very clearly and definitely produced, not by some "iron" elemental law, but by human enactments about land, about taxes, and about property. There is one set of laws by which any quantity of land may belong to private people, and may pass from one to another by inheritance, or by will, or may be sold; there is another set of laws by which every one must pay the taxes demanded of him unquestioningly; and there is a third set of laws to the effect that any quantity of articles, by whatever means acquired, may become the absolute property of the people who hold them. And in consequence of these laws slavery exists.

Many constitutions have been devised, beginning with the English and the American, and ending with the Japanese and the Turkish, according to which people are to believe that all laws established in their country are established at their desire. But every one knows that not in despotic countries only, but also in the countries nominally most free—England, America, France—the laws are made not by the will of all, but by the will of those who have power; and, therefore, always and everywhere are only such as are profitable to those who have power, whether they are many, a few, or only one man. Everywhere and always the laws are enforced by the only means that has compelled, and still compels, some people to obey the will of others—that is, by blows, by deprivation of liberty, and by murder. There can be no other way. It cannot be otherwise; for laws are demands to execute certain rules; and to compel some people to obey certain rules (that is, to do what other people want of them) cannot be done except by blows, by deprivation of liberty, and by murder. If there are laws there must be the force that can compel people to obey them, and there is only one force that can compel people to obey rules (that is, to obey the will of others), and that is violence; not the simple violence which people use to one another in moments of passion, but the organized violence used by people who have power, in order to compel others to obey the laws they (the powerful) have made; in other words, to do their will. And so the essence of legislation does not lie in the subject or object, in rights or in the idea of the dominion of the collective will of the people, or in other such indefinite and confused conditions; but it lies in the fact that people who wield organized violence have the power to compel others to obey them and to do as they like. So that the exact and irrefutable definition of legislation, intelligible to all, is that: Laws are rules made by people who govern by means of organized violence, for non-compliance with which the non-complier is subjected to blows, to loss of liberty, or even to being murdered. This definition furnishes the reply to the question, What is it that renders it possible for people to make laws? The same thing makes it possible to establish laws as enforces obedience to them—organized violence.

The cause of the miserable condition of the workers is slavery. The cause of slavery is legislation. Legislation rests on organized violence. It follows that an improvement in the condition of the people is possible only through the abolition of organized violence. "But organized violence is government, and how can we live without governments? Without governments there will be chaos, anarchy; all the achievements of civilization will perish, and the people will revert to their primitive barbarism." But why should we suppose this? Why think that non-official people could not arrange their life themselves as well as government people arrange it, not for themselves, but for others? We see, on the contrary, that in the most diverse matters people in our times arrange their own lives incomparably better than those who govern them arrange for them. Without the least help from government, and often in spite of the interference of government, people organize all sorts of social undertakings—workmen's unions, co-operative societies, railway companies, and syndicates. If collections for public works are needed, why should we suppose that free people could not without violence voluntarily collect the necessary means, and carry out all that is carried out by means of taxes, if only the undertakings in question are really useful for anybody? Why suppose that there cannot be tribunals without violence? Trial by people trusted by the disputants has always existed and will exist, and needs no violence. We are so depraved by long-continued slavery that we can hardly imagine administration without violence. And yet, again, that is not true: Russian communes migrating to distant regions, where our government leaves them alone, arrange their own taxation, administration, tribunals, and police, and always prosper until government violence interferes with their administration. And in the same way, there is no reason to suppose that people could not, by common consent, decide how the land is to be apportioned for use.

The robber generally plundered the rich, the governments generally plunder the poor and protect those rich who assist in their crimes. The robber doing his work risked his life, while the governments risk nothing, but base their whole activity on lies and deception. The robber did not compel anyone to join his band, the governments generally enrol their soldiers by force. All who paid the tax to the robber had equal security from danger. But in the state, the more any one takes part in the organized fraud the more he receives not merely of protection, but also of reward. Most of all, the emperors, kings and presidents are protected (with their perpetual bodyguards), and they can spend the largest share of the money collected from the taxpaying subjects; next in the scale of participation in the governmental crimes come the commander in chief, the ministers, the heads of police, governors, and so on, down to the policemen, who are least protected, and who receive the smallest salaries of all. Those who do not take any part in the crimes of government, who refuse to serve, to pay taxes, or to go to law, are subjected to violence, as among the robbers. The robber does not intentionally vitiate people, but the governments, to accomplish their ends, vitiate whole generations from childhood to manhood with false religions and patriotic instruction.

How Can Governments Be Abolished?—Slavery results from laws, laws are made by governments, and, therefore, people can only be freed from slavery by the abolition of governments. But how can governments be abolished? All attempts to get rid of governments by violence have hitherto, always and everywhere, resulted only in this: that in place of the deposed governments new ones established themselves, often more cruel than those they replaced. Not to mention past attempts to abolish governments by violence, according to the Socialist theory, the coming abolition of the rule of the capitalists—that is, the communalization of the means of production and the new economic order of society—is also to be carried out by a fresh organization of violence, and will have to be maintained by the same means. So that attempts to abolish violence by violence neither have in the past nor, evidently, can in the future emancipate people from violence, nor, consequently, from slavery. It cannot be otherwise. Apart from outbursts of revenge or anger, violence is used only in order to compel some people, against their own will, to do the will of others. But the necessity to do what other people wish against your own will is slavery. And, therefore, as long as any violence, designed to compel some people to do the will of others, exists, there will be slavery. All the attempts to abolish slavery by violence are like extinguishing fire with fire, stopping water with water, or filling up one hole by digging another. People must feel that their participation in the criminal activity of governments, whether by giving part of their work in the form of money, or by direct participation in military service, is not, as is generally supposed, an indifferent action, but, besides being harmful to one's self and to one's brothers, is a participation in the crimes unceasingly committed by all governments and apreparation for new crimes, which governments are always preparing by maintaining disciplined armies.

The age for the veneration for governments, notwithstanding all the hypnotic influence they employ to maintain their position, is more and more passing away. And it is time for people to understand that governments not only are not necessary, but are harmful and most highly immoral institutions, in which a self-respecting, honest man cannot and must not take part, and the advantages of which he cannot and should not enjoy. And as soon as people clearly understand that, they will naturally cease to take part in such deeds—that is, cease to give the governments soldiers and money. And as soon as a majority of people ceases to do this the fraud which enslaves people will be abolished. Only in this way can people be freed from slavery. And in order not to do the evil which produces misery for himself and for his brothers, he should, first of all, neither willingly nor under compulsion take any part in governmental activity, and should, therefore, be neither a soldier, nor a field-marshal, nor a minister of state, nor a tax-collector, nor a witness, nor an alderman, nor a juryman, nor a governor, nor a member of Parliament, nor, in fact, hold any office connected with violence. That is one thing. Secondly, such a man should not voluntarily pay taxes to governments, either directly or indirectly; nor should he accept money collected by taxes, either as salary, or as pension, or as a reward; nor should he make use of governmental institutions, supported by taxes collected by violence from the people. That is the second thing. Thirdly, a man who desires not to promote his own well-being alone, but to better the position of people in general, should not appeal to governmental violence for the protection of his own possessions in land or in other things, nor to defend him and his near ones; but should only possess land and all products of his own or other people's toil in so far as others do not claim them from him.

XX
BENJAMIN R. TUCKER

Benjamin R. Tucker, born at South Dartmouth in 1854. From 1870 to 1872, studied technology in Boston; traveled in England, France, and Italy. In 1877 took the temporary editorship of *The Word*, published at Princeton, Mass.; published the quarterly *The Radical Review*, in New Bedford, 1878; but only four numbers appeared; in 1881, in Boston, founded the semi-monthly paper *Liberty*; for ten years was one of the editorial staff of the *Globe*. From 1892 to 1907 lived in New York and published *Liberty*. Tucker's teaching about law, the State and property is contained mainly in his articles in *Liberty*. Wrote *Instead of a Book*, an exposition of philosophical Anarchism, 1893; translated and published *The Kreutzer Sonata* and two volumes of Proudhon, and many other works. He is at present (1913) living in France, devoting his time to study and research.

The selections are from *Liberty* and *Instead of a Book*.

The people cannot afford to be enslaved for the sake of being insured.

The motto on our flag is not "Liberty a Natural Right," but "Liberty the Mother of Order."

Just as truly as Liberty is the mother or order, is the State the mother of violence.

There is no such depth of poltroonery as that of the man who does not dare to run.

If there were more extremists in evolutionary periods, there would be no revolutionary periods.

No man can make himself so much a slave as to forfeit the right to issue his own emancipation proclamation.

Man has but little to gain from liberty unless that liberty includes the liberty to control what he produces.

The invader, whether an individual or a government, forfeits all claim to consideration from the invaded.

Force of offence is the principle of the state, while force of defence is one aspect of the principle of liberty.

Apart from the right of might, no individual has a right to anything, except as he creates his right by contract with his neighbor.

Evolution is "leading us up to liberty" simply because it

has already led us in nearly every other direction and made a failure of it.

The voice of the majority saves bloodshed, but it is no less the arbitrament of force than is the decree of the most absolute of despots backed by the most powerful of armies.

The art of war, on which government finally rests, has, like government itself, its laws and regulations and customs, which, in the eyes of the military devotee, must be observed at all hazards. Beside them human life is a mere bagatelle.

Anarchism may be described as the doctrine that all the affairs of men should be managed by individuals or voluntary associations, and that the State should be abolished.

Relation of the State to the Individual
Address before the Unitarian Ministers' Institute, Salem, Mass., Oct. 14, 1890.

The future of the tariff, of taxation, of finance, of property, of woman, of marriage, of the family, of the suffrage, of education, of invention, of literature, of science, of the arts, of personal habits, of private character, of ethics, of religion, will be determined by the conclusion at which mankind shall arrive as to whether and how far the individual owes allegiance to the State.

Anarchism, in dealing with this subject, has found it necessary, first of all, to define its terms. Popular conceptions of the terminology of politics are incompatible with the rigorous exactness required in scientific investigation. To be sure, a departure from the popular use of language is accompanied by the risk of misconception by the multitude, who persistently ignore the new definitions; but, on the other hand, conformity thereto is attendant by the still more deplorable alternative of confusion in the eyes of the competent, who would be justified in attributing inexactness of thought where there is inexactness of expression. Take the term "State," for instance, with which we are especially concerned today. It is a word that is on every lip. But how many of those who use it have any idea of what they mean by it? And, of the few who have, how various are their conceptions! We designate by the term "State" institutions that embody absolutism in its extreme form and institutions that temper it with more or less liberality. We apply the word alike to institutions that do nothing but aggress and to institutions that, besides aggressing, to some extent protect and defend. But which is the State's essential function, aggression or defense, few seem to know or care. Some champions of the State evidently consider aggression its principle, although they disguise it alike from themselves and from the people under the term "administration," which they wish to extend in every possible direction. Others, on the contrary, consider defense its principle, and wish to limit it accordingly to the performance of police duties. Still others seem to think that it exists for both aggression and defense, combined in varying proportions according to the momentary interests, or may be only whims, of those happening to control it. Brought face to face with these diverse views, the Anarchists, whose mission in the world is the abolition of aggression and all the evils that result therefrom, perceived that, to be understood, they must attach some definite and avowed significance to the terms which they are obliged to employ, and especially to the words "State" and "government." Seeking, then, the elements common to all the institutions to which the name "State" has been applied, they have found them two in number: first, aggression; second, the assumption of sole authority over a given area and all within it, exercised generally for the double purpose of more complete oppression of its subjects and extension of its boundaries. That this second element is common to all States, I think, will not be denied,—at least, I am not aware that any State has ever tolerated a rival State within its borders; and it seems plain that any State which should do so would thereby cease to be a State and to be considered as such by any. The exercise of authority over the same area by two States is a contradiction. That the first element, aggression, has been and is common to all States will probably be less generally admitted. Nevertheless, I shall not attempt to reenforce here the conclusion of Spencer, which is gaining wider acceptance daily,—that the State had its origin in aggression, and has continued as an aggressive institution from its birth. Defense was an afterthought, prompted by necessity; and its introduction as a State function, though effected doubtless with a view to the strengthening of the State, was really and in principle the initiation of the State's destruction. Its growth in importance is but an evidence of the tendency of progress toward the abolition of the State. Taking this view of the matter, the Anarchists contend that defense is not an essential of the State, but that aggression is. Now what is aggression? Aggression is simply another name for government. Aggression, invasion, government, are interconvertible terms. The essence of government is control, or the attempt to control. He who attempts to control another is a governor, an aggressor, an invader; and the nature of such invasion is not changed, whether it is made by one man upon another man, after the manner of the ordinary criminal, or by one man upon all other men, after the manner of an absolute monarch, or by all other men upon one man, after the manner of a modern democracy. On the other hand, he who resists another's attempt to control is not an aggressor, an invader, a governor, but simply a defender, a protector; and the nature of such resistance is not changed whether it be offered by one man to all other men, as when one declines to obey an oppressive law, or by all other men to one man, as when a subject people rises against a despot, or as when the members of a community voluntarily unite to restrain a criminal. This distinction between invasion and resistance, between government and defense, is vital. Without it there can be no valid philosophy of politics. Upon this distinction and the other considerations just outlined, the Anarchists frame the desired definitions. This, then, is the Anarchistic definition of government: the subjection of the non-invasive individual to an external will. And this is the Anarchistic definition of the State: the embodiment of the principle of invasion in an individual, or a band of individuals, assuming to act as representatives or masters of the entire people within a given area. As to the meaning of the remaining term in the subject under discussion, the word "individual," I think there is little difficulty. Putting aside the subtleties in which certain metaphysicians have indulged, one may use this word without danger of being misunderstood. Whether the definitions thus arrived at prove generally acceptable or not is a matter of minor consequence. I submit that they are reached scientifically, and serve the purpose of a clear conveyance of thought. The Anarchists, having by their adoption taken due care to be explicit, are entitled to have their ideas judged in the light of these definitions.

Now comes the question proper: What relations should exist between the State and the individual? The general method of determining these is to apply some theory of ethics involving a basis of moral obligation. In this method the Anarchists have no confidence. The idea of moral obligation, of inherent rights and duties, they totally discard. They look upon all obligations, not as moral, but as social, and even then not really as obligations except as these have been consciously and voluntarily assumed. If a man makes an agreement with men, the latter may combine to hold him to his agreement; but, in the absence of such agreement, no man, so far as the Anarchists are aware, has made any agreement with God or with any other power of any order whatsoever. The Anarchists are not only utilitarians, but egoists in the farthest and fullest sense. So far as inherent right is concerned, might is its only measure. Any man, be his name Bill Sykes or Alexander Romanoff, and any set of men, whether the Chinese highbinders or the Congress of the United States, have the right, if they have the power, to kill or coerce other men and to make the entire world subservient to their ends. Society's right to enslave the individual and the individual's right to enslave society are unequal only because their powers are unequal.

If this, then, were a question of right, it would be, according to the Anarchist, purely a question of strength. But, fortunately, it is not a question of right: it is a question of expediency, of knowledge, of science,—the science of living together, the science of society. The history of humanity has been largely one long and gradual discovery of the fact that the individual is the gainer by society exactly in proportion as society is free, and of the law that the condition of a permanent and harmonious society is the greatest amount of individual liberty compatible with equality of liberty. The average man of each new generation has said to himself more clearly and consciously than his predecessor: "My neighbor is not my enemy, but my friend, and I am his, if we would but mutually recognize the fact. We help each other to a better, fuller, happier living; and this service might be greatly increased if we would cease to restrict, hamper, and oppress each other. Why can we not agree to let each live his own life, neither of us transgressing the limit that separates our individualities?" It is by this reasoning that mankind is approaching the real social contract, which is not, as Rousseau thought, the origin of society, but rather the outcome of a long social experience, the fruit of its follies and disasters. It is obvious that this contract, this social law, developed to its perfection, excludes all aggression, all violation of equality of liberty, all invasion of every kind. Considering this contract in connection with the Anarchistic definition of the State as the embodiment of the principle of invasion, we see that the State is antagonistic to society; and, society being essential to individual life and development, the conclusion leaps to the eyes that the relation of the State to the individual and of the individual to the State must be one of hostility, enduring till the State shall perish.

"But," it will be asked of the Anarchists at this point in

the argument, "what shall be done with those individuals who undoubtedly will persist in violating the social law by invading their neighbors?" The Anarchists answer that the abolition of the State will leave in existence a defensive association, resting no longer on a compulsory but on a voluntary basis, which will restrain invaders by any means that may prove necessary. "But that is what we have now," is the rejoinder. "You really want, then, only a change of name?" Not so fast, please. Can it be soberly pretended for a moment that the State, even as it exists here in America, is purely a defensive institution? Surely not, save by those who see of the State only its most palpable manifestation—the policeman on the street corner. And one would not have to watch him very closely to see the error of this claim. Why, the very first act of the State, the compulsory assessment and collection of taxes, is itself an aggression, a violation of equal liberty, and, as such, vitiates every subsequent act, even those acts which would be purely defensive if paid for out of a treasury filled by voluntary contributions. How is it possible to sanction, under the law of equal liberty, the confiscation of a man's earnings to pay for protection which he has not sought and does not desire? And, if this is an outrage, what name shall we give to such confiscation when the victim is given, instead of bread, a stone; instead of protection, oppression? To force a man to pay for the violation of his own liberty is indeed an addition of insult to injury. But that is exactly what the State is doing. Read the Congressional Record; follow the proceedings of the State legislatures; examine our statute-books; test each act separately by the law of equal liberty,—you will find that a good nine-tenths of existing legislation serves, not to enforce that fundamental social law, but either to prescribe the individual's personal habits, or, worse still, to create and sustain commercial, industrial, financial, and proprietary monopolies which deprive labor of a large part of the reward that it would receive in a perfectly free market.

This leads to another consideration that bears powerfully upon the problem of the invasive individual, who is such a bugbear to the opponents of Anarchism. Is it not such treatment as has just been described that is largely responsible for his existence? I have heard or read somewhere of an inscription written for a certain charitable institution:

> This hospital a pious person built,
> But first he made the poor wherewith to fill't.

And so, it seems to me, it is with our prisons. They are filled with criminals which our virtuous State has made what they are by its iniquitous laws, its grinding monopolies, and the horrible social conditions that result from them. We enact many laws that manufacture criminals, and then a few that punish them. Is it too much to expect that the new social conditions which must follow the abolition of all interference with the production and distribution of wealth will in the end so change the habits and propensities of men that our jails and prisons, our policemen and our soldiers,—in a word, our whole machinery and outfit of defense,—will be superfluous? That, at least, is the Anarchists' belief. It sounds Utopian, but it really rests on severly economic grounds.

It (Government) is the cause of the money monopoly, the land monopoly, the tariff monopoly, and the patent monopoly.

First in the importance of its evil influence is the money monopoly, which consists of the privilege given by the government to certain individuals, or to individuals holding certain kinds of property, of issuing the circulating medium, a privilege which is now enforced in this country by a national tax of ten per cent upon all other persons who attempt to furnish a circulating medium, and by State laws making it a criminal offense to issue notes as currency. It is claimed that the holders of this privilege control the rate of interest, the rate of rent of houses and buildings, and the prices of goods,—the first directly, and the second and third indirectly. For, if the business of banking were made free to all, more and more persons would enter into it until the competition should become sharp enough to reduce the price of lending money to the labor cost, which statistics show to be less than three-fourths of one per cent. In that case the thousands of people who are now deterred from going into business by the ruinously high rates which they must pay for capital with which to start and carry on business will find their difficulties removed. If they have property which they do not desire to convert into money by sale, a bank will take it as collateral for a loan of a certain proportion of its market value at less than one per cent discount. If they have no property, but are industrious, honest, and capable, they will generally be able to get their individual notes endorsed by a sufficient number of known and solvent parties; and on such business paper they will be able to get a loan at a bank on similarly favorable terms. Thus interest will fall at a blow. The banks will really not be lending capital at all, but will be doing business on the capital of their customers, the business consisting in an exchange of the known and widely available credits of the banks for the unknown and unavailable, but equally good credits of the customers, and a charge therefor of less than one per cent, not as interest for the use of capital, but as pay for the labor of running the banks. This facility of acquiring capital will give an unheard-of impetus to business, and consequently create an unprecedented demand for labor,— a demand which will always be in excess of the supply, directly the contrary of the present condition of the labor market. Then will be seen an exemplification of the words of Richard Cobden, that, when two laborers are after one employer, wages fall, but when two employers are after one laborer, wages rise. Labor will then be in a position to dictate its wages, and will thus secure its natural wage, its entire product. Thus the same blow that strikes interest down will send wages up. But this is not all. Down will go profits also. For merchants, instead of buying at high prices on credit, will borrow money of the banks at less than one per cent, buy at low prices for cash, and correspondingly reduce the prices of their goods to their customers. And with the rest will go house-rent. For no one who can borrow capital at one per cent with which to build a house of his own will consent to pay rent to a landlord at a higher rate than that.

Second in importance comes the land monopoly, the evil effects of which are seen principally in exclusively agricultural countries, like Ireland. This monopoly consists in the enforcement by government of land titles which do not rest upon personal occupancy and cultivation. As soon as individuals are no longer protected by their fellows in anything but personal occupancy and cultivation of land, ground-rent will disappear, and so usury have one less leg to stand on. The very small fraction of ground-rent which rests, not on monopoly, but on superiority of soil or site, will continue to exist for a time and perhaps forever, though tending constantly to a minimum under conditions of freedom. But the inequality of soils which gives rise to the economic rent of land, like the inequality of human skill which gives rise to the economic rent of ability, is not a cause for serious alarm even to the most thorough opponent of usury, as its nature is not that of a germ from which other and graver inequalities may spring, but rather that of a decaying branch which may finally wither and fall.

Third, the tariff monopoly, which consists in fostering production at high prices and under unfavorable conditions by visiting with the penalty of taxation those who patronize production at low prices and under favorable conditions. The evil to which this monopoly gives rise might more properly be called misusury than usury, because it compels labor to pay, not exactly for the use of capital, but rather for the misuse of capital. The abolition of this monopoly would result in a great reduction in the prices of all articles taxed, and this saving to the laborers who consume these articles would be another step towards securing to the laborer his natural wage, his entire product. To abolish this monopoly before abolishing the money monopoly would be a cruel and disastrous policy, first, because the evil of scarcity of money, created by the money monopoly, would be intensified by the flow of money out of the country which would be involved in an excess of imports over exports, and, second, because that fraction of the laborers of the country which is now employed in the protected industries would be turned adrift to face starvation without the benefit of the insatiable demand for labor which a competitive money system would create.

Fourth, the patent monopoly, which consists in protecting inventors and authors against competition for a period long enough to enable them to extort from the people a reward enormously in excess of the labor measure of their services,—in other words, in giving certain people a right of property for a term of years in laws and facts of Nature, and the power to exact tribute from others for the use of this natural wealth, which should be open to all. The abolition of this monopoly would fill its beneficiaries with a wholesome fear of competition which would cause them to be satisfied with pay for their services equal to that which other laborers get for theirs, and to secure it by placing their products and works on the market at the outset at prices so low that their lines of business would be no more tempting to competitors than any other lines.

Liberty will abolish interest; it will abolish profit; it will abolish monopolistic rent; it will abolish taxation; it will abolish the exploitation of labor; it will abolish all means whereby any laborer can be deprived of any of his product; but it will not abolish the limited inequality between one laborer's product and another's. Now, because it has not this power last named, there are people who say: We will have no liberty, for we must have absolute equality. I am not of them. If I can go through life free and rich, I shall not cry because my neighbor, equally free, is richer. Liberty will ultimately make all men rich; it will not make all men equally rich. Authority may (and may not) make all men equally rich in purse; it certainly will make them equally poor in all that makes life best worth living.

A greater equality than is compatible with liberty is undesirable. The moment we invade liberty to secure equality we enter upon a road which knows no stopping-place short of the annihilation of all that is best in the human race. If absolute equality is the ideal; if no man must have the slightest advantage over another,—then the man who achieves greater results through superiority of muscle or skill or brain must not be allowed to enjoy them. All that he produces in excess of that which the weakest and stupidest produce must be taken from him and distributed among his fellows. The economic rent, not of land only, but of strength and skill and intellect and superiority of every kind, must be confiscated. And a beautiful world it would be when absolute equality had been thus achieved! Who would live in it? Certainly no freeman.

The Anarchists are simply unterrified Jeffersonian Democrats. They believe that "the best government is that which governs least," and that that which governs least is no government at all. Even the simple police function of protecting person and property they deny to governments supported by compulsory taxation. Protection they look upon as a thing to be secured, as long as it is necessary, by voluntary association and co-operation for self-defense, or as a commodity to be purchased, like any other commodity, of those who offer the best article at the lowest price. In their view it is in itself an invasion of the individual to compel him to pay for or suffer a protection against invasion that he has not asked for and does not desire. And they further claim that protection will become a drug in the market after poverty and consequently crime have disappeared through the realization of their economic program. Compulsory taxation is to them the life principle of all the monopolies, and passive, but organized, resistance to the tax-collector they contemplate, when the proper time comes, as one of the most effective methods of accomplishing their purposes.

Their attitude on this is a key to their attitude on all other questions of a political or social nature. In religion they are atheistic as far as their own opinions are concerned, for they look upon divine authority and the religious sanction of morality as the chief pretext put forward by the privileged classes for the exercise of human authority. "If God exists," said Proudhon, "he is man's enemy." And, in contrast to Voltaire's famous epigram, "If God did not exist, it would be necessary to invent him," the great Russian Nihilist, Michael Bakounine, placed this antithetical proposition, "If God existed, it would be necessary to abolish him." But although, viewing the divine hierarchy as a contradiction of Anarchy, they do not believe in it, the Anarchists none the less firmly believe in the liberty to believe in it. Any denial of religious freedom they squarely oppose.

Upholding thus the right of every individual to be or select his own priest, they likewise uphold his right to be or select his own doctor. No monopoly in theology, no monopoly in medicine. Competition everywhere and always; spiritual advice and medical advice alike to stand or fall on their own merits. And not only in medicine, but in hygiene, must this principle of liberty be followed. The individual may decide for himself not only what to do to get well, but what to do to keep well. No external power must dictate to him what he must and must not eat, drink, wear, or do.

Nor does the Anarchistic scheme furnish any code of morals to be imposed upon the individual. "Mind your own busines" is its only moral law. Interference with another's business is a crime and the only crime, and as such may properly be resisted. In accordance with this view the Anarchists look upon attempts to arbitrarily suppress vice as in themselves crimes. They believe liberty and the resultant social well-being to be a sure cure for all the vices. But they recognize the right of the drunkard, the gambler, the rake, and the harlot to live their lives until they shall freely choose to abandon them.

In the matter of the maintenance and rearing of children the Anarchists would neither institute the communistic nursery which the State Socialists favor nor keep the communistic school system which now prevails. The nurse and the teacher, like the doctor and the preacher, must be selected voluntarily, and their services must be paid for by those who patronize them. Parental rights must not be taken away, and parental responsibilities must not be foisted upon others.

Even in so delicate a matter as that of the relations of the sexes the Anarchists do not shrink from the application of their principle. They acknowledge and defend the right of any man and woman, or any men or women, to love each other for as long or as short a time as they can, will, or may. To them legal marriage and legal divorce are equal absurdities. They look forward to a time when every individual, whether man or woman, shall be self-supporting, and when each shall have an independent home of his or her own, whether it be a separate house or rooms in a house with others, when the love relations between these independent individuals shall be as varied as are individual inclinations and attachments; and when the children born of these relations shall belong exclusively to the mothers until old enough to belong to themselves.

Anarchism being neither more nor less than the principle of equal liberty, property, in an Anarchistic society, must accord with this principle. The only form of property which meets this condition is that which secures each in the possession of his own products, or of such products of others as he may have obtained unconditionally without the use of fraud or force and in the realization of all titles to such products which he may hold by virtue of free contact with others. Possession, unvitiated by fraud or force, of values to which no one else holds a title unvitiated by fraud or force, and the possession of similarly unvitiated titles to values, constitute the Anarchistic criterion of ownership. By fraud I do not mean that which is simply contrary to equity, but deceit and false pretense in all their forms.

That society is a concrete organism the Anarchists do not deny; on the contrary, they insist upon it. Consequently they have no intention or desire to abolish it. They know that its life is inseparable from the lives of individuals; that it is impossible to destroy one without destroying the other. But, though society cannot be destroyed, it can be greatly hampered and impeded in its operations, much to the disadvantage of the individuals composing it, and it meets its chief impediment in the State. The State, unlike society, is a discreet organism. If it should be destroyed tomorrow, individuals would still continue to exist. Production, exchange, and association would go on as before, but much more freely, and all those social functions upon which the individual is dependent would operate in his behalf more usefully than ever. The individual is not related to the State as the tiger's paw is related to the tiger. Kill the tiger, and the tiger's paw no longer performs its office; kill the State, and the individual still lives and satisfies his wants. As for society, the Anarchists would not kill it if they could, and could not if they would.

If "government" confined itself to the protection of equal liberty, Anarchists would have no quarrel with it; but such protection they do not call government. Criticism of the Anarchistic idea which does not consider Anarchistic definitions is futile. The Anarchist defines government as invasion, nothing more or less. Protection against invasion, then, is the opposite of government. Anarchists, in favoring the abolition of governmet, favor the abolition of invasion, not of protection against invasion. It may tend to a clearer understanding if I add that all States, to become non-invasive, must abandon first the primary act of invasion upon which all of them rest,—the collection of taxes by force,—and that Anarchists look upon the change in social conditions which will result when economic freedom is allowed as far more efficiently protective against invasion than any machinery of restraint, in the absence of economic freedom, possibly can be.

Value.—In a letter to the London *Herald of Anarchy*, Mr. J. Greevz Fisher asserts that "government does not, and never can, fix the value of gold or any other commodity," and cannot even affect such value except by the slight additional demand which it creates as a consumer. It is true that government cannot fix the value of a commodity, because its influence is but one of several factors that combine to govern value. But its power to affect value is out of all proportion to the extent of its consumption. Government's consumption of commodities is an almost infinitesimal influence upon value in comparison with its prohibitory power. One of the chief factors in the constitution of value is, as Mr. Fisher himself states, utility; and as long as government exists, utility is largely dependent upon their arbitrary decrees. When government prohibits the manufacture and sale of liquor, does it not thereby reduce the value of everything that is used in such manufacture and sale? If government were to allow theatrical performances on Sundays, would not the value of every building that contains a theatre rise? Have not we, here in America, just seen the McKinley bill change the value of nearly every article that the people use? If government were to decree that all plates shall be made of tin, would not the value of tin rise and the value of china fall? Unquestionably. Well, a precisely parallel thing occurs when government decrees that all money shall be made of or issued against gold or silver; these metals immediately take on an artificial, government-created value, because of the new use which arbitrary power enables them to monopolize, and all other commodities, which are at the same time forbidden to be put to this use, correspondingly lose value. How absurd, then, in view of these indisputable facts, to assert that government can affect values only in the ratio of its consumption! And yet Mr. Fisher makes this assertion the starting-point of a lecture to the editor of the *Herald of Anarchy* delivered in that dogmatic, know-it-all style which only those are justified in assuming who can sustain their statements by facts and logic.

Voluntary Co-operation.—Liberty always, say the Anarchists. No use of force, except against the invader; and in those cases where it is difficult to tell whether the alleged offender is an invader or not, still no use of force except where the necessity of immediate solution is so imperative that we must use it to save ourselves. And in these few cases where we must use it, let us do so frankly and squarely, acknowledging it as a matter of necessity, without seeking to harmonize our action with any political ideal or constructing any far-fetched theory of a State or collectivity having prerogatives and rights superior to those of individuals and aggregations of individuals and exempted from the operation of the ethical principles which individuals are expected to observe. This is the best rule that I can frame as a guide to voluntary co-operators. To apply it to only one case, I think that under a system of Anarchy, even if it were admitted that there was some ground for considering an unvaccinated person an invader, it would be generally recognized that such invasion was not of a character to require treatment by force, and that any attempt to treat by force would be regarded as itself an invasion of a less doubtful and more immediate nature, requiring as such to be resisted.

Compulsory co-operation is simply one form of invading the liberty of others, and voluntary co-operators will not be justified in restoring to it—that is, in becoming compulsory co-operators—any more than resorting to any other form of invasion.

The Proletaire and Strikes.—The whole industrial and commercial world is in a state of internecine war, in which the proletaires are massed on one side and the proprietors on the other. This is the fact that justifies strikers in subjecting society to what the *Nation* calls a "partial paralysis." It is a war measure. The laborer sees that he does not get his due. He knows that the capitalists have been intrusted by society, through its external representative, the State, with privileges which enable them to control production and distribution; and that, in abuse of these privileges, they have seen to it that the demand for labor should fall far below the supply, and have then taken advantage of the necessities of the laborer and reduced his wages. The laborer and his fellows, therefore, resort to the policy of uniting in such numbers in a refusal to work at the reduced rate that the demand for labor becomes very much greater than the supply, and then they take advantage of the necessities of the capitalists and society to secure a restoration of the old rate of wages, and perhaps an increase upon it. Be the game fair or foul, two can play at it; and those who begin it should not complain when they get the worst of it. If society objects to being "paralyzed," it can very easily avoid it. All it needs to do is to adopt the advice which *Liberty* has long been offering it and withdraw from the monopolists the privileges which it has granted them.

We are here to let in the light of Liberty upon political superstition, and from that policy can result no captivity to corruption, no subserviency to monopoly, only a world of free laborers controlling the products of their labor and growing richer every day. Fortunately for liberty, there is no oppressive respect for Law. Men, to be sure, glibly talk about Law, but what are the facts? What do men do when the law and the pocket collide? Which is the stronger influence—economic interest or the shalt-nots of the Law? Let the corporations and trusts answer. They are vehement upholders of the law—at the expense of union labor, for example. Let the violent strikers and their sympathizers answer. These, too, want plenty of law—for the capitalists. Let the tariff-dodging importers answer, the adulterators of foods, and so on, and so on.

Anarchists work for the abolition of the State, but by this they mean not its overthrow but, as Proudhon put it, its dissolution in the economic organism. This being the case, the question before us is not what measures and means of interference we are justified in instituting, but which ones of those already existing we should first lop off. And to this the Anarchists answer that unquestionably the first to go should be those that interfere most fundamentally with a free market, and that the economic and moral changes that would result from this would act as a solvent upon all the remaining forms of interference.

It is true that labor never gains anything by extravagant claims, but no claim is extravagant that does not exceed justice. It is equally true that labor always loses by foolish concessions; and in this industrial struggle every concession is foolish that falls short of justice.

The Ballot.—Now, what is the ballot? It is neither more nor less than a paper representative of the bayonet, the billy, and the bullet. It is a labor-saving device for ascertaining on which side force lies and bowing to the inevitable. The voice of the majority saves bloodshed, but it is no less the arbitrament of force than is the decree of the most absolute of despots backed by the most powerful of armies. Of course it may be claimed that the struggle to attain to the majority involves an incidental use of intellectual and moral processes; but these influences would exert themselves still more powerfully in other channels if there were no such thing as the ballot, and, when used as subsidiary to the ballot, they represent only a striving for the time when physical force can be substituted for them. Reason devoted to politics fights for its own dethronement. The moment the minority becomes the majority, it ceases to reason and persuade, and begins to command and enforce and punish. If this be true, it follows that to use the ballot for the modification of government is to use force for the modification of government.

Methods of Anarchists.—In the first place the policy to be pursued by individual and isolated Anarchists is dependent upon circumstances. It is not wise warfare to throw your ammunition to the enemy unless you throw it from the cannon's mouth. But if you can compel the enemy to waste his ammunition by drawing his fire on some thoroughly protected spot; if you can, by annoying and goading and harassing him in all possible ways, drive him to the last resort of stripping bare his tyrannous and invasive purposes and put him in the attitude of a designing villain assailing honest men for purposes of plunder,—there is no better strategy. Let no Anarchist, then, place his property within reach of the sheriff's clutch. But some year, when he feels exceptionally strong and independent, when his conduct can impair no serious personal obligations, when on the whole he would a little rather go to jail than not, and when his property is in such shape that he can successfully conceal it, let him declare to the assessor property of a certain value, and then defy the collector to collect. Or, if he have no property, let him decline to pay his poll tax. The State will then be put to its trumps. Of two things, one,—either it will let him alone, and then he will tell his neighbors all about it, resulting the next year in an alarming disposition on their part to keep their own money in their own pockets; or else it will imprison him, and then by the requisite legal processes he will demand and secure all the rights of a civil prisoner and live thus a decently comfortable life until the State shall get tired of supporting him and the increasing number of persons who will follow his example. Unless, indeed, the State, in desperation, shall see fit to make its laws regarding imprisonment for taxes more rigorous, and then, if our Anarchist be a determined man, we shall find out how far a republican government, "deriving its just powers from the consent of the governed," is ready to go to procure that "consent,"—whether it will stop at solitary confinement in a dark cell or join with the Czar of Russia in administering torture by electricity. The farther it shall go the better it will be forAnarchy, as every student of the history of reform well knows. Who can estimate the power for propagandism of a few cases of this kind, backed by a well-organized force of agitators without the prison walls? So much, then, for individual resistance.

But, if individuals can do so much, what shall be said of the ernomous and utterly irresistible power of a large and intelligent minority, comprising say one-fifth of the population in any given locality? I conceive that on this point I need do no more than call attention to the wonderfully instructive history of the Land League movement in Ireland (1881), the most potent and instantly effective revolutionary force the world has ever known so long as it stood by its original policy of "Pay no rent," and which lost nearly all its strength the day it abandoned that policy. It abandoned it because there the peasantry, instead of being an intelligent minority following the lead of principles, were an ignorant, though enthusiastic and earnest, body of men following blindly the lead of unscrupulous politicians like Parnell.

Thrown into jail by the government, these leaders, to secure their release, withdrew the "No Rent Manifesto," which they had issued in the first place not with any intention of freeing the peasants from the burden of "an immoral tax," but simply to make them the tools of their political advancement. Had the people realized the power they were exercising and understood the economic situation, they would not have resumed the payment of rent at Parnell's bidding, and today they might have been free. The Anarchists do not propose to repeat their mistake. That is why they are devoting themselves entirely to the inculcation of principles, especially of economic principles.

But it was pursued far enough to show that the British government was utterly powerless before it; and it is scarcely too much to say, in my opinion, that, had it been persisted in, there would not today be a landlord in Ireland. Within a few short months from the inauguration of the "No-Rent" policy landlordry found itself upon the verge of dissolution. It was at its wits' end. Confronted by this intangible power, it knew not what to do. It wanted nothing so much as to madden the stubborn peasantry into becoming an actively belligerent mob which could be mowed down with gatling guns. But, barring a paltry outbreak here and there, it was impossible to goad the farmers out of their quiesence, and the grip of the landlords grew weaker every day.

It is easier to resist taxes in this country than it is to resist rent in Ireland; and such a policy would be as much more potent here than there as the intelligence of the people is greater, providing always that you can enlist in it a sufficient number of earnest and determined men and women. If one-fifth of the people were to resist taxation, it would cost more to collect their taxes, or try to collect them, than the other four-fifths would consent to pay into the treasury. The force needed for this bloodless fight *Liberty* is slowly but surely recruiting, and sooner or later it will organize for action. Then, Tyranny and Monopoly, down goes your house!

Passive and Non-Resistance.—The chief difference between passive resistance and non-resistance is this: passive resistance is regarded by its champions as a mere policy, while non-resistance is viewed by those who favor it as a principle or universal rule. Believers in passive resistance consider it as generally more effective than active resistance, but think that there are certain cases in which the opposite is true; believers in non-resistance consider either that it is immoral to actively resist or else that it is always unwise to do so.

"Passive resistance," said Ferdinand Lassalle, with an obtuseness thoroughly German, "is the resistance which does not resist." Never was there a greater mistake. It is the only resistance which in these days of military discipline resists with any result. There is not a tyrant in the civilized world today who would not do anything in his power to precipitate a bloody revolution rather than see himself confronted by any large fraction of his subjects determined not to obey. An insurrection is easily quelled; but no army is willing or able to train its guns on inoffensive people who do not even gather in the streets but stay at home and stand back on their rights. Neither the ballot nor the bayonet is to play any great part in the coming struggle.

Power feeds on its spoils, and dies when its victims refuse to be despoiled. They can't persuade it to death, they can't vote it to death, they can't shoot it to death; but they can always starve it to death. When a determined body of people, sufficiently strong in numbers and force of character to command respect and make it unsafe to imprison them, shall agree to quietly close their doors in the faces of the tax collector and the rent collector, and shall, by issuing their own money in defiance of legal prohibition, at the same time cease paying tribute to the money lord, government, with all the privileges which it grants and the monopolies which it sustains, will go by the board.

I care little how the State goes, but I insist that it shall really go,—that it shall be abolished, not reformed. That it cannot be abolished until there shall exist some considerable measure and solid weight of absolute and well-grounded disbelief in it as an institution is a truth too nearly axiomatic for demonstration. In the absence of such disbelief the existing State might be destroyed by the blindly rebellious or might fall through its own rottenness, but another would at once arise in its stead. Why should it not, how could it be otherwise, when all believe in the necessity of the State? Now, it is to create this measure and weight of disbelief that the Anarchist is working. He is simply addressing himself to such persons as are amenable to reason to the end that these may unite and here and now enter upon the work of laying the foundations of liberty, knowing that, these foundations once laid, the structure must rise upon them, the work of all men's hands, as a matter of economic necessity. This is a work that must be done sooner or later, and the sooner the better.

The idea that Anarchy can be inaugurated by force is as

fallacious as the idea that it can be sustained by force. Force cannot preserve Anarchy; neither can it bring it. In fact, one of the inevitable influences of the use of force is to postpone Anarchy. The only thing that force can ever do for us is to save us from extinction, to give us a longer lease of life in which to try to secure Anarchy by the only methods that can ever bring it. But this advantage is always purchased at immense cost, and its attainment is always attended by frightful risk. The attempt should be made only when the risk of any other course is greater. When a physician sees that his patient's strength is being exhausted so rapidly by the intensity of his agony that he will die of exhaustion before the medical processes inaugurated have a chance to do their curative work, he administers an opiate. But a good physician is always loth to do so, knowing that one of the influences of the opiate is to interfere with and defeat the medical processes themselves. He never does it except as a choice of evils. It is the same with the use of force, whether of the mob or of the State, upon diseased society; and not only those who prescribe its indiscriminate use as a sovereign remedy and a permanent tonic, but all who ever propose it as a cure, and even all who would likely and unnecessarily resort to it, not as a cure, but as an expedient, are social quacks.

The right to resist oppression by violence is beyond doubt; it is only the policy of exercising this right that Anarchists at this juncture have to consider. In *Liberty's* view but one thing can justify its exercise on any large scale,—namely, the denial of free thought, free speech, and a free press. Even then its exercise would be unwise unless suppression were enforced so stringently that all other means of throwing it off had become hopeless. Bloodshed in itself is pure loss. When we must have freedom of agitation, and when nothing but bloodshed will secure it, then bloodshed is wise. But it must be remembered that it can never accomplish the Social Revolution proper; that that can never be accomplished except by means of agitation, investigation, experiment, and passive resistance; and that, after all the bloodshed, we shall be exactly where we were before, except in our possession of the power to use these means.

It is because peaceful agitation and passive resistance are, in Liberty's hands, weapons more deadly to tyranny than any others that I uphold them, and it is because force strengthens tyranny that I condemn it. War and Authority are companions; Peace and Liberty are companions. It is foolish in the extreme, not only to resort to force before necessity compels, but especially to madly create the conditions that will lead to this necessity.

Anarchists believe in trial by jury.—Jury trial in its original form differed from its present forms both in the manner of selecting the jury and in the powers of the jury selected. It was originally selected by drawing twelve names from a wheel containing the names of the whole body of citizens, instead of by putting a special panel of jurors through a sifting process of examination; and by its original powers it was judge, not of the facts alone, as is generally the case now, but of the law and the justice of the law and the extent and nature of the penalty. (*Further information on this subject may be found in Lysander Spooner's chapter on "Trial by Jury."*)

XXI
PIERRE A. KROPOTKIN

Pierre Alexeyevitch Kropotkin, born at Moscow, 1842; Russian Socialist and Anarchist; member of the Russian nobility; studied geology and geography at St. Petersburg; became secretary of the Geographical Society, and was appointed chamberlain to the czarina. He was arrested as an Anarchist in 1873, but escaped in 1876 to England; went to Switzerland in 1877, but was expelled from that country in 1881. He was imprisoned in France, 1883, under a law directed against the International Workingmen's Association, of which he was a member, and pardoned in 1886. Since then he has lived in England. He is the author of *Memoirs of a Revolutionist,* 1885; *In Russian and French Prisons,* 1887; *The Conquest of Bread,* 1892 (G. P. Putnam's Sons, New York); *Mutual Aid a Factor in Evolution,* 1902 (McClure-Phillips Co.); *Fields, Factories and Workshops,* and other books and pamphlets.

The selections are from *The Conquest of Bread* and *Mutual Aid.*

Mutual Aid.—As soon as we study animals—not in laboratories and museums only, but in the forest and prairie, in the steppe and in the mountains—we at once perceive that though there is an immense amount of warfare and extermination going on amidst various species, and especially amidst various classes of animals, there is, at the same time, as much, or perhaps even more, of mutual support, mutual aid, and mutual defence amidst animals belonging to the same species or, at least, to the same society. Sociability is as much a law of nature as mutual struggle. Of course it would be extremely difficult to estimate, however roughly, the relative numerical importance of both these series of facts. But if we resort to an indirect test, and ask Nature: "Who are the fittest: those who are continually at war with each other, or those who support one another?" we at once see that those animals which acquire habits of mutual aid are undoubtedly the fittest. They have more chances to survive, and they attain, in their respective classes, the highest development of intelligence and bodily organization. If the numberless facts which can be brought forward to support this view are taken into account, we may safely say that mutual aid is as much a law of animal life as mutual struggle, but that, as a factor of evolution, it most probably has a far greater importance, inasmuch as it favors the development of such habits and characters as insure the maintenance and further development of the species, together with the greatest amount of welfare and enjoyment of life for the individual, with the least waste of energy.

Facts illustrating mutual aid amidst the termites, the ants, and the bees are so well known to the general reader, especially through the works of Romanes, L. Buchner, and Sir John Lubbock, that I may limit my remarks to a very few hints. If we take an ants' nest, we not only see that every description of work—rearing of progeny, foraging, building, rearing of aphides, and so on—is performed according to the principles of voluntary mutual aid; we must also recognize, with Forel, that the chief, the fundamental feature of the life of any species of ants is the fact and the obligation for every ant of sharing its food, already swallowed and partly digested, with every member of the community which may apply for it. Two ants belonging to two different species or to two hostile nests when they occasionally meet together will avoid each other. But two ants belonging to the same nest or to the same colony of nests will approach each other, exchange a few movements with the antennae, and "if one of them is hungry or thirsty, and especially if the other has its crop full, . . . it immediately asks for food." The individual thus requested never refuses; it sets apart its mandibles, takes a proper position, and regurgitates a drop of transparent fluid, which is licked up by the hungry ant. Regurgitating food for other ants is so prominent a feature in the life of ants (at liberty), and it so constantly recurs both for feeding hungry comrades and for feeding larvae, that Forel considers the digestive tube of the ants as consisting of two different parts, one of which, the posterior, is for the special use of the individual, and the other, the anterior part, is chiefly for the use of the community. If an ant which has its crop full has been selfish enough to refuse feeding a comrade, it will be treated as an enemy, or even worse. If the refusal has been made while its kinsfolk were fighting with some other species, they will fall back upon the greedy individual with greater vehemence than even upon the enemies themselves. And if an ant has not refused to feed another ant belonging to an enemy species, it will be treated by the kinsfolk of the latter as a friend. All this is confirmed by most accurate observation and decisive experiments.

The same is true as regards the bees. These small insects, which so easily might become the prey of so many birds, and whose honey has so many admirers in all classes of animals from the beetle to the bear, also have none of the protective features derived from mimicry or otherwise, without which an isolatedly-living insect hardly could escape wholesale destruction; and yet, owing to the mutual aid they practice, they obtain the wide extension which we know and the intelligence we admire. By working in common they multiply their individual forces; by resorting to a temporary division of labor combined with the capacity of each bee to perform every kind of work when required, they attain such a degree of well-being and safety as no isolated animal can ever expect to achieve, however strong or well-armed it may be. In their combinations they are often more successful than man, when he neglects to take advantage of a well-planned mutual assistance. Thus, when a new swarm of bees is going to leave the hive in search of a new abode, a number of bees will make a preliminary exploration of the neighborhood, and if they discover a convenient dwelling-place—say, an old basket, or anything of the kind—they will take possession of it, clean it, and guard it, sometimes for a whole week, till the swarm comes to settle therein. But how many human settlers will perish in new countries simply for not having understood the necessity of combining their efforts! By combining their individual intelligences they succeed in coping with adverse circumstances, even quite unforeseen and unusual, like those bees of the Paris Exhibition which fastened with their resinous propolis the shutter to a glass plate fitted in the wall of their hive. Besides, they display none of the sanguinary proclivities and love of useless fighting with which many writers so readily endow animals. The sentries which guard the entrance to the hive pitilessly put to death the robbing bees which attempt entering the hive; but those stranger bees which come to the hive by mistake are left unmolested, especially if they come laden with pollen, or are young individuals which can easily go astray. There is no more warfare than is strictly required.

The sociability of the bees is the more instructive as predatory instincts and laziness continue to exist among the bees as well, and reappear each time that their growth is favored by some circumstances. It is well known that there always are a number of bees which prefer a life of robbery to the laborious life of a worker; and that both periods of scarcity and periods of an unusually rich supply of food lead to an increase of the robbing class. When our crops are in and there remains but little to gather in our meadows and fields, robbing bees become of more frequent occurrence; while, on the other side, about the sugar plantations of the West Indies and the sugar refineries of Europe, robbery, laziness, and very often drunkenness become quite usual with the bees. We thus see that anti-social instincts continue to exist amidst the bees as well; but natural selection continually must eliminate them, because in the long run the practice of solidarity proves much more advantageous to the species than the development of individuals endowed with predatory inclinations. The cunningest and the shrewdest are eliminated in favor of those who understand the advantages of sociable life and mutual support.

Certainly, neither the ants, nor the bees, nor even the termites, have risen to the conception of a higher solidarity embodying the whole of the species.

It would be quite impossible to enumerate here the various hunting associations of birds; but the fishing associations of the pelicans are certainly worthy of notice for the remarkable order and intelligence displayed by these clumsy birds. They always go fishing in numerous bands, and after having chosen an appropriate bay, they form a wide half-circle in face of the shore, and narrow it by paddling towards the shore, catching all fish that happen to be enclosed in the circle. On narrow rivers and canals they even divide into two parties, each of which draws up on a half-circle, and both paddle to meet each other, just as if two parties of men dragging two long nets should advance to capture all fish taken between the nets when both parties come to meet. As the night comes they fly to their resting-places—always the same for each flock—and no one has ever seen them fighting for the possession of either the bay or the resting-place. In South America they gather in flocks of from forty to fifty thousand individuals, part of which enjoy sleep while the others keep watch, and others again go fishing.

It is evident that it would be quite contrary to all that we know of nature if men were an exception to so general a rule; if a creature so defenseless as man was at his beginnings should have found his protection and his way to progress, not in mutual support, like other animals, but in a reckless competition for personal advantages, with no regard to the interests of the species. To a mind accustomed to the idea of unity in nature, such a proposition appears utterly indefensible. And yet, improbable and unphilosophical as it is, it has never found a lack of supporters. There always were writers who took a pessimistic view of mankind. They knew it, more or less superficially, through their own limited experience; they knew of history what the annalists, always watchful of wars, cruelty, and oppression, told of it, and little more besides; and they concluded that mankind is nothing but a loose aggregation of beings, always ready to fight with each other, and only prevented from so doing by the intervention of some authority.

Hobbes took that position; and while some of his eighteenth

century followers endeavored to prove that at no epoch of its existence—not even in its most primitive condition—mankind lives in a state of perpetual warfare; that men have been sociable even in "the state of nature," and that want of knowledge, rather than the natural bad inclinations of man, brought humanity to all the horrors of its early historical life,—his idea was, on the contrary, that the so-called "state of nature" was nothing but a permanent fight between individuals, accidentally huddled together by the mere caprice of their bestial existence. True, that science has made some progress since Hobbes's time, and that we have safer ground to stand upon than the speculations of Hobbes or Rousseau. But the Hobbesian philosophy has plenty of admirers still; and we have had of late quite a school of writers who, taking possession of Darwin's terminology rather than of his leading ideas, made of it an argument in favor of Hobbes's views upon primitive man, and even succeeded in giving them a scientific appearance. Huxley, as is known, took the lead of that school, and in a paper written in 1888 he represented primitive men as a sort of tigers or lions, deprived of all ethical conceptions, fighting out the struggle for existence to its bitter end, and living a life of "continual free fight"; to quote his own words, "beyond the limited and temporary relations of the family, the Hobbesian war of each against all was the normal state of existence."

It has been remarked more than once that the chief error of Hobbes, and the eighteenth century philosophers as well, was to imagine that mankind began its life in the shape of small straggling families, something like the "limited and temporary" families of the bigger carnivores, while in reality it is now positively known that such was not the case. Of course, we have no direct evidence as to the modes of life of the first man-like beings. We are not yet settled even as to the time of their first appearance, geologists being inclined at present to see their traces in the pliocene, or even the miocene, deposits of the Tertiary period. But we have the indirect method which permits us to throw some light even upon that remote antiquity. A most careful investigation into the social institutions of the lowest races has been carried on during the last forty years, and it has revealed among the present institutions of primitive folk some traces of still older institutions which have long disappeared, but nevertheless left unmistakable traces of their previous existence. A whole science devoted to the embryology of human institutions has thus developed in the hands of Bachofen, MacLennen, Morgan, Edwin Tylor, Maine, Post, Kovalevsky, Lubbock, and many others. And that science has established beyond any doubt that mankind did not begin its life in the shape of small isolated families.

Far from being a primitive form of organization, the family is a very late product of human evolution. As far as we can go back in the paleo-ethnology of mankind, we find men living in societies—in tribes similar to those of the highest mammals; and an extremely slow and long evolution was required to bring these societies to the gentile, or clan organization, which, in its turn, had to undergo another, also very long evolution, before the first germs of family, polygamous or monogamous, could appear. Societies, bands, or tribes—not families—were thus the primitive form of organization of mankind and its earliest ancestors. That is what ethnology has come to after its painstaking researches. And in so doing it simply came to what might have been foreseen by the zoologist. None of the higher mammals, save a few carnivores and a few undoubtedly decaying species of apes (orang-outangs and gorillas), live in small families, isolatedly straggling in the woods. All others live in societies. And Darwin so well understood that isolately living apes never could have developed into man-like beings, that he was inclined to consider man as descended from some comparatively weak but social species, like the chimpanzee, rather than from some stronger but unsociable species, like the gorilla. Zoology and paleo-ethnology are thus agreed in considering that the band, not the family, was the earliest form of social life. The first human societies simply were a further development of those societies which constitute the very essence of life of the higher animals.

Sociability and need of mutual aid and support are such inherent parts of human nature that at no time of history can we discover men living in small isolated families, fighting each other for the means of subsistence.

Far from being the fighting animals they have often been compared to, the barbarians of the first centuries of our era (like so many Mongolians, Africans, Arabs, and so on, who still continue in the same barbarian stage) invariably preferred peace to war. With the exception of a few tribes which had been driven during the great migrations into unproductive deserts or highlands, and were thus compelled periodically to prey upon their better-favored neighbors—apart from these, the great bulk of the Teutons, the Saxons, the Celts, the Slavonians, and so on, very soon after they had settled in their newly-conquered abodes reverted to the spade or to their herds. The earliest barbarian codes already represent to us societies composed of peaceful agricultural communities, not hordes of men at war with each other. These barbarians covered the country with villages and farmhouses; they cleared the forests, bridged the torrents, and colonized the formerly quite uninhabited wilderness; and they left the uncertain warlike pursuits to brotherhoods, scholae, or "trusts" of unruly men, gathered round temporary chieftains, who wandered about, offering their adventurous spirit, their arms, and their knowlege of warfare for the protection of populations, only too anxious to be left in peace. The warrior bands came and went, prosecuting their family feuds; but the great mass continued to till the soil, taking but little notice of their would-be rulers, so long as they did not interfere with the independence of their village communities. The new occupiers of Europe evolved the systems of land tenure and soil culture which are still in force with hundreds of millions of men; they worked out their systems of compensation for wrongs, instead of the old tribal blood-revenge; they learned the first rudiments of industry; and while they fortified their villages with palisaded walls, or erected towers and earthen forts whereto to repair in case of a new invasion, they soon abandoned the task of defending these towers and forts to those who made of war a specialty.

The very peacefulness of the barbarians, certainly not their supposed warlike instincts, thus became the source of their subsequent subjection to the military chieftains. It is evident that the very mode of life of the armed brotherhoods offered them more facilities for enrichment than the tillers of the soil could find in their agricultural communities. Even now we see that armed men occasionally come together to shoot down Matabeles and to rob them of their droves of cattle, though the Matabeles only want peace and are ready to buy it at a high price.

Social Bonds.—Under the present social system, all bonds of union among the inhabitants of the same street or neighborhood have been dissolved. In the richer parts of the large towns, people live without knowing who are their next-door neighbors. But in the crowded lanes people know each other perfectly, and are continually brought into mutual contact. Of course, petty quarrels go their course, in the lanes as elsewhere; but groupings in accordance with personal affinities grow up, and within their circle mutual aid is practiced to an extent of which the richer classes have no idea. If we take, for instance, the children of a poor neighborhood who play in a street or a churchyard, or on a green, we notice at once that a close union exists among them, notwithstanding the temporary fights, and that that union protects them from all sorts of misfortunes. As soon as a mite bends inquisitively over the opening of a drain—"Don't stop there," another mite shouts out, "fever sits in the hole!" "Don't climb over that wall, the train will kill you if you tumble down! Don't come near to the ditch!

Don't eat those berries—poison! you will die!" Such are the first teachings imparted to the urchin when he joins his mates out-doors. How many of the children whose play-grounds are the pavements around "model workers' dwellings," or the quays and bridges of the canals, would be crushed to death by the carts or drowned in the muddy waters, were it not for that sort of mutual support! And when a fair Jack has made a slip into the unprotected ditch at the back of the milkman's yard, or a cherry-cheeked Lizzie has, after all, tumbled down into the canal, the young brood raises such cries that all the neighborhood is on the alert, and rushes to the rescue.

Then comes in the alliance of the mothers. "You could not imagine" (a lady-doctor who lives in a poor neighborhood told me lately) "how much they help each other. If a woman has prepared nothing, or could prepare nothing, for the baby which she expected—and how often that happens!—all the neighbors bring something for the new-comer. One of the neighbors always takes care of the children, and some other always drops in to take care of the household, so long as the mother is in bed." This habit is general. It is mentioned by all those who have lived among the poor. In a thousand small ways the mothers support each other and bestow their care upon children that are not their own. Some training—good or bad, let them decide it for themselves—is required in a lady of the richer classes to render her able to pass by a shivering and hungry child in the street without noticing it. But the mothers of the poorer classes have not that training. They cannot stand the sight of a hungry child; they must feed it, and so they do. "When the school children beg bread, they seldom or rather never meet with a refusal"—a lady friend, who has worked several years in Whitechapel in connection with a workers' club, writes to me. But I may, perhaps, as well transcribe a few more passages from her letter:—

"Nursing neighbors, in cases of illness, without any shade of remuneration, is quite general among the workers. Also, when a woman has little children, and goes out for work, another mother always takes care of them.

"If, in the working classes, they would not help each other, they could not exist. I know families which continually help each other—with money, with food, with fuel, for bringing up the little children, in cases of illness, in cases of death.

"The mine and thine is much less sharply observed among the poor than among the rich. Shoes, dress, hats, and so on,—what may be wanted on the spot—are continually borrowed from each other, also all sorts of household things.

"Last winter the members of the United Radical Club had brought together some little money, and began after Christmas to distribute free soup and bread to the children going to school. Gradually they had 1,800 children to attend to. The money came from outsiders, but all the work was done by the members of the club. Some of them, who were out of work, came at four in the morning to wash and to peel the vegetables; five women came at nine or ten (after having done their own household work) for cooking, and stayed till six or seven to wash the dishes. And at meal time, between twelve and half-past one, twenty to thirty workers came in to aid in serving the soup, each one staying what he could spare of his meal time. This lasted for two months. No one was paid."

To every one who has any idea of the life of the laboring classes it is evident that without mutual aid being practiced among them on a large scale they never could pull through all their difficulties. It is only by chance that a worker's family can live its lifetime without having to face such circumstances as the crisis described by the ribbon weaver, Joseph Gutteridge, in his autobiography. And if all do not go to the ground in such cases, they owe it to mutual help. In Gutteridge's case it was an old nurse, miserably poor herself, who turned up at the moment when the family was slipping towards a final catastrophe, and brought in some bread, coal, and bedding, which she had obtained on credit. In other cases, it will be some one else, or the neighbors will take steps to save the family. But without some aid from other poor, how many more would be brought every year to irreparable ruin!

Mr. Plimsoll, after he had lived for some time among the poor, on 7s. 6d. a week, was compelled to recognize that the kindly feelings he took with him when he began this life "changed to hearty respect and admiration" when he saw how the relations between the poor are permeated with mutual aid and support, and learned the simple ways in which that support is given. After many years' experience, his conclusion was that "when you come to think of it, such as these men were, so were the vast majority of the working classes." As to bringing up orphans, even by the poorest families, it is so widely-spread a habit, that it may be described as a general rule; thus among the miners it was found, after the two explosions at Warren Vale and at Lund Hill, that "nearly one-third of the men killed, as the respective committees can testify, were thus supporting relations other than wife and child. Have you reflected," Mr. Plimsoll added, "what this is? Rich men, even comfortably-to-do men do this, I don't doubt. But consider the difference." Consider what a sum of one shilling, subscribed by each worker to help a comrade's widow, or 6d. to help a fellow-worker to defray the extra expense of a funeral, means for one who earns 16s. a week and has a wife, and in some cases five or six children to support. But such subscriptions are a general practice among the workers all over the world, even in much more ordinary cases than a death in the family, while aid in work is the commonest thing in their lives.

Voluntary Associations.—It is known that every year more than a thousand ships are wrecked on the shores of England. At sea a good ship seldom fears a storm. It is near the coasts that danger threatens—rough seas that shatter her sternpost, squalls that carry off her masts and sails, currents that render her unmanageable, reefs and sand banks on which she runs aground.

Even in olden times, when it was a custom among inhabitants of the coasts to light fires in order to attract vessels onto reefs, and to seize their cargoes, they always strove to save the crew. Seeing a ship in distress, they launched their nutshells and went to the rescue of shipwrecked sailors, only too often finding a watery grave themselves. Every hamlet along the seashore has its legends of heroism, displayed by woman as well as by man, to save crews in distress.

No doubt the State and men of science have done something to diminish the number of casualties. Lighthouses, signals, charts, meteorological warnings have diminished them greatly, but there remain a thousand ships and several thousand human lives to be saved every year.

To this end a few men of good will put their shoulders to the wheel. Being good sailors and navigators themselves, they invented a lifeboat that could weather a storm without being torn to pieces or capsizing, and they set to work to interest the public in their venture, to collect the necessary funds for constructing boats, and for stationing them along the coasts, wherever they could be of use.

These men, not being Jacobins, did not turn to the government. They understood that to bring their enterprise to a successful issue they must have the co-operation, the enthusiasm, the local knowledge, and especially the self-sacrifice of sailors. They also understood that to find men who at the first signal would launch their boat at night, in a chaos of waves, not suffering themselves to be deterred by darkness or breakers, and struggling five, six, ten hours against the tide before reaching a vessel in distress—men ready to risk their lives to save those of others, there must be a feeling of solidarity, a spirit of sacrifice not to be bought with galloon. It was therefore a perfectly spontaneous movement, sprung from agreement and individual initiative. Hundreds of local groups arose along the coasts. The initiators had the common sense not to pose as masters. They looked for sagacity in the fishermen's hamlets, and when a lord sent £1000 to a village on the coast to erect a lifeboat station, and his offer was accepted, he left the choice of a site to the local fishermen and sailors.

Models of new boats were not submitted to the Admiralty. We read in a Report of the Association: "As it is of importance that lifeboatmen should have full confidence in the vessel they man, the Committee will make a point of constructing and equipping the boats according to the lifeboatmen's expressed wish." In consequence every year brings with it new improvements.

The work is wholly conducted by volunteers organizing in committees and local groups; by mutual aid and agreement!— Oh, Anarchists!—Moreover, they ask nothing of ratepayers, and in a year they may receive £40,000 in spontaneous subscriptions.

As to the results, here they are: In 1891 the Association possessed 293 lifeboats. The same year it saved 601 shipwrecked sailors and 33 vessels. Since its foundation it has saved 32,671 human beings.

In 1886, three lifeboats with all their men having perished at sea, hundreds of new volunteers entered their names, organized themselves into local groups, and the agitation resulted in the construction of twenty additional boats. As we proceed, let us note that every year the Association sends to the fishermen and sailors excellent barometers at a price three times less than their sale price. It propagates meteorological knowledge, and warns the parties concerned of the sudden changes predicted by men of science.

Let us repeat, that these hundreds of committees and local groups are not organized hierarchically, and are composed exclusively of volunteers, lifeboatmen, and people interested in the work. The Central Committee, which is more of a center for correspondence, in no wise interferes.

It is true that when voting on a question of education or local taxation takes place in a district, these committees do not, as such, take part in the deliberations, a modesty which unfortunately the members of elected bodies do not imitate. But, on the other hand, these brave men do not allow those who have never faced a storm to legislate for them about saving life. At the first signal of distress they rush forth, concert, and go ahead. There are no galloons, but much goodwill.

Let us take another society of the same kind, that of the Red Cross. The name matters little; let us examine it.

Imagine somebody saying twenty-five years ago: "The State, capable as it is of massacring twenty thousand men in a day, and of wounding fifty thousand more, is incapable of helping its own victims; as long as war exists private initiative must intervene, and men of goodwill must organize internationally for this humane work!" What mockery would not have met the man who had dared thus to speak! To begin with he would have been called Utopian, and if that did not silence him he would have been told: "Volunteers will be found wanting precisely where they are most needed, your hospitals will be centralized in a safe place, while what is indispensable will be wanting in the ambulances. National rivalry will cause poor soldiers to die without help." Disheartening remarks are only equalled by the number of speakers. Who of us has not heard men hold forth in this strain?

Now we know what happened. Red Cross societies organized themselves freely, everywhere, in all countries, in thousands of localities; and when the war of 1870-1 broke out, the volunteers set to work. Men and women offered their services. Thousands of hospitals and ambulances were organized; trains were started carrying ambulances, provisions, linen, and medicaments for the wounded. The English committees sent entire convoys of food, clothing, tools, grain to sow, beasts of draught, even steam-ploughs with their attendants to help in the tillage of departments devastated by the war! Only consult *La Croix Rouge,* by Gustave Moynier, and you will be really struck by the immensity of the work performed.

As to the prophets ever ready to deny other men's courage, good sense, and intelligence, and believing themselves to be the only ones capable of ruling the world with a rod, none of their predictions were realized. The devotion of the Red Cross volunteers was beyond all praise. They were only too glad to occupy the most dangerous posts; and whereas the salaried doctors of the State fled with their staff when the Prussians approached, the Red Cross volunteers continued their work under fire, enduring the brutalities of Bismarck's and Napoleon's officers, lavishing their care on the wounded of all nationalities. Dutch, Italians, Swedes, Belgians, even Japanese and Chinese agreed remarkably well. They distributed their hospitals and their ambulances according to the needs of the occasion. They vied with one another especially in the hygiene of their hospitals. And there is many a Frenchman who still speaks with deep gratitude of the tender care he received from a Dutch or German volunteer in the Red Cross ambulances. But what is this to an authoritarian? His ideal is the regiment doctor, salaried by the State. What does he care for the Red Cross and its hygienic hospitals, if the nurses be not functionaries?

Here is then an organization, sprung up but yesterday, and which reckons its members by hundreds of thousands; possesses ambulances, hospital trains, elaborates new processes for treating wounds, and so on, and is due to the spontaneous initiative of a few devoted men.

Perhaps we shall be told that the State has something to do with this organization. Yes, States have laid hands on it to seize it. The directing committees are presided over by those whom flunkeys call princes of the blood. Emperors and queens lavishly patronize the national committees. But it is not to this patronage that the success of the organization is due. It is to the thousand local committees of each nation; to the activity of individuals, to the devotion of all those who try to help the victims of war. And this devotion would be far greater if the State did not meddle with it.

In any case, it was not by the order of an International Directing Committee that Englishmen and Japanese, Swedes and Chinamen, bestirred themselves to send help to the wounded in 1871. It was not by order of an international ministry that hospitals rose on the invaded territory and that ambulances were carried on to the battlefield. It was by the initiative of volunteers from each country. Once on the spot, they did not get hold of one another by the hair as foreseen by Jacobins; they all set to work without distinction of nationality.

We may regret that such great efforts should be put to the service of so bad a cause, and ask ourselves like the poet's child: "Why inflict wounds if you are to heal them afterwards?" In striving to destroy the power of capital and bourgeois authority, we work to put an end to massacres, and we would far rather see the Red Cross volunteers put forth their activity to bring about (with us) the suppression of war; but we had to mention this immense organization as another illustration of results produced by free agreement and free aid.

Communism.—We find in all modern history a tendency, on the one hand, to retain all that remains of the partial Communism of antiquity, and, on the other, to establish the Communistic principle in the thousand developments of modern life.

As soon as the communes of the tenth, eleventh, and twelfth centuries had succeeded in emancipating themselves from their lords, ecclesiastical or lay, their communal labor and communal consumption began to extend and develop rapidly. The township—and not private persons—freighted ships and equipped expeditions, and the benefit arising from the foreign trade did not accrue to individuals, but was shared by all. The townships also bought provisions for their citizens. Traces of these institutions have lingered on into the nineteenth century, and the folk piously cherish the memory of them in their legends.

All that has disappeared. But the rural township still struggles to preserve the last traces of this Communism, and it succeeds—except when the State throws its heavy sword into the balance.

Meanwhile new organizations, based on the same principle—to every man according to his needs—spring up under a thousand forms; for without a certain leaven of Communism the present societies could not exist. In spite of the narrowly egoistic turn given to men's minds by the commercial system, the tendency towards Communism is constantly appearing, and influences our activities in a variety of ways.

The bridges, for the use of which a toll was levied in the old days, are now become public property and free to all; so are the high roads, except in the East, where a toll is still exacted from the traveler for every mile of his journey. Museums, free libraries, free schools, free meals for children; parks and gardens open to all; streets paved and lighted, free to all; water supplied to every house without measure or stint—all such arrangements are founded on the principle: "Take what you need."

The tramways and railways have already introduced monthly and annual season tickets, without limiting the number of journeys taken; and two nations, Hungary and Russia, have introduced on their railways the zone system, which permits the holder to travel five hundred or a thousand miles for the same price. It is but a short step from that to a uniform charge, such as already prevails in the postal service. In all these innovations, and a thousand others, the tendency is not to measure the individual consumption. One man wants to travel a thousand miles, another five hundred. These are personal requirements. There is no sufficient reason why one should pay twice as much as the other because his need is twice as great. Such are the signs which appear even now in our invividualist societies.

Moreover, there is a tendency, though still a feeble one, to consider the needs of the individual, irrespective of his past or possible services to the community. We are beginning to think of society as a whole, each part of which is so intimately bound up with the others that a service rendered to one is a service rendered to all.

When you go into a public library—not indeed the National Library of Paris, but, say, into the British Museum or the Berlin Library—the librarian does not ask what services you have rendered to society before giving you the book, or the fifty books, which you require, and he comes to your assistance if you do not know how to manage the catalogue. By means of uniform credentials—and very often a contribution of work is preferred—the scientific society opens its museums, its gardens, its library, its laboratories, and its annual conversaziones to each of its members, whether he be a Darwin, or a simple amateur.

At St. Petersburg, if you are pursuing an invention, you go into a special laboratory or a workshop, where you are given a place, a carpenter's bench, a turning lathe, all the necessary tools and scientific instruments, provided only you know how to use them; and you are allowed to work there as long as you please. There are the tools; interest others in your idea, join with fellow workers skilled in various crafts, or work alone if you prefer it. Invent a flying machine, or invent nothing—that is your own affair. You are pursuing an idea—that is enough.

In the same way, those who man the lifeboat do not ask credentials from the crew of a sinking ship; they launch their boat, risk their lives in the raging waves, and sometimes perish, all to save men whom they do not even know. And what need to know them? "They are human beings, and they need our aid—that is enough, that establishes their right—To the rescue!"

Thus we find a tendency, eminently communistic, springing up on all sides, and in various guises, in the very heart of theoretically individualist societies.

Suppose that one of our great cities, so egotistic in ordinary times, were visited tomorrow by some calamity—a siege, for instance—that same selfish city would decide that the first needs to satisfy were those of the children and the aged. Without asking what services they had rendered, or were likely to render to society, it would first of all feed them Then the combatants would be cared for, irrespective of the courage or the intelligence which each has displayed, and thousands of men and women would outvie each other in unselfish devotion to the wounded.

This tendency exists and is felt as soon as the most pressing needs of each are satisfied, and in proportion as the productive power of the race increases. It becomes an active force every time a great idea comes to oust the mean preoccupations of everyday life.

How can we doubt, then, that when the instruments of production are placed at the service of all, when business is conducted on Communistic principles, when labor, having recovered its place of honor in society, produces much more than is necessary to all—how can we doubt but that this force (already so powerful) will enlarge its sphere of action till it becomes the ruling principle of social life?

But ours is neither the Communism of Fourier and the Phalansterians, nor of the German State-Socialists. It is Anarchist Communism,—Communism without government— the Communism of the Free. It is the synthesis of the two ideals pursued by humanity throughout the ages—Economic and Political Liberty.

In taking "Anarchy" for our ideal of political organization we are only giving expression to another marked tendency of human progress. Whenever European societies have developed up to a certain point they have shaken off the yoke of authority and substituted a system founded roughly more or less on the principles of individual liberty. And history shows us that these periods of partial or general revolution, when the governments were overthrown, were also periods of sudden progress both in the economic and the intellectual field. Now it is the enfranchisement of the communes, whose monuments, produced by the free labor of the guilds, have never been surpassed; now it is the peasant rising which brought about the Reformation and imperiled the papacy; and then again it is the society, free for a brief space, which was created at the other side of the Atlantic by the malcontents from the Old World.

Further, if we observe the present development of civilized peoples we see, most unmistakably, a movement ever more and more marked to limit the sphere of action of the Government, and to allow more and more liberty to the individual. This evolution is going on before our eyes, though cumbered by the ruins and rubbish of old institutions and old superstitions. Like all evolutions, it only waits a revolution to overthrow the old obstacles which block the way, that it may find free scope in a regenerated society.

After having striven long in vain to solve the insoluble problem—the problem of constructing a government "which will constrain the individual to obedience without itself ceasing to be the servant of society," men at last attempt to free themselves from every form of government and to satisfy their need for organization by a free contract between individuals and groups pursuing the same aim. The independence of each small territorial unit becomes a pressing need; mutual agreement replaces law, and everywhere regulates individual interests in view of a common object.

All that once was looked on as a function of the Government, is today called in question. Things are arranged more easily and more satisfactorily without the intervention of the State. And in studying the progress made in this direction, we are led to conclude that the tendency of the human race is to reduce Government interference to zero, in fact, to abolish the State, the personification of injustice, oppression, and monopoly.

These organizations, free and infinitely varied, are so natural an outcome of our civilization; they expand so rapidly and group themselves with so much ease; they are so necessary a result of the continual growth of the needs of civilized man; and lastly, they so advantageously replace governmental interference that we must recognize in them a factor of growing importance in the life of societies. If they do not yet spread over the whole of the manifestations of life, it is that they find an insurmountable obstacle in the poverty of the worker, in the castes of present society, in the private appropriation of capital, and in the State. Abolish these obstacles and you will see them covering the immense field of civilized man's activity.

The history of the last fifty years furnishes a living proof that Representative Government is impotent to discharge the functions we have sought to assign to it. In days to come the nineteenth century will be quoted as having witnessed the failure of parliamentarianism.

But this impotence is becoming evident to all; the faults of parliamentarianism, and the inherent vices of the representative principle, are self-evident, and the few thinkers who have made a critical study of them (J. S. Mill and Laveleye) did but give literary form to the popular dissatisfaction It is not difficult, indeed, to see the absurdity of naming a few men and saying to them, "Make laws regulating all our spheres of activity, although not one of you knows anything about them!"

We are beginning to see that government by majorities means abandoning all the affairs of the country to the tide-waiters who make up the majorities in the House and in election committees; to those, in a word, who have no opinion of their own. But mankind is seeking and already finding new issues.

The International Postal Union, the railway unions, and the learned societies give us examples of solutions based on free agreement in place and stead of law.

Today, when groups scattered far and wide wish to organize themselves for some object or other, they no longer elect an international parliament of Jack-of-all-trades. No, where it is not possible to meet directly or come to an agreement by correspondence, delegates versed in the question at issue are sent to treat, with the instructions: "Endeavor to come to an agreement on such or such a question, and then return not with a law in your pocket, but with a proposition of agreement which we may or may not accept."

Such is the method of the great industrial companies, the learned societies, and the associations of every description, which already cover Europe and the United States. And such should be the method of an emancipated society. While bringing about expropriation, society cannot continue to organize itself on the principle of parliamentary representation. A society founded on serfdom is in keeping with absolute monarchy; a society based on the wage system and the exploitation of the masses by the capitalists finds its political expression in parliamentarianism. But a free society, regaining possession of the common inheritance, must seek, in free groups and free federations of groups, a new organization, in harmony with the new economic phase of history.

Every economic phase has a political phase corresponding to it, and it would be impossible to touch property without finding at the same time a new mode of political life.

XXII
WILLIAM B. GREENE

William B. Greene, 1819-1878, American reformer and writer. One of the first men in America to advocate freedom in banking. He taught that interest for the use of money was caused by the State monopoly of banking, and the monopoly of gold and silver as money; that the monetization of all wealth and the organization of credit through Mutual Banks of Issue would reduce interest on money to cost, and that profits and interest on capital would fall. Held a debate on the Mutual Bank with Edward Atkinson in the town hall of Brookline, Mass., in the early seventies. Author of *Mutual Banking*, showing the radical deficiency of the present circulating medium and the advantages of a free currency; *Socialistic, Communistic, Mutualistic, and Financial Fragments*, including *A Short History of Marriage* and the *Address to the Working People's International Association;* and *The Sovereignty of the People*. The selections are from *Mutual Banking*.

Freedom in Money.—The most concise and expressive definition of the term "capital" which we have seen in the writings of the political economists is the one furnished by J. Stuart Mill, in his table of contents. He says: "Capital is wealth appropriated to reproductive employment." There is, indeed, a certain ambiguity attached to the word wealth; but let that pass: we accept the definition. A tailor has five dollars in money, which he proposes to employ in his business. This money is unquestionably capital, since it is wealth appropriated to reproductive employment; but it may be expended in the purchase of cloth, in the payment of journeymen's wages, or in a hundred other ways; what kind of capital, then, is it? It is, evidently, disengaged capital. Let us say that the tailor takes his money, and expends it for cloth; this cloth is also devoted to reproductive employment, and is therefore still capital; but what kind of capital? Evidently, engaged capital. He makes his cloth into a coat. But the coat is no longer capital; for it is no longer (so far at least as the occupation of the tailor is concerned) capable of being appropriated to reproductive employment; what is it then? It is that for the creation of which the capital was originally appropriated;

it is product. The tailor takes this coat, and sells it in the market for eight dollars, which dollars become to him a new disengaged capital. The circle is complete; the coat becomes engaged capital to the purchaser; and the money is disengaged capital, with which the tailor may commence another operation. Money is disengaged capital, and disengaged capital is money. Capital passes, therefore, through various forms: first it is disengaged capital, then it becomes engaged capital, then it becomes product, afterwards it is transformed again into disengaged capital, thus recommencing its circular progress.

The community is happy and prosperous when all professions of men easily exchange with each other the products of their labor; that is, the community is happy and prosperous when money circulates freely, and each man is able with facility to transform his product into disengaged capital, for with disengaged capital, or money, men may command such of the products of labor as they desire, to the extent, at least, of the purchasing power of their money.

The community is unhappy, unprosperous, miserable, when money is scarce, when exchanges are effected with difficulty. For notice that, in the present state of the world, there is never real overproduction to any appreciable extent; for, whenever the baker has too much bread, there are always laborers who could produce that of which the baker has too little, and who are themselves in want of bread. It is when the tailor and the baker cannot exchange that there is want and overproduction on both sides. Whatever, therefore, has power to withdraw the currency from circulation has power also to cause trade to stagnate; power to overwhelm the community with misery; power to carry want, and its correlative, overproduction, into every artisan's house and workshop. For the transformation of product into disengaged capital is one of the regular steps of production; and whatever withdraws the disengaged capital, or money, from circulation, at once renders this step impossible, and thus puts a drag on all production.

But all money is not the same money. There is one money of gold, another of silver, another of brass, another of leather, and another of paper; and there is a difference in the glory of these different kinds of money. There is one money that is a commodity, having its exchangeable value determined by the law of supply and demand, which money may be called (though somewhat barbarously) merchandise-money, as, for instance, gold, silver, brass, bank bills, etc.; there is another money, which is not a commodity, whose exchangeable value is altogether independent of the law of supply and demand, and which may be called mutual money.

The Usury Laws.—A young man goes to a capitalist, saying: "If you will lend me $100, I will go into a certain business, and make $1,500 in the course of the present year; and my profits will thus enable me to pay you back the money you lend me, and another $100 for the use of it. Indeed, it is nothing more than fair that I should pay you as much as I offer; for, after all, there is a great risk in the business, and you do me a greater favor than I do you." The capitalist answers: "I cannot lend you money on such terms; for the transaction would be illegal; nevertheless, I am willing to help you all I can, if I can devise a way. What do you say to my buying such rooms and machinery as you require, and letting them to you on the terms you propose? For, though I cannot charge more than six per cent. on money loaned, I can let buildings whose total value is only $100, at a rate of $100 per annum, and violate no law. Or, again, as I shall be obliged to furnish you with the raw material consumed in your business, what do you say to our entering into a partnership, so arranging the terms of agreement that the profits will be divided in fact, as they would be in the case that I loaned you $100 at 100 per cent. interest per annum?" The young man will probably permit the capitalist to arrange the transaction in any form he pleases, provided the money is actually forthcoming. If the usury laws speak any intelligible language to the capitalist, it is this: "The legislature does not intend that you shall lend money to any young man to help in his business, where the insurance upon the money you trust in his hands, and which is subjected to the risk of his transactions, amounts to more than six per cent. per annum on the amount loaned." And, in this speech, the deep wisdom of the legislature is manifested! Why six, rather than five or seven? Why any restriction at all?

Now for the other side; for we have thus far spoken of the usury laws as they bear on mere personal credit. If a man borrows $1,500 on the mortgage of a farm, worth, in the estimation of the creditor himself, $2,000, why should he pay six per cent. interest on the money borrowed? What does this interest cover? Insurance? Not at all; for the money is perfectly safe, as the security given is confessedly ample: the insurance is 0. Does the interest cover the damage which the creditor suffers by being kept out of his money for the time specified in the contract? This cannot be the fact,—for the damage is also 0,—since a man who lends out money at interest, on perfect security, counts the total amount of interest as clear gain, and would much prefer letting the money at one-half per cent. to permitting it to remain idle. The rate of interest upon money lent on perfect security is commensurate, not with the risk the creditor runs of losing his money—for that risk is 0; not with the inconvenience to which the creditor is put by letting the money go out of his hands,—for that inconvenience is also 0, since the creditor lends only such money as he himself does not wish to use; but it is commensurate with the distress of the borrower. One per cent. per annum interest on money lent on perfect security is, therefore, too high a rate; and all levying of interest money on perfect security is profoundly immoral, since such interest-money is the fruit of the speculation of one man upon the misfortune of another. Yet the legislature permits one citizen to speculate upon the misfortune of another to the amount of six-hundreths per annum of the extent to which he gets him into his power! This is the morality of the usury laws in their bearing on real credit.

Legitimate Credit.—All the questions connected with credit, the usury laws, etc., may be forever set at rest by the establishment of Mutual Banks. Whoever goes to the Mutual Bank, and offers real property in pledge, may always obtain money; for the Mutual Bank can issue money to any extent; and that money will always be good, since it is all of it based on actual property, that may be sold under the hammer. The interest will always be at a less rate than one per cent. per annum, since it covers, not the insurance of the money loaned, there being no such insurance required, as the risk is 0; since it covers, not the damage which is done the bank by keeping it out of its money, as that damage is also 0, the bank having always an unlimited supply remaining on hand, so long as it has a printing-press and paper; since it covers, plainly and simply, the mere expenses of the institution,—clerk-hire, rent, paper, printing, etc. And it is fair that such expenses should be paid under the form of a rate of interest; for thus each one contributes to bear the expenses of the bank, and in the precise proportion of the benefits he individually experiences from it. Thus the interest, properly so called, is 0; and we venture to predict that the Mutual Bank will one day give all the real credit that will be given; for, since this bank will give at 0 per cent. interest per annum, it will be difficult for other institutions to compete with it for any length of time. The day is coming when everything that is bought will be paid for on the spot, and in mutual money; when all payments will be made, all wages settled, on the spot. The Mutual Bank will never, of course, give personal credit; for it can issue bills only on real credit. It cannot enter into partnership with anybody; for, if it issues bills where there is no real guaranty furnished for their repayment, it vitiates the currency, and renders itself unstable. Personal credit will one day be given by individuals only; that is, capitalists will one day enter into partnership with enterprising and capable men who are without capital, and the profits will be divided between the parties according as their contract of partnership may run. Whoever, in the times of the Mutual Bank, has property will have money also; and the laborer who has no property will find it very easy to get it; for every capitalist will seek to secure him as a partner. All services will then be paid for in ready money; and the demand for labor will be increased three, four, and five fold.

As for credit of the kind that is idolized by the present generation, credit which organized society on feudal principles, confused credit, the Mutual Bank will obliterate it from the face of the earth. Money furnished under the existing system to individuals and corporations is principally applied to speculative purposes, advantageous perhaps to those individuals and corporations, if the speculations answer; but generally disadvantageous to the community, whether they answer or whether they fail. If they answer, they generally end in a monopoly of trade, great or small, and in consequent high prices; if they fail, the loss falls on the community. Under the existing system, there is little safety for the merchant. The utmost degree of caution practicable in business has never yet enabled a company or individual to proceed for any long time without incurring bad debts.

The existing organization of credit is the daughter of hard money, begotten upon it incestuously by that insufficiency of circulating medium which results from laws making specie the sole legal tender. The immediate consequences of confused credit are want of confidence, loss of time, commercial frauds, fruitless and repeated applications for payment, complicated with irregular and ruinous expenses. The ultimate consequences are compositions, bad debts, expensive accommodation-loans, lawsuits, insolvency, bankruptcy, separation of classes, hostility, hunger, extravagance, distress, riots, civil war, and, finally, revolution. The natural consequences of mutual banking are, first of all, the creation of order, and the definitive establishment of due organization in the social body; and, ultimately, the cure of all the evils which flow from the present incoherence and disruption in the relations of production and commerce.

Our plan for a Mutual Bank is as follows:

1. Any person, by pledging actual property to the bank, may become a member of the Mutual Banking Company.

2. Any member may borrow the paper money of the bank, on his own note running to maturity (without indorsement), to an amount not to exceed one-half of the value of the property by himself pledged.

3. Each member binds himself in legal form, on admission, to receive in all payments, from whomsoever it may be, and at par, the paper of the Mutual Bank.

4. The rate of interest at which said money shall be loaned shall be determined by, and shall, if possible, just meet and cover, the bare expenses of the institution. As for interest in the common acceptation of the word, its rate shall be, at the Mutual Bank, precisely 0.

5. No money shall be loaned to any persons who are not members of the company; that is, no money shall be loaned, except on a pledge of actual property.

6. Any member, by paying his debts to the bank, may have his property released from pledge, and be himself released from all obligations to the bank, or to the holders of the bank's money, as such.

7. As for the bank, it shall never redeem any of its notes in specie; nor shall it ever receive specie in payments, or the bills of specie-paying banks, except at a discount of one-half of one per cent.

Ships and houses that are insured, machinery, in short, anything that may be sold under the hammer, may be made a basis for the issue of mutual money. Mutual banking opens the way to no monopoly; for it simply elevates every species of property to the rank which has hitherto been exclusively occupied by gold and silver. It may be well (we think it will be necessary) to begin with real estate; we do not say it would be well to end there!

As interest-money charged by Mutual Banks covers nothing but the expenses of the institutions, such banks may lend money, at a rate of less than one per cent. per annum, to persons offering good security.

It may be asked: What advantage does mutual banking hold out to individuals who have no real estate to offer in pledge? We answer this question by another: What advantage do the existing banks hold out to individuals who desire to borrow, but are unable to offer adequate security? If we knew of a plan whereby, through an act of the legislature, every member of the community might be made rich, we would destroy this petition, and draw up another embodying that plan. Meanwhile, we affirm that no system was ever devised so beneficial to the poor as the system of mutual banking; for, if a man, having nothing to offer in pledge, has a friend who is a farmer, or other holder of real estate, and that friend is willing to furnish security for him, he can borrow money at the Mutual Bank at one per cent. interest per annum, whereas, if he should borrow at the existing banks, he would be obliged to pay six per cent. Again: as mutual banking will make money exceedingly plenty, it will cause a rise in the rate of wages, thus benefiting the man who has no property but his bodily strength; and it will not cause a proportionate increase in the price of the necessaries of life, for the price of provisions, etc., depends on supply and demand, and mutual banking operates, not directly on supply and demand, but to the diminution of the rate of interest on the medium of exchange. Mutual banking will indeed cause a certain rise in the price of commodities by creating a new demand; for, with mutual money, the poorer classes will be able to purchase articles which, under the present currency, they never dream of buying.

But certain mechanics and farmers say: "We borrow no

money, and therefore pay no interest. How, then, does this thing concern us?" Hearken, my friends! let us reason together. I have an impression on my mind that it is precisely the class who have no dealings with the banks, and derive no advantages from them, that ultimately pay all the interest-money that is paid. When a manufacturer borrows money to carry on his business, he counts the interest he pays as a part of his expenses, and therefore adds the amount of interest to the price of his goods. The consumer who buys the goods pays the interest when he pays for the goods; and who is the consumer, if not the mechanic and the farmer? If a manufacturer could borrow money at one per cent., he could afford to undersell all his competitors, to the manifest advantage of the farmer and mechanic. The manufacturer would neither gain nor lose; the farmer and mechanic, who have no dealings with the bank, would gain the whole difference; and the bank—which, were it not for the competition of the Mutual Bank, would have loaned the money at six per cent. interest—would lose the whole difference. It is the indirect relation of the bank to the farmer and mechanic, and not its direct relation to the manufacturer and merchant, that enables it to make money. When foreign competition prevents the manufacturer from keeping up the price of his goods, the farmer and mechanic, who are consumers, do not pay the interest-money; but still the interest is paid by the class that derive no benefit from the banks; for, in this case, the manufacturer will save himself from loss by cutting down the wages of his workmen, who are producers. Wages fluctuate, rising and falling (other things being equal) as the rate of interest falls or rises. If the farmer, mechanic, and operative are not interested in the matter of banking, we know not who is.

Let us suppose the Mutual Bank to be at first established in a single town, and its circulation to be confined within the limits of that town. The trader who sells the produce of that town in the city, and buys there such commodities—tea, coffee, sugar, calico, etc.—as are required for the consumption of his neighbors, sells and buys on credit. He does not pay the farmer cash for his produce; he does not sell that produce for cash in the city; neither does he buy his groceries, etc., for cash from the city merchant: but he buys of the farmer at, say, eight months' credit; and he sells to the city merchant at, say, six months' credit. He finds, moreover, as a general thing, that the exports of the town which pass through his hands very nearly balance the imports that he brings into the town for sale: so that, in reality, the exports—butter, cheese, pork, beef, eggs, etc.—pay for the imports,—coffee, sugar, etc. And how, indeed, could it be otherwise? It is not to be supposed that the town has silver mines and a mint; and, if the people pay for their imports in money, it will be because they have become enabled so to do by selling their produce for money. It follows, therefore, that the people in a country town do not make the money, whereby they pay for store-goods, off each other, but that they make it by selling their produce out of the town. There are, therefore, two kinds of trade going on at the same time in the town,—one trade of the inhabitants with each other, and another of the inhabitants, through the store, with individuals living out of town. And these two kinds of trade are perfectly distinct from each other. The mutual money would serve all the purposes of the internal trade, leaving the hard money, and paper based on hard money, to serve exclusively for the purposes of trade that reaches out of the town. The mutual money will not prevent a single dollar of hard money, or paper based on hard money, from coming into the town; for such hard money comes into the town, not in consequence of exchanges made between the inhabitants themselves, but in consequence of produce sold abroad. So long as produce is sold out of the town, so long will the inhabitants be able to buy commodities that are produced out of the town; and they will be able to make purchases to the precise extent that they are able to make sales. The mutual money will therefore prove to them an unmixed benefit; it will be entirely independent of the old money, and will open to them a new trade entirely independent of the old trade. So far as it can be made available, it will unquestionably prove itself to be a good thing; and, where it cannot be made available, the inhabitants will only be deprived of a benefit that they could not have enjoyed,—mutual money, or no mutual money. Besides, the comparative cost of the mutual money is almost nothing; for it can be issued to any amount on good security, at the mere cost of printing, and the expense of looking after the safety of the mortgages. If the mutual money should happen, at any particular time, not to be issued to any great extent, it would not be as though an immense mass of value was remaining idle; for the interest on the mutual money is precisely 0. The mutual money is not itself actual value, but a mere medium for the exchange of actual values,—a mere medium for the facilitation of barter.

We have remarked that, when the trader, who does the out-of-town business of the inhabitants, buys coffee, sugar, etc., he does not pay cash for them, but buys them at, say, six months' credit. Now, the existing system of credit causes, by its very nature, periodical crises in commercial affairs. When one of these crises occurs, the trader will say to the city merchant: "I owe you so much for groceries; but I have no money, for times are hard: I will give you, however, my note for the debt." Now, we leave it to the reader, would not the city merchant prefer to take the mutual money of the town to which the trader belongs, money that holds real estate and produce in that town, rather than the private note of a trader who may fail within a week?

If, under the existing system, all transactions were settled on the spot in cash, things might be different; but, as almost all transactions are conducted on the credit system and as the credit system necessarily involves periodical commercial crises, the mutual money will find very little difficulty in ultimately forcing itself into general circulation. The Mutual Bank is like the stone cut from the mountain without hands, for let it be once established in a single village, no matter how obscure, and it will grow till it covers the whole earth. Nevertheless, it would be better to obviate all difficulty by starting the Mutual Bank on a sufficiently extensive scale at the very beginning.

The Measure of Value.—The bill of a Mutual Bank is not a standard of value, since it is itself measured and determined in value by the silver dollar. If the dollar rises in value, the bill of the Mutual Bank rises also, since it is receivable in lieu of a silver dollar. The bills of a Mutual Bank are not standards of value, but mere instruments of exchange; and as the value of mutual money is determined, not by the demand and supply of mutual money, but by the demand and supply of the precious metals, the Mutual Bank may issue bills to any extent, and those bills will not be liable to any depreciation from excess of supply. And, for like reasons, mutual money will not be liable to rise in value if it happens at any time to be scarce in the market. The issues of mutual money are therefore susceptible of any contraction or expansion which may be necessary to meet the wants of the community, and such contraction or expansion cannot by any possibility be attended with any evil consequences whatever: for the silver dollar, which is the standard of value, will remain throughout at the natural valuation determined for it by the general demand and supply of gold and silver through the whole world.

The bills of Mutual Banks act merely as a medium of exchange; they do not and cannot pretend to be measures or standards of value. The medium of exchange is one thing; the measure of value is another; and the standard of value still another. The dollar is the measure of value. Silver and gold, at a certain degree of fineness, are the standard of value. The bill of a Mutual Bank is a bill of exchange, drawn by all the members of the banking company upon themselves, indorsed and accepted by themselves, payable at sight, but only in services and products. The members of the company bind themselves to receive their own money at par; that is, in lieu of as many silver dollars as are denoted by the denomination on the face of the bill. Services and products are to be estimated in dollars, and exchanged for each other without the intervention of specie.

Mutual money, which neither is nor can be merchandise, escapes the law of supply and demand, which is applicable to merchandise only.

Advantages of a Mutual Currency.—Mutual Banks would furnish an adequate currency; for, whether money were hard or easy, all legitimate paper would be discounted by them. At present banks draw in their issues when money is scarce (the very time when a large issue is desirable), because they are afraid there will be a run upon them for specie; but Mutual Banks, having no fear of a run upon them,—as they have no metallic capital, and never pretend to pay specie for their bills,—can always discount good paper.

It may appear to some readers, notwithstanding the explanations already given, that we go altogether farther than we are warranted when we affirm that the creation of an immense mass of mutual money would produce no depreciation in the price of the silver dollar. The difficulty experienced in understanding this matter results from incorrect notions respecting the standard of value, the measure of value, and the nature of money. This may be made evident by illustration. The yard is a measure of length; and a piece of wood, or a rod of glass or metal, is a corresponding standard of length. The yard, or measure, being ideal, is unvarying; but all the standards we have mentioned contract or expand by heat or cold, so that they vary (to an almost imperceptible degree, perhaps) at every moment. It is almost impossible to measure off a yard, or any other given length, with mathematical accuracy. The measure of value is the dollar; the standard of value, as fixed by law, is silver or gold at a certain degree of fineness. Corn, land, or any other merchantable commodity might serve as a standard of value; but silver and gold form a more perfect standard, on account of their being less liable to variation; and they have accordingly been adopted, by the common consent of all nations, to serve as such. The dollar, as simple measure of value, has—like the yard, which is a measure of length—an ideal existence only. In Naples the ducat is the measure of value; but the Neapolitans have no specific coin of that denomination. Now, it is evident that the bill of a Mutual Bank is, like a note of hand, or like an ordinary bank bill, neither a measure nor a standard of value. It is (1) not a measure; for, unlike all measures, it has an actual, and not a merely ideal, existence. The bill of a Mutual Bank, being receivable in lieu of a specified number of silver dollars, presupposes the existence of the silver dollar as measure of value, and acknowledges itself amendable to that measure. The silver dollar differs from a bill of a Mutual Bank receivable in lieu of a silver dollar, as the measure differs from the thing measured. The bill of a Mutual Bank is (2) not a standard of value, because it has in itself no intrinsic value, like silver and gold; its value being legal, and not actual. A stick has actual length, and therefore may serve as a standard of length; silver has actual intrinsic value, and may therefore serve as a standard of value; but the bill of a Mutual Bank, having a legal value only, and not an actual one, cannot serve as a standard of value, but is referred, on the contrary, to silver and gold as that standard, without which it would itself be utterly unintelligible.

If ordinary bank-bills represented specie actually existing in the vaults of the banks, no mere issue or withdrawal of them could effect a fall or rise in the value of money; for every issue of a dollar-bill would correspond to the locking-up of a specie dollar in the banks' vaults; and every canceling of a dollar-bill would correspond to the issue by the banks of a specie dollar. It is by the exercise of banking privileges—that is, by the issue of bills purporting to be, but which are not, controvertible—that the banks effect a depreciation in the price of the silver dollar. It is this fiction (by which legal value is assimilated to, and becomes, to all business intents and purposes, actual value) that enables bank-notes to depreciate the silver dollar. Substitute verity in the place of fiction, either by permitting the banks to issue no more paper than they have specie in their vaults, or by effecting an entire divorce between bank-paper and its pretended specie basis, and the power of paper to depreciate specie is at an end. So long as the fiction is kept up, the silver dollar is depreciated, and tends to emigrate for the purpose of traveling in foreign parts; but, the moment the fiction is destroyed, the power of paper over metal ceases. By its intrinsic nature specie is merchandise, having its value determined, as such, by supply and demand; but, on the contrary, paper-money is, by its intrinsic nature, not merchandise, but the means whereby merchandise is exchanged, and, as such, ought always to be commensurate in quantity with the amount of merchandise to be exchanged, be that amount great or small. Mutual money is measured by specie, but is in no way assimilated to it; and therefore its issue can have no effect whatever to cause a rise or fall in the price of the precious metals.

Credit.—We are obliged to make a supposition by no means flattering to the individual presented to the reader. Let us suppose, therefore, that some miserable mortal, who is utterly devoid of any personal good quality to recommend him, makes his advent on the stage of action, and demands credit. Are there circumstances under which he can obtain it? Most certainly. Though he possesses neither energy, morality, nor business capacity, yet, if he own a farm worth $2,000, which he is willing to mortgage as security for $1,500 that he desires to borrow, he will be considered as eminently deserving of credit. He is neither industrious, punctual, capable, nor virtuous; but he owns a farm clear of debt, worth $2,000, and verily he shall raise the $1,500!

Personal credit is one thing; real credit is another and a very different thing. In one case, it is the man who receives credit; in the other, it is the property, the thing. Personal credit is in the nature of partnership; real credit is in the nature of a sale, with a reserved right to repurchase under conditions. By personal credit two or more men are brought into voluntary mutual relations; by real credit a certain amount of fixed property is transformed, under certain conditions and for a certain time, into circulating medium; that is, a certain amount of engaged capital is temporarily transformed into disengaged capital.

XXIII
AUBERON HERBERT

Auberon Herbert, 1838-1906, well-known English politician and journalist, son of the third earl of Carnavon. "I have often laughed," Herbert says in his chapter on "Spencer and the Great Machine," "and said that, as far as I myself was concerned, he (Spencer) spoilt my political life. I went into the House of Commons, as a young man, believing we might do much for the people by a bolder and more unsparing use of the power that belonged to the great law-making machine; and great, as it then seemed to me, were those still unexhausted resources of united national action on behalf of the common welfare. It was at that moment that I had the privilege of meeting Mr. Spencer, and the talk which we had—a talk that will always remain very memorable to me—set me busily to work to study his writings. As I read and thought over what he taught, a new window was opened in my mind. I lost my faith in the great machine; I saw that thinking and acting for others had always hindered, not helped, the real progress; that every evil violently stamped out still persisted, almost in a worse form, when driven out of sight, and festered under the surface." Author of *The Danes in Camp*, 1864; *Letters from Sonderberg*; *The Sacrifice of Education to Examination*; *Letters from All Sorts and Conditions of Men*, edited by Herbert, 1889; *A Politician in Trouble About His Soul*, 1884; *True Line of Deliverance*, 1891. The selections are from *A Voluntarist's Creed* and *A Politician in Sight of Haven*.

Liberty and Majority Rule.—On what foundation does Mr. Spencer place political liberty? He founds it on the right of every man to use the faculties he possesses. It is evident, as he insists, that all sciences rest on certain axioms. You remember Euclid's axioms, such as "a whole is greater than its parts," and you can easily perceive that any science, however complicated it may be, owing to its dependence on other sciences that have preceded it, must rest on its own axioms. Now politics are the science of determining the relations in which men can live together with the greatest happiness, and you will find that the axioms on which they depend are, (1) that happiness consists in the exercise of faculties; (2) that as men have these faculties there must be freedom for their exercise; (3) that this freedom must rest on equal and universal conditions, no unequal conditions satisfying our moral sense. Place before your mind the opposite of these statements, and try to construct a definite social system out of them. Happiness is not the exercise of faculties; men having faculties ought not to exercise them; the conditions as regards their exercise should be unequal and varying. Can you seriously maintain any of these statements? When you propose unequal conditions of freedom do you offer a standing ground which men universally could accept, which they could look upon as the perfect condition of their existence? What does any man or any race want more than freedom for themselves? Admit that any one may take more than his share; that is, in other words, that he may restrain by force the exercise of the faculties of others, and in what a sea of moral confusion you are at once plunged. Who is to decide which is the better man or the more civilized race, or how much freedom is to be allowed or disallowed? To settle this question men must act as judges in their own case; and this means that the strongest will declare themselves the most civilized, and will assign such portions of freedom as they choose to the rest of the nation, or the rest of the world, as the case may be. Are you prepared for this? . . .

Those people who wish to make their fellow-men wise, or temperate, or virtuous, or comfortable, or happy, by some rapid exercise of power, little dream of the sterility that belongs to the universal systems which they so readily inflict on them. Some day they will open their eyes and see that there never yet has been a great system sustained by force under which all the best faculties of men have not slowly withered. . . .

Majority rule is not founded—any more than emperor's rule—on reason or justice. There is no reason or justice in making two men subject to three men. The opinions of two men are just as sacred for them as the opinions and interests of three men are for them. Nobody has the moral right to seek his own advantage by force. That is the one unalterable, inviolable condition of a true society. Whether we are many, or whether we are few, we must learn only to use the weapons of reason, discussion, and persuasion. . . .

What does representative government mean? It means the rule of the majority and the subjection of the minority; the rule of every three men out of five, and the subjection of every two men. It means that all rights go to the three men, no rights to the two men. The lives and fortunes, the actions, the faculties and property of the two men, in some cases their beliefs and thoughts, so far as these last can be brought within the control of machinery, are all vested in the three men, as long as they can maintain themselves in power. The three men represent the conquering race, and the two men—*vae victis* as of old—the conquered race. As citizens, the two men are de-citizenized; they have lost all share for the time in the possession of their country, they have no recognized part in the guidance of its fortunes; as individuals they are de-individualized, and hold all their rights—if rights they have—on sufferance. The ownership of their bodies, and the ownership of their minds and souls—so far as you can transfer by machinery the ownership of mind and soul from the rightful owners to the wrongful owners—no more belongs to them, but belongs to those who hold the position of the conquering race. Now that is I believe a true and uncolored description of the system, as it is in its nakedness, as it is in its real self, under which we are content to live. It is not an exaggerated description—there is not a touch in the picture with which you can fairly quarrel.

Why should either two men live at the discretion of three, or three at the discretion of two? Both propositions are absurd from a reasonable point of view. If being a slave and owning a slave are both wrong relations, what difference does it make whether there are a million slave-owners and one slave, or one slave-owner and a million slaves? Do robbery and murder cease to be what they are if done by ninety-nine per cent. of the population? . . .

You cannot serve two masters. You cannot devote yourself to the winning of power, and remain faithful to the great principles. The great principles, and the tactics of the political campaign, can never be made one, never be reconciled. In that region of mental and moral disorder, which we call political life, men must shape their thoughts and actions according to the circumstances of the hour, and in obedience to the tyrant necessity of defeating their rivals. When you strive for power, you may form a temporary, fleeting alliance with the great principles, if they happen to serve your purpose of the moment, but the hour soon comes, as the great conflict enters a new phase, when they will not only cease to be serviceable to you, but are likely to prove highly inconvenient and embarrassing. If you really mean to have and to hold power, you must sit lightly in your saddle, and make and remake your principles with the needs of each new day; for you are as much under the necessity of pleasing and attracting, as those who gain their livelihood in the street. We all know that the course which our politicians of both parties will take, even in the near future, the wisest man cannot foresee. We all know that it will probably be a zig-zag course; that it will have "sharp curves," that it may be in self-evident contradiction to its own past; that although there are many honorable and high-minded men in both parties, the interest of the party, as a party, ever tends to be the supreme influence, overriding the scruples of the truer-judging, the wiser and more careful. Why must it be so, as things are to-day? Because this conflict for power over each other is altogether different in its nature to all other— more or less useful and stimulating—conflicts in which we engage in daily life. As soon as we place unlimited power in the hands of those who govern, the conflict which decided who is to possess the absolute sovereignty over us involves deepest interests, involves all our rights over ourselves, all our relations to each other, all that we most deeply cherish, all that we have, all that we are in ourselves. It is a conflict of such supreme fateful importance, as we shall presently see in more detail, that once engaged in it we must win, whatever the cost; and we can hardly suffer anything, however great or good in itself, to stand between us and victory. In that conflict affecting all the supreme issues of life, neither you nor I, if we are on different sides, can afford to be beaten. Think carefully what this conflict and what the possession of unlimited power in plainest matter of fact means. If I win, I can deal with you and yours as I please; you are my creature, my subject for experiment, my plastic material, to which I shall give any shape that I please; if you win, you in the same way can deal with me and mine, just as you please; I am your political plaything, "your chattel, your anything." Ought we to wonder that, with so vast a stake flung down on the table, even good men forget and disregard all the restraints of their higher nature, and in the excitement of the great game become utterly unscrupulous? There are grim stories of men who have staked body and soul in the madness of their play; are we after all so much unlike them—we gamesters of the political table—staking all rights, all liberties, and the very ownership of ourselves? And what results, what must result from our consenting to enter into this reckless soul-destroying conflict for power over each other? Will there not necessarily be the ever-present, the haunting, the maddening dread of how I shall deal with you if I win; and how you will deal with me if you win? That dread of each other, vague and undefined, yet very real, is perhaps the worst of all the counsellors that men can admit to their hearts. A man who fears, no longer guides and controls himself; right and wrong become shadowy and indifferent to him; the grim phantom drives, and he betakes himself to the path—whatever it is—that seems to offer the best chance of safety. We see the same vague dread acting upon the nations. At times you may have an aggressive and ambitious government, planning a world-policy for its own aggrandizement, that endangers the peace of all other nations; but in most cases it is the vague dread of what some other rival nation will do with its power that slowly leads up to those disastrous and desolating international conflicts. So it is with our political parties. We live dreading each other, and become the reckless slaves of that dread, losing conscience, losing guidance and definite purpose, in our desperate effort to escape from falling under the subjection of those whose thoughts and beliefs and aims are all opposed to our own. True it is that the leaders of a party may have their own higher desires, their own personal sense of right, but it is a higher desire and sense of right which they must often with a sigh—or without a sigh—put away into their pockets, bowing themselves before the ever-present necessity of winning the conflict and saving their own party from defeat. The stake is too great to allow room for scruples, or the more delicate balancings of what is right and wrong in itself. We all know—"Need must, when the devil drives." "Skin for a skin, what will a man not do for his skin."

Now let us look how that winning of the political battle has to be done? Winning means securing for our side the larger crowd; and that can only be done, as we know in our hearts, though we don't always put it into words, by clever baiting of the hook which is to catch the fish. It is of little use throwing the bare hook into the salmon pool; you must have the colors brightly and artistically blended—the colors that suit the particular pool, the state of the water, the state of the weather. Unless you are learned in the fisherman's art, it is but few fish you will carry home in your basket. So in the political pool you must skillfully combine all the glittering attractions that you have to offer; you must appeal to all the different special interests, using the well chosen lure for each. It is true that there may be exceptional moments with all nations when the political arts lose much of their importance, when some great matter rises above special interests, and the people also rise above themselves. But that is human nature at its best; and not the human nature as we have to deal with it on most days of the week. It is also true that the best men in every party stoop unwillingly; but, as I have said, they are not their own masters; they are acting under forces which decide for them the course they must follow, and reduce to silence the voice within them. They have gone in for the winning of power, and those who play for that stake must accept the conditions of the game. You can't make resolutions—it is said—with rosewater; and you can't play at politics, and at the same time listen to what your soul has to say in the matter. The soul of a high-minded man is one thing; and the great game of politics is another thing. You are now part of a machine with a purpose of its own—not the purpose of serving the fixed and supreme principles—the great game laughs at all things that stand before and above itself, and brushes them scornfully aside, but the purpose of securing victory; and to that purpose all the more scrupulous men must conform, like the weaker brethren, or—as the noblest men do occasionally—stand aside. As our system works, it is the party interests that rule and compel us to do their bidding. It must be so; for without unity in the party there is no victory, and without victory no power to be enjoyed. When once we have taken our place in the great game, all choice as regards ourselves is at an end. We must win; and we must do the things which mean winning, even if those things are not very beautiful in themselves. And what is it that we have to do? In plain words—and plainness of thought, directness of speech, is the only wholesome course—we must buy the larger half of the nation; and buying the nation means setting up before all the various groups, of which it is composed, the supreme object, the idol of their own special interests. We must offer something that makes it worth while for each group to give us their support, and that something must be more than our rivals offer. Put your own self-interests in the first place, and see that you get them—is the watchword of all politics—though we don't often express it in those crude and unashamed terms. Political art has, like many another accomplishment, its own refinements for half veiling the real meanings. If we wish to do our work in the finer fashion, in the artist's way, we must use the light and skilful hand; we must mix in the attractive phrases, appeal to patriotic motives, borrow—a little cautiously—such assistance as we can from the great principles—a slight passing bow that does not too deeply commit us to their acquaintance as regards the future—and throw dexterously over it all—as a clever cook introduces into her dishes her choicest seasoning—a flavor of noble and disinterested purpose. It is a fine art of its own, to buy, and at the same time to gild and beautify the buying; to get the voter into the net, and at the same time to inspire him with the happy consciousness that, whilst he is getting what he wants, he is through it all the devoted patriot, serving the great interests of his country. And then also you must study and understand human nature; you must play—as the skilled musician plays on his instrument—on all the strings—both the higher and the lower—of that nature; you must utilize all ambitions, desires, prejudices, passions and hatreds—lightly touching, as occasion offers, on the higher notes. But in this matter, as in all other matters, underneath the fine words, business remains business; and the business of politics is to get the votes, without which the great prize of power could not by any possibility be won. Votes must be had—the votes of the crowd, both the rich and the poor crowd, whatever may be the price which the market of the day exacts from those who are determined to win.

So rolls the ball. We follow the inevitable course that seeking for power forces upon us. Politics, in spite of all better desires and motives, become a matter of traffic and bargaining; and in the rude process of buying, we find ourselves treading not only on the interests, but on the rights of others, and we soon learn to look on it as a quite natural and unavoidable part of the great game. Keener and keener the competition, more heart and brain-absorbing grows the great conflict, and the people and the politicians cannot help mutually corrupting each other. This buying up of the groups is so distinctly recognized nowadays, that lately a *Times* correspondent—whose letters we read with much interest—speaking of a newly formed ministry abroad, wrote, with unconscious cynicism, that it would have to choose between leaning on the extreme right or the extreme left.

Power.—Is unlimited power—whether with or without good sense and fairness—a right or wrong thing in itself? Can we in any way make it square with the great principles? Can we morally justify the putting of the larger part of our mind and body—in some cases almost the whole—under the rule of others; or the subjecting of others in the same way to ourselves? If you answer that it is a right thing—then see plainly what follows. You are putting the force of the most numerous, or perhaps of the most cunning, who often lead the most numerous—which, disguise and polish the external form of it as much as you like, will always remain true to its own essentially brutal and selfish nature—in the first place, making of it our supreme principle; and if unlimited power—remember it is unlimited power— power to do whatever the governing majority thinks right— is a right thing, must you not leave it—whatever may be your own personal views—to those who possess it to decide how they will employ it? You can't dictate to others, in the hour of their victory, as to what they will do or not do; and they can't dictate to you, in the hour of your victory. Unlimited power— as the term expresses—can only be defined and limited by itself; if it were subject to any limiting principle, it would cease to be unlimited, and become something of a different nature. And remember always—when once you entered into the struggle for the possession of this unlimited power, that you sanctioned its existence, as a lawful prize, for which we may all rightly contend; and if the prize does not fall to you, it will only remain for you to accept the consequences of your consent to take part in the reckless and dangerous competition. By entering into that conflict, by competing for that prize you sanctioned the ownership of some men by other men; you sanctioned the taking away from some men—say two-fifths of the nation—all the great rights, and the reducing of them to mere cyphers, who have lost power over themselves. Once you have sanctioned the act of stripping the individual of his own intelligence and will and conscience, and of the self-guidance which depends upon these things, you cannot then turn your back upon yourself, and indignantly point to the mass of unhappy individuals who are now writhing under the stripping process. You should have thought of all this before you consented to put up the ownership of the individual to public auction, before you consented to throw all these rights into the great melting-pot. In your desire to have power in your own hands, you threw away all restraints, all safeguards, all limits as regards the using of it; you wanted to be able to do just as you yourself pleased with it, when once you possessed it; and what good reason have you now to complain, when your rivals—or shall I say your conquerors—in their turn do just what they please with it? You entered into the game with all its possible penalties; you made your bed, it only remains for you to lie on it.

Let us follow a little further this rightfulness of unlimited power in which you believe. If it is a right thing in itself, who shall give any clear and certain rule to tell us when and where it ceases to be a right thing? Is any right thing by being pushed a little further, and then a little further, and yet a little further, transformed at some definite point into a wrong thing, unless some new element, that changes its nature, comes into the matter? The question of degree can hardly change right into wrong in any authoritative way, that men with their many varying opinions will agree to accept. We may, and should forever dispute over such movable boundary lines—lines that each man according to his own views and feeling would draw for himself. If it is right to use unlimited power to take the one-tenth of a man's property, is it also right to take one-half or the whole? If it is not right to take the half, where is the magical undiscoverable point at which right is suddenly converted into wrong? If it is right to restrict a man's faculties—not employed for an act of aggression against his neighbor—

in one direction, is it right to restrict them in half a dozen or a dozen different directions? Who shall say? It is a matter of opinion, taste, feeling. Perhaps you answer—we will judge each case on its merits; but then once more you are in the illusory region of words, for, apart from any fixed principle, the merits will be always determined by our varying personal inclinations. It is all slope, ever falling away into slope, with no firm level standing place to be found anywhere. Nor do I feel quite sure, if we speak the truth, that any of us are much inclined to accept the rule of moderation and good sense in this matter. You and I, who have entered into this great struggle for unlimited power, have made great efforts and sacrifices to obtain it; now that we have won our prize, why should we not reap the full fruits of victory; why should we be sparing and moderate in our use of it? Is not the laborer worthy of his wage; is not the soldier to receive his prize money? If power was worth winning, it must be worth using. If power is a good thing, why should we hold back our hand; why not do all we can with it, and extract from it its full service and usefulness? Our efforts, our sacrifices of time, money and labor, and perhaps of principle—if that is worth counting—were not made for the possession of mere fragmentary pieces of power, but for power to do exactly as we please with our fellow-men. It is rather late in the day, now that we have won the stake, to tell us that we must leave the larger part of it lying on the table; that, having defeated the enemy, we must evacuate his territory, and not even ask for an indemnity to compensate us for our sacrifices. Do you not see, first, that—as a mental abstract—physical force is directly opposed to morality; and, secondly, that it practically drives out of existence the moral forces? How can an act done under compulsion have any moral element in it, seeing that what is moral is the free act of an intelligent being? If you tie a man's hands there is nothing moral about his not committing murder. Such an abstaining from murder is a mechanical act; and just the same in kind, though less in degree, are all the acts which men are compelled to do under penalties imposed upon them by their fellow-men. Those who would drive their fellow-men into the performance of any good actions do not see that the very elements of morality —the free act following on the free choice—are as much absent in those upon whom they practice their legislation as in a flock of sheep penned in by hurdles. You cannot see too clearly that force and reason—which last is the essence of the moral act—are at the two opposite poles. When you act by reason you are not acting under the compulsion of other men; when you act under compulsion you are not acting under the guidance of reason. The one is a force within you and the other is a force without. Moreover, physical force in a man's hand is an instrument of such brutal character that its very nature destroys and excludes the kindlier or better qualities of human nature. The man who compels his neighbor is not the man who reasons with and convinces him, who seeks to influence him by example, who rouses him to make exertions to save himself He takes upon himself to treat him, not as a being with reason, but as an animal in whom reason is not. The old saying, that any fool can govern with bayonets, is one of the truest sayings which this generation has inherited and neglected.

Force and Power.—Deny human rights, and however little you may wish to do so, you will find yourself abjectly kneeling at the feet of that old-world god Force—that grimmest and ugliest of gods that men have ever carved for themselves out of the lusts of their hearts; you will find yourselves hating and dreading all other men who differ from you; you will find yourselves obliged by the law of the conflict into which you have plunged, to use every means in your power to crush them before they are able to crush you; you will find yourselves day by day growing more unscrupulous and intolerant, more and more compelled by the fear of those opposed to you, to commit harsh and violent actions, of which you would once have said "Is thy servant a dog that he should do these things?" you will find yourselves clinging to and welcoming Force, as the one and only form of protection left to you, when you have once destroyed the rule of the great principles. When once you have plunged into the strife for power, it is the fear of those who are seeking for power over you that so easily persuades to all the great crimes. Who shall count up the evil brood that is born from power—the pitiful fear, the madness, the despair, the overpowering craving for revenge, the treachery, the unmeasured cruelty? It is liberty alone, broad as the sky above our heads, and planted deep and strong as the great mountains, that allows the better and higher part of our nature to rule in us, and subdues those passions that we share with the animals.

Those who bid you use force are merely using language of the same kind as every blood-stained ruler has used in the past, the language of those who paid their troops by pillage, the language of the war-loving German general, who in old days looked down from the heights surrounding Paris, and whispered with a gentle sigh—"What a city to sack!" It is the language of those who through all the past history of the world have believed in the right of conquering, in the right of making slaves, who have set up force as their god, who have tried to do by the violent hand whatever smiled to their own desires, and who only brought curses upon themselves, and a deluge of blood and tears upon the world. Force—whatever form it takes—can do nothing for you. It can redeem nothing; it can give you nothing that is worth the having, nothing that will endure; it cannot even give you material prosperity. There is no salvation for you or for any living man to be won by the force that narrows rights, and always leaves men lower and more brutal in character than it found them. It is, and ever has been the evil genius of our race. It calls out the reckless, violent, cruel part of our nature, it wastes precious human effort in setting men to strive one against the other; it turns us into mere fighting animals; and ends, when men at last become sick of the useless strife and universal confusion, in "the man on the black horse" who calls himself and is greeted as "the saviour of society." Make the truer, the nobler choice. Resist the blind and sordid appeal to your interests of the moment, and take your place once and for good on the side of the true liberty, that calls out all the better and higher part of our nature, and knows no difference between rulers and ruled, majorities and minorities, rich and poor.

Our great purpose is to get rid of force, to banish it wholly from our dealings with each other, to give it notice to quit from this changed world of ours; but as long as some men—like Bill Sykes and all his tribe—are willing to make use of it for their own ends, or to make use of fraud, which is only force in disguise, wearing a mask, and evading our consent, just as force with violence openly disregards it—so long we must use force to restrain force. That is the one and only one rightful employment of force—force in the defence of the plain simple rights of liberty, of the exercise of faculties, and therefore of the rights of property, public or private, in a word, of all the rights of self-ownership—force used defensively against force used aggressively. The only true use of force is for the destruction, the annihilation of itself, to rid the world of its own mischief making existence. Even when used defensively, it still remains an evil, only to be tolerated in order to get rid of the greater evil. It is the one thing in the world to be bound down with chains, to be treated as a slave, and only as a slave, that must always act under command of something better and higher than itself. Wherever and whenever we use it, we must surround it with the most stringent limits, looking on it, as we should look on a wild and dangerous beast, to which we deny all will and free movement of its own. It is one of the few things in our world to which liberty must be forever denied. Within those limits the force that keeps a clear and open field for every effort and enterprise of human activity—that are in themselves untainted by force and fraud—such force is in our present world a necessary and useful servant, like the fire which burns in the fireplaces of our rooms and the ranges of our kitchen; force, which, once it passes beyond that purely defensive office, becomes our worst, our most dangerous enemy, like the fire which escapes from our fireplaces and takes its own wild course. If then we are wise and clear-seeing, we shall keep the fire in the fireplace, and never allow it to pass away from our control.

Under no circumstances can we afford to depart from the great principle that we must never abandon our own personality, that we must only strive for the ends in which we ourselves believe, and never consent to enter into combinations, in which we either are used against our convictions, or use others against their convictions. Whenever we descend to "log rolling"— your services to pay for my services—we are lost in a sea of intrigue and corruption, and all true guidance disappears. There is no true guidance for any of us, except in our own best and highest selves, in our own personal sense of what is true and right. When that goes, there is little, if anything, worth the saving.

Progress depends upon a great number of small changes and adaptations and experiments, constantly taking place— each carried out by those who have strong beliefs and clear perceptions of their own in the matter; for the only true experimenter is he who finds and follows his own way, and is free to try his experiment from day to day. But this true experimentation is impossible under universal systems. An experiment can only be tried on a small scale by those who are the clearer-sighted amongst us, and are aiming at some particular end, and when those who are affected by it are willing to take the risk. You can't rightly experiment with a whole nation; and the consequence is that the sin and mistakes of every universal system go on silently accumulating, until the time for the next periodical tearing up by the roots of what exists comes due, and once more we start afresh.

Has not the real prosperity, the happiness, the peace of a nation increased just in proportion as it has broken all the bonds and disabilities that impeded its life, just in proportion as it has let liberty replace force; just in proportion as it has chosen and established for itself all rights of opinion, of meeting, of discussion, rights of free trade, rights of the free use of faculties, rights of self-ownership as against the wrongs of subjection? And do you think that these new bonds and restrictions in which the nations of today have allowed themselves to be entangled—the conscription which sends men out to fight, consenting or not consenting, which treats them as any other war-material, as the guns and the rifles dispatched in batches to do their work; or the great systems of taxation, which make of the individual mere tax-material, as conscription makes of him mere war-material; or the great systems of compulsory education, under which the State on its own unavowed interest tries to exert more and more of its own influence and authority over the minds of the children, tries—as we see specially in other countries—to mould and to shape those young minds for its own ends—"Something of religion will be useful—school-made patriotism will be useful—drilling will be useful"—so preparing from the start docile and obedient State-material, ready made for taxation, ready made for conscription—ready made for the ambitious aims and ends of the rulers—do you think that any of these modern systems, though they are more veiled, more subtle, less frank and brutal than the systems of the older governments, though the poison in them is more thickly smeared with the coating of sugar, will bear different fruit, will work less evil amongst us all, will endure longer than those other broken and discredited attempts, which men again and again in their madness and presumption have made to possess themselves of and to rule the bodies and minds of others? No! one and all they belong to the same evil family; they are all part of the same conspiracy against the true greatness of human nature; they are all marked broad across the forehead with the same old curse; and they will all end in the same shameful and sorrowful ending. Over us all is the great unchanging law, ever the same.

Liberty and Society.—And now place before yourselves the picture of the nation that not simply out of self-interest but for right's sake and conscience sake took to its heart the great cause of true liberty, and was determined that all men and women should be left free to guide themselves and take charge of their own lives; that was determined to oppress and persecute and restrain the actions of no single person in order to serve any interest or any opinion or any class advantage; that flung out of its hands the bad instrument of force—using force only for its one clear, simple and rightful purpose of restraining all acts of force and fraud, committed by one citizen against another, of safeguarding the lives, the actions, the property of all, and thus making a fair open field for all honest effort; think, under the influences of liberty and her twin-sister peace—for they are inseparably bound together—neither existing without the other—how our character as a people would grow nobler and at the same time softer and more generous—think how the old useless enmities and jealousies and strivings would die out; how the unscrupulous politician would become a reformed character, hardly recognizing his old self in his new and better self; how men of all classes would learn to co-operate together for every kind of good and useful purpose; how, as the results of this free co-operation, innumerable ties of friendship and kindliness would spring up amongst us all of every class and condition, when we no longer sought to humble and crush each other, but invited all who were willing to work freely with us; how much truer and more real would be the campaign against the besetting vices and weakness of our nature, when we sought to change that nature, not simply to tie men's hands and restrain external action, no longer setting up and establishing in all parts of life that poor weak motive—the fear of punishment—those clumsy useless penalties, evaded and laughed at by the cunning, that have never yet turned sinner into saint;

how we should rediscover in ourselves the good vigorous stuff that lies hidden there, the power to plan, to dare and to do; how we should see in clearer light our duty towards other nations, and fulfil, more faithfully our great world-trust; how we should cease to be a people divided into three or four quarrelsome unscrupulous factions—ready to sacrifice all the great things to their intense desire for power—and grow into a people really one in heart and mind, because we frankly recognized the right to differ, the right of each one to choose his own path because we respected and cherished the will, the intelligence, the free choice of others, as much as we respect and cherish these things in ourselves, and were resolved never to trample, for the sake of any plea, for any motive, on the higher parts of human nature, resolved that—come storm or sunshine—we would not falter in our allegiance to liberty and her sister peace, that we would do all, dare all and suffer all, if need be, for their sake, then at last the regeneration of society would begin, the real promised land, not the imaginary land of vain and mocking desires, would be in sight.

XXIV
G. BERNARD SHAW

George Bernard Shaw, British dramatist, critic, novelist, humanitarian; born at Dublin, Ireland, 1856. Music and art critic; Shakespeare enthusiast; one of the founders of the Fabian Society; at present devoting his time to lecturing on social and ethical questions, and writing. His works include the novels, *The Irrational Knot, Love Among the Artists, Cashel Byron's Profession*, and *An Unsocial Socialist; Fabianism and the Empire*, 1900; *Fabianism and the Fiscal Question*, 1904; *The Sanity of Art*, 1898; *The Perfect Wagnerite*, 1898; *Dramatic Criticisms;* and plays, including *Plays Pleasant and Unpleasant* (1898), *Three Plays for Puritans* (1900), *The Admirable Bashville* (1901), *Major Barbara* (1905), *Getting Married* (1908), *Press Cuttings* (1909), *The Doctor's Dilemma, The Showing Up of Blanco Posnet* (1908), *Fanny's First Play* (1912), etc.

The selections are from *The Quintessence of Ibsenism* (1891) and *Man and Superman* (1903).

Imprisonment is as irrevocable as death.

In heaven an angel is nobody in particular.

Liberty means responsibility. That it is why most men dread it.

It is dangerous to be sincere unless you are also stupid.

Self-sacrifice enables us to sacrifice other people without blushing.

Self-denial is not a virtue: it is only the effect of prudence on rascality.

Martyrdom is the only way in which a man can become famous without ability.

Your breathing goes wrong the moment your conscious self meddles with it.

No man dares say so much of what he thinks as to appear to himself an extremist.

Vice is waste of life. Poverty, obedience and celibacy are the canonical vices.

A king nowadays is only a dummy put up to draw your fire off the real oppressors of society.

Beware of the man who does not return your blow: he neither forgives you nor allows you to forgive yourself.

If you begin by sacrificing yourself to those you love, you will end by hating those to whom you have sacrificed yourself.

Disobedience, the rarest and most courageous of the virtues, is seldom distinguished from neglect, the laziest and commonest of the vices.

(In the Fabian Society) no one of us is strong enough to impose his will on the rest, or weak enough to allow himself to be overridden.

Every fool believes what his teachers tell him, and calls his credulity science or morality as confidently as his father called it divine revelation.

I can no longer be satisfied with fictitious morals and fictitious good conduct, shedding fictitious glory on overcrowding, disease, crime, drink, war, cruelty, infant mortality, and all the other commonplaces of civilization which drive men to the theater to make foolish pretences that these things are progress, science, morals, religion, patriotism, imperial supremacy, national greatness, and all the other names the newspapers call them.

How to Beat Children.—If you strike a child, take care that you strike it in anger, even at the risk of maiming it for life. A blow in cold blood neither can nor should be forgiven.

If you beat children for pleasure, avow your object frankly, and play the game according to the rules, as a foxhunter does; and you will do comparatively little harm. No foxhunter is such a cad as to pretend that he hunts the fox to teach it not to steal chickens, or that he suffers more acutely than the fox at the death. Remember that even in child-beating there is the sportsman's way and the cad's way.

The Perfect Gentleman.—The fatal reservation of the gentleman is that he sacrifices everything to his honor except his gentility.

A gentleman of our days is one who has money enough to do what every fool would do if he could afford it: that is, consume without producing.

The true diagnostic of modern gentility is parasitism.

No elaboration of physical or moral accomplishment can atone for the sin of parasitism.

A moderately honest man with a moderately faithful wife, moderate drinkers both, in a moderately healthy house: that is the true middle class unit.

The Golden Rule.—Do not do unto others as you would that they should do unto you. Their tastes may not be the same.

Never resist temptation: prove all things: hold fast that which is good.

Do not love your neighbor as yourself. If you are on good terms with yourself it is an impertinence: if on bad, an injury.

The golden rule is that there are no golden rules.

Idolatry.—The art of government is the organization of idolatry.

The bureaucracy consists of functionaries; the aristocracy, of idols; the democracy, of idolaters.

The populace cannot understand the bureaucracy: it can only worship the national idols.

The savage bows down to idols of wood and stone: the civilized man to idols of flesh and blood.

A limited monarchy is a device for combining the inertia of a wooden idol with the credibility of a flesh and blood one.

When the wooden idol does not answer the savage's prayer, he beats it: when the flesh and blood idol does not satisfy the civilized man, he cuts its head off.

He who slays a king and he who dies for him are alike idolaters.

Democracy.—If the lesser mind could measure the greater as a foot-rule can measure a pyramid, there would be finality in universal suffrage. As it is, the political problem remains unsolved.

Democracy substitutes election by the incompetent many for appointment by the corrupt few.

Democratic republics can no more dispense with national idols than monarchies with public functionaries.

Government presents only one problem: the discovery of a trustworthy anthropometric method.

Social progress takes effect through the replacement of old institutions by new ones; and since every institution involves the recognition of the duty of conforming to it, progress must involve the repudiation of an established duty at every step. If the Englishman had not repudiated the duty of absolute obedience to his king, his political progress would have been impossible. If women had not repudiated the duty of absolute submission to their husbands, and defied public opinion as to the limits set by modesty to their education, they would never have gained the protection of the Married Women's Property Act or the power to qualify themselves as medical practitioners. If Luther had not trampled on his duty to the head of his Church and on his vow of chastity, our priests would still have to choose between celibacy and profligacy. There is nothing new, then, in the defiance of duty by the reformer: every step of progress means a duty repudiated, and a scripture torn up. And every reformer is denounced accordingly, Luther as an apostate, Cromwell as a traitor, Mary Wollstonecraft as an unwomanly virago, Shelley as a libertine, and Ibsen as all the things enumerated in the *Daily Telegraph.*

Women.—Now of all the idealist abominations that make society pestiferous, I doubt if there be any so mean as that of forcing self-sacrifice on a woman under pretence that she likes it; and, if she ventures to contradict the pretence, declaring her no true woman. In India they carried this piece of idealism to the length of declaring that a wife could not bear to survive her husband, but would be prompted by her own faithful, loving, beautiful nature to offer up her life on the pyre which consumed his dead body. The astonishing thing is that women, sooner than be branded as unsexed wretches, allowed themselves to be stupefied with drink, and in that unwomanly condition burnt alive.

The domestic career is no more natural to all women than

the military career is natural to all men; although it may be necessary that every able-bodied woman should be called on to risk her life in childbed just as it may be necessary that every man should be called on to risk his life in the battlefield. It is of course quite true that the majority of women are kind to children and prefer their own to other people's. But exactly the same thing is true of the majority of men, who nevertheless do not consider that their proper sphere is the nursery. The case may be illustrated more grotesquely by the fact that the majority of women who have dogs are kind to them, and prefer their own dogs to other people's; yet it is not proposed that women should restrict their activities to the rearing of puppies. If we have come to think that the nursery and the kitchen are the natural sphere of a woman, we have done so exactly as English children come to think that a cage is the natural sphere of a parrot—because they have never seen one anywhere else. No doubt there are Philistine parrots who agree with their owners that it is better to be in a cage than out, so long as there is plenty of hempseed and Indian corn there. There may even be idealist parrots who persuade themselves that the mission of a parrot is to minister to the happiness of a private family by whistling and saying "Pretty Polly," and that it is in the sacrifice of its liberty to this altruistic pursuit that a true parrot finds the supreme satisfaction of its soul. I will not go so far as to affirm that there are theological parrots who are convinced that imprisonment is the will of God because it is unpleasant; but I am confident that there are rationalist parrots who can demonstrate that it would be a cruel kindness to let a parrot out to fall a prey to cats, or at least to forget its accomplishments and coarsen its naturally delicate fibres in an unprotected struggle for existence. Still, the only parrot a free-souled person can sympathize with is the one that insists on being let out as the first condition of its making itself agreeable. A selfish bird, you may say: one that puts its own gratification before that of the family which is so fond of it—before even the greatest happiness of the greatest number: one that, in aping the independent spirit of a man, has unparroted itself and become a creature that has neither the home-loving nature of a bird nor the strength and enterprise of a mastiff. All the same, you respect that parrot in spite of your conclusive reasoning; and if it persists, you will have either to let it out or kill it.

Duty.—The sum of the matter is that unless woman repudiates her womanliness, her duty to her husband, to her children, to society, to the law, and to everyone but herself, she cannot emancipate herself. But her duty to herself is no duty at all, since a debt is canceled when the debtor and creditor are the same person. Its payment is simply a fulfilment of the individual will, upon which all duty is a restriction, founded on the conception of the will as naturally malign and devilish. Therefore, woman has to repudiate duty altogether. In that repudiation lies her freedom; for it is false to say that woman is now directly the slave of man: she is the immediate slave of duty; and as man's path to freedom is strewn with the wreckage of the duties and ideals he has trampled on, so must hers be. She may indeed mask her iconoclasm by proving in rationalist fashion, as man has often done for the sake of a quiet life, that all these discarded idealist conceptions will be fortified instead of shattered by her emancipation.

No one ever feels helpless by the side of the self-helper; whilst the self-sacrificer is always a drag, a responsibility, a reproach, an everlasting and unnatural trouble with whom no really strong soul can live. Only those who have helped themselves know how to help others, and to respect their right to help themselves.

Love and Marriage.—Although romantic idealists generally insist on self-surrender as an indispensable element in true womanly love, its repulsive effect is well known and feared in practice by both sexes. The extreme instance is the reckless self-abandonment seen in the infatuation of passionate sexual desire. Every one who becomes the object of that infatuation shrinks from it instinctively. Love loses its charm when it is free; and whether the compulsion is that of custom and law, or of infatuation, the effect is the same: it becomes valueless. The desire to give inspires no affection unless there is also the power to withhold; and the successful wooer, in both sexes alike, is the one who can stand out for honorable conditions, and, failing them, go without. Such conditions are evidently not offered to either sex by the legal marriage of today; for it is the intense repugnance inspired by the compulsory character of the legalized conjugal relation that leads, first to the idealization of marriage whilst it remains indispensable as a means of perpetuating society; then to its modification by divorce and by the abolition of penalties for refusal to comply with judicial orders for restitution of conjugal rights; and finally to its disuse and disappearance as the responsibility for the maintenance and education of the rising generation is shifted from the parent to the community.

First there was man's duty to God, with the priest as assessor. That was repudiated; and then came man's duty to his neighbor, with Society as the assessor. Will this too be repudiated, and be succeeded by Man's duty to himself, assessed by himself? And if so, what will be the effect on the conception of duty in the abstract?

Duty arises at first, a gloomy tyranny, out of man's helplessness, his self-mistrust, in a word, his abstract fear. He personifies all that he abstractly fears as God, and straightway becomes the slave of his duty to God. He imposes that slavery fiercely on his children, threatening them with hell, and punishing them for their attempts to be happy. When, becoming bolder, he ceases to fear everything, and dares to love something, this duty of his to what he fears evolves into a sense of duty to what he loves. Sometimes he again personifies what he loves as God; and the God of Wrath becomes the God of Love: sometimes he at once becomes a humanitarian, an altruist, acknowledging only his duty to his neighbor. This stage is correlative to the rationalist stage in the evolution of philosophy and the capitalist phase in the evolution of industry. But in it the emancipated slave of God falls under the dominion of society, which, having just reached a phase in which all the love is ground out of it by the competitive struggle for money, remorselessly crushes him until, in due course of the further growth of his spirit or will, a sense at last arises in him of his duty to himself. And when this sense is fully grown, which it hardly is yet, the tyranny of duty is broken; for now the man's God is himself; and he, self-satisfied at last, ceases to be selfish. The evangelist of this last step must therefore preach the repudiation of duty. This, to the unprepared of his generation, is indeed the wanton masterpiece of paradox. What! after all that has been said by men of noble life as to the secret of all right conduct being only "Duty, duty, duty," is he to be told now that duty is the primal curse from which we must redeem ourselves before we can advance another step on the road along which, as we imagine—having forgotten the repudiations made by our fathers—duty and duty alone has brought us thus far? But why not? God was once the most sacred of our conceptions; and he had to be denied. Then reason became the infallible Pope, only to be deposed in turn. Is duty more sacred than God or reason?

XXV
THEODORE HERTZKA

Theodore Hertzka, 1845, a Viennese economist, representative of the Manchester school of political economy. Economic editor of *Neue Freie Presse,* 1872; founded Society of Austrian National Economists, 1874; published *Die Gesetze der Handels und Socialpolitik,* 1880; *Die Gesetze der Sozialentwickelung,* 1886; founded (1889) and still edits the weekly *Zeitschrift fur Staats und Volkswirthschaft;* published *Freiland,* 1890. In response to *Freiland,* local societies, since united into an International Freeland Society, were organized in many of the larger towns and cities of Austria and Germany. It is anticipated by the society that a Freeland Colony will be formed on a tract of land in East Africa which has been placed at the disposal of the society.

The selections which follow are from *Freeland* (1904).

Economics.—In former epochs of human culture it was impossible to create abundance and leisure for all—it was impossible because the means of production would not suffice to create abundance for all even if all without exception labored with all their physical power; and therefore much less would they have sufficed if the workers had indulged in the leisure which is as necessary to the development of the higher intellectual powers as abundance is to the maturing of the higher intellectual needs. And since it was not possible to guarantee to all the means of living a life worthy of human beings, it remained a sad, but not less inexorable, necessity of civilization that the majority of men should be stinted even in the little that fell to their share, and that the booty snatched from the masses should be used to endow a minority who might thus attain to abundance and leisure. Servitude was a necessity of civilization, because that alone made possible the development of the tastes and capacities of civilization in at least a few individuals, while without it barbarism would have been the lot of all.

It is, moreover, a mistake to suppose that servitude is as old as the human race: it is only as old as civilization. There was a time when servitude was unknown, when there were neither masters nor servants, and no one could exploit the labor of his fellow-men; that was not the Golden, but the Barbaric, Age of our race. While man had not yet learned the art of producing what he needed, but was obliged to be satisfied with gathering or capturing the voluntary gifts of nature, and every competitor was therefore regarded as an enemy who strove to get the same goods which each individual looked upon as his own special prey, so long did the struggle for existence among men necessarily issue in reciprocal destruction instead of subjection and exploitation. It did not then profit the stronger or the more cunning to force the weaker into his service—the competitor had to be killed; and as the struggle was accompanied by hatred and superstition, it soon began to be the practice to eat the slain. A war of extermination waged by all against all, followed generally by cannibalism, was therefore the primitive condition of our race.

This first social order yielded, not to moral or philosophical considerations, but to a change in the character of labor. The man who first thought of sowing corn and reaping it was the deliverer of mankind from the lowest, most sanguinary stage of barbarism, for he was the first producer—he first practised the art not only of collecting, but of producing, food. When this art so improved as to make it possible to withdraw from the worker a part of his produce without positively exposing him to starvation, it was gradually found to be more profitable to use the vanquished as beasts of labor than as beasts for slaughter. Since slavery thus for the first time made it possible for at least a favored few to enjoy abundance and leisure, it became the first promoter of higher civilization. But civilization is power, and so it came about that slavery or servitude in one form or another spread over the world.

But it by no means follows that the domination of servitude must, or even can, be perpetual. Just as cannibalism—which was the result of that minimum productiveness of human labor by means of which the severest toil sufficed to satisfy only the lowest animal needs of life—had to succumb to servitude as soon as the increasing productiveness of labor made any degree of abundance possible, so servitude—which is nothing else but the social result of that medium measure of productiveness by which labor is able to furnish abundance and leisure to a few but not to all—must also succumb to another, a higher social order, as soon as this medium measure of productiveness is surpassed, for from that moment servitude has ceased to be a necessity of civilization, and has become a hindrance to its progress.

And for generations this has actually been the case. Since man has succeeded in making the forces of nature serviceable in production—since he has acquired the power of substituting the unlimited elemental forces for his own muscular force—there has been nothing to prevent his creating abundance and leisure for all; nothing except that obsolete social institution, servitude, which withholds from the masses the enjoyment of abundance and leisure. We not merely can, but we shall be compelled to make social justice an actual fact, because the new form of labor demands this as imperatively as the old forms of labor demanded servitude. Servitude, once the vehicle of progress, has become a hindrance to civilization, for it prevents the full use of the means of civilization at our disposal. As it reduces to a minimum the things consumed by most of our brethren, and therefore does not call into play more than a very small part of our present means of production, it compels us to restrict our productive labor within limits far less than those to which we should attain if an effective demand existed for what would then be the inevitable abundance of all kinds of wealth.

I sum up thus: Economic equality of rights could not be realized in earlier epochs of civilization, because human labor was not then sufficiently productive to supply wealth to all, and equality therefore meant poverty for all, which would have been synonymous with barbarism. Economic equality of rights not only can but must now become a fact, because—thanks to the power which has been acquired of using the forces of nature—abundance and leisure have become possible for all; but the full utilization of the now acquired means of civilization is dependent on the condition that everyone enjoys the product of his own industry.

I think it has been incontrovertibly shown that economic equality of rights was formerly impossible, and that it can now be realized; but why it must now be realized does not seem to me to have been yet placed beyond a doubt. So long as the productiveness of labor was small, the exploitation of man by man was a necessity of civilization—that is plain; this is no longer the case, since the increased productiveness of labor is now capable of creating wealth enough for all—this is also as clear as day. But this only proves that economic justice has become possible, and there is a great difference between the possible and the necessary existence of a state of things. It has been said—and the experience of the exploiting world seems to justify the assertion—that full use cannot be made of the control which science and invention have given to men over the natural forces, while only a small part of the fruits of the thus increased effectiveness of labor is consumed; and if this can be irrefutably shown to be inherent in the nature of the thing, there remains not the least doubt that servitude in any form has become a hindrance to civilization. For an institution that prevents us from making use of the means of civilization which we possess is in and of itself a hindrance to civilization; and since it restrains us from developing wealth to the fullest extent possible, and wealth and civilization are power, there can consequently be no doubt as to why and in what manner such an institution must in the course of economic evolution become obsolete. The advanced and the strong everywhere and necessarily impose their laws and institutions upon the unprogressive and the weak; economic justice must therefore—though with bloodless means—as certainly and as universally supplant servitude as formerly servitude—when it was the institution which conferred a higher degree of civilization and power—supplanted cannibalism. I have already admitted that the modern exploiting society is in reality unable to produce that wealth which would correspond to the now existing capacity of production: hence it follows as a matter of fact that the exploiting society is very much less advanced than one based upon the principle of economic justice, and it also quite as incontrovertibly follows that the former cannot successfully compete with the latter.

But before we have a right to jump to the conclusion that the principles of economic justice must necessarily be everywhere victorious, it must be shown that it is the essential nature of the exploiting system, and not certain transitory accidents connected with it, which makes it incapable of calling forth all the capacity of highly productive labor. Why is the existing exploiting society not able to call forth all this capacity? Because the masses are prevented from increasing their consumption in a degree corresponding to the increased power of production—because what is produced belongs not to the workers but to a few employers. Right. But, it would be answered, these few would make use of the produce themselves. To this the rejoinder is that that is impossible, because the few owners of the produce of labor can use—that is, actually consume—only the smallest portion of such an enormous amount of produce; the surplus, therefore, must be converted into productive capital, the employment of which, however, is dependent upon the consumption of those things that are produced by it. Very true. No factories can be built if no one wants the things that would be manufactured in them. But have the masters really only this one way of disposing of the surplus—can they really make no other use of it? In the modern world they do as a matter of fact make no other use of it. As a rule, their desire is to increase or improve the agencies engaged in labor—that is, to capitalize their profits—

without inquiring whether such an increase or improvement is needed; and since no such increase is needed, so over-production—that is, the non-disposal of the produce—is the necessary consequence. But because this is the fact at present, must it necessarily be so? What if the employers of labor were to perceive the true relation of things, and to find a way of creating an equilibrium by proportionally reducing their capitalization and increasing their consumption? If that were to happen, then, it must be admitted, all products would be disposed of, however much the productiveness of labor might increase. The consumption by the masses would be stationary as before; but luxury would absorb all the surplus with the exception of such reserves as were required to supply the means of production, which means would themselves be extraordinarily increased on account of the enormously increased demand caused by luxury.

Labor—Of the means of production there are two classes—the powers of nature and capital. Without these means of production, the most exact information as to which are the branches of labor whose products are in greatest demand, and which, therefore, yield the highest profits, would be of as little use as the most perfect skill in such branches of production. A man can utilize his power to labor only when he has command both of the materials and forces supplied by nature, and of the appropriate instruments and machines; and if he is to compete with his fellow-workers he must possess both classes of the means of production as fully and as completely as they. In order to grow wheat, a man must not only have land at his command, but he must have land that is equally good for growing wheat as is the land of the other wheat-growers, otherwise he will labor with less profit and possibly with actual loss. And possession of the most fertile land will not make the work possible, or at any rate equally profitable, unless the worker possesses the requisite agricultural implements, or if he possesses them in a less degree than his competitors.

No one has produced the land, therefore no one has a claim of ownership upon it, and everyone has a right to use it. But not merely has no one produced the land, no one can produce it; the land, therefore, exists in a limited quantity, and, moreover, the existing land is not all of the same quality. Now, in spite of all this, how is it possible to satisfy everyone's claim not merely to land, but to produce-bearing land?

In order to make this clear, the third and, in reality, most fundamental predicate of economic justice must be expounded. When every worker is promised the undiminished produce of his own labor, it is necessarily assumed that the worker himself is the sole and exclusive producer of the whole of this produce. But this he was, by no means, according to the old economic system. The worker as such produced only a part of the product, while another part was produced by the employer, whether he was landowner, capitalist, or undertaker. Without the organizing disciplinary influence of the latter the toil of the worker would have been fruitless, or at least much less fruitful; formerly the worker supplied merely the power, while the organizing mind was supplied by the employer.

It is not implied by this that the more intellectual element in the work of production was formerly to be found exclusively or necessarily on the side of the employer: the technicians and directors who superintend the great productive establishments belong essentially to the wage-earners; and it will be readily admitted that in many cases the higher intelligence is to be found not in the employers, but in the workers. Nevertheless, in all cases where a number of workers have had to be brought together and accustomed to work in common, this work of organizing has been the business of the employer. Hitherto the worker has been able to produce for himself only in isolation; whenever a number had to be brought together, in one enterprise, a "master" has been necessary, a master who with a whip—which may be made either of thongs or of the paragraphs in a set of factory regulations—has kept the rebellious together, and therefore—not because of his higher intelligence—has swept the profits into his own pocket, leaving to the workers, whether they belonged to the proletariat or to the so-called intelligent classes, only so much as sufficed to sustain them. Hitherto the workers have made no attempt to unite their productive labors without a master, as free, self-competent men, and not as servants. The employment of those powerful instruments and contrivances which science and invention have placed in the hands of men, and which so indefinitely multiply the profits of human activity, presupposes the united action of many; and hitherto this united action has been taken only hand in hand with servitude. The productive associations of a Shulze-Delitzsch and others have effected no change in the real character of servitude; they have merely altered the name of the masters. In these associations there are still the employers and the workers; to the former belongs the profit; the latter receive stall and manger like the biped beasts of burden of the single employer or of the joint-stock societies whose shareholders do not happen to be workers. In order that labor may be free and self-controlling, the workers must combine as such, and not as small capitalists; they must not have over them any employer of any land or any name, not even an employer consisting of an association of themselves. They must organize themselves as workers, and only as such; for only as such have they a claim to the full produce of their labor. This organization of work without the slightest remnant of the old servile relationship to an employer of some kind or other, is the fundamental problem of social emancipation: if this problem be successfully solved, everything else will follow of itself.

Value.—Labor alone is not the source of value, though most Socialists adopt this error of the so-called classical economists as the ground of their demands. If all value were derived from labor and from labor alone, everything would be in favor of the workers, for the workers have control over their working power. The misery is due to the fact that the workers have no control over the other things which are requisite for the creation of value, namely, the product of previous work—i. e. capital, and the forces and materials derived from nature. Labor should have the whole of what it assists to produce. But we do not base this right upon the erroneous proposition that labor is the sole source of the value of what it produces, but upon the proposition that the worker has the same claim to the use of those other factors requisite for the creation of value as he has to his working-power. But this is only by the way. Eeven if labor were the only source of and the only ingredient in value, it would still be in any case the worst conceivable measure of value; for it is of all things that possess value the one the value of which is most liable to variations. Its value rises with every advance in human dexterity and industry; that is, a labor-day or a labor hour is continuously being transformed into an increasing quantity of all imaginable other kinds of value. That the value of the product of labor differs as the labor-power is well or badly furnished with tools, well or badly applied, cannot be questioned, and never has been seriously questioned. Perfect and unlimited freedom of labor to apply itself at any time to whatever will then create the highest value brings about, if not an absolute yet a relative equilibrium of values; but, in order that this may be brought about, there must exist an unchangeable and reliable standard by which the value of the things produced by labor can be measured.

If we concluded that the things which required an equal time to produce were of equal value because they were produced in an equal time, we might soon find ourselves producing shoes which no one wanted, while we were suffering from a lack of textile fabrics; and we might see with unconcern the superfluity of turnery wares, the production of which was increasing, while perhaps all available hands were required in order to correct a disastrous lack of cereals. To make the labor-day the measure of value—if it were not, for other reasons, impossible—involves Communism, which, instead of leaving the adjustment of the relations between supply and demand to free commerce, fixes those relations by authority; doing this, of course, without asking anyone what he wishes to enjoy, or what he wishes to do, but authoritatively prescribing what everyone shall consume, and what he shall produce.

But we strive after what is the direct opposite of Communism —namely, individual freedom. Consequently, we need a measure of value as accurate and reliable as possible—that is, one the exchange-power of which, with reference to all other things, is exposed to as little variation as possible This best possible, most constant, standard the civilized world has hitherto found rightly in gold. There is no difference in value between two equal quantities of gold, whilst one labor-day may be very materially more valuable than another; and there is no means of ascertaining with certainty the difference in value of the two labor-days except by comparing them both with one and the same thing which possesses a really constant value. Yet this equality in value of equal quantities of gold is the least of the advantages possessed by gold over other measures of value. Two equal quantities of wheat are of nearly equal value. But the value of gold is exposed to less variation than is the value of any other thing. Two equal quantities of wheat are of equal value at the same time; but tomorrow they may both be worth twice as much as today, or they may sink to half their present value; while gold can change its value but very little in a short time. If its exchange-relation to any commodity whatever alters suddenly and considerably, it can be at once and with certainty assumed that it is the value not of the gold, but of the other commodity, which has suddenly and considerably altered. And this is a necessary conclusion from that most unquestionable law of value according to which the price of everything is determined by supply and demand, if we connect with this law the equally unquestionable fact that the supply and demand of no other thing is exposed to so small a relative variation as are those of gold. This fact is not due to any mysterious quality in this metal, but to its peculiar durability, in consequence of which in the course of thousands of years there has been accumulated, and placed at the service of those who can command it, a quantity of gold sufficient to make the greatest temporary variations in its production of no practical moment. Whilst a good or a bad wheat harvest makes an enormous difference in the supply of wheat for the time being, because the old stock of wheat is of very subordinate importance relatively to the results of the new harvest, the amount of gold in the world remains relatively unaltered by the variations, however great they may be, of even several years of gold production, because the existing stock of gold is enormously greater than the greatest possible gold-production of any single year. If all the gold mines in the world suddenly ceased to yield any gold, no material influence would be produced upon the quantity of available gold; whilst a single general failure in the cereal crop would at once and inevitably produce the most terrible corn-famine. This, then, is the reason why gold is the best possible, though by no means an absolutely perfect, measure of value. But labor-time would be the worst conceivable measure of value, for neither are two equal periods of labor necessarily of equal value, nor does labor-time in general possess an unalterable value, but its exchange-power in relation to all other things increases with every step forward in the methods of labor.

Capital is indispensible to a highly developed production, and the working masses of the outside world are mostly without capital; but they are without it only because they are powerless servants, and even when in exceptional cases they possess capital they do not know how to do anything with it without the aid of masters. Yet it is frequently the capital of the servants themselves by means of which—through the intervention of the savings-bank—the undertaker carries on the work of production; it none the less follows that he pockets the proceeds and leaves to the servants nothing but a bare subsistence over and above the interest. Or the servants club their savings together for the purpose of engaging in productive work on their own account; but as they are not able to conceive of discipline without servitude, cannot even understand how it is possible to work without a master who must be obeyed, because he can hire and discharge, pay and punish—in brief, because he is master; and as they would be unable to dispose of the produce, or to agree over the division of it, though this might be expected from them as possessors of the living labor-power,—they therefore set themselves in the character of a corporate capitalist as master over themselves in the character of workmen.

Interest is charged for a real and tangible service essentially different from the service rendered by the undertaker and the landowner. Whilst, namely, the economic service of the two latter consists in nothing but the exercise of a relation of mastership, which becomes superfluous as soon as the working masses have transformed themselves from servants working under compulsion into freely associated men, the capitalist offers the worker an instrument which gives productiveness to his labor under all circumstances. And whilst it is evident that, with the establishment of industrial freedom, both undertaker and landowner become, not merely superfluous, but altogether objectless—ipso facto cease to exist—with respect to the capitalist, the possessor of savings, it can even be asserted that society is dependent upon him in an infinitely higher degree when free than when enslaved, because it can and must employ much more capital in the former case than in the latter. Moreover, it is not true that service rendered by capital—the giving wings to production—is compensated for by the mere return of the capital. After a full repayment, there remains to the worker, in proportion as he has used the capital wisely—

which is his affair and not the lender's—a profit which in certain circumstances may be very considerable, the increase of the proceeds of labor obtained by the aid of capital. Why should it be considered unreasonable or unjust to hand over a part of this gain to the capitalist—to him, that is, to whose thrift the existence of the capital is due? The saver, so said the earlier Socialists, has no right to demand any return for the service which he has rendered the worker; it costs him nothing, since he receives back his property undiminished when and how he pleases (the premium for risk, which may have been charged as security against the possible bad faith or bankruptcy of the debtor, has nothing to do with the interest proper). Granted; but what right has the borrower, who at any rate derives the advantage from the service rendered, to retain all the advantage himself? And what certainty has he of being able to obtain this service, even though it costs the saver nothing to render it, if he (the borrower) does not undertake to render any service in return? It is quite evident that the interest is paid in order to induce the saver to render such a friendly service. How could we, without communistic coercion, transfer capital from the hands of the saver into those of the capital-needing producer? For the community to save and to provide producers with capital from this source is a very simple way out of the difficulty, but the right to do this must be shown. No profound thinker will be satisfied with the communistic assertion that the capital drawn from the producers in one way is returned to them in another, for by this means there does not appear to be established any equilibrium between the burden and the gain of the individual producers. The tax for the accumulation of capital must be equally distributed among all the producers; the demand for capital, on the other hand, is a very unequal one. But how could we take the tax paid by persons who perhaps require but little capital, to endow the production of others who may happen to require much capital? What advantage do we offer to the former for their compulsory thrift?

And yet the answer lies close at hand. It is true that in the exploiting system of society the creditor does not derive the slightest advantage from the increase in production which the debtor effects by means of the creditor's savings; on the other hand, in the system of society based upon social freedom and justice both creditor and debtor are equally advantaged.

Interest disappears of itself, just like profit and rent, for the sole but sufficient reason that the freely associated worker is his own capitalist, as well as his own undertaker and landlord.

Machinery.—In countries, where the wages of labor and the profit of labor are fundamentally different things, there is a fundamental distinction between the profitableness of a business and the theoretical perfection of the machinery used in it. In order to be theoretically useful a machine must simply save labor—that is, the labor required for producing and working the machine must be less than that which is saved by using it. The steam-plough, for example, is a theoretically good and useful machine if the manufacture of it, together with the production of the coal consumed by it, swallows up less human labor than on the other hand is saved by ploughing with steam instead of with horses or cattle. But the actual profitableness of a machine is quite another thing. In order to be profitable, the steam-plough must save, not labor, but value or money—that is, it must cost less than the labor which it has saved would have cost. But it by no means follows that it costs less because the amount of labor saved is greater than that consumed by the manufacture of the steam-plough and the production of the coal it uses. For whilst the labor which the improved plough saves receives merely its "wages," with the bought plough and the bought coal there have to be paid for not only the labor required in producing them, but also three items of "gain"—namely, ground-rent, interest, and undertaker's salary. Thus it may happen that the steam-plough, between its first use and its being worn out, saves a million hours of labor, whilst in its construction and in the total quantity of coal it has required, it may have consumed merely 100,000 hours of labor; and yet it may be very unprofitable—that is, it may involve very great loss to those, who, relying upon the certainty of such an enormous saving of labor, should buy and use it. For the million hours of labor saved mean no more than a million hours of wages saved; therefore, for example, £10,000, if the wages are merely £1 for a hundred hours of labor. For the construction of the plough and for the means of driving it 100,000 hours of labor are required, which alone certainly will have cost £1000. But then the rent which the owners of the iron-pits and the coal-mines charge, and the interest for the invested capital, must be paid, and finally the profits of the iron-manufacturer and the coal-producer. All this may, under certain circumstances, amount to more than the difference of £9,000 between cost of labor in the two cases respectively; and when that is the case the Western employer loses money by buying a machine which saves a thousand per cent of his labor.

That only the relatively rich nations—that is, those whose masses are relatively in the best condition—very largely employ machinery in production, could not possibly long escape the most obtuse-minded; but this undeniable phenomenon is wrongly explained. It is held that the English or the American people live in a way more worthy of human nature than, for example, the Chinese or the Russians, because they are richer; and that for the same reason—namely, because the requisite capital is more abundant—the English and Americans use machinery while the Chinese and Russians employ merely human muscles. This leaves unexplained the principal question, whence comes this difference in wealth? and also directly contradicts the facts that the Chinese and the Russians make no use of the capital so liberally and cheaply offered to them, and that machine-labor is unprofitable in their hands as long as their wage-earners are satisfied with a handful of rice or with half-rotten potatoes and a drop of spirits. But it is a part of the credo of the orthodox political economy, and is therefore accepted without examination. Yet he who does not use his eyes merely to shut them to facts, or his mind merely to harbor obstinately the prejudices which he has once acquired, must sooner or later see that the wealth of the nations is nothing else than their possession of the means of production; that this wealth is great or small in proportion as the means of production are many and great, or few and small; and that many or few means of production are needed according as there is a great or small use of those things which are created by these means of production—therefore solely in proportion to the large or small consumption. Where little is used little can be produced, and there will therefore be few instruments of production, and the people must remain poor.

Neither can the export trade make any alteration; for the things which are exported must be exchanged for other things, whether food, or instruments of labor, or money, or some other commodity, and for that which is imported there must be some use; which, however, is impossible if there is no consumption, for in such a case the imported articles will find as little sale as the things produced at home. Certainly those commodities which are produced by a people who use neither their own productions nor those of other people, may be lent to other nations. But this again depends upon whether foreigners have a use for such a surplus above what is required at home; and as this is not generally the case, it remains, once for all, that any nation can produce only so much as it has a use for, and the measure of its wealth is therefore the extent of its requirements.

Naturally this applies to only those nations whose civilization has reached such a stage that the employment of complex instruments of labor is prevented, not by their ignorance, but simply by their social political helplessness. To such nations, however, applies in full the truth that they are poor simply because they cannot eat enough to satisfy themselves; and that the increase of their wealth is conditioned by nothing else than the degree of energy with which the working classes struggle against their misery. The English and the Americans will eat meat, and therefore do not allow their wages to sink below the level at which the purchase of meat is possible; this is the only reason why England and America employ more machinery than China and Russia, where the people are contented with rice or potatoes.

Land.—If, in order to labor productively, we required the undertaker, no power in heaven or earth could save us from giving up to him what was due to him as master of the process of production, while we contented ourselves with a bare subsistence. I would add that we should also be compelled to pay the tribute due to the landlord for the use of the ground, if we could not till the ground without having a landlord. For property in land was always based upon the supposition that unowned land could not be cultivated. Men did not understand how to plough and sow and reap without having the right to prevent others from ploughing and sowing and reaping upon the same land. Whether it was an individual, a community, a district, or a nation, that in this way acquired an exclusive right of ownership of the land, was immaterial: it was necessarily an exclusive right, otherwise no one would put any labor into the land. Hence it happened, in course of time, that the individual owner of land acquired very considerable advantages in production over the many-headed owner; and the result was that common property in land gradually passed into individual ownership. The land—so far as it is used as a means of production and not as sites for dwelling-houses—should be masterless, free as air; it belongs neither to one nor to many: everyone who wishes to cultivate the soil should be at liberty to do so where he pleases, and to appropriate his part of the produce. Therefore, no ground-rent, which is nothing else than the owner's interest for the use of the land.

For, according to my views, there is no right of property in land, and therefore not in the building-site of the house; and the right to appropriate such ground to one's own house is simply a right of usufruct for a special purpose. Just as, for example, the traveller by rail has a claim to the seat which he occupies, but only for the purpose of sitting there, and not for the purpose of unpacking his goods or of letting it to another, so I have the right to reserve for myself, merely for occupation, the spot of ground upon which I wish to fix my home; and no one has any more right to settle upon my building-site than he has to occupy my cushion in the railway, even if it should be possible to crowd two persons into the one seat. But neither am I at liberty to make room for a friend upon my seat; for my fellow-travellers are not likely to approve of the inconvenience thereby occasioned, and they may protest that the legs and elbows of the sharer of my seat crowd them too much, and that the air-space calculated for one pair of lungs is by my arbitrary action shared by two pair.

XXVI
EDWARD CARPENTER

Edward Carpenter, poet, philosophical writer, humanitarian; born at Brighton, England, 1844. Educated at Cambridge, became fellow of his college in 1868, took orders in 1869 and was a curate under Frederick Denison Maurice. Left Cambridge in 1873, gave up his fellowship and devoted seven years to University Extension movement, lecturing on astronomy, physical science, music, etc. In 1881 built cottage near Sheffield, gardened and wrote *Towards Democracy*, published 1883. Joined Sheffield Socialists and became active propagandist, 1886. Visited Whitman in America several times and has been living in America for a number of years; devotes time to literature and philosophy. Works: *Civilization, Its Cause and Cure; England's Ideal; Love's Coming of Age; Angel's Wings; The Story of Eros and Psyche; Chants of Labor; Iolaus; Adam's Peak to Elephanta; An Unknown People; The Promised Land*, a drama of a people's deliverance. Selections are from *Love's Coming of Age*.

Woman in Freedom.—It is clear enough that what woman most needs today, and is mostly seeking for, is a basis of independence for her life. Nor is her position likely to be improved until she is able to face man on an equality; to find, self-balanced, her natural relation to him; and to dispose of herself and her sex perfectly freely, and not as a thrall must do.

Doubtless if man were an ideal creature his mate might be secure of equal and considerate treatment from him without having to insist upon an absolute economic independence; but as that is only too obviously not the case there is nothing left for her today but to unfold the war-flag of her "rights," and (dull and tiresome as it may be) to go through a whole weary round of battles till peace is concluded again upon a better understanding.

Yet it must never be forgotten that nothing short of large social changes, stretching beyond the sphere of women only, can bring about the complete emancipation of the latter. Not until our whole commercial system, with its barter and sale of human labor and human love for gain, is done away, and not till a whole new code of ideals and customs of life has come in, will women really be free. They must remember that their cause is also the cause of the oppressed laborer over the whole earth, and the laborer has to remember that his cause is theirs.

The modern woman sees plainly enough that no decent advance of her sex is possible until this whole equstion is fairly faced—involving, as of course it will do, a life very different from her present one, far more in the open air, with real bodily exercise and development, some amount of regular manual work, a knowledge of the laws of health and physiology, an altogether wider mental outlook, and greater self-reliance and nature-hardihood. But when once these things are granted, she sees that she will no longer be the serf, but the equal, the mate, and the comrade of Man.

The commercial prostitution of love is the last outcome of our whole social system, and its most clear condemnation. It flaunts in our streets, it hides itself in the garment of respectability under the name of matrimony, it eats in actual physical disease and death right through our midst; it is fed by the oppression and the ignorance of women, by their poverty and denied means of livelihood, and by the hypocritical puritanism which forbids them by millions not only to gratify but even to speak of their natural desires; and it is encouraged by the callousness of an age which has accustomed men to buy and sell for money every most precious thing—even the life-long labor of their brothers, therefore why not also the very bodies of their sisters?

Here there is no solution except the freedom of woman—which means of course also the freedom of the masses of the people, men and women, and the ceasing altogether of economic slavery. There is no solution which will not include the redemption of the terms "free woman" and "free love" to their true and rightful significance. Let every woman whose heart bleeds for the sufferings of her sex, hasten to declare herself and to constitute herself, as far as she possibly can, a free woman. Let her accept the term with all the odium that belongs to it; let her insist on her right to speak, dress, think, act, and above all to use her sex, as she deems best; let her face the scorn and ridicule; let her "use her own life" if she likes; assured that only so can come deliverance, and that only when the free woman is honored will the prostitute cease to exist. And let every man who really would respect his counterpart, entreat her also to act so; let him never by word or deed tempt her to grant as a bargain what can only be precious as a gift; let him see her with pleasure stand a little aloof; let him help her to gain her feet; so at last, by what slight sacrifices on his part such a course may involve, will it dawn upon him that he has gained a real companion and helpmate on life's journey.

The whole evil of commercial prostitution arises out of the domination of man in matters of sex. Better indeed were a Saturnalia of free men and women than the spectacle which as it is our great cities present at night. Here in sex, the women's insticts are, as a rule, so clean, so direct, so well-rooted in the needs of the race, that except for man's domination they would scarcely have suffered this preversion. Sex in man is an unorganized passion, an individual need or impetus; but in woman it may more properly be termed a constructive instinct, with the larger signification that that involves. Even more than man should woman be "free" to work out the problem of her sex-relations as may commend itself best to her—hampered as little as possible by legal, conventional, or economic considerations, and relying chiefly on her own native sense and tact in the matter. Once thus free—free from the mere cash-nexus to a husband, from the money-slavery of the streets, from the nameless terrors of social opinion, and from the threats of the choice of perpetual virginity or perpetual bondage—would she not indeed choose her career (whether that of wife and mother, or that of free companion, or one of single blessedness) far better for herself than it is chosen for her today—regarding really in some degree the needs of society, and the welfare of children, and the sincerity and durability of her relations to her lovers, and less the petty motives of profit and fear?

The point is that the whole conception of a nobler womanhood for the future has to proceed candidly from this basis of her complete freedom as to the disposal of her sex, and from the healthy conviction that, with whatever individual aberrations, she will on the whole use that freedom rationally and well. And surely this—in view too of some decent education of the young on sexual matters—is not too great a demand to make on our faith in women. If it is, then indeed we are undone—for short of this we can only retain them in servitude—and society in its form of the hell on earth which it largely is today.

Refreshing therefore in its way is the spirit of revolt which is spreading on all sides. Let us hope such revolt will continue. If it leads here and there to strained or false situations, or to temporary misunderstandings—still, declared enmity is better than unreal acquiescence. Too long have women acted the part of mere appendages to the male, suppressing their own individuality and fostering his self-conceit. In order to have souls of their own they must free themselves, and greatly by their own efforts. They must learn to fight. Whitman in his poem "A Woman Waits for Me," draws a picture of a woman who stands in the sharpest possible contrast with the feeble bourgeois ideal—a woman who can "swim, row, ride, wrestle, shoot, run, strike, retreat, defend herself," etc.; and Bebel, in his book on woman, while pointing out that in Sparta, "where the greatest attention was paid to the physical development of both sexes, boys and girls went about naked till they had reached the age of puberty, and were trained together in bodily exercises, games and wrestling," compains that nowadays "the notion that women require strength, courage and resolution is regarded as very heterodox." But the truth is that qualities of courage and independence are not agreeable in a slave, and that is why man during all these centuries has consistently discountenanced them—till at last the female herself has come to consider them "unwomanly." Yet this last epithet is absurd; for if tenderness is the crown and glory of woman, nothing can be more certain than that true tenderness is only found in strong and courageous natures; the tenderness of a servile person is no tenderness at all.

It has not escaped the attention of thinkers on these subjects that the rise of Women into freedom and larger social life here alluded to—and already indeed indicated by the march of events—is likely to have a profound influence on the future of our race. It is pointed out that among most of the higher animals, and indeed among many of the early races of mankind, the males have been selected by the females on account of their prowess or superior strength or beauty, and this has led to the evolution in the males and in the race at large of a type which (in a dim and unconscious manner) was the ideal of the female.

But as soon as in the history of mankind property-love set in, and woman became the chattel of man, this action ceased. She, being no longer free, could not possibly choose man, but rather the opposite took place, and man began to select woman for the characteristics pleasing to him. The latter now adorned herself to gratify his taste, and the female type and consequently the type of the whole race have been correspondingly affected. With the return of woman to freedom the ideal of the female may again resume its sway. It is possible indeed that the more dignified and serious attitude of women towards sex may give to sexual selection when exercised by them a nobler influence than when exercised by the males. Anyhow it is not difficult to see that women really free would never countenance for their mates the many mean and unclean types of men who today seem to have things all their own way, nor consent to have children by such men; nor is it difficult to imagine that the feminine influence might thus sway to the evolution of a more manly and dignified race than has been disclosed in these last days of commercial civilization!

The social enthusiasm and activity shown by women in Britain, Russia, and the United States is so great and well-rooted that it is impossible to believe it a mere ephemeral event; and though in the older of these countries it is at present confined to the more wealthy classes, we can augur from that—according to a well-known principle—that it will in time spread downwards to the women of the nation.

Important as is the tendency of women in the countries mentioned to higher education and brain development, I think it is evident that the widening and socialization of their interests is not taking place so much through mere study of books and the passing of examinations in political economy and other sciences, as through the extended actual experience which the life of the day is bringing to them. Certainly the book-studies are important and must not be neglected; but above all is it imperative (and men, if they are to have any direct sway in the future destinies of the other sex, must look to it) that women so long confined to the narrowest mere routine and limited circle of domestic life, should see and get experience, all they can, of the actual world. The theory happily now exploding, of keeping them "innocent" through sheer ignorance partakes too much of the "angel and idiot" view. To see the life of slum and palace and workshop, to enter into the trades and professions, to become doctors, nurses, and so forth, to have to look after themselves and to hold their own as against men, to travel, to meet with sexual experience, to work together in trade-unions, to join in social and political uprisings and rebellions, etc., is what women want just now. And it is evident enough that at any rate among the more prosperous sections in this country such a movement is going on apace. If the existence of the enormous hordes of unattached females that we find living on interest and dividends today is a blemish from a socialistic point of view; if we find them on the prowl all over the country, filling the theaters and concert rooms and public entertainments in the proportion of three to one male, besetting the trains, swarming onto the tops of the 'buses, dodging on bicycles under the horses' heads, making speeches at street corners, blocking the very pavements in the front of fashionable shops, we must not forget that for the objects we have just sketched, even this class is going the most direct way to work, and laying in stores of experience which will make it impossible for it ever to return to the petty life of times gone by.

Marriage.—As long as man is only half-grown, and woman is a serf or a parasite, it can hardly be expected that marriage should be particularly successful. Two people come together, who know but little of each other, who have been brought up along different lines, who certainly do not understand each other's nature, whose mental interests and occupations are different, whose worldly interests and advantages are also different; to one of whom the subject of sex is probably a sealed book; to the other perhaps a book whose most dismal page has been opened first. The man needs an outlet for his passion; the girl is looking for a "home" and a proprietor. A glamor of illusion descends upon the two, and drives them into each other's arms. It envelops in a gracious and misty halo all their differences and misapprehensions. They marry without misgiving; and their hearts overflow with gratitude to the white-surpliced old gentleman who reads the service over them.

But at a later hour, and with calmer thought, they begin to realize that it is a life-sentence which he has so suavely passed upon them—not reducable (as in the case of ordinary convicts) even to a term of twenty years. The brief burst of their first satisfaction has been followed by satiety on the physical plane, then by mere vacuity of affection, then by boredom, and even nausea. The girl, full perhaps of tender emotion, and missing the sympathy and consolation she expected in the man's love, only to find its more materialistic side—"This, then is what

I am wanted for;" the man, who looked for a companion, finding he can rouse no mortal interest in his wife's mind save in the most exasperating trivialities;—whatever the cause may be, a veil has fallen from before their faces and there they sit held together now by the least honorable interests, the interests which they themselves can least respect, but to which Law and Religion lend all their weight. The monetary dependence of the woman, the mere sex-needs of the man, the fear of public opinion, all form motives, and motives of the meanest kind, for maintaining the seeming tie; and the relation of the two hardens down into a dull neutrality, in which lives and characters are narrowed and blunted, and deceit becomes the common weapon which guards divided interests.

A sad picture! and of course in this case a portrayal deliberately of the seamy side of the matter. But who shall say what agonies are often gone through in those first few years of married life? Anyhow, this is the sort of problem which we have to face today, and which shows its actuality by the amazing rate at which it is breaking out in literature on all sides.

It may be said—and often of course is said—that such cases as these only prove that marriage was entered into under the influence of a passing glamor and delusion, and that there was not much real devotion to begin with. And no doubt there is truth enough in such remarks. But—we may say in reply—because two people make a mistake in youth, to condemn them, for that reason, to lifelong suffering and mutual degradation, or to see them so condemned, without proposing any hope or way of deliverance, but with the one word "serves you right" on the lips, is a course which can commend itself only to the grimmest and dullest Calvinist. Whatever safeguards against a too frivolous view of the relationship may be proposed by the good sense of society in the future, it is certain that the time has gone past when marriage can continue to be regarded as a supernatural institution to whose maintenance human bodies and souls must be indiscriminately sacrificed; a humaner, wiser, and less panic-striken treatment of the subject must set in; and if there are difficulties in the way they must be met by patient and calm consideration of human welfare—superior to any law, however ancient and respectable.

Today, however, there are thousands of women—and every day more thousands—to whom such a lop-sided alliance is detestable; who are determined that they will no longer endure the arrogant lordship and egoism of men, nor countenance in themselves or other women the craft and servility which are the necessary complements of the relation; who see too clearly in the oak-and-ivy marriage its parasitism on the one hand and strangulation on the other to be sensible of any picturesqueness; who feel too that they have capacities and powers of their own which need space and liberty, and some degree of sympathy and help, for their unfolding; and who, believe that they have work to do in the world, as important in its own way as any that men do in theirs. Such women have broken into open warfare— not against marriage, but against a marriage which makes true and equal love an impossibility. They feel that as long as women are economically dependent they cannot stand up for themselves and insist on those rights which men from stupidity and selfishness will not voluntarily grant them.

On the other hand there are thousands—and one would hope every day more thousands—of men who (whatever their forerunners may have thought) do not desire or think it delightful to have a glass continually held up for them to admire themselves in; who look for a partner in whose life and pursuits they can find some interest, rather than for one who has no interest but in them; who think perhaps that they would rather minister than be (like a monkey fed with nuts in a cage) the melancholy object of another person's ministrations, and who at any rate feel that love, in order to be love at all, must be absolutely open and sincere, and free from any sentiment of dependence or inequality. They see that the present cramped condition of women is not only the cause of the false relation between the sexes, but that it is the fruitful source—through its debarment of any common interests—of that fatal boredom of which we have spoken, and which is the bugbear of marriage; and they would gladly surrender all of that masterhood and authority which is supposed to be their due, if they could only get in return something like a frank and level comradeship.

Thus while we see in the present inequality of the sexes an undoubted source of marriage troubles and unsatisfactory alliances, we see also forces at work which are tending to reaction, and to bringing the two nearer again to each other—so that while differentiated they will not perhaps in the future be quite so much differentiated as now, but only to a degree which will enhance and adorn, instead of destroying their sense of mutual sympathy.

From all which the only conclusion seems to be that marriage must be either alive or dead. As a dead thing it can of course be petrified into a hard and fast formula, but if it is to be a living bond, that living bond must be trusted to, to hold the lovers together; nor be too forcibly stiffened and contracted by private jealousy and public censorship, lest the thing that it would preserve for us perish so, and cease altogether to be beautiful. It is the same with this as with everything else. If we would have a living thing we must give that thing some degree of liberty—even though liberty bring with it risk. If we would debar all liberty and all risk, then we can have only the mummy and dead husk of the thing.

In all men who have reached a certain grade of evolution, and certainly in almost all women, the deep rousing of the sexual nature carries with it a romance and tender emotional yearning towards the object of affection, which lasts on and is not forgotten, even when the sexual attraction has ceased to be strongly felt. This, in favorable cases, forms the basis of what may almost be called an amalgamated personality. That there should exist one other person in the world toward whom all openness of interchange should establish itself, from whom there should be no concealment; whose body should be as dear to one in every part, as one's own; with whom there should be no sense of Mine or Thine in property or possession, into whose mind one's thoughts should naturally flow, as it were to know themselves and to receive a new illumination; and between whom and oneself there should be a spontaneous rebound of sympathy in all the joys and sorrows and experiences of life; such is perhaps one of the dearest wishes of the soul. It is obvious however, that this state of affairs can not be reached at a single leap, but must be the gradual result of years of intertwined memory and affection. For such a union Love must lay the foundation, but patience and gentle consideration and self-control must work unremittingly to perfect the structure. At length each lover comes to know the complexion of the other's mind, the wants, bodily and mental, the needs, the regrets, the satisfactions of the other, almost as his or her own—and without prejudice in favor of self rather than in favor of the other; above all, both parties come to know in course of time, and after perhaps some doubts and trials, that the great want, the great need, which holds them together, is not going to fade away into thin air; but is going to become stronger and more indefeasible as the years go on. There falls a sweet, an irresistible, trust over their relation to each other, which consecrates as it were the double life, making both feel that nothing can now divide; and robbing each of all desire to remain, when death has indeed (or at least in outer semblance) removed the other.

Looking back to the historical and physiological aspects of the question it might of course be contended—and probably with some truth—that the human male is, by his nature and needs, polygamous. Nor is it necessary to suppose that polgamy in certain countries and races is by any means so degrading or unsuccessful an institution as some folk would have it to be. But, as Letourneau in his "Evolution of Marriage" points out, the progress of society in the past has on the whole been from confusion to distinction; and we may fairly suppose that with the progress of our own race (for each race no doubt has its special genius in such matters), and as the spiritual and emotional sides of man develop in relation to the physical, there is probably a tendency for our deeper alliances to become more unitary. Though it might be said that the growing complexity of man's nature would be likely to lead him into more rather than fewer relationships, yet on the other hand it is obvious that as the depth and subtelty of any attachment that will really hold him increases, so does such attachment become more permanent and durable, and less likely to be realized in a number of persons. Woman, on the other hand, cannot be said to be by her physical nature polyandrous as man is polygynous. Though of course there are plenty of examples of women living in a state of polyandry both among savages and civilized peoples, yet her more limited sexual needs and her long periods of gestation, render one mate physically sufficient for her; while her more clinging affectional nature perhaps accentuates her capacity of absorption in the one.

In both man and woman then we may say that we find a distinct tendency towards the formation of this double unit of wedded life—(I hardly like to use the word monogamy on account of its sad associations)—and while we do not want to stamp such natural unions with any false irrevocability or dogmatic exclusiveness, what we do want is a recognition today of the tendency to their formation as a natural fact, independent of any artificial laws, just as one might believe in the natural bias of two atoms of certain different chemical substances to form a permanent compound atom or molecule.

It might not be so very difficult to get quite young people to understand this—to understand that even though they may have to contend with some superfluity of passion in early years, yet that the most deeply rooted desire within them will probably in the end point to a permanent union with one mate; and that towards this end they must be prepared to use self-control against the aimless straying of their passions, and patience and tenderness towards the realization of the union when its time comes. Probably most youths and girls, at the age of romance, would easily appreciate this position; and it would bring to them a much more effective and natural idea of the sacredness of Marriage than they ever get from the artificial thunder of the Church and the State on the subject.

No doubt the suggestion of the mere possibility of any added freedom of choice and experience in the relations of the sexes will be very alarming to some people—but it is so, I think, not because they are at all ignorant that men already take to themselves considerable latitude, and that a distinct part of the undoubted evils that accompany that latitude springs from the fact that it is not recognized; not because they are ignorant that a vast number of respectable women and girls suffer frightful calamities and anguish by reason of the utter inexperience of sex in which they are brought up and have to live; but because such good people assume that the least loosening of the formal barriers between the sexes must mean (and must be meant to mean) an utter dissolution of all ties, and the reign of mere licentiousness. They are convinced that nothing but the most unyielding and indeed exasperating strait-jacket can save society from madness and ruin.

To those, however, who can look facts in the face, and who see that as a matter of fact the reality of Marriage is coming more and more to be considered in the public mind in comparison with its formalities, the first thought will probably be one of congratulation that after such ages of treatment as a mere formality there should be any sense of the reality of the tie left; and the second will be the question how to give this reality its natural form and expression. Having satisfied ourselves that the formation of a more or less permanent double unit is—for our race and our kind—on the whole the natural and ascendant law of sex-union, slowly and with whatever exceptions establishing and enforcing itself independently of any artifiicial enactments that exist, then we shall not feel called upon to tear our hair or rend our garments at the prospect of added freedom for the operation of this force, but shall rather be anxious to consider how it may best be freed and given room for its reasonable development and growth.

Love when felt at all deeply has an element of transcendentalism in it, which makes it the most natural thing in the world for the two lovers—even though drawn together by a passing sex-attraction—to swear eternal troth to each other; but there is something quite diabolic and mephistophelean in the practice of the Law, which creeping up behind, as it were, at the critical moment, and overhearing the two pledging themselves, claps its book together with a triumphant bang and exclaims: "There now you are married and done for, for the rest of your natural lives."

What actual changes in Law and Custom the collective sense of society will bring about is a matter which in its detail we cannot of course foresee or determine. But that the drift will be, and must be, towards greater freedom, is pretty clear. Ideally speaking it is plain that anything like a perfect union must have perfect freedom for its condition; and while it is quite supposable that a lover might out of the fullness of his heart make promises and give pledges, it is really almost inconceivable that anyone having that delicate and proud sense which marks deep feeling, could possibly demand a promise from his loved one. As there is undoubtedly a certain natural reticence in sex, so perhaps the most decent thing in true Marriage would be to say nothing, make no promises—either for a year or a life time. Promises are bad at any time, and when the heart is full silence befits it best. Practically however, since a love of this kind is slow to be realized, since social custom is slow to change, and since the partial dependence and slavery of woman must yet for a while continue, it is likely for such period that formal contracts of some kind will still be made; only these (it may be hoped) will lose their irrevocable and rigid character, and become in some degree adapted to the needs of the contracting parties.

Such contracts might, of course, if adopted, be very various in respect to conjugal rights, conditions of termination, division of property, responsibility for and rights over children, etc. In some cases possibly they might be looked upon as preliminary to a later and more permanent alliance; in others they would provide, for disastrous marriages, a remedy free from the inordinate scandals of the present divorce courts. It may, however, be said that rather than adopt any new system of contracts, public opinion in this country would tend to a simple facilitation of divorce, and that if the latter were made (with due provision for the children) to depend on mutual consent, it would become little more than an affair of registration, and the scandals of the proceeding would be avoided. In any case we think that marriage contracts, if existing at all, must tend more and more to become matters of private arrangement as far as the relations of husband and wife are concerned, and that this is likely to happen in proportion as woman becomes more free, and therefore more competent to act in her own right. It would be felt intolerable, in any decently constituted society, that the old blunderbus of the Law should interfere in the delicate relations of wedded life. As it is today the situation is most absurd. On the one hand, having been constituted from times back in favor of the male, the Law still gives to the husband barbarous rights over the person of his spouse; on the other hand, to compensate for this, it rushes in with the farcicalities of breech of promise; and in any case, having once pronounced its benediction over a pair—how hateful the alliance may turn out to be to both parties, and however obvious its failure to the whole world—the stupid old thing blinks owlishly on at its work, and professes itself totally unable to undo the knot which once it tied!

The inner laws of the sex-passion of love, and of all human

relationship must gradually appear and take the lead, since they alone are the powers which can create and uphold a rational society; and that the outer laws—since they are dead and lifeless things—must inevitably disappear. Real love is only possible in the freedom of society; and freedom is only possible when love is a reality. The subjection of sex-relations to legal conventions is an intolerable bondage, but of course it is a bondage inescapable as long as people are slaves to a merely physical desire. The two slaveries in fact form a sort of natural counterpoise, the one to the other. When love becomes sufficient of a reality to hold the sex-passion as its powerful yet willing servant, the absurdity of law will be at an end.

XXVII
OLIVE SCHREINER

Olive Schreiner, born in England, 1863; one of our foremost contemporary feminist philosophers; sociologist, humanitarian; daughter of Lutheran clergyman, who settled with his family in Cape Town, South Africa, in the early seventies. At age of seventeen wrote novel, *The Story of an African Farm*, which took the literary world by storm and which she brought to England in 1883 for publication under pseudonym of "Ralph Iron." Published *Dreams*, 1890, which were allegories originally included in chapters of her unpublished *Musings on Woman and Labor*, the preparation of which occupied a large part of her life and which was destroyed in a raid during the Boer War, 1900; *Dream Life and Real Life*, 1893. On the side of literature, Olive Schreiner is, perhaps, our greatest woman stylist. The following selections are from *Woman and Labor*, 1911 (F. A. Stokes Co.), a philosophical exposition of modernism and the woman's movement from the evolutionary viewpoint.

Freedom and Woman.—I saw a woman sleeping. In her sleep she dreamed Life stood before her, and held in each hand a gift—in the one Love, in the other Freedom. And she said to the woman, "Choose!" And the woman waited long: and said, "Freedom!" And Life said: "Thou hast well chosen. If thou hadst said, "Love," I would have given thee that thou didst ask for; and I would have gone from thee, and returned to thee no more. Now, the day will come when I shall return. In that day I shall bear both gifts in one hand." I heard the woman laugh in her sleep.

Our woman's movement resembles strongly the gigantic religious and intellectual movement which for centuries convulsed the life of Europe, and had, as its ultimate outcome, the final emancipation of the human intellect and the freedom of the human spirit. Looked back upon from the vantage-point of the present, it presents the appearance of one vast, steady, persistent movement, proceeding always in one ultimate direction, as though guided by some controlling human intellect. But, to the mass of human individuals taking part in it, it presented an appearance far otherwise. It was fought out, now here, now there, by isolated individuals and small groups, and often for what appeared small and almost personal ends, having sometimes, superficially, little in common. Now it was a Giordano Bruno, burnt in Rome in defense of abstract theory with regard to the nature of the First Cause; then an Albigense hurled from his rocks because he refused to part with the leaves of his old Bible; now a Dutch peasant woman, walking serenely to the stake because she refused to bow her head before two crossed rods; then a Servetus burnt by Protestant Calvin at Geneva; or a Spinoza cut off from his tribe and people because he could see nothing but God anywhere; and then it was an exiled Rousseau or Voltaire, or a persecuted Bradlaugh; till, in our own day, the last sounds of the long fight are dying about us, as fading echoes, in the guise of a few puerile attempts to enforce trivial disabilities on the ground of abstract convictions. The vanguard of humanity has won its battle for freedom of thought.

It is often said of those who lead in this attempt at the readeption of woman's relation to life, that they are "New Women;" and they are at times spoken of as though they were a something portentous and unheard-of in the order of human life.

But, the truth is, we are not new. We who lead in this movement today are of that old, old Teutonic womanhood, which twenty centuries ago plowed its march through European forests and morasses beside its male companion; which marched with the Cimbri to Italy, and with the Franks across the Rhine, with the Varagians into Russia, and the Alamani into Switzerland; which peopled Scandinavia, and penetrated to Britain; whose priestesses had their shrines in German forests, and gave out the oracle for peace or war. We have in us the blood of a womanhood that was never bought and never sold; that wore no veil, and had no foot bound; whose realized ideal of marriage was sexual companionship and an equality in duty and labor;

who stood side by side with the males they loved in peace or war, and whose children, when they had borne them, sucked manhood from their breasts, and even through their fetal existence heard a brave heart beat above them. We are women of a breed whose racial ideal was no Helen of Troy, passed passively from male hand to male hand, as men pass gold or lead; but that Brynhild whom Segurd found, clad in helm and byrnie, the warrior maid, who gave him counsel, "the deepest that ever yet was given to living man," and "wrought on him to the performing of great deeds;" who, when he died, raised high the funeral pyre and lay down on it beside him, crying, "Nor shall the door swing to at the heel of him as I go in beside him!" We are of a race of women that of old knew no fear, and feared no death; and if today some of us have fallen on evil and degenerate times, there moves in us yet the throb of the old blood. If it be today on no physical battlefield that we stand beside our men, and on no march through an external forest or morass that we have to lead; it is yet the old spirit which, undimmed by two thousand years, stirs within us in deeper and subtler ways; it is yet the cry of the old, free Northern woman which makes the world today. Though the battle be now for us all, in the laboratory or the workshop, in the forum or the study, in the assembly and in the mart, with the pen and not the sword, of the head and not the arm; we will stand side by side with the men we love, "to dare with them in war and to suffer with them in peace," as the Roman wrote of our old Northern womanhood.

Those women of whom the old writers tell us, who, barefooted and white robed, led their northern hosts on that long march to Italy, were animated by the thought that they led their people to a land of warmer sunshine and richer fruitage; we, today, believe we have caught sight of a land bathed in a nobler than any material sunlight, with a fruitage richer than any which the senses only can grasp. And behind us, we believe, there follows a longer train than any composed of our own race and people; the sound of the tread we hear behind us is that of all earth's women, bearing within them the entire race. The footpath, yet hardly perceptible, which we tread down today, will, we believe, be life's broadest and straightest road, along which the children of men will pass to a higher co-ordination and harmony. The banner which we unfurl today is not new: it is the standard of the old, free, monogamous laboring woman, which, twenty hundred years ago, floated over the forests of Europe. We shall bear it on, each generation as it falls passing it into the hand of that which follows, till we plant it so high that all nations of the world shall see it; till the women of the humblest human races shall be gathered beneath its folds, and no child enter life that was not born within its shade.

We are not new! If you would understand us, go back two thousand years, and study our descent; our breed is our explanation. We are the daughters of our fathers as well as of our mothers. In our dreams we still hear the clash of the shields of our forbears as they struck them together before battle and raised the shout of "Freedom!" In our dreams it is with us still, and when we wake it breaks from our own lips! We are the daughters of those men.

But, it may be said, "Are there not women among you who would use the shibboleth of freedom and labor as a means for opening a door to a greater and more highly flavored self-indulgence, to a more lucrative and enjoyable parasitism? Are there not women who, under the guise of 'work,' are seeking only increased means of pleasure and self-indulgence, to whom intellectual training and the opening to new fields of labor side by side with man, mean merely new means of *self-advertisement* and parasitic success?"

We answer: There may be such truly; among us—but not of us! This at least is true, that we, ourselves, are seldom deceived by them; the sheep generally recognize the wolf however carefully fitted the sheepskin under which he hides, though the onlookers may not; and though the sheep may not always be able to drive him from the flock! The outer world may be misled; we, who stand shoulder to shoulder with them, know them; they are not many; neither are they new. They are one of the oldest survivals, and among the most primitive relics in the race. They are as old as Loki among the gods, as Lucifer among the Sons of the Morning, as the serpent in the Garden of Eden, as pain and dislocation in the web of human life.

Such women are as old as that first primitive woman who, when she went with her fellows to gather wood for the common household, put grass in the center of the bundle that she might appear to carry as much as they, yet carry nothing; she is as old as the first man who threw away his shield in battle, and yet, when it was over, gathered with the victors to share the spoils; as old as cowardice and lust in the human and animal world; only to cease from being when, perhaps, an enlarged and expanded humanity shall have cast the last slough of its primitive skin.

Every army has its camp-followers, not among its accredited soldiers, but who follow in its train, ready to attack and rifle the fallen on either side. To lookers-on, they may appear soldiers; but the soldiers know who they are. At the Judean supper there was one Master, and to the onlooker there may have seemed twelve apostles; in truth only twelve were of the company, and one was not of it. There has always been this thirteenth figure at every sacramental gathering since the world began, wherever the upholders of a great cause have broken spiritual bread; but it may be questioned whether in any instance this thirteenth figure has been able to destroy, or even vitally to retard, any great human movement. Judas could betray his Master by a kiss; but he could not silence the voice which for a thousand years rang out of that Judean grave. Again and again, in social, political, and intellectual movements, the betrayer betrays; and the cause marches on over the body of the man.

There are women, as there are men, whose political, social,

intellectual, or philanthropic labors are put on, as the harlot puts on paint, and for the same purpose, but they can no more retard the progress of the great bulk of vital and sincere womanhood, than the driftwood on the surface of a mighty river can ultimately prevent its waters from reaching the sea.

When one considers the part which sexual attraction plays in the order of sentient life on the globe, from the almost unconscious attractions which draw ameboid globule to ameboid globule, on through the endless progressive forms of life; till in monogamous birds it expresses itself in song and complex courtship and the life-long conjugal affection of mates; and which, in the human race itself, passing through various forms, from the imperative but almost purely physical attraction of savage male and female for each other, till in the highly developed male and female it assumes its esthetic and intellectual but not less imperative form, couching itself in the songs of the poet and the deathless fidelity of fully developed man and woman to each other, we find it not only everywhere forming the groundwork on which is based sentient existence, never eradicable, though infinitely varied in its external forms of expression. When we consider that in the human world, from the battles and dances of savages to the intrigues and entertainments of modern courts and palaces, the attraction of man and woman for each other has played an unending part; and that the most fierce ascetic religious enthusiasm through the ages, the flagellations and starvations in endless nunneries and monasteries, have never been able to extirpate nor seriously to weaken for a moment the master dominance of this emotion; that the lowest and most brutal ignorance, and the highest intellectual culture leave mankind, equally, though in different forms, amenable to its mastery; that, whether in the brutal guffaw of sex laughter which rings across the drinking bars of our modern cities, and rises from the comfortable armchairs in fashionable clubs; or in the poet's dreams, and the noblest conjugal affection of men and women linked together for life, it plays still today on earth the part it played when hoary monsters plowed through Silurian slime, and that still it forms as ever the warp on which in the loom of human life the web is woven, and runs as a thread never absent through every design and pattern which constitutes an individual existence on earth:—not only does sexual attraction appear ineradicable, but it is ridiculous to suppose that that attraction of sex toward sex, which, with hunger and thirst, lie, as the triune instincts, at the base of animal life, should ever be exterminable or in any way modifiable by the comparatively superficial changes resulting from the performance of this or that form of labor, or the little more or less of knowledge in one direction or another.

That the female who runs steam-driven looms, producing scores of yards of linen in a day, should therefore desire less the fellowship of her corresponding male than had she toiled at a spinning-wheel with hand and foot to produce one yard; that the male should desire less of the companionship of the woman who spends the morning in doctoring babies in her consulting-room, according to the formularies of the pharmacopeia, than she who of old spent it on the hillside collecting simples for remedies; that the woman who paints a modern picture or designs a modern vase should be less lovable by man than her ancestor who shaped the first primitive pot and ornamented it with zigzag patterns was to the man of her day and age; that the woman who contributes to the support of her family by giving legal opinions will less desire motherhood and wifehood than she who in the past contributed to the support of her household by bending on hands and knees over her grindstone, or scrubbing floors, and that the former should be less valued by man than the latter—these are suppositions which it is difficult to regard as consonant with any knowledge of human nature and the laws by which it is dominated.

On the other hand, if it be supposed that the possession of wealth or the means of earning it makes the human female objectionable to the male, all history and all daily experience negate it. The eager hunt for heiresses, in all ages and social conditions, makes it obvious that the human male has a strong tendency to value the female who can contribute to the family expenditure; and the case is yet, we believe, unrecorded of a male who, attracted to a female, becomes averse to her on finding she has material good. The female doctor or lawyer earning a thousand a year will always, and today certainly does, find more suitors than had she remained a governess or cook, laboring as hard, earning thirty pounds.

While if the statement that the female entering on new fields of labor will cease to be lovable to the male be based on the fact that she will then be free, all history and all human experience yet more negate its truth. The study of all races in all ages proves that the greater the freedom of woman, the higher the sexual value put upon her by the males of that society. The three squaws who walk behind the Indian, whom he has captured in battle or bought for a few axes or lengths of tobacco, and over whom he exercises the right of life and death, are probably all three of infinitesimal value in his eyes, compared with the value of his single, free wife to one of our ancient, monogamous German ancestors; while the hundred wives and concubines purchased by a Turkish pasha have probably not even an approximate value in his eyes, when compared with the value thousands of modern European males set upon the one comparatively free woman, whom they have won, often only after a long and tedious courtship.

So axiomatic is the statement that the value of the female to the male varies as her freedom, that, given an account of any human society in which the individual female is highly valued, it will be perfectly safe to infer the comparative social freedom of woman; and, given a statement as to the high degree of freedom of woman in any society, it will be safe to infer the great sexual value of the individual woman to man.

When we examine narrowly the statement, that the entrance

of woman into the new fields of labor, with its probably resulting greater freedom of action, economic independence and wider culture, may result in a severance between the sexes, it becomes clear what that fallacious appearance is, which suggests this.

The entrance of a woman into new fields of labor, though bringing her increased freedom and economic independence, and necessitating increased mental training and wider knowledge, could not extinguish the primordial physical instinct which draws sex to sex throughout all the orders of sentient life; and still less could it annihilate that subtler mental need, which, as humanity develops, draws sex to sex for emotional fellowship and close intercourse; but, it might, and undoubtedly would, powerfully react; and readjust the relations of certain men with certain women!

While the attraction, physical and intellectual, which binds sex to sex would remain the same in volume and intensity, the forms in which it would express itself, and, above all, the relative power of individuals to command the gratification of their instincts and desires, would be fundamentally altered, and in many cases inverted.

In the barbarian state of societies, where physical force dominates, it is the most muscular and pugilistically and brutally and animally successful male who captures and possesses the largest number of females; and no doubt he would be justified in regarding any social change which gave to woman a larger freedom of choice, and which would so perhaps give to the less brutal but perhaps more intelligent male whom the woman might select, an equal opportunity for the gratification of his sexual wishes and for the producing of offspring, as a serious loss. And, from the purely personal standpoint, he would undoubtedly he right in dreading anything which tended to free woman. But he would manifestly not have been justified in asserting that woman's increased freedom of choice, or the fact that the other men would share his advantage in the matter of obtaining female companionship, would in any way lessen the amount of sexual emotion or the tenderness of relation between the two halves of humanity. He would not by brute force possess himself of so many females nor have so large a circle of choice, under the new conditions; but what he lost, others would gain; and the intensity of the sex emotions and the nearness and passion of the relation between the sexes be in no way touched.

In our civilized societies, as they exist today, woman possesses (more often perhaps in appearance than reality!) a somewhat greater freedom of sexual selection; in modern societies she is no longer captured by muscular force, but there are still conditions entirely unconnected with sex attractions and affections, which yet largely dominate the sex relations.

It is not the man of the strong arm, but the man of the long purse, who unduly and artificially dominates in the sexual world today. Practically, wherever in the modern world woman is wholly or partially dependent for her means of support on the existence of her sexual functions, she is dependent more or less on the male's power to support her in their exercise, and her freedom of choice is practically so far limited. Probably three-fourths of the sexual unions in our modern European societies, whether in the illegal or recognized legal forms, are dominated by or largely influenced by the sex purchasing power of the male. With regard to the large and savage institution of prostitution, which still lies as a cancer inbedded in the heart of all our modern civilized societies, this is obviously and nakedly the case; the wealth of the male as compared to the female being, with hideous obtrusiveness, its foundation and source of life. But the purchasing power of the male as compared with the poverty of the female is not less painfully, if a little less obtrusively, displayed in those layers of society lying nearer the surface. From the fair, effete young girl of the wealthier classes and her city boudoir, who weeps copiously as she tells you she cannot marry the man she loves, because he has only two hundred a year and cannot afford to keep her, to the father who demands frankly of his daughter's suitor how much he can settle on her before consenting to his acceptance, the fact remains, that, under existing conditions, not the amount of sex affection and attraction, but the extraneous question of the material possessions of the male, determines to a large extent the relation of the sexes. The parasitic, helpless youth who has failed in his studies, who possesses neither virility, nor charm of person, nor strength of mind, but who possesses wealth, has a far greater chance of securing the life companionship of the fairest maid, than her brother's tutor, who may be possessed of every manly and physical grace and mental gift; and the ancient libertine, possessed of material good, has, especially among the so-called upper classes of our societies, a far greater chance of securing the sex companionship of any woman he desires as wife, mistress, or prostitute, than the most physically attractive and mentally developed male, who may have nothing to offer to the dependent female but affection and sexual companionship.

To the male, whenever and wherever he exists in our societies, who depends mainly for his power for procuring the sex relation he desires, not on his power of winning and retaining personal affection, but on the purchasing power of his possessions as compared to the poverty of the females of his society, the personal loss would be seriously and at once felt, of any social change which gave to the woman a larger economic independence and therefore greater freedom of sexual choice. It is not an imaginary danger which the young dude—of that type which sits in the front row of the stalls in the theater, with sloping forehead and feeble jaw, sucking at intervals the top of his gilt-headed cane, and watching the unhappy women who dance for gold—sees looming before him, as he lisps out his deep disapproval of increased knowledge and the freedom of obtaining the means of subsistence in intellectual fields by woman, and expresses his vast preference for the uncultured ballet-girl over all types of cultured and productive, laboring womanhood in the universe. A subtle and profound instinct warns him, that, with the increased intelligence and economic freedom of woman, he, and such as he, might ultimately be left sexually companionless; the undesirable, the residuary, male old-maids of the human race.

On the other hand, there is undoubtedly a certain body of females who would lose, or imagine they would lose, heavily by the advance of woman as a whole to a condition of free labor and economic independence. That female, willfully or organically belonging to the parasite class, having neither the vigor of intellect nor the vitality of body to undertake any form of productive labor, and desiring to be dependent only upon passive performance of sex function merely, would, whether as prostitute or wife, undoubtedly lose heavily by any social change which demanded of woman increased knowledge and activity.

It is exactly by these two classes of persons that the objection is raised that the entrance of woman into the new fields of labor and her increased freedom and intelligence will dislocate the relations of the sexes; and while, from the purely personal standpoint, they are undoubtedly right, viewing human society as a whole they are fundamentally wrong. The loss of a small and unhealthy section will be the gain of human society as a whole.

In the male voluptuary of feeble intellect and unattractive individuality, who depends for the gratification of his sexual instincts, not on his power of winning and retaining the personal affection and admiration of woman, but on her purchasable condition, either in the blatantly barbarous field of sex traffic that lies beyond the pale of legal marriage, or the not less barbarous though more veiled traffic within that pale, the entrance of woman into the new fields of labor, with an increased intellectual culture and economic freedom, means little less than social extinction. But, to those males who, even at the present day, constitute the majority in our societies, and who desire

the affection and fellowship of woman rather than a mere
material possession; for the male who has the attributes and
gifts of mind or body, which, apart from any weight of material
advantage, would fit him to hold the affection of woman, however great her freedom of choice, the gain will be correspondingly
great. Given a society in which the majority of women should
be so far self-supporting, that, having their free share open to
them in the modern fields of labor, and reaping the full economic
rewards of their labor, marriage or some form of sexual sale was
no more a matter of necessity to them; so far from this condition causing a diminution in the number of permanent sex
unions, one of the heaviest bars to them would be removed.
It is universally allowed that one of the disease spots in our
modern social condition is the increasing difficulty which bars
conscientious men from entering on marriage and rearing families, if limited means would in the case of their death or disablement throw the woman and their common offspring comparatively helpless into the fierce stream of our modern economic
life. If the woman could justifiably be looked to, in case of
the man's disablement or death, to take his place as an earner,
thousands of valuable marriages which cannot now be contracted
could be entered on; and the serious social evil, which arises
from the fact that while the self-indulgent and selfish freely
marry and produce large families, the restrained and conscientious are often unable to do so, would be removed. For
the first time in the history of the modern world, prostitution,
using that term in the broadest sense to cover all sexual relationships based, not on the spontaneous affection of the woman
for the man, but on the necessitous acceptance by woman of
material good in exchange for the exercise of her sexual functions, would be extinct; and the relation between men and
women become a co-partnership between freemen.

So far from the economic freedom and social independence
of the woman exterminating sexual love between man and
woman, it would for the first time fully enfranchise it. The

element of physical force and capture which dominated the most primitive sex relations, the more degrading element of seduction and purchase by means of wealth or material good offered to woman in our modern societies, would then give place to the untrammeled action of attraction and affection alone between the sexes, and sexual love, after its long pilgrimage in the deserts, would be enabled to return at last, a king crowned.

We have called the woman's movement of our age an endeavor on the part of women among modern civilized races to find new fields of labor as the old slip from them, as an attempt to escape from parasitism and an inactive dependence upon sex function alone; but, viewed from another side, the woman's movement might not less justly be called a part of a great movement of the sexes towards each other, a movement towards common occupations, common interests, common ideals, and an emotional tenderness and sympathy between the sexes more deeply founded and more indestructible than any the world has yet seen.

XXVIII
OSCAR WILDE

Oscar Wilde, born at Dublin, Ireland, 1856; died at Paris, 1900. A British writer and a leader in the "esthetic" movement. He was a son of Sir William Wilde, the oculist, and was educated at Oxford, where he won the Newdigate prize in 1878 with a poem, *Ravenna*. His poems were published in 1881, and *The Happy Prince and Other Tales* in 1882. He also wrote *The Picture of Dorian Gray*, 1890; a number of plays, among which are *Vera* (1882), *The Duchess of Padua* (1891), *Lady Windemere's Fan* (1892); *Salome*, 1893 (in French, written for Sarah Bernhardt), and *A Woman of No Importance; The Ballad of Reading Gaol*, 1896; *De Profundis*, 1905, which was written during the last months of his imprisonment. The selections are from *The Soul of Man Under Socialism*.

Liberty in Art.—An individual who has to make things for the use of others, and with reference to their wants and their wishes, does not work with interest, and consequently cannot put into his work what is best in him. Upon the other hand, whenever a community or a powerful section of a community, or a government of any kind, attempts to dictate to the artist what he is to do, Art either entirely vanishes, or becomes stereotyped, or degenerates into a low and ignoble form of craft. A work of art is the unique result of a unique temperament. Its beauty comes from the fact that the author is what he is. It has nothing to do with the fact that other people want what they want. Indeed, the moment that an artist takes notice of what other people want, and tries to supply the demand, he ceases to be an artist, and becomes a dull or an amusing craftsman, an honest or a dishonest tradesman. He has no further claim to be considered as an artist. Art is the most intense mode of individualism that the world has known. I am inclined to say that it is the only real mode of individualism that the world has known. Crime, which, under certain conditions, may seem to have created individualism, must take cognizance of other people and interfere with them. It belongs to the sphere of action. But alone, without any reference to his neighbors, without any interference, the artist can fashion a beautiful thing; and if he does not do it solely for his own pleasure, he is not an artist at all.

And it is to be noted that it is the fact that Art is this intense form of individualism that makes the public try to exercise over it an authority that is as immoral as it is ridiculous, and as corrupting as it is contemptible. It is not quite their fault. The public has always, and in every age, been badly brought up. They are continually asking Art to be popular, to please their want of taste, to flatter their absurd vanity, to tell them what they have been told before, to show them what they ought to be tired of seeing, to amuse them when they feel heavy after eating too much, and to distract their thoughts when they are wearied of their own stupidity. Now Art should never try to be popular. The public should try to make itself artistic. There is a very wide difference. If a man of science were told that the results of his experiments, and the conclusions that he arrived at, should be of such a character that they would not upset the received popular notions on the subject, or disturb popular prejudice, or hurt the sensibilities of people who knew nothing about science; if a philosopher were told that he had a perfect right to speculate in the highest spheres of thought, provided that he arrive at the same conclusions as were held by those who had never thought in any sphere at all—well, nowadays the man of science and the philospher would be considerably amused. Yet it is really a very few years since both philosophy and science were subjected to brutal popular control, to authority in fact—the authority of either the general ignorance of the community, or the terror and greed for power of an ecclesiastical or governmental class. Of course, we have to a very great extent got rid of any attempt on the part of the community, or the church, or the government, to interfere with the individualism of speculative thought, but the attempt to interfere with the individualism of imaginative art still lingers. In fact, it does more than linger: it is aggressive, offensive and brutalizing.

In England, the arts that have escaped best are the arts in which the public takes no interest. Poetry is an instance of what I mean. We have been able to have fine poetry in England because the public does not read it, and consequently does not influence it. The public likes to insult poets because they are individual, but once they have insulted them they leave them alone. In the case of the novel and the drama, arts in which the public does take an interest, the result of the exercise of popular authority has been absolutely ridiculous. No country produces such badly written fiction, such tedious, common work in the novel-form, such silly, vulgar, plays as in England. It must necessarily be so. The popular standard is of such a character that no artist can get to it. It is at once too easy and too difficult to be a popular novelist. It is too easy, because the requirements of the public as far as plot, style, psychology, treatment of life and treatment of literature are concerned, are within the reach of the very meanest capacity and the most uncultivated mind. It is too difficult, because to meet such requirements the artist would have to do violence to his temperament, would have to write not for the artist joy of writing, but for the amusement of half-educated people, and so would have to suppress his individualism, forget his culture, annihilate his style, and surrender everything that is valuable in him. In the case of the drama, things are a little better: the theater-going public likes the obvious, it is true, but it does not like the tedious: and burlesque and farcical comedy, the two most popular forms, are distinct forms of art. Delightful work may be produced under burlesque and farcical conditions, and in works of this kind the artist in England is allowed very great freedom. It is when one comes to the higher forms of the drama that the result of popular control is seen. The one thing that the public dislikes is novelty. Any attempt to extend the subject-matter of art is extremely distasteful to the public; and yet the vitality and progress of art depend in a large measure on the continual extension of subject-matter. The public dislikes novelty because it is afraid of it. It represents to them a mode of Individualism, an assertion on the part of the artist that he selects his own subject, and treats it as he chooses. The public is quite right in its attitude. Art is Individualism, and Individualism is a disturbing and disintegrating force. Therein lies its immense value. For what it seeks to disturb is monotony of type, slavery of custom, tyranny of habit, and the reduction of man to the level of a machine. In Art, the public accepts what has been because they cannot alter it, not because they appreciate it. They swallow their classics whole, and never taste them. They endure them as the inevitable and, as they cannot mar them, they mouth about them. Strangely enough, or not strangely, according to one's own views, this acceptance of the classics does a great deal of harm. The uncritical admiration of the Bible and Shakespeare in England is an instance of what I mean. With regard to the Bible, considerations of ecclesiastical authority enter into the matter, so that I need not dwell upon the point.

But in the case of Shakespeare it is quite obvious that the public really sees neither the beauties nor the defects of his plays. If they saw the beauty, they would not object to the development of the drama; and if they saw the defects, they would not object to the development of the drama either. The fact is, the public makes use of the classics of a country as a means of checking the progress of Art. They degrade the classics into authorities. They use them as bludgeons for preventing the free expression of Beauty in new forms. They are always asking a writer why he does not write like somebody else, or a painter why he does not paint like somebody else, quite oblivious of the fact that if either of them did anything of the kind he would cease to be an artist. A fresh mode of Beauty is absolutely distasteful to them, and whenever it appears they get so angry and bewildered that they always use two stupid expressions—one is that the work of art is grossly unintelligible; the other, that the work of art is grossly immoral. What they mean by these words seems to me to be this: When they say a work is grossly unintelligible, they mean that the artist has said or made a beautiful thing that is new; when they describe a work as grossly immoral, they mean that the artist has said or made a beautiful thing that is true. The former expression has reference to style; the latter to subject-matter. But they probably use the words very vaguely, as an ordinary mob will use ready-made paving-stones. There is not a single real poet or prose-writer of this century, for instance, on whom the British public has not solemnly conferred diplomas of immorality, and these diplomas practically take the place, with us, of what in France is the formal recognition of an Academy of Letters, and fortunately make the establishment of such an institution quite unnecessary in England. Of course the public is very reckless in its use of the word. That they should have called Wordsworth an immoral poet was only to be expected. Wordsworth was a poet. But that they should have called Charles Kingsley an immoral novelist is extraordinary. Kingsley's prose was not of a very fine quality. Still, there is the word, and they use it as best they can. An artist is, of course, not disturbed by it. The true artist is a man who believes absolutely in himself, because he is absolutely himself. But I can fancy that if an artist produced a work of art in England that immediately on its appearance was recognized by the public, through its medium, which is the public press, as a work that was quite intelligible and highly moral, he would begin seriously to question whether in its creation he had really been himself at all, and consequently whether the work was not quite unworthy of him, and either of a thoroughly second-rate order, or of no artist value whatsoever.

Perhaps, however, I have wronged the public in limiting them to such words as "immoral," "unintelligible," "exotic," and "unhealthy." There is one other word that they use. That word is "morbid." They do not use it often. The meaning of the word is so simple that they are afraid of using it. Still, they use it sometimes and, now and then, one comes across it in popular newspapers. It is, of course, a ridiculous word to apply to a work of art. For what is morbidity but a mood of emotion or a mode of thought that one cannot express? The public are all morbid, because the public can never find expression for anything. The artist is never morbid. He expresses everything. He stands outside his subject, and through its medium produces incomparable and artistic effects. To call an artist morbid because he deals with morbidity as his subject-matter is as silly as if one called Shakespeare mad because he wrote King Lear.

On the whole, an artist in England gains something by being attacked. His individuality is intensified. He becomes more completely himself. Of course the attacks are very gross, very impertinent, and very contemptible. But then no artist expects grace from the vulgar minds, or style from the suburban intellect. Vulgarity and stupidity are two very vivid facts in modern life. One regrets them, naturally. But there they are. They are subjects for study, like everything else. And it is only fair to state, with regard to modern journalists, that they always apologize to one in private for what they have written against one in public.

Within the last few years two other adjectives, it may be mentioned, have been added to the very limited vocabulary of art abuse that is at the disposal of the public. One is the word "unhealthy," the other is the word "exotic." The latter merely expresses the rage of the momentary mushroom against the immortal, entrancing, and exquisitely lovely orchid. It is a tribute. But a tribute of no importance. The word "unhealthy," however, admits of analysis. It is a rather interesting word. In fact, it is so interesting that the people who use it do not know what it means.

What does it mean? What is a healthy, or an unhealthy work of art? All terms that one applies to a work of art, provided that one applies them rationally, have reference to either its style or its subject, or to both together. From the point of view of style, a healthy work of art is one whose style recognizes the beauty of the material it employs, be that material one of words or of bronze, of color or of ivory, and uses that beauty as a factor in producing the esthetic effect. From the point of view of subject, a healthy work of art is one the choice of whose subject is conditioned by the temperament of the artist, and comes directly out of it. In fine, a healthy work of art is one that has both perfection and personality. Of course, form and substance cannot be separated in a work of art; they are always one. But for purposes of analysis, and setting the wholeness of esthetic impression aside for a moment, intellectually we can so separate them. An unhealthy work of art, on the other hand, is a work whose style is obvious, old-fashioned and common, and whose subject is deliberately chosen, not because the artist has any pleasure in it, but because he thinks that the public will pay him for it. In fact, the popular novel that the public calls healthy is always a thoroughly unhealthy production; and what the public calls an unhealthy novel is always a beautiful and healthy work of art.

I have pointed out that the arts which have escaped best in England are the arts in which the public has not been interested. They are, however, interested in the drama, and as a certain advance has been made in the drama within the last ten or fifteen years, it is important to point out that this advance is entirely due to a few individual artists refusing to accept the popular want of taste as their standard, and refusing to regard art as a mere matter of demand and supply. With his marvelous and vivid personality, with a style that has really a true color-element in it, with his extraordinary power, not over mere mimicry but over imaginative and intellectual creation, Mr. Irving, had his sole object been to give the public what it wanted, could have produced the commonest plays in the commonest manner, and made as much success and money as a man could possibly desire. But his object was not that. His object was to realize his own perfection as an artist, under certain conditions, and in certain forms of Art. At first he appealed to the few: now he has educated the many. He had created in the public both taste and temperament. The public appreciates his artistic success immensely. I often wonder, however, whether the public understands that that success is entirely due to the fact that he did not accept their standard, but realized his own. With their standard the Lyceum would have been a sort of second-rate booth, as some of the popular theaters in London are at present. Whether they understand it or not the fact however remains, that taste and temperament have, to a certain extent, been created in the public, and that the public is capable of developing these qualities. The problem then is, why does not the public become more civilized? They have the capacity. What stops them?

The thing that stops them, it must be said again, is their desire to exercise authority over the artist and over works of art. To certain theaters, such as the Lyceum and the Haymarket, the public seems to come in a proper mood. In both of these theaters there have been individual artists, who have succeeded in creating in their audiences—and every theater in London has its own audience—the temperament to which Art appeals. And what is that temperament? It is the temperament of receptivity. That is all.

If a man approaches a work of art with any desire to exercise authority over it and the artist, he approaches it in such a spirit that he cannot receive any artistic impression from it at all. The work of art is to dominate the spectator: the spectator is not to dominate the work of art. The spectator is to be receptive. He is to be the violin on which the master is to play. And the more completely he can suppress his own silly views, his own foolish prejudices, his own absurd ideas of what Art should be or should not be, the more likely he is to understand and appreciate the work of art in question. This is, of course, quite obvious in the case of the vulgar theater-going public of English men and women. But it is equally true of what are called educated people. For an educated person's ideas of Art are drawn naturally from what Art has been, whereas the new work of art is beautiful by being what Art has never been; and to measure it by the standard of the past is to measure it by a standard on the rejection of which its real perfection depends. A temperament capable of receiving, through an imaginative medium, and under imaginative conditions, new and beautiful impressions is the only temperament that can appreciate a work of art. And true as this is in the case of the appreciation of sculpture and painting, it is still more true of the appreciation of such arts as the drama. For a picture and a statue are not at war with Time. They take no count of its succession. In one moment their unity may be apprehended. In the case of literature it is different. Time must be traversed before the unity of effect is realized. And so, in the drama, there may occur in the first act of the play something whose real artistic value may not be evident to the spectator till the third or fourth act is reached. Is the silly fellow to get angry and call out, and disturb the play, and annoy the artists? No. The honest man is to sit quietly, and know the delightful emotions of wonder, curiosity and suspense. He is not to go to the play to lose a vulgar temper. He is to go to the play to realize an artistic temperament. He is to go to the play to gain an artistic temperament. He is not the arbiter of the work of art. He is one who is admitted to contemplate the work of art, and, if the work be fine, to forget in its contemplation all the egotism that mars him—the egotism of his ignorance, or the egotism of his information. This point about the drama is hardly, I think, sufficiently recognized. I can quite understand that were Macbeth produced for the first time before a modern London audience, many of the people present would strongly and vigorously object to the introduction of the witches in the first act, with their grotesque phrases and their ridiculous words. But when the play is over one realizes that the laughter of the witches in Macbeth is as terrible as the laughter of madness in Lear, more terrible than the laughter of Iago in the tragedy of the Moor. No spectator of art needs a more perfect mood of receptivity than the spectator of a play. The moment he seeks to exercise authority he becomes the avowed enemy of Art and of himself. Art does not mind. It is he who suffers.

With the novel it is the same thing. Popular authority and the recognition of popular authority are fatal. Thackeray's Esmond is a beautiful work of art because he wrote it to please himself. In his other novels, in Pendennis, in Philip, in Vanity Fair even, at times, he is too conscious of the public, and spoils his work by appealing directly to the sympathies of the public, or by directly mocking at them. A true artist takes no notice whatever of the public. The public is to him non-existent. He has no poppied or honeyed cakes through which to give the monster sleep or sustenance. He leaves that to the popular novelist. One incomparable novelist we have now in England, Mr. George Meredith. There are better artists in France, but France has no one whose view of life is so large, so varied, so imaginatively true. There are tellers of stories in Russia who have a more vivid sense of what pain in fiction may be. But to him belongs philosophy in fiction. His people not merely live, but they live in thought. One can see them from myriad points of view. They are suggestive. There is soul in them and around them. They are interpretative and symbolic. And he who made them, those wonderful quickly moving figures, made them for his own pleasure, and has never asked the public what they wanted, has never cared to know what they wanted, has never allowed the public to dictate to him or influence him in any way, but has gone on intensifying his own personality, and producing his own individual work. At first none came to him. That did not matter. Then the few came to him. That did not change him. The many have come now. He is still the same. He is an incomparable novelist.

With the decorative arts it is not different. The public clung with really pathetic tenacity to what I believe were the direct traditions of the Great Exhibition of international vulgarity, traditions that were so appalling that the houses in which people lived were only fit for blind people to live in. Beautiful things began to be made, beautiful colors came from the dyer's hands, beautiful patterns from the artist's brain, and the use of beautiful things and their value and importance were set forth. The public was really very indignant. They lost their temper. They said silly things. No one minded. No one was a whit the worse. No one accepted the authority of public opinion. And now it is almost impossible to enter any modern house without seeing some recognition of good taste, some recognition of the value of lovely surroundings, some sign of appreciation of beauty. In fact, people's houses are, as a rule, quite charming nowadays. People have been to a very great extent civilized. It is only fair to state, however, that the extraordinary success of the revolution in house-decoration and furniture and the like has not really been due to the majority of the public developing a very fine taste in such matters. It has been chiefly due to the fact that the craftsmen of things so appreciated the pleasure of making what was beautiful, and woke to such a vivid consciousness of the hideousness and vulgarity of what the public had previously wanted, that they simply starved the public out. It would be quite impossible at the present moment to furnish a room as rooms were furnished a few years ago, without going for everything to an auction of second-hand furniture from some third-rate lodging-house. The things are no longer made. However they may object to it, people must nowadays have something charming in their surroundings. Fortunately for them, their assumption of authority in these art-matters came to entire grief.

It is evident, then, that all authority in such things is bad.

People sometimes inquire what form of government is most suitable for an artist to live under. To this question there is only one answer. The form of government that is most suitable to the artist is no government at all. Authority over him and his art is ridiculous. It has been stated that under despotisms artists have produced lovely work. This is not quite so. Artists have visited despots, not as subjects to be tyrannized over, but as wandering wonder-makers, as fascinating vagrant personalities, to be entertained and charmed and suffered to be at peace, and allowed to create. There is this to be said in favor of the despot, that he, being an individual, may have culture, while the mob, being a monster, has none. One who is an emperor and king may stoop down to pick up a brush for a painter, but when the democracy stoops down it is merely to throw mud. And yet the democracy have not so far to stoop as the emperor. In fact, when they want to throw mud they have not to stoop at all. But there is no necessity to separate the monarch from the mob; all authority is equally bad.

There are three kinds of despots. There is the despot who tyrannizes over the body. There is the despot who tyrannizes over the soul. There is the despot who tyrannizes over soul and body alike. The first is called the Prince. The second is called the Pope. The third is called the People. The Prince may be cultivated. Many princes have been. Yet in the Prince there is danger. One thinks of Dante at the bitter feast in Verona, of Tasso in Ferrara's madman's cell. It is better for the artist not to live with princes. The Pope may be cultivated. Many popes have been; the bad popes have been. The bad popes loved Beauty almost as passionately, nay, with as much passion as the good popes hated Thought. To the wickedness of the papacy humanity owes much. The goodness of the papacy owes a terrible debt to humanity. Yet, though the Vatican has kept the rhetoric of its thunders and lost the rod of its lightning, it is better for the artist not to live with popes. It was a pope who said of Cellini to a conclave of cardinals that common laws and common authority were not made for men such as he; but it was a pope who thrust Cellini into prison, and kept him there till he sickened with rage, and created unreal visions for himself, and saw the gilded sun enter his room and grew so enamored of it that he sought to escape, and crept out from tower to tower, and falling through dizzy air at dawn maimed himself, and was by a vine-dresser covered with vine leaves and carried in a cart to one who, loving beautiful things, had care of him. There is danger in popes. And as for the People, what of them and their authority? Perhaps of them and their authority one has spoken enough. Their authority is a thing blind, deaf, hideous, grotesque, tragic, amusing, serious and obscene. It is impossible for the artist to live with the People. All despots bribe. The people bribe and brutalize. Who told them to exercise authority? They were made to live, to listen, and to love. Some one has done them a great wrong. They have marred themselves by imitation of their inferiors. They have taken the scepter of the Prince. How should they use it? They have taken the triple tiara of the Pope. How should they carry its burden? They are as a clown whose heart is broken. They are as a priest whose soul is not yet born. Let all who love Beauty pity them. Though they themselves love not Beauty, let them pity themselves. Who taught them the trick of tyranny?

Despotism is unjust to everybody, including the despot, who was probably made for better things. Oligarchies are unjust to the many, and ochlocracies are unjust to the few. High hopes were once formed of democracy; but democracy means simply the bludgeoning of the people by the people for the people. It has been found out. I must say that it was high time, for all authority is quite degrading. It degrades those who exercise it, and degrades those over whom it is exercised. When it is violently, grossly and cruelly used, it produces a good effect, by creating, or at any rate bringing out, the spirit of revolt and individualism that is to kill it. When it is used with a certain amount of kindness, and accompanied by prizes and rewards, it is dreadfully demoralizing. People, in that case, are less conscious of the horrible pressure that is being put on them, and so go through their lives in a sort of coarse comfort, like petted animals, without ever realizing that they are probably thinking other people's thoughts, living by other people's standards, wearing practically what one may call other people's second-hand clothes, and never being themselves for a single moment. "He who would be free," says a fine thinker, "must not conform." And authority, by bribing people to conform, produces a very gross kind of overfed barbarism amongst us.

There are many other things that one might point out. One might point out how the Renaissance was great, because it sought to solve no social problem, and busied itself not about such things, but suffered the individual to develop freely, beautifully and naturally, and so had great and individual artists, and great and individual men. One might point out how Louis XIV, by creating the modern state, destroyed the individualism of the artist, and made things monstrous in their monotony of repetition, and contemptible in their conformity to rule, and destroyed throughout all France all those fine freedoms of expression that had made tradition new in beauty, and new modes one with antique form. But the past is of no importance. The present is of no importance. It is with the future that we have to deal. For the past is what man should not have been. The present is what man ought not to be. The future is what artists are.

It will come of course to be said that such a scheme as is set forth here is quite unpractical, and goes against human nature. This is perfectly true. It is unpractical, and it goes against human nature. This is why it is worth carrying out, and that is why one proposes it. For what is a practical scheme? A practical scheme is either a scheme that is already in existence, or a scheme that could be carried out under existing conditions.

But it is exactly the existing conditions that one objects to; and any scheme that could accept these conditions is wrong and foolish. The conditions will be done away with, and human nature will change. The only thing that one really knows about human nature is that it changes. Change is the one quality we can predicate of it. The systems that fail are those that rely on the permanency of human nature, and not on its growth and development. The error of Louis XIV was that he thought human nature would always be the same. The result of his error was the French Revolution. It was an admirable result. All the results of the mistakes of governments are quite admirable.

It is to be noted also that Individualism does not come to man with any sickly cant about duty, which merely means doing what other people want because they want it; or any hideous cant about self-sacrifice, which is merely a survival of savage mutilation. In fact, it does not come to man with any claims upon him at all. It comes naturally and inevitably out of man. It is the point to which all development tends. It is the differentiation to which all organisms grow. It is the perfection that is inherent in every mode of life, and towards which every mode of life quickens. And so Individualism exercises no compulsion over man. On the contrary, it says to man that he should suffer no compulsion to be exercised over him. It does not try to force people to be good. It knows that people are good when they are let alone. Man will develop Individualism out of himself. Man is now so developing Individualism. To ask whether Individualism is practical is like asking whether Evolution is practical. Evolution is the law of life, and there is no evolution except towards Individualism. Where this tendency is not expressed, it is a case of artificially arrested growth, or of disease, or of death.

XXIX
FRANCISCO FERRER

Francisco Ferrer, founder of the Modern School in Spain, born near Barcelona, Spain, 1859. Parents were well-to-do farmers and devout Catholics, but he became a Freethinker when very young. In 1879 proclaimed himself a republican; took part in revolution led by General Villacampa; fled to Paris, became secretary to Spanish republican leader, Ruix Zorrilla. Returned to Spain, 1901, and started the first of his Modern Schools; used as text-books one of the greatest radical and scientific works of the day and tore education in Spain from the cloisters. The Roman Catholic Church bitterly opposed his Modern Schools and looked for excuses to suppress them; accused Ferrer of complicity in bomb-throwing at King and Queen, imprisoned him for one year, but could not prove anything; accused him again, in 1909, when uprising took place in Barcelona inspired by indignation against unjust war in Morocco; arrested on charge of being head of uprising, a charge which later investigations by the State proved to be false, and was condemned to death by a court-martial and shot at Montjuich fortress Oct. 13, 1909. His last words were: "Long live the Modern School." The selections are from *The Modern School.*

The Modern School

To those who wish to renovate the education of children two methods are open: To work for the transformation of the school by studying the child, so as to prove scientifically that the present organization of education is defective and to bring about progressive modification; or, to found new schools in which shall be directly applied those principles corresponding directly to the ideal of society and of its units, as held by those who eschew the conventionalities, prejudices, cruelties, trickeries, and falsehoods, upon which modern society is based.

The first method certainly offers great advantages. It corresponds to that evolutionary conception which all men of science defend, and which alone, according to them, can succeed. In theory they are right, and we are quite ready to recognize it.

It is evident that experiments in psychology and physiology must lead to important changes in matters of education: that teachers, being better able to understand the child, will know better how to adapt their instruction to natural laws. I even grant that such evolution will be in the direction of liberty, for I am convinced that constraint arises only from ignorance, and that the educator who is really worthy of the name will obtain his results through the spontaneous response of the child, whose desires he will learn to know, and whose development he will try to further by giving it every possible gratification.

But in reality, I do not believe that those who struggle for human emancipation can expect much from this method. Governments have ever been careful to hold a high hand over the education of the people. They know, better than anyone else, that their power is based almost entirely on the school. Hence, they monopolize it more and more. The time is past when they opposed the diffusion of instruction, and when they sought to restrain the education of the masses. These tactics were formerly possible, because the economic life of the nations allowed the prevalence of popular ignorance, that ignorance which renders mastery easy. But circumstances have changed. The progress of science, discoveries of all kinds, have revolutionized the conditions of labor and production. It is no longer possible for a people to remain ignorant: it must be educated in order that the economic situation of one country may hold its own and make headway against the universal competition. In consequence, governments want education; they want a more and more complete organization of the school, not because they hope for the renovation of society through education, but because they need individuals, workmen, perfected instruments of labor, to make their industrial enterprises and the capital employed in them profitable. And we have seen the most reactionary governments follow this movement; they have realized perfectly that their former tactics were becoming dangerous to the economic life of the nations, and that it is necessary to adapt popular education to new necessities.

But it would be a great mistake to suppose that the directors have not foreseen the dangers which the intelligent development of the people might create for them, and that it was necessary for them to change their methods of keeping the mastery. These methods have likewise been adapted to the new conditions of life, and they have labored to keep a hold over the evolution of ideas. At the same time that they seek to preserve the beliefs upon which social discipline was formerly based, they have sought to give to conceptions born of scientific effort a signification which could do no harm to established institutions. And to that end they took possession of the school. They who formerly left the priests in charge of the education of the people, because the priests were perfectly suited to the task, their instruction being at the service of authority, now took up everywhere the direction of scholarly education.

The danger, for them, lay in the awakening of human intelligence to the new outlook on life; the awakening, in the depths of men's consciousness, of a will towards emancipation. It would have been foolish to combat the evolving forces; they had to be driven into channels. That is the reason why, far from adhering to the old procedures of government, they adopted new ones, and evidently efficacious ones. It did not require great genius to find this solution; the simple pressure of facts led the men in power to understand what they must oppose to the apparent perils.

Oh, what have people not expected, what do they not expect still, from education! The majority of progressive men expect everything from it, and it is only in these later days that some begin to understand that it offers nothing but illusions. We perceive the utter uselessness of this learning, acquired in the schools by the systems of education at present in practice; we see that we expected and hoped in vain. It is because the organization of the school, far from spreading the ideal which we imagined, has made education the most powerful means of enslavement in the hands of the governing powers today. Their teachers are only the conscious or unconscious instruments of these powers, modeled moreover according to their principles; they have from their youth up, and more than any one else, been subjected to the discipline of their authority; few indeed are those who have escaped the influence of this domination; and these remain powerless, because the school organization constrains them so strongly that they cannot but obey it. It is not my purpose here to examine the nature of this organization. It is sufficiently well known for me to characterize it in one word: *constraint*. The school imprisons children physically, intellectually, and morally, in order to direct the development of their faculties in the paths desired. It deprives them of contact with nature, in order to model them after its own pattern. And this is the explanation of all which I have here set forth: The care which governments have taken to direct the education of the people, and the bankruptcy of the hopes of believers in liberty. The education of today is nothing more than drill. I refuse to believe that the systems employed have been combined with any exact design for bringing about the results desired. That would presuppose genius. But things take place precisely as if this education responded to some vast entire conception in a manner really remarkable. It could not have been better done. What accomplished it, was simply that the leading inspiration was the principle of discipline and of authority which guides social organizers at all times. They have but one clearly defined idea, one will, viz.: Children must be accustomed to obey, to believe, to think, according to the social dogmas which govern us. Hence, education cannot be other than what it is today. It is not a matter of seconding the spontaneous development of the faculties of the child, of leaving it free to satisfy its physical, intellectual, and moral needs; it is a matter of imposing ready-made ideas upon it; a matter even of preventing it from ever thinking otherwise than is willed for the maintenance of the institutions of this society; it is a matter of making it an individual strictly adapted to the social mechanism.

No one should be astonished that such an education has this evil influence upon human emancipation. I repeat, it is but a means of domination in the hands of the governing powers. They have never wanted the uplift of the individual, but his enslavement; and it is perfectly useless to hope anything from the school of today.

Now, what has been resulting up until today will continue to result in the future. There is no reason for governments to change their systems. They have succeeded in making education serve their advantage; they will likewise know how to make use of any improvements that may be proposed to their advantage.

It is sufficient that they maintain the spirit of the school, the authoritarian discipline which reigns therein, for all innovations to be turned to their profit. And they will watch their opportunity; be sure of that.

I would like to call the attention of my readers to this idea: All the value of education rests in respect for the physical, intellectual, and moral will of the child. Just as in science no demonstration is possible save by facts, just so there is no real education save that which is exempt from all dogmatism, which leaves to the child itself the direction of its effort, and confines itself to the seconding of that effort. Now there is nothing easier than to alter this purpose, and nothing harder than to respect it. Education is always imposing, violating, constraining; the real educator is he who can best protect the child against his (the teacher's) own ideas, his peculiar whims; he who can best appeal to the child's own energies.

One may judge by this with what ease education receives the stamp they wish to put upon it, and how easy is the task of those who wish to enslave the individual. The best methods become in their hands only the more powerful and perfect instruments of domination. Our own ideal is certainly that of science, and we demand that we be given the power to educate the child by favoring its development through the satisfaction of all its needs, in proportion as these arise and grow.

We are convinced that the education of the future will be of an entirely spontaneous nature; certainly we cannot as yet realize it, but the evolution of methods in the direction of a wider comprehension of the phenomena of life, and the fact that all advances toward perfection mean the overcoming of some constraint,—all this indicates that we are in the right when we hope for the deliverance of the child through science. . . .

We shall follow the labors of the scientists who study the child with the greatest attention, and we shall eagerly seek for means of applying their experience to the education we wish to build up, in the direction of an ever fuller liberation of the individual. But how can we attain our end? Shall it not be by putting ourselves directly to the work favoring the foundation of new schools, which shall be ruled as much as possible by this spirit of liberty, which we forefeel will dominate the entire work of education in the future?

A trial has been made which, for the present, has already given excellent results. We can destroy all which in the present school answers to the organization of constraint, the artificial surroundings by which the children are separated from nature and life, the intellectual and moral discipline made use of to impose ready-made ideas upon them, beliefs which deprave and annihilate natural bent. Without fear of deceiving ourselves, we can restore the child to the environment which entices it, the environment of nature in which he will be in contact with all that he loves, and in which impressions of life will replace fastidious book-learning. If we did no more than that, we should already have prepared in great part the deliverance of the child.

In such conditions we might already freely apply the data of science, and labor most fruitfully.

I know very well that we could not thus realize all our hopes, that we should often be forced, for lack of knowledge, to employ undesirable methods; but a certitude would sustain us in our effort, namely, that even without reaching our aim completely we should do more and better in our still imperfect work than the present school accomplishes. I like the free spontaneity of a child who knows nothing, better than the world-knowledge and intellectual deformity of a child who has been subjected to our present education. . . . .

Every cultivated person of my acquaintance has agreed with me as to the best means to be employed in order to make men and create strong and good types of humanity, and of these means education and instruction were those most apropos.

I detest the shedding of blood; I labor for the regeneration of humanity, and I love the good for the good's own sake. That which violence wins for us today, another act of violence may wrest from us tomorrow. Those stages of progress are alone durable which have rooted themselves in the mind and conscience of mankind before receiving the final sanction of legislators. The only means of realizing what is good is to teach it by education and propagate it by example.

XXX
MARIA MONTESSORI

Professoressa Maria Montessori, 1870, one of the foremost modern educators, doctor of philosophy, anthropologist, psychotherapist, professor of psychiatrics at University of Rome. Was first woman medical student at University of Rome. Treated nervous diseases and insanity, and, following the steps of Itard and Seguin, experimented and worked for many years with feeble-minded children, evolving a highly efficient didactic apparatus for training the senses; idiot children passed the same examination as normal children taught by the old method for the same length of time. Has overwhelmed contemporary educators by completely revolutionizing present methods of training young children. She demands for the child complete freedom for development; against the restrictive discipline of the common school, whose idea of goodness is absolute immobility, and which, more often than not, annihilates the individuality of the child and converts him into an automaton, she has established the principle of discipline through liberty. Useful activity is her key to discipline and self-control. Through self-imposed tasks children learn muscular control. The sense of touch, with its spinal nerve supply, is the base of her sense training. A retentive muscular memory of shapes, sizes, textures, etc., is developed, and causes the phenomenon of "explosion into writing" which has aroused so much discussion. (Children of four years are suddenly able to read and write without being conscious of the steps by which they have arrived; so in place of the laborious, mechanical, ineffective process of our common schools there is keen interest and tireless application in their play-tasks.) Doctor Montessori transformed the worst tenements in Rome into child gardens called "Houses of Childhood." Models of her houses of childhood have been formed all over the civilized world and her didactic apparatus is now sold and used in a number of schools. An English translation of her book, *The Montessori Method*, appeared in 1912 (F. A. Stokes Co.), and in response to popular demand Doctor Montessori, in 1913, opened a training class in Rome for a limited number of pupils. Her scientific training, her exhaustive study of child psychology, together with her personal experimentation and teaching of children, her sympathy for and keen understanding of the needs of the child, make Doctor Montessori a unique figure in the educational world. The selections are from *The Montessori Method* and from the articles of Josephine Tozier in *McClure's Magazine*, 1911-12.

Discipline.—The pedagogical method of observation has for its base the liberty of the child; and liberty is activity.

Discipline must come through liberty. Here is a great principle which it is difficult for followers of common-school methods to understand. How shall one obtain discipline in a class of free children? Certainly in our system we have a concept of discipline very different from that commonly accepted. If discipline is founded upon liberty, the discipline itself must necessarily be *active*. We do not consider an individual disciplined only when he has been rendered as artificially silent as a mute and as immovable as a paralytic. He is an invidual *annihilated*, not *disciplined*.

We call an individual disciplined when he is master of himself, and can, therefore, regulate his own conduct when it shall be necessary to follow some rule of life. Such a concept of *active discipline* is not easy either to comprehend or to apply. But certainly it contains a great educational principle, very different from the old-time absolute and undiscussed coercion to immobility.

A special technique is necessary to the teacher who is to lead the child along such a path of discipline, if she is to make it possible for him to continue in this way all his life, advancing indefinitely toward perfect self-mastery. Since the child now learns to *move* rather than to sit still, he prepares himself not for the school, but for life; for he becomes able, through habit and through practice, to perform easily and correctly the simple acts of social or community life. The discipline to which the child here habituates himself is, in its character, not limited to the school environment, but extends to society.

The liberty of the child should have as its *limit* the collective interest; as its form, what we universally consider good breeding. We must, therefore, check in the child whatever offends or annoys others, or whatever tends toward rough or ill-bred acts. But all the rest,—every manifestation having a useful scope, whatever it be, and under whatever form it expresses itself,—must not only be permitted, but must be observed by the teacher. Here lies the essential point; from her scientific preparation, the teacher must bring not only the capacity, but the desire, to observe natural phenomena. In our system, she must become a passive, much more than an active, influence, and her passivity shall be composed of anxious scientific curiosity, and of absolute respect for the phenomenon which she wishes to observe. The teacher must understand and feel her position of observer: the activity must lie in the phenomenon.

Such principles assuredly have a place in schools for little children who are exhibiting the first psychic manifestations of their lives. We cannot know the consequences of suffocating a spontaneous action at the time when the child is just beginning to be active: perhaps we suffocate life itself. Humanity shows itself in all its intellectual splendour during this tender age as the sun shows itself at the dawn, and the flower in the first unfolding of the petals; and we must respect religiously, reverently, these first indications of individuality. If any educational act is to be efficacious, it will be only that which tends to help toward the complete unfolding of this life. To be thus helpful it is necessary rigorously to avoid the arrest of spontaneous movements and the imposition of arbitrary tasks. It is, of course, understood that here we do not speak of useless or dangerous acts, for these must be suppressed, destroyed.

The first idea that the child must acquire, in order to be actively disciplined, is that of the difference between good and evil; and the task of the educator lies in seeing that the child does not confound good with immobility, and evil with activity, as often happens in the case of the old-time discipline. And all this because our aim is to discipline for activity, for work, for good; not for immobility, not for passivity, not for obedience.

A room in which all the children move about usefully, intelligently, and voluntarily, without committing any rough or rude act, would seem to me a classroom very well disciplined indeed.

If we can, when we have established individual discipline, arrange the children, sending each one to his own place, in order, trying to make them understand the idea that thus placed they look well, and that it is a good thing to be thus placed in order, that it is a good and pleasing arrangement in the room, this ordered and tranquil adjustment of theirs—then their remaining in their places, quiet and silent, is the result of a species of lesson, not an imposition. To make them understand the idea, without calling their attention too forcibly to the practice, to have them assimilate a principle of collective order—that is the important thing.

If, after they have understood this idea, they rise, speak, change to another place, they no longer do this without knowing and without thinking, but they do it because they wish to rise, to speak, etc.; that is, from that state of repose and order, well understood, they depart in order to undertake some voluntary action; and knowing that there are actions which are prohibited, this will give them a new impulse to remember to discriminate between good and evil.

The movements of the children from the state of order become always more co-ordinated and perfect with the passing of the days; in fact they learn to reflect upon their own acts. Now (with the idea of order understood by the children) the observation of the way in which the children pass from the first disordered movements to those which are spontaneous and ordered—this is the book of the teacher; this is the book which must inspire her actions; it is the only one in which she must read and study if she is to become a real educator.

For the child with such exercises makes, to a certain extent, a selection of his own tendencies, which were at first confused in the unconscious disorder of his movements. It is remarkable how clearly individual differences show themselves, if we proceed in this way; the child, conscious and free, reveals himself.

Our idea of liberty for the child cannot be the simple concept of liberty we use in the observation of plants, insects, etc.

The child, because of the peculiar characteristics of helplessness with which he is born, and because of his qualities as a social individual, is circumscribed by bonds which limit his activity.

An educational method that shall have liberty as its basis

must intervene to help the child to a conquest of these various obstacles. In other words, his training must be such as shall help him to diminish, in a rational manner, the social bonds which limit his activity.

Little by little, as the child grows in such an atmosphere, his spontaneous manifestations will become more and more clear, with the clearness of truth, revealing his nature. For all these reasons, the first form of educational intervention must tend to lead the child toward independence.

Independence.—No one can be free unless he is independent: therefore, the first, active manifestations of the child's individual liberty must be so guided that through this activity he may arrive at independence. Little children, from the moment in which they are weaned, are making their way toward independence.

What is a weaned child? In reality, it is a child that has become independent of the mother's breast. Instead of this one source of nourishment he will find various kinds of food; for him the means of existence are multiplied, and he can to some extent make a selection of his food, whereas he was first limited absolutely to one form of nourishment.

Nevertheless, he is still dependent, since he is not yet able to walk, and cannot wash and dress himself, and since he is not yet able to ask for things in a language which is clear and easily understood. He is still in this period to a great extent the slave of everyone. By the age of three, however, the child should have been able to render himself to a great extent independent and free.

That we have not yet thoroughly assimilated the highest concept of the term independence, is due to the fact that the social form in which we live is still servile. In an age of civilization where servants exist, the concept of that form of life which is independence cannot take root or develop freely. Even so in the time of slavery, the concept of liberty was distorted and darkened. Our servants are not our dependents, rather it is we who are dependent upon them. It is not possible to accept universally as a part of our social structure such a deep human error without feeling the general effects of it in the form of moral inferiority. We often believe ourselves to be independent simply because no one commands us, and because we command others; but the nobleman who needs to call a servant to his aid is really a dependent through his own inferiority. The paralytic who cannot take off his boots because of a pathological fact, and the prince who dare not take them off because of a social fact, are in reality reduced to the same condition.

Any nation that accepts the idea of servitude and believes that it is an advantage for man to be served by man, admits servility as an instinct, and indeed we all too easily lend ourselves to obsequious service, giving to it such complimentary names as courtesy, politeness, charity. In reality, he who is served is limited in his independence. This concept will be the foundation of the dignity of the man of the future: "I do not wish to be served, because I am not an impotent." And this idea must be gained before men can feel themselves to be really free.

Any pedagogical action, if it is to be efficacious in the training of little children, must tend to help the children to advance upon this road of independence. We must help them to learn to walk without assistance, to run, to go up and down stairs, to lift up fallen objects, to dress and undress themselves, to bathe themselves, to speak distinctly, and to express their own needs clearly. We must give such help as shall make it possible for children to achieve the satisfaction of their own individual aims and desires. All this is a part of education for independence.

I spent two years, with the help of my colleagues, in preparing the teachers of Rome for a special method of observation and education of feeble-minded children. Not only did I train teachers, but, what was much more important, after I had been in London and Paris for the purpose of studying in a practical way the education of deficients, I gave myself over completely to the actual teaching of the children, directing at the same time the work of other teachers in our institute.

I succeeded in teaching a number of the idiots from the asylums both to read and to write so well that I was able to present them at a public school for an examination together with normal children. And they passed the examination successfully.

These results seemed almost miraculous to those who saw them. To me, however, the boys from the asylums had been able to compete with the normal children only because they had been taught in a different way. They had been helped in their psychic development, and the normal children had, instead, been suffocated, held back. I found myself thinking that if, some day, the special education which had developed these idiot children in such a marvelous fashion, could be applied to the development of normal children, the "miracle" of which my friends talked would no longer be possible. The abyss between the inferior mentality of the idiot and that of the normal brain can never be bridged if the normal child has reached his full development.

While every one was admiring the progress of my idiots, I was searching for the reasons which could keep the happy healthy children of the common schools on so low a plane that they could be equaled in tests of intelligence by my unfortunate pupils!

Other Libertarians

THE INTERNATIONAL

Mikhail Bakunin's address on the Working-People's International Association: 1867

1. The International claims for each worker the full product of his labor: finding it wrong that there should be in society so many men who, producing nothing at all, can maintain their insolent riches only by the work of others. The International, like the apostle St. Paul, maintains that "if any would not work, neither should he eat."

The International recognizes the right to this noble name of labor as belonging only to productive labor. Some years ago, the young king of Portugal, having come to pay a visit to his august father-in-law, was presented in the working people's association at Turin; and there, surrounded by workingmen, he said to them these memorable words: "Gentlemen, the present century is the century of labor. We all labor. I, too, labor for the good of my people." However flattering this likening of royal labor to workingmen's labor may appear, we cannot accept it. We must recognize that royal labor is a labor of absorption and not of production; capitalists, proprietors, contractors, also labor; but all their labor, having no other object than to transfer the real products of labor from their workingmen into their own pockets, cannot be considered by us as productive labor. In this sense thieves and brigands labor also, and roughly, risking every day their liberty and their life.

The International clearly recognizes intellectual labor—that of men of science as well as of the application of science to industry, and that of the organizers and administrators of industrial and commercial affairs—as productive labor. But it demands for all men a participation as much in manual labor as in labors of the mind, suited not to birth nor to social privileges which must disappear, but to the natural capacities of each, developed by equal education and instruction. Only then will disappear the gulf which today separates the classes which are called intelligent and the working masses.

2. The International declares that, so long as the working masses shall remain plunged in misery, in economic servitude and in this forced ignorance to which economic organization and present society condemn them, all the political reforms and revolutions, without excepting even those which are projected and promised by the Republican Alliance of Mazzini, will avail them nothing.

3. That consequently in their own interest, material as well as moral, they should subordinate all political questions to economic questions, the material means of an education and an existence really human being for the proletariat the first condition of liberty, morality, and humanity.

4. That the experience of past centuries as well as of all present facts ought to have sufficiently convinced the working masses that they can and should expect no social amelioration of their lot from the generosity nor even from the justice of the privileged classes; that there has never been and that there will never be a generous class, a just class, justice is able to exist only in equality, and equality involving necessarily the abolition of privileges and classes; that the classes actually existing—clergy, bureaucracy, plutocracy, nobility, bourgeoisie —dispute for power only to consolidate their own strength and to increase their profits; and that consequently the proletariat must take henceforth the direction of its own affairs into its own hands.

5. That, once clearly understanding itself and organized

nationally and internationally, there will be no power in the world that can resist it.

6. That the proletariat ought to tend, not to the establishment of a new rule or of a new class for its own profit, but to the definitive abolition of all rule, of every class, by the organization of justice, liberty, and equality for all human beings, without distinction of race, color, nationality, or faith,—all to fully exercise the same duties and enjoy the same rights.

7. That the cause of the workingmen of the entire world is solidary, across and in spite of all State frontiers. It is solidary and international because, pushed by an inevitable law which is inherent in it, bourgeois capital, in its threefold employment,—in industry, in commerce, and in banking speculations,—has evidently been tending, since the beginning of this century, towards an organization more and more international and solidary, enlarging each day more, and simultaneously in all countries, the abyss which already separates the working world from the bourgeois world; whence it results that for every workingman endowed with intelligence and heart, for every proletaire who has affection for his companions in misery and servitude, and who at the same time is conscious of his situation and of his only actual interests, the real country is henceforth the international camp of labor, opposed, across the frontiers of all countries, to the much older international camp of exploiting capital; that to every workingman truly worthy of the name, the workingmen of foreign countries who suffer and who are oppressed like himself, are infinitely nearer and more like brothers than the bourgeoisie of his own country, who enrich themselves to his detriment.

8. That the oppression and exploitation of which the toiling masses are victims in all countries, being in their nature and by their present organization internationally solidary, the deliverance of the proletariat must also be so; that the economic and social emancipation (foundation and preliminary condition of political emancipation) of the working-people

of a country will be forever impossible, if it is not effected simultaneously at least in the majority of the countries with which it finds itself bound by means of credit, industry and commerce; and that, consequently, by the duty of fraternity as well as by enlightened self-interest, in the interest of their own salvation and of their near deliverance, the working-people of all trades are called upon to establish, organize, and exercise the strictest practical solidarity, communal, provincial, national, and international, beginning in their workshop, and then extending it to all their trade societies and to the federation of all the trades,—a solidarity which they ought above all to scrupulously observe and practice in all the developments, in all the catastrophes, and in all the incidents of the incessant struggle of the labor of the workingman against the capital of the bourgeois, such as strikes, demands for decrease of the hours of work and increase of wages, and, in general, all the claims which relate to the conditions of labor and to the existence, whether material or moral, of the working-people.

Economic Interpretation of History.—From the truth which I have just laid down as a principle flows another consequence as important as the first,—that all religions and all systems of morality which prevail in a society are always the ideal expression of its real, material situation, that is to say, of its economic organization first of all, but also of its political organization, the latter being, moreover, nothing but the legal and violent consecration of the former.

The revolt of the laborers and the spontaneous organization of human solidary labor through the free federation of the working-men's groups! This, then, is the answer to the enigma which the Eastern Sphinx forces us today to solve, threatening to devour us if we do not solve it. The principle of justice, liberty, and equality by all and in solidary labor which is agitating today the working masses of America and Europe must penetrate the East equally and completely. The salvation of Europe is to be had only at this price, for this is the true, the only constitutive principle of humanity, and no people can be completely and solidarily free in the human sense of the word, unless all humanity is free.

(It has been) stated, that Protestantism established liberty in Europe. This is a great error. It is the economic, material emancipation of the bourgeois class on the one hand, and on the other its necessary accompaniment, the intellectual, anti-Christian, and anti-religious emancipation of this class, which in spite of Protestantism, have created that exclusively political and bourgeois liberty which is today easily confounded with the grand, universal, human liberty which only the proletariat can create, because its essential condition is the disappearance of those centers of authority called States, and the complete emancipation of labor, the real base of human society.

The human race, like all the other animal races, has inherent principles which are peculiar to it, and all these principles are summed up in or reducible to a single principle which we call Solidarity. This principle may be formulated thus: no human individual can recognize his own humanity, or, consequently, realize it in life, except by recognizing it in others and by co-operating in its realization for others. No man can emancipate himself save by emancipating with him all the men about him. My liberty is the liberty of everybody, for I am really free, free not only in idea, but in fact, only when my liberty and my right find their confirmation, their sanction, in the liberty and right of all men, my equals. What all other men are is of great importance to me, because, however independent I may imagine myself or may appear by my social position, whether I am pope, czar, or emperor, or even prime minister, I am always the product of the lowest among them; if they are ignorant, miserable, enslaved, my life is determined by their ignorance, misery, and slavery. I, an enlightened or intelligent man, for example—if such is the case—am foolish with their folly; I, a brave man, am the slave of their slavery;

I, a rich man, tremble before their misery; I, a privileged man, turn pale before their justice. In short, wishing to be free, I cannot be, because all the men around me do not yet wish to be free, and, not wishing it, they become instruments of my oppression.

The true, human liberty of a single individual implies the emancipation of all; because, thanks to the law of solidarity which is the natural basis of all human society, I cannot be, feel, and know myself really, completely free, if I am not surrounded by men as free as myself, and because the slavery of each is my slavery.

SYNDICALISM
Emma Goldman

In view of the fact that the ideas embodied in Syndicalism have been practised by the workers for the last half century, even if without the background of social consciousness; that in this country five men had to pay with their lives because they advocated Syndicalist methods as the most effective in the struggle of labor against capital; and that, furthermore, Syndicalism has been consciously practised by the workers of France, Italy and Spain since 1895, it is rather amusing to witness some people in America and England now swooping down upon Syndicalism as a perfectly new and never before heard-of proposition.

Already as far back as 1848 a large section of the workers realized the utter futility of political activity as a means of helping them in their economic struggle. At that time already the demand went forth for direct economic measures, as against the useless waste of energy along political lines. This was the case not only in France, but even prior to that in England, where Robert Owen, the true revolutionary Socialist, propagated similar ideas.

After years of agitation and experiment the idea was incorporated by the first convention of the *Internationale* in 1867, in the resolution that the economic emancipation of the workers must be the principal aim of all revolutionists, to which everything else is to be subordinated.

In fact, it was this determined radical stand which eventually brought about the split in the revolutionary movement of that day, and its division into factions: the one, under Marx and Engels, aiming at political conquest; the other, under Bakunin and the Latin workers, forging ahead along industrial and Syndicalist lines. The further development of those two wings is familiar to every thinking man and woman: the one has gradually centralized into a huge machine, with the sole purpose of conquering political power within the existing capitalist State; the other is becoming an ever more vital revolutionary factor, dreaded by the enemy as the greatest menace to its rule.

The fundamental difference between Syndicalism and the old trade union methods is this: while the old trade unions, without exception, move within the wage system and capitalism, recognizing the latter as inevitable, Syndicalism repudiates and condemns present industrial arrangements as unjust and criminal, and holds out no hope to the workers for lasting results from this system.

Of course Syndicalism, like the old trade unions, fights for immediate gains, but it is not stupid enough to pretend that labor can expect humane conditions from inhuman economic arrangements in society. Thus it merely wrests from the enemy what it can force him to yield; on the whole, however, Syndicalism aims at, and concentrates its energies upon, the complete overthrow of the wage system. Indeed, Syndicalism goes further: it aims to liberate labor from every institution that has not for its object the free development of production for the benefit of all humanity. In short, the ultimate purpose of Syndicalism is to reconstruct society from its present centralized, authoritative and brutal state to one based upon the free, federated grouping of the workers along lines of economic and social liberty.

With this object in view, Syndicalism works in two directions: first, by undermining the existing institutions; secondly, by developing and educating the workers and cultivating their spirit of solidarity, to prepare them for a full, free life, when capitalism shall have been abolished.

Syndicalism is, in essence, the economic expression of Anarchism. That circumstance accounts for the presence of so many Anarchists in the Syndicalist movement. Like Anarchism, Syndicalism prepares the workers along direct economic lines, as conscious factors in the great struggles of today, as well as conscious factors in the task of reconstructing society along autonomous industrial lines, as against the paralyzing spirit of centralization with its bureaucratic machinery of corruption, inherent in all political parties.

As a logical sequence Syndicalism, in its daily warfare against capitalism, rejects the contract system, because it does not consider labor and capital equals, hence cannot consent to an agreement which the one has the power to break, while the other must submit to without redress.

Syndicalism has grown out of the disappointment of the workers with politics and parliamentary methods. In the course of its development Syndicalism has learned to see in the State—with its mouthpiece, the representative system—one of the strongest supports of capitalism; just as it has learned that the army and the church are the chief pillars of the State. It is therefore that Syndicalism has turned its back upon parliamentarism and political machines, and has set its face toward the economic arena wherein a lone gladiator Labor can meet his foe successfully.

Equally so has experience determined their anti-military attitude. Time and again has the army been used to shoot down strikers and to inculcate the sickening idea of patriotism, for the purpose of dividing the workers against themselves and helping the masters to the spoils. The inroads that Syndicalist agitation has made into the superstition of patriotism are evident from the dread of the ruling class for the loyalty of the army, and the rigid persecution of the anti-militarists. Naturally, for the ruling class realizes much better than the workers that when the soldiers will refuse to obey their superiors, the whole system of capitalism will be doomed.

Indeed, why should the workers sacrifice their children that the latter may be used to shoot their own parents? Therefore, Syndicalism is not merely logical in its anti-military agitation; it is most practical and far-reaching, inasmuch as it robs the enemy of his strongest weapon against labor.

Direct Action: Conscious individual or collective effort to protest against, or remedy, social conditions through the systematic assertion of the economic power of the workers.

One of the objections of politicians to the General Strike is that the workers also would suffer for the necessaries of life. In the first place, the workers are past masters in going hungry; secondly, it is certain that a General Strike is surer of prompt settlement than an ordinary strike. Witness the transport and miner strikes in England: how quickly the lords of State and capital were forced to make peace. Besides, Syndicalism recognizes the right of the producers to the things which they have created—namely, the right of the workers to help themselves if the strike does not meet with speedy settlement.

These ideas and methods of Syndicalism some may consider entirely negative, though they are far from it in their effect upon society today. But Sydicalism has also a directly positive aspect. In fact, much more time and effort is being devoted to that phase than to the others. Various forms of Syndicalist activity are designed to prepare the workers, even within present social and industrial conditions, for the life of a new and better society. To that end the masses are trained in the spirit of mutual aid and brotherhood, their initiative and self-reliance developed, and an *esprit de corps* maintained whose very soul is solidarity of purpose and the community of interests of the international proletariat.

Chief among these activities are the *mutualitees*, or mutual aid societies, established by the French Syndicalists. Their object is, foremost, to secure work for unemployed members, and to further that spirit of mutual assistance which rests upon the consciousness of labor's identity of interests throughout the world.

In his *The Labor Movement in France*, Mr. L. Levine states that during the year 1902 over 74,000 workers, out of a total of 99,000 applicants, were provided with work by these societies, without being compelled to submit to the extortion of the employment bureau sharks. These latter are a source of the deepest degradation, as well as of most shameless exploitation, of the worker. Especially does it hold true of America, where the employment agencies are in many cases also masked detective agencies, supplying workers in need of employment to strike regions, under false promises of steady, remunerative employment. The French Confederation had long realized the vicious role of employment agencies as leeches upon the jobless worker and nurseries of scabbery. By the threat of a General Strike the French Syndicalist forced the government to abolish the employment bureau sharks, and the workers' own *mutualitees* have almost entirely superseded them, to the great economic and moral advantage of labor.

Besides the *mutualitees*, the French Syndicalists have established other activities tending to weld labor in closer bonds of solidarity and mutual aid. Among these are the efforts to assist workingmen journeying from place to place. The practical as well as ethical value of such assistance is inestimable. It serves to instill the spirit of fellowship and gives a sense of security in the feeling of oneness with the large family of labor. This is one of the vital effects of the Syndicalist spirit in France and other Latin countries. What a tremendous need there is for just such efforts in this country! Can anyone doubt the significance of the consciousness of workingmen coming from Chicago, for instance, to New York, sure to find there among their comrades welcome lodging and food until they have secured employment? This form of activity is entirely foreign to the labor bodies of this country, and as a result the traveling workman in search of a job—the "blanket stiff"—is constantly at the mercy of the constable and policeman, a victim of the vagrancy laws, and the unfortunate material whence is recruited, through stress of necessity, the army of scabdom.

I have repeatedly witnessed while at the headquarters of the Confederation, the cases of workingmen who came with their union cards from various parts of France, and even from other countries of Europe, and were supplied with meals and lodging, and encouraged by every evidence of brotherly spirit, and made to feel at home by their fellow-workers of the Confederation. It is due, to a great extent, to these activities of the Syndicalists that the French government is forced to employ the army for strikebreaking, because few workers are willing to lend themselves for such service, thanks to the efforts and tactics of Syndicalism.

No less in importance than the mutual aid activities of the Syndicalists is the co-operation established by them between the city and the country, the factory worker and the peasant or farmer, the latter providing the workers with food supplies during strikes, or taking care of the strikers' children. This form of practical solidarity has for the first time been tried in this country during the Lawrence strike, with inspiring results. And all these Syndicalist activities are permeated with a spirit of educational work, carried on systematically by evening classes on all vital subjects treated from an unbiased, libertarian standpoint—not the adulterated "knowledge" with which the minds are stuffed in our public schools. The scope of the education is truly phenomenal, including sex hygiene, the care of women during pregnancy and confinement, the care of home and children, sanitation and general hygiene; in fact, every branch of human knowledge—science, history, art—receives thorough attention, together with the practical application in the established workingmen's libraries, dispensaries, concerts and festivals, in which the greatest artists and literateurs of Paris consider it an honor to participate.

One of the most vital efforts of Syndicalism is to prepare the workers, *now*, for their role in a free society. Thus the Syndicalist organizations supply its members with textbooks on every trade and industry, of a character that is calculated to make the worker an adept in his chosen line, a master of his craft, for the purpose of familiarizing him with all the branches of his industry, so that when labor finally takes over production and distribution, the people will be fully prepared to manage successfully their own affairs.

A demonstration of the effectiveness of this educational campaign of Syndicalism is given by the railroad men of Italy, whose mastery of all the details of transportation is so great that they could offer to the Italian government to take over the railroads of the country and guarantee their operation with greater economy and fewer accidents than is at present done by the government.

Their ability to carry on production has been strikingly proved by the Syndicalists in connection with the glassblowers' strike in Italy. There the strikers, instead of remaining idle during the progress of the strike, decided themselves to carry on the production of glass. The wonderful spirit of solidarity resulting from the Syndicalist propaganda enabled them to build a glass factory within an incredibly short time. An old building, rented for the purpose and which would have ordinarily required months to be put into proper condition, was turned into a glass factory within a few weeks, by the solidaric efforts of the strikers, aided by their comrades who toiled with them after working hours. Then the strikers began operating the glassblowing factory, and their co-operative plan of work and distribution during the strike has proved so satisfactory in every way that the experimental factory has been made permanent and a part of the glassblowing industry in Italy is now in the hands of the co-operative organization of the workers.

This method of applied education not only trains the worker in his daily struggle, but serves also to equip him for the battle royal and the future, when he is to assume his place in society as an intelligent, conscious being and useful producer, once capitalism is abolished.

Nearly all leading Syndicalists agree with the Anarchists that a free society can exist only through voluntary association, and that its ultimate success will depend upon the intellectual and moral development of the workers who will supplant the wage system with a new social arrangement, based on solidarity and economic well-being for all. That is Syndicalism, in theory and practice.

FREEDOM IN MUSIC
James Huneker

Have not all great composers been anarchs—from Bach to Strauss? At first blush the hard-plodding Johann Sebastian of the *Well-Tempered Clavichord* seems a doubtful figure to drape with the black flag of revolt. He grew a forest of children, he worked early and late, and he played the organ in church of Sundays; but he was a musical revolutionist nevertheless. His music proves it. And he quarreled with his surroundings like any good social democrat. He even went out for a drink during a prosy sermon, and came near being discharged for returning late. If Lombroso were cognizant of this suspicious fact, he might build a terrifying structure of theories, with all sorts of inferential subcellars. However, it is Bach's music that still remains revolutionary. Mozart and Gluck depended too much on aristocratic patronage to play the role of Solitaries. But many tales are related of their refusal to lick the boots of the rich, to curve the spine of the suppliant. Both were by nature gentlemen, and both occasionally arose to the situation and snubbed their patrons outrageously. Handel! A fighter, a born revolutionist, a hater of rulers. John Runciman—himself an anarchistic critic—calls Handel the most magnificent man that ever lived. He was certainly the most virile among musicians.

I recall the story of Beethoven refusing to uncover in the presence of royalty, though his companion, Goethe, doffed his hat. Theoretically I admire Beethoven's independence, yet there is no denying that the great poet was the politer of the two and doubtless a pleasanter man to consort with. The mythic William Tell and his contempt for Gessler's hat were translated into action by the composer.

Handel, despite the fact that he could not boast Beethoven's peasant ancestry, had a contempt for rank and its entailed snobberies, that was remarkable. And his music is like a blow from a muscular fist. Haydn need not be considered. He was henpecked, and for the same reason as was Socrates. The Croatian composer's wife told some strange stories of that merry little blade, her chamber-music husband. As I do not class Mendelssohn among the great composers, he need not be discussed. His music was Bach watered for general consumption. Schubert was an anarch all his short life. He is said to have loved an Esterhazy girl, and being snubbed he turned sour-souled. He drank "far more than was good for him," and he placed on paper the loveliest melodies the world has ever heard. Beethoven was the supreme anarch of art, and put into daily practice the radicalism of his music.

Because of its opportunities for soul expansion, music has ever attracted the strong free sons of earth. The most profound truths, the most blasphemous things, the most terrible ideas, may be incorporated within the walls of a symphony, and the police be none the wiser. Suppose that some Russian professional supervisor of artistic anarchy really knew what arrant doctrines Tschaikowsky preached! It is its freedom from the meddlesome hand of the censor that makes of music a playground for great brave souls. Richard Wagner in Siegfried, and under the long nose of royalty, preaches anarchy, puts into tone, words, gestures, lath, plaster, paint, and canvas an allegory of humanity liberated from the convention of authority, from what Bernard Shaw would call the Old Man of the Mountain, the Government.

I need only adduce the names of Schumann, another revolutionist like Chopin in the psychic sphere; Liszt, bitten by the socialistic theories of Saint-Simon, a rank hater of conventions in art, though in life a silken courtier; Brahms, a social democrat and freethinker; and Tschaikowsky, who buried more bombs in his work than ever Chopin with his cannon among roses or Bakunin with his terrible prose of a nihilist. Years ago I read and doubted Mr. Ashton-Ellis's interesting "1849," with its fallacious denial of Wagner's revolutionary behavior. Wagner may not have shouldered a musket during the Dresden uprising, but he was, with Mikhail Bakunin, its prime inspirer. His very ringing of the church bells during the row is a symbol of his attitude. And then he ran away, luckily enough for the world of music, while his companions, Roeckel and Bakunin, were captured and imprisoned. Wagner might be called the Joseph Proudhon of composers—his music is anarchy itself, coldly deliberate like the sad and logical music we find in the great Frenchman's *Philosophy of Misery* (a subtitle, by the way).

And what a huge regiment of painters, poets, sculptors, prosateurs, journalists, and musicians might not be included under the roof of the House Beautiful! Verhaeren of Belgium, whose powerful bass hurls imprecations at the present order; Georges Eckhoud, Maurice Maeterlinck; Constantin Meunier, whose eloquent bronzes are a protest against the misery of the proletarians; Octave Mirbeau, Richepin, William Blake, William Morris, Swinburne, Maurice Barres, the late Stephane Mallarme, Walt Whitman, Ibsen, Strindberg; Felicien Rops, the sinister author of love and death; Edvard

Munch, whose men and women with staring eyes and fuliginous faces seem to discern across the frame of his pictures febrile visions of terror; and the great Scandinavian sculptors, Vigeland and Sinding; and Zola, Odilon Redon, Huysmans, Heine, Baudelaire, Poe, Richard Strauss, Shaw,—is not the art of these men, and many more left unnamed, direct personal expression of anarchic revolt?

Nor is there cause for alarm in the word of anarchy, which means in its ideal state unfettered self-government. If we all were self-governed, governments would be sinecures. Anarchy often expresses itself in rebellion against conventional art forms—the only kind of anarchy that interests me. A most signal example is Henry James. Surprising it is to find this fastidious artist classed among the anarchs of art, is it not? He is one, as surely as was Turgenieff, the de Goncourts, or Flaubert.

I have left Berlioz and Strauss for the last. The former all his life long was a flaming individualist. His books, his utterances, his conduct, prove it. Hector of the Flaming Locks, fiery speech, and crimson scores, would have made a picturesque figure on the barricades waving a red flag or casting bombs. His *Fantastic Symphony* is full of the tonal commandments of anarchic revolt.

Strauss, who is a psychological realist in symphonic art, withal a master symbolist; back of his surface eccentricities there is a foundational energy, an epic largeness of utterance, a versatility of manner, that rank him as the unique anarchist of music. He taps the tocsin of revolt, and his velvet sonorities do not disguise either their meagre skein of spirituality or the veiled ferocities of his aristocratic insurgency. Sufficient to add that as in politics he is a social democrat, so in his vast and memorial art he is the anarch of anarchs. Not as big a fellow in theme-making as Beethoven, he far transcends Beethoven in harmonic originality. His very scheme of harmonization is the sign of a soul insurgent.

OBSCENITY LAWS
Theodore Schroeder

Obscenity is not a quality inherent in a book or picture, but solely and exclusively a contribution of the reading mind, and hence cannot be defined in terms of the qualities of a book or picture.

Has it ever occurred to you that the witchcraft superstition was almost identical, in its essence, with the present superstitious belief in the reality of the "obscene," as a thing outside the mind? Think it over.

Fanatical men and pious judges, otherwise intelligent, have affirmed the reality of both, and, on the assumption of their inerrancy in this, have assumed to punish their fellowmen. It is computed from historical records that 9,000,000 persons were put to death for witchcraft after 1484. The opponents of witch-belief were denounced just as the disbelievers in the "obscene" are now denounced. Yet witches ceased to be, when men no longer believed in them. Think it over and see if the "obscene" will not also disappear when men cease to believe in it.

In 1661, the learned Sir Mathew Hale, "a person than whom no one was more backward to condemn a witch without full evidence," used this language: "That there are such angels (as witches) it is without question." Then he made a convincing argument from Holy Writ, and added: "It is also confirmed to us by daily experience of the power and energy of these evil spirits in witches and by them." (See *Annals of Witchcraft*, by Drake, preface, page 11.)

A century later, the learned Sir William Blackstone, since then the mentor of every English and American lawyer, joined with the witch-burners in bearing testimony to the existence of these spook-humans, just as our own courts today join with the obscenity-burners to affirm that obscenity is in a book and not in the reading minds, and that, therefore, the publisher and not the reader shall go to jail for being "obscene."

And yet when men ceased to believe in witches, they ceased to be, and so when men shall cease to believe in the "obscene" they will also cease to find that. Obscenity and witches exist only in the minds and emotions of those who believe in them, and, neither dogmatic judicial dictum nor righteous vituperation can ever give to them any objective existence.

In the "good old days," when a few, wiser than the rest, doubted the reality of witches, if not themselves killed as being bewitched they were cowed into silence by an avalanche of vituperation such as "infidel," "atheist," or "emissary of Satan," "the enemy of God," "the Anti-christ," and some witch-finder would get on his trail to discover evidence of this heretic's compact with the devil.

How this is duplicated in the attitude of the nasty-minded portion of the public toward those who disbelieve in the objectivity of "obscenity"! Whether obscenity is a sense-perceived quality of a book, or resides exclusively in the reading mind, is a question of science, and, as such, a legitimate matter of debate. Try to prove its non-existence by the scientific method, and the literary scavengers, instead of answering your arguments, by showing the fallacy of its logic or error of fact, show their want of culture, just as did the witch-burners. They tell you that you are "either an ignoramus or so ethereal that there is no suitable place on earth for you," except in jail. They further hurl at you such illuminating epithetic arguments as "immoral," "smut dealer," "moral cancer-planter," etc., etc. It is a regrettable fact that the miscalled "moral" majority is still too ignorant to know that such question-begging epithets, when unsupported, are not argument, and its members are too obsessed with sensual images to be open to any proof against their resultant "obscene" superstition.

Think it over and see if when you cease to believe in the existence of "obscenity," you must not also cease to find it. If that be true, then it exists only in the minds and the emotions of those who believe in the superstition. Connect your mind with a sewer, and empty therein all the ideational and emotional associations which the miscalled "pure" people have forced into your thoughts. Having done this, you may be prepared to believe that "unto the pure, all things are pure, but unto them that are defiled and unbelieving, is nothing pure, but even their mind and conscience is defiled." (Titus, i:15.) Not till thus cleansed can you join in these words: "I know and am persuaded by the Lord Jesus that there is nothing unclean of itself, but to him that esteemeth anything to be unclean, to him it is unclean." (Romans, xiv:14.)

When you have cleansed your own mind of the "obscene" superstition, proclaim a real purity on the highways and byways, until other minds are likewise cleansed, and then our obscenity laws will soon die a natural death, and healthy-mindedness will have a chance to control the normal functioning of a healthy body.

Once let the public become sufficiently clean-minded to allow every adult access to all that is to be known about the physiology, psychology, hygiene and ethics of sex, and in two generations we will have a new humanity, with more health and joy, fewer wrecked nerves and almost no divorces. All morbid curiosity will then be dispelled, and thus the dealer in bawdy art and literature will be bankrupted. Our sanitariums, and hospitals and insane asylums in that day will be uninhabited by those hundreds of thousands of inmates who are now there because of compulsory ignorance of their own sex nature. All these present evils are the outgrowth of that enforced sexual ignorance resulting from our legalized prudery, brought about by our general acquiescence in the "obscene" superstition, forced upon us by the vehement insistence of our over-sexed, prurient prudes. Let all clean-minded persons unite to abolish this twin to the witchcraft superstition and secure the annulment of all present laws against "obscene" literature. Thus you can best further the interest of humanity by promoting a sane and scientific physical and moral culture.

MAJORITY VS. MINORITY
Henrik Ibsen in letters to George Brandes

And what can be said of the attitude assumed by the press of these leaders of the people who speak and write of freedom of thought, and at the same time make themselves the slaves of the supposed opinions of their subscribers? I receive more and more corroboration of my conviction that there is something demoralizing in engaging in politics and in joining parties. It will never, in any case, be possible for me to join a party that has the majority on its side. Bjornson says: "The majority is always right;" and as a practical politician he is bound, I suppose, to say so. I, on the contrary, must of necessity say, "The minority is always right." Naturally I am not thinking of that minority of stagnationists who are left behind by the great middle party, which with us is called Liberal; but I mean that minority which leads the van, and pushes on to points which the majority has not yet reached. . . .

Liberty, equality, and fraternity are no longer the things they were in the days of the late lamented guillotine. This is what politicians will not understand, and therefore I hate them. What they want is special revolutions, revolutions in externals, in the political sphere. But all this is mere trifling. What is really wanted is a revolution of the spirit of man. . . .

The struggle for liberty is nothing but the constant active appropriation of the idea of liberty. He who possesses liberty otherwise than as an aspiration possesses it soulless, dead. One of the qualities of liberty is that, as long as it is being striven after, it goes on expanding. Therefore, the man who stands still in the midst of the struggle and says, "I have it," merely shows by so doing that he has just lost it. Now this very contentedness in the possession of a dead liberty is characteristic of the so-called State, and, as I have said, it is not a good characteristic. No doubt the franchise, self taxation, etc., are benefits—but to whom? To the citizen, not to the individual. Now, reason does not imperatively demand that the individual should be a citizen. Far from it. The State is the curse of the individual. With what is Prussia's political strength bought? With the absorption of the individual in the political and geographical idea. The waiter is the best soldier. And on the other hand, take the Jewish people, the aristocracy of the human race—how is it they have kept their place apart, their poetical halo, amid surroundings of coarse cruelty? By having no State to burden them. Had they remained in Palestine, they would long ago have lost their individuality in the process of their State's construction, like all other nations. Away with the State! I will take part in that revolution. Undermine the whole conception of a state, declare free choice and spiritual kinship to be the only all-important conditions of any union, and you will have the commencement of a liberty that is worth something. Changes in forms of government are pettifogging affairs—a degree less or a degree more, mere foolishness. The State has its root in time, and will ripe and rot in time. Greater things than it will fall—religion, for example. Neither moral conceptions nor art forms have an eternity before them. How much are we really in duty bound to pin our faith to? Who will guarantee me that on Jupiter two and two do not make five? . . .

I have not the gifts that go to make a good citizen, nor yet the gift of orthodoxy; and what I possess no gift for I keep out of. Liberty is the first and highest condition for me. At home they do not trouble much about liberty, but only about liberties, a few more or a few less, according to the standpoint of their party.

OPTIONAL SINGLE TAX
Alexander Horr

The Single Tax movement is no exception to the general principle in matters social, as its adherents consist of an individualistic and socialistic wing; of a libertarian and authoritarian group.

The authoritarian Single Taxers, misled by the language of political economy, insist that rent is an indestructible, natural phase of economic life, that land monopoly is inevitable; and, like the humane persons they are, they would prefer public to private monopoly, just as the Greenbackers and Populists preferred public monopoly to private monopoly in banking and transportation.

The Spencerian principle of the law of equal freedom, that "every man may claim the fullest liberty to exercise his faculties, compatible with the like claim of every other man," negates such a theory, and libertarians like Col. Greene, Lysander Spooner, Benj. R. Tucker, Victor Yarros and others, have long insisted that banking, insurance, railroading, etc., are competitive, are not naturally monopolies; hence, that government is not necessary to abolish interest or profit. Rent, according to Ricardo, is caused by the "excess of the productivity of a given piece of land over that of the best free land." Waiving all technical difficulties in this definition, I deny the implied fact (the bottom fact of the authoritarian Single Taxer when he claims that rent is natural) that rent could exist unless the government was ready to secure the ownership of this "excess of . . . productivity" to somebody. Rent is thus artificially created by the State—just as are interest and profit—by a denial of equal freedom. If all mankind had access to all land, then with the "open group system" of land tenure advocated by Duehring and Hertzka, a larger number of workers would be gathered on the more productive land, and through the free mobilization of labor, in consequence of the well known economic law of increasing and diminishing returns on unit land, by the continued application of additional units of labor and capital (as in intensive cultivation), the productivity of all land would be equalized according to work performed; and thus rent would be abolished (made non-existent, not merged into wages). . . . .

The optional single tax has the further merit that it could be the nucleus of all other non-invasive social forms, and thus could be universally applied (the one great test of Emerson for the validity of any moral principle). There would be nothing to prevent the Communists from practising their theories among themselves; they could not enforce Communism on others of course, but if they wished to form a closed group (exclude non-Communists) and were the occupiers of valuable land, they could pay a single tax on the annual value of their land, and divide their own product among themselves in their own way. Ditto with the Mutualists, Freelanders, Single Taxers, or any group of collectivists who would refrain from invading the liberties of their neighbors and content themselves with their own products, which they could divide among themselves (like the Communists) according to any non-competitive basis that appealed to their sense of justice or to their sentiments. These group methods would, of course, be themselves subject to competition, and thus be kept at their best. Any group that could not show a good balance-sheet would be subjected to close scrutiny, to criticism; and if it did not or could not mend its ways, would be disciplined by the abandonment of it by its members for better methods or for other groups which could show better results, either in efficiency, general well-being, or social achievement. . . . .

MR. DOOLEY ON LIBERTY
Peter F. Dunne

It takes vice to hunt vice. That accounts f'r polisman.

I care not who makes th' laws iv a nation, if I can get out an injunction.

No matther whether th' constitution follows th' flag or not, th' Supreme Coort follows th' iliction returns.

Laws ar-re made to throuble people, an' th' more throuble they make th' longer they stay on the stachoo books.

Gover'mint, me boy, is a case iv me makin' ye do what I want, an' if I can't do it with a song, I'll do it with a shovel.

Th' pope, improrrs, kings, an' women haven't th' right to make laws, but they have th' privilege iv breakin' thim, which is bettther.

Di-plomacy has become a philanthropic pursoot like shop-keepin', but politics, me lords, is still th' same ol' spoort iv highway robbry.

If I wanted to keep me money so that me gran'childer might get it f'r their ol' age, I'd appeal it to th' Supreme Coort.

Why is it that th' fair sect wudden't be seen talkin' to a polisman, but if ye say "Sojer" to thim, they're all out iv th' window but th' feet.

A man that'd expect to train lobsters to fly in a year is called a loonytic; but a man that thinks men can be tur-rned into angels be an iliction is called a rayformer an' remains at large.

Hinceforth th' policy iv this gover'mint will be, as befure, not to bully a sthrong power or wrong a weak, but will remain thrue to th' principle iv wrongin' th' sthrong an' bullyin' th' weak.

If we'd begun a few years ago shuttin' out folks that wudden't mind handin' a bomb to a king, they wudden't be enough people in Mattsachoosets to make a quorum f'r th' Anti-Impeeryal S'ciety.

If me ancestors were not what Hogan calls regicides, 'twas not because thay were not ready an' willin,' on'y a king niver came their way.

An autocrat's a ruler that does what th' people wants, an' takes th' blame f'r it. A constitootional ixicutive, Hinnissy, is a ruler that does as he dam pleases, an' blames th' people.

LIBERTY IN ART
W. L. Judson

Time was when the Egyptian artist painted by formula at the direction of an over-fed priesthood, the basest and least progressive era of painting with which we are acquainted.

In a later time painting, like everything else, fell under the sacredotal yoke again. It became a soulless convention and relapsed into absolute imbecility. There is no surer sign of the decadence of art than the search after formulae, striving to lay down rules in imitation of the methods of the past, as if discovery were dead.

The modern renaissance of art was simultaneous with its emancipation from tradition. Almost every rule and dogma of the old painters finds refutation in some splendid recent canvas. It is no longer safe to lay down rules of composition. Some mannerless fellow is sure to prove their futility tomorrow. The best we can do is to make some suggestions showing how others have succeeded, which will at least be helpful for a beginning. There are, in fact, men great enough to override all the theories ever expounded and plenty of men who seek to prove their greatness by breaking all the rules they ever heard of. Any conventional treatment of chiaroscuro should be regarded only as a temporary expedient. Every young artist will base his method on the work of some master, perhaps many masters in succession Gradually his own individuality begins to emerge and he adopts a manner of his own. Every man has his own ideal or personal convention in composition by which he selects his subject or into which he makes his subject fit.

MEDICAL FREEDOM
Dr. J. H. Greer

The acquisition of authority and the exclusive privilege of controlling the bodies of others for mercenary purposes appears to be the chief aim of the medical fraternity. To aid in accomplishing their designs, by deception and wily subterfuge they have secured the enactment of unconstitutional laws and the appropriation of State funds to be placed at their disposal. Thus have they established and do they maintain one of the most gigantic trusts that ever cursed a free-born people. Medical monopoly is the last remnant of mercenary priestcraft to thrive upon mankind's afflictions and misfortunes. But its chains, forged centuries ago by ignorance and superstition, have gradually weakened by the continuous strain put upon them by education and enlightenment. Tighter and tighter does it seek to draw those weakened chains, and greater and greater grows the resistance afforded by increased public knowledge. Before long the fetters must give way, and humanity will be free to enjoy the liberty of striving to know all things and of exercising the right of self-preservation.

LIBEL
C. L. Swartz

Under a rational conception of free speech there can be no such thing as libel, considered as an invasive act. Speech after all is not a complete act. An indispensable complement is the hearing of what is said. And even then the thing does not attain to the dignity of an act. An invasion must be an overt act. To determine an invasion, the consequences of the overt act must be considered. To say a thing, no matter how untrue, outside of the hearing of anyone, is, it is clear, of no consequence. There is no reason, therefore, to believe that the situation changes, in so far as the speaker is concerned, when the thing spoken is heard. And neither does the simple fact of its being heard alter the conditions. It is only when the hearer thinks or takes action that any person lied about can feel the effect of the lie. He could not be injured by it if it were not heard; he could not be injured by it if it were heard and not believed; he could not be injured by it if it were heard and believed if no action were taken by the person hearing and believing it. It is only when a person hears a lie, believes it, and then takes some action toward the person lied about that the latter can be injured. After the liar has told his lie, three things must take place before it can have any injurious effect, and these three things are in no wise connected with the liar. What, then, has the liar to do with it anyway?

LIBERTY AND DUTY
George E. Macdonald

Liberty is always consistent with itself, as one fact fits every other fact, while one law always repeals its predecessor and needs a third law to correct its own mistakes.

The only time that law makes angels of men is when it hangs them.

It is not in the nature of politics that the best men should be elected. The best men do not want to govern their fellowmen, and, anyhow, there are not enough of them to fill the offices.

By arguments from psychology, Mr. Theodore Schroeder, attorney for the Free Speech League, proves that the quality of a thing which is defined as "obscenity" has existence, not in the thing itself, but only in the mind of the person who imagines that he detects its presence there. It follows that, when the courts have been brought around to this view, the man who charges "obscenity" against a picture or print will be locked up for improper exposure of his mind. And the law will do justice then oftener than it does now, because it will catch the fellows who made it.

Mr. Roosevelt says: "The performance of duty stands ahead of the insistence upon one's rights." I conceive duties (towards others) to be what others have the right to exact. If, then, as Mr. Roosevelt says, our duty to others is greater than our right, the said duty being their right, it follows that their right is greater than ours. And then, from their point of view, we ourselves become others, when, according to Mr. Roosevelt, their duties toward us stands ahead of their own right; and this duty of theirs, being now the same as our right, enlarges our right so that it stands ahead of our duty, which duty, as premised, is equivalent to their right, and so on. If Mr. Roosevelt can demonstrate that duty is ahead of right, he can prove that every man in the world owes more than is coming to him. This is pure altruism, enticing as a theory, but unlikely to work out when you come to collect.

LAND, LIBERTY AND JUSTICE
Louis F. Post

No nation or class has ever forced its dominion upon another for the good of the latter, and none ever will. The desire for mastership is the most evil of all passions; and however it may mask its designs in philanthropic pretensions, the nation or class that seeks to govern others does so for its own aggrandizement. "It is not for my breakfast that you invite me down," said the goat in the fable to the wolf who had urged him to descend to the foot of the cliff where rich grass would give him a better breakfast, "but for your own."

Popular liberties never have been and never will be destroyed by the power of usurpers. They are destroyed by the free consent of the people themselves. When a free people turn from the principles of liberty to worship its lifeless symbols, they are in condition to become easy dupes of the first bold leader who has the shrewdness to conjure them with those symbols. No free people can lose their liberties while they are jealous of liberty. But the liberties of the freest people are in danger when they set up symbols of liberty as fetishes, worshiping the symbol instead of the principle it represents.

Since in justice rights are equal, there must in justice be equal rights to land. Without land man cannot sustain life. It is to him as water to the fish or air to the bird—his natural environment. And if to get land whereby to support life, any man is compelled to give his labor or the products of his labor to another, to that extent his liberty is denied him and his right to pursue happiness is obstructed. Enforced toil without pay is the essence of slavery, and permission to use land can be no pay for toil; he who gives it parts with nothing that any man ever earned, and he who gets it acquires nothing that nature would not freely offer him but for the interference of land monopolists.

EGOISM
Dr. James L. Walker

What is good? What is evil? These words express only appreciations. A good fighter is a "good man" or a "bad man"! both words expressing the same idea of ability, but from different points of view. To the beggar a generous giver is a good man. To the master a servant is good when he cheerfully slaves for the master. A good subject is one obedient to his prince. A good citizen is one who gives no trouble to the State, but contributes to its revenues and stability. Evil is only what we do not find to our good, but what we have to combat. A horse is not good because strong and swift if he be "vicious"; that is, if we find him hard to tame. A breed of dogs is good if readily susceptible of training to hunt all day or watch all night for the benefit of the owner. A wife is "good" if she will not be good to any man but her husband.

The love of money within reason is conspicuously an Egoistic manifestation, but when the passion gets the man, when money becomes his ideal, his god, we must class him as an Altruist. There is the characteristic of "devotion to another," no matter that that other is neither a person nor the social welfare, nothing but the fascinating golden calf or a row of figures. We Egoists draw the line of distinction between the Egoist and the devotee. It is the same logically when a person becomes bewitched with another of the opposite sex so as to lose judgment and self-control, though this species of fascination is usually curable by experience, while the miser's insanity cannot be reached. The love-sick man or woman has the illusion dispelled by contact with the particular person that caused it; but in certain cases absence or death prevents the remedy from being applied, and in some of these instances the mental malady is lifelong.

Laconics

Where there is but one there is neither liberty nor slavery. Where there are more than one there may be despotism (sometimes called "government," sometimes "absolute liberty") for one or more, and liberty for one or more, or there may be approximate equal liberty for all.

In a word, the conception and the facts of liberty and slavery result from association, not isolation; and the sparseness or density of population, the simplicity or complexity of association, will create the customs, rules and laws governing human relations. Therefore, what the solitary man rightfully may do is no measure of what he rightfully may do when he comes into contact with another man. The liberty of one is conditioned by the liberty of the other.

Thomas Paine wrote these words in *The Crisis:* "The Grecians and the Romans were strongly possessed of the spirit of liberty but not the principle, for at the time they were determined not to be slaves themselves, they employed their power to enslave the rest of mankind."

The kind of equal liberty possible is determined by environment. It is not a matter of guesswork, of intuition; it is not indicated by the undisciplined spirit of mastership which sometimes expresses itself today in the demand for "absolute" freedom. It is to be ascertained by the activities of brain and tested by ethics, ethics here meaning the conception of fair play, of the nearest possible equality of opportunity. For equal liberty simply means fair play.

Of course "equal liberty" does not mean equal liberty to invade, to indulge in "self-expression" careless of the thus denied self-expression of others, to rob, to tyrannize, as careless or unbalanced thinkers sometimes have said, but equal freedom from invasion, from robbery, from the exaction of tyranny. Fair play (liberty) cannot exist in the atmosphere of absolutism, whether the absolutism be that of czar, majority, or lawless individual outside of formal government.—*Edwin C. Walker.*

In all ages, the truest lovers of mankind have toiled to imbue their fellows with the spirit of open-mindedness. The cause of free-speech numbers the most glorious martyrs in history, Socrates, whose name we hold in reverence today, was murdered by the Athenian people, for seeking to lead them to think for themselves. Bruno in death and Galileo in imprisonment paid the penalty of loving truth more than public opinion. Roger Bacon upheld the cause of scientific research against unnumbered persecutions. Milton perceived that no error was so fatal as the suppression of thought, and penned his glorious *Areopagitica,* which remains to this day an unanswerable argument to all who, either from mental weakness or from a tyrannous disposition, seek to set bounds to human speculation or expression. Voltaire, Paine and a host of others have followed in demonstrating that free minds and free lips were necessary, in order that men might grow and learn. In our own land, Elijah Lovejoy gave his life for the principle of freedom of the press; and from his martyrdom was born the grand apostleship of Wendell Phillips in the cause of freedom. We stand indeed on holy ground, when we approach the sublime company of those who, through the ages, have striven to secure, not only for themselves, but for all mankind, the right of unfettered utterance on every theme. Well for us, if we are found worthy to tread in their footsteps, and to bear the most humble part in this great work.—*James F. Morton.*

The philosophy of Egoism, which is merely the doctrine of evolution applied to psychology, teaches us that each individual always seeks his own greatest happiness. Any interference with an individual in the pursuit of his happiness is unwarranted, as no one can know better than the person himself in what direction his happiness lies. Individual freedom is necessary to the attainment of individual happiness. Any restraint of the free activities of the individual are certain to violate the conditions of social progress.

If freedom is the condition of progress, all invasion of that freedom is bad and should be resisted, whether it is practiced by one upon another, by one upon many, or by many upon one. In other words, individual freedom presupposes the suppression of the invader, whether that invader appears as an individual criminal or as the corporate criminal—the State,—and whether as the Republican or as the Imperial form of State.

The first essentials of freedom are, of course, the freedom to live unmolested and the freedom of the producer to retain unrestricted the full product of his toil. While there may be serious differences of opinion in regard to the definitions of "producer" and "product," I think no one will deny that crimes against person and property—murder, assault, theft, etc.— are violations of Equal Freedom.—*Francis D. Tandy*.

No man ever ruled other men for their own good; no man was ever rightly the master of the minds or bodies of his brothers; no man ever ruled other men for anything except for their undoing and for his own brutalization. The possession of power over others is inherently destructive both to the possessor of the power and to those over whom it is exercised. And the great man of the future, in distinction from the great man of the past, is he who will seek to create power in the people, and not gain power over them. The great man of the future is he who will refuse to be great at all, in the historic sense; he is the man who will literally lose himself, who will altogether diffuse himself, in the life of humanity. All that any man can do for a people, all that any man can do for another man, is to set the man or the people free. Our work, whensoever and wheresoever we would do good, is to open to men the gates of life—to lift up the heavenly doors of opportunity. . . . . Give men opportunity and opportunity will give you men.— *George D. Herron*.

It is the fundamental condition of liberty that no one shall be deprived of the opportunity of securing the full product of his labor. Economic independence is consequently the first demand of Anarchism; the abolition of the exploitation of man by man. That exploitation is made impossible: by the freedom of banking, i. e. liberty in the matter of furnishing a medium of exchange free from the legal burden of interest; by the freedom of credit, i. e. the organization of credit on the basis of the principle of mutualism, of economic solidarity; by the freedom of home and foreign trade, i. e. liberty of unhindered exchange of values from hand to hand as from land to land; the freedom of land, i. e. liberty in the occupation of land for the purpose of personal use, if it is not already occupied by others for the same purpose; or, to epitomize all these demands: the exploitation of man by man is made impossible by the freedom of labor.—*John Henry Mackay.*

I have lived with communities of savages in South America and in the East, who have no laws or law-courts but the public opinion of the village freely expressed. Each man scrupulously respects the rights of his fellow, and any infraction of those rights rarely or never takes place. In such a community all are nearly equal. There are none of those wide distinctions of education and ignorance, wealth and poverty, master and servant, which are the production of our civilization. There is none of that wide-spread division of labor, which, while it increases wealth, produces also conflicting interests. There is not that severe competition and struggle for existence or for wealth which the dense population of civilized countries inevitably creates. All incitements to great crimes are thus wanting, and petty ones are suppressed partly by the influence of public opinion, but chiefly by that natural sense of justice and his neighbor's right which seem to be in some degree inherent in every race of men.—*Alfred Russell Wallace.*

Liberty is the most jealous and exacting mistress that can beguile the brain and soul of man. From him who will not give her all, she will have nothing. She knows that his pretended love serves but to betray. But when once the fierce heat of her quenchless, lustrous eyes has burned into the victim's heart, he will know no other smile but hers. Liberty will have none but the great devoted souls, and by her glorious visions, by her lavish promises, her boundless hopes, her infinitely witching charms, she lures these victims over hard and stony ways, by desolate and dangerous paths, through misery, obloquy and want to a martyr's cruel death. Today we pay our last sad homage to the most devoted lover, the most abject slave, the fondest, wildest, dreamiest victim that ever gave his life to liberty's immortal cause.—*Clarence S. Darrow, at Altgeldt's funeral.*

To be governed, is to be watched, inspected, spied, directed, law-ridden, regulated, penned up, indoctrinated, preached at, checked, appraised, seized, censured, commanded, by beings who have neither title nor knowledge nor virtue. To be governed is to have every operation, every transaction, every movement noted, registered, counted, rated, stamped, measured, numbered, assessed, licensed, refused, authorized, indorsed, admonished, prevented, reformed, redressed, corrected. To be governed is, under pretext of public utility and in the name of the general interest, to be laid under contribution, drilled, fleeced, exploited, monopolized, extorted from, exhausted, hoaxed and robbed; then, upon the slightest resistance, at the first word of complaint, to be repressed, fined, vilified, annoyed, hunted down, pulled about, beaten, disarmed, bound, imprisoned, shot, mitrailleused, judged, condemned, banished, sacrificed, sold, betrayed, and, to crown all, ridiculed, derided, outraged, dishonored.—*Proudhon.*

Every attempt to gag the free expression of thought is an unsocial act, a crime against society. That is why judges and juries who try to enforce these laws make themselves ridiculous. It is very hard for a robber to convince his victims that he is acting in their behalf and for their good. Is there no parallel between the gag of the burglar and the gag of the law? Why does the burglar use a gag? It is because he wants to get away with your goods, and he doesn't want you to make an outcry and call the neighbors. He knows that he cannot convince you by argument that he is entitled to the goods and that it is really to your best interest to pass them over to him. Capitalism holds up the toilers; it robs them of their labor and is enjoying life to its fullest on the result of its plunder. Naturally it doesn't want to be deprived of its special privilege, therefore it puts the gag of the law in the mouth of anyone who attempts to make an outcry.—*Jay Fox.*

Make no laws whatever concerning speech, and speech will be free; so soon as you make a declaration on paper that speech shall be free, you will have a hundred lawyers proving that "freedom does not mean abuse, nor liberty license;" and they will define and define freedom out of existence. Let the guarantee of free speech be in every man's determination to use it, and we shall have no need of paper declarations. On the other hand, so long as the people do not care to exercise their freedom, those who wish to tyrannize will do so; for tyrants are active and ardent, and will devote themselves in the name of any number of gods, religious and otherwise, to put shackles upon sleeping men.—*Voltairine De Cleyre.*

Of course if we knew the whole truth Liberty would not be so necessary as far as the race is concerned. But because we do not know the truth we must leave all the avenues for its discovery open, and hence every individual must have perfect liberty to follow his own inclination and desire. In this way all of society would be transformed into one great sociological laboratory in which all the isms in each succeeding age would be subjected to laboratory tests and only the truths remain. Not only does Liberty solve all of our sociological problems but it is the only possible source for material advancement. The innumerable social advantages that have come from individual inventions and discoveries illustrate this. Thus it must be perfectly plain that if the race is to climb to higher levels and make still farther advances the one big prime necessity for such advancement is Liberty.—*Dr. Claude Riddle.*

Instead of defending "free love," which is a much-abused term capable of many interpretations, we ought to strive for the freedom of love; for while the former has come to imply freedom for any sort of love, the latter must only mean freedom for a feeling which is worthy the name of love. This feeling, it may be hoped, will gradually win for itself the same freedom in life as it already possesses in poetry. The flowering, as well as the budding of love, will then be a secret between the lovers, and only its fruits will be a matter between them and society. As always, poetry has pointed out the way to development. A great poet has seldom sung of lawfully wedded happiness, but often of free and secret love; and in this respect, too, the time is coming when there will no longer be one standard of morality for poetry and another for life. To anyone tender of conscience, the ties formed by a free connection are stronger than the legal ones, since in the former case he has made a choice more decisive to his own and the other's personality than if he had followed law and custom.—*Ellen Key.*

God so made us, and put such instincts in us, that to gratify them is wrong, and to crush them is right; to be happy is wicked, while to be miserable is righteousness. The old asceticism said: "Be virtuous, and you will be happy." The new hedonism says: "Be happy and you will be virtuous." Self-development is greater than self-sacrifice. It will make each in the end more helpful to humanity. To be sound in mind and limb; to be healthy of body and mind; to be educated, to be emancipated, to be free, to be beautiful,—these things are ends towards which all should strain, and by attaining which all are happier in themselves, and more useful to others. That is the central idea of the new hedonism.—*Grant Allen.*

Men mistake when they imagine the Single Tax agitation to aim only at fiscal change, a new method of taxation. Its sole purpose is to secure the larger freedom of the race. It is not the method but the result that is precious. For it is idle to talk of the equal rights of men when the one thing essential to such equality is withheld. The Physiocrats of France grasped the central truth, and saw that freedom of natural opportunity, comprised in the term land, was the foundation-stone of freedom and justice. Had the French Revolution proceeded on their line, it would have had a different ending. The succeeding spectre of Napoleon, devastating Europe and wading through the blood of his sacrificed countrymen to the throne, would not have affrighted mankind. The fruits of liberty would have been gathered.—*William Lloyd Garrison.*

It is vain to echo Nietzsche's mad cry for absolute freedom— the freedom of the strong to enslave the weak, of the cunning to rob the candid. That we already have and it does not satisfy. The personal life cannot satisfy the growing sympathies of man. The demand of the centuries, never so virile and insistent as today, is for equal freedom. The modern Everyman asks not for himself what all may not have. The asking were vain, indeed, for there is no freedom till all are free. Master and slave are bound by the same thong. Human solidarity is not a moral fancy but a stern fact.—*Luke North (Editor of Everyman).*

The Single Tax does not intend to add to or multiply the already almost infinite statutory enactments now confusing and befuddling the social state, but rather means to abolish, one after the other, every law on the statute books granting a special privilege to any one man or body of men that is at the expense of the unprivileged mass of society. This will destroy the petty and grand larceny now preying upon the social body.

Aside from the million of petty privileges granted by municipalities, states and the nation to individuals, the great and glorious pillage shows itself in privileges and monopoly in labor-saving inventions, trade restrictions and the private ownership of natural resources, the major part of which is a matter of taxation; therefore, the Single Tax would abolish all taxes on barter, trade, exchange, personal property and improvements, commensurately raising all taxes from the value of land alone, till there was in existence but one single tax upon the value of bare land exclusive of improvements. This would be a single tax on land value—not on land, for some land would pay no tax while other land would pay much tax.

For instance, one acre of land worth a million dollars would pay as much tax as a million acres worth only one dollar per acre.—*Edmund Norton.*

So long as society is founded on injustice, the function of the laws will be to defend and sustain injustice. And the more unjust they are, the more respectable they will seem. Observe also that, being ancient, for the most part, they do not represent altogether present iniquity, but a past iniquity—rougher and more brutal. They are the monuments of barbarous times which have survived to a gentler period.—*Anatole France.*

If that is the best government which governs least, is no government at all the *summum bonum*? What use for Church or State if man, with every burden cast off, every bond broken, rises to his full stature and development, with a spirit purified into selflessness by very surrender to the instincts of self! What is this but the sublimation, the apotheosis of Herbert Spencer's enlightened self-interest? What is it but Prof. James' Pragmatism—the idea that there is no good but what is good to me? —*William Marion Reedy.*

The people, the standpatters, who for profit, or for an unthinking but sincere conservatism, try to suppress radical tendencies because they fear revolution and destruction, are themselves fostering revolution and destruction. The force and power of their reactionary intolerance tend to make the idealist desperate and induce him to resort to violence; he, therefore, who stands in the way of free speech and free expression in art, politics or industry is an enemy of society.—*Hutchins Hapgood.*

This government was established to protect primarily the

rights of men in social union, not the rights of property-holders, merely as such. Therefore, traffic in ideas is more important than traffic in merchandise. To suppress the former on pretense of protecting the latter, even in the use of streets, is an unpardonable outrage which becomes quite intolerable when done by arbitrary police violence, or with favoritism for approved opinions.—*Leonard Abbott.*

The political franchise for women is a strike in the direction of equal justice to all, regardless of sex, but woman has been endowed by nature with a franchise incomparably more important than any that man can bestow upon her, namely, the right to elect whether she shall become a mother or not, the right to elect her masculine helper in the creative process, and the added right to elect the economic conditions, the home surroundings under which she will consent to become a mother.
—*Moses Harman.*

Noble souls wish not to have anything for nothing.

The crowd will follow a leader who marches twenty steps in advance; but if he is a thousand steps in front of them, they do not see and do not follow him, and any literary freebooter who chooses may shoot him with impunity.—*George Brandes.*

It can never be unpatriotic for a man to take his country's side against his government; it must always be unpatriotic for a man to take his government's side against his country.
—*Steven T. Byington.*

What is freedom? To have the will to be responsible for one's self.

Whosoever will be free, must make himself free: freedom is no fairy's gift to fall into any man's lap.

Whatever the State saith is a lie; whatever it hath is a theft: all is counterfeit in it, the gnawing, sanguinary, insatiate monster. It even bites with stolen teeth. Its very bowels are counterfeit.

We carry faithfully what we are given, on hard shoulders, over rough mountains! And when perspiring, we are told:

"Yea, life is hard to bear!" But man himself only is hard to bear! The reason is that he carrieth too many strange things on his shoulders. Like the camel he kneeleth down and alloweth the heavy load to be put on his back.—*Nietzsche*.

More liberty, not less, is demanded by every rational thinker in the world today, but the clergy are not in that category, so we still see them sitting on the lid, so to speak, trying their best to keep liberty in check. Liberty to them is the most offensive word in the English language, and to keep the mass of mankind from enjoying it, has always been the prime object of priestcraft.—*Channing Severance*.

The glorification of the State as a kind of all-wise Providence has neither historic nor logical foundation. The quixotic belief of the Socialists that the State can be captured by the proletariat and used to expropriate the capitalists, then afterwards carry on all the industrial functions of society on collectivist principles, is as economically unsound as it is chimerical. —*William Bailie*.

Liberty, divinest word ever coined by human brain or uttered by human tongue. It is the spirit of liberty that today undermines the empires of the old world, sets crowns and mitres askew, and in its onward elemental sweep is shaking the institutions of capitalism in this nation as frail weeds are shaken in the blasts of the storm king's fury.—*Eugene V. Debs*.

As for discussions about my one ideal form of government, they are simply idle.

The ideal form of government is no government at all.

The existence of government in any shape is a sign of man's imperfection.—*Professor E. A. Freeman*.

Only a monopoly which prevented a free supply could for any length of time command tribute for the use of land, money, plant, or commodities.—*J. K. Ingalls*.

In general the art of government consists in taking as much money as possible from one part of the citizens to give it to another.—*Voltaire*.

INDEX

Abbott, Leonard, 538.
Acton, Lord, 33, 34.
Allen, Grant, 536.
Altgeld, 35.
Anarchism, 335, 378, 533.
Anarchists, Methods of, 352.
Andrews, J. A., 48.
Andrews, Stephen Pearl, 236.
Art, Liberty in, 472, 524.
Bailie, Wm., 540.
Bakounine, Mikhail, 501.
Ballot, 352.
Banks and banking, 341, 386, 388, 389, 533.
Beecher, Henry Ward, 38.
Belief, 45.
Bentham, Jeremy, 46.
Bible, 38.
Bigotry, 41.
Blackstone, 40.
Bradlaugh, Charles, 40.
Brandes, George, 539.
Bright, John, 33.
Brougham, Lord, 38.
Buckle, 51.
Burke, Edmund, 60.
Byington, Steven T., 539.
Byron, 33, 45.

Capital, 256, 382, 434.
Capital punishment, 88.
Carlyle, 45.
Carpenter, Edward, 442.
Carter, James Coolidge, 16.
Children, 172, 417, 487, 494, 495.
Church, The, 162, 255.
Church and State, 55, 105, 283.
Church taxation, 56.
Cicero, 33.
Civil disobedience, The duty of, 192.
Civilization, 75, 424.
Clifford, Dr., 34.
Clifford, William Kingdon, 34.
Communism, 375.
Connecticut, Constitution of, 36.
Constitution, The, 154.
Cooper, Thomas, 52.
Co-operation, 326, 350, 512.
Cowper, 43.
Credit, 386, 396, 533.
Creed, Ingersoll's, 283.
Crimes and criminals, 23, 100, 251, 287, 341.
Cromwell, 34.
Crosby, Ernest, 54.
Curtis, George William, 34.
Custom (usage), 16.

Dana, Chas. A., 42.
Darrow, C. S., 533.
Debs, Eugene V., 540.
De Cleyre, Voltairine, 535.
Democracy, 418.
Despots, 483.
Discipline, 494.
Dooley, Mr., 34, 35, 37, 523.

Draper, Dr. J. W., 39.
Dunne, Peter F., see Mr. Dooley.
Duty, 421, 527.
Economic interpretation of history, 504.
Education, 487, 494.
Egoism, 174, 210, 277, 529, 531.
Emerson, Ralph Waldo, 142, 144, 150.
Equal freedom, 19, 214, 537.
Ethics, 109, 214.
Ethics of power, 406.

Ferguson, Rev. Chas., 40.
Ferrer, Francisco, 487.
Feuerbach, 41.
Flags, 31.
Fiske, John, 36.
Fox, Jay, 534.
France, Anatole, 538.
Franklin, 34, 50.
Free press, see Liberty of the press.
Free speech, see Liberty of speech.
Free trade and protection, 303, 343, 533.
Freedom, see Liberty.
Freeman, Prof. E. A., 540.

Garrison, William Lloyd, 154.
Garrison, William Lloyd Jr., 536.
George, Henry, 291.
Gilman, Charlotte Perkins, 35.
Godwin, William, 93.
Goethe, 37.
Golden Rule, 418.
Goldman, Emma, 506.
Goldsmith, Oliver, 33.
Gordak, 44.
Government, 20, 43, 46, 65, 76, 83, 102, 105, 150, 163, 192, 230, 247, 258, 264, 324, 332, 523, 534.
Government, Definition of, 337.
Grant, U. S., 55.
Green, Prof. T. H., 51.
Greene, Wm. B., 382.
Greer, Dr. J. H., 525.

Hapgood, Hutchins, 538.
Harman, Moses, 539.
Harrison, Frederick, 34.
Hay, John, 37.
Hedonism, 537.
Heine, 33.
Helvetius, 47.
Henry, Patrick, 36.
Herbert, Auberon, 41, 398.
Herron, George D., 532.
Hertzka, Theodore, 424.
Hobbes, 33.
Holmes, Rev. Sidney, 34.
Holyoake, George Jacob, 44.
Horr, Alexander, 521.
Hugo, Victor, 40.
Humboldt, Wilhelm von, 105.
Hume, 48.
Huneker, James, 513.
Huxley, 37, 45.

Ibsen, Henrik, 520.
Idolatry, 418.
Individual, The, and the State, 335.
Individualism, 236, 486.
Individuality, 111, 169, 236, 275.
Industrialism, 29.
Ingalls, J. K., 540.
Ingersoll, Robt. G., 272.
Interest, 342, 384, 435, 533.
International, The, 501.
Internationalism, 246.
Intolerance, see Religious liberty.
Jefferson, Thomas, 82.
Johnson, Dr. S., 35.
Jones, Sam M., 44.
Judson, W. L., 524.
Junius, 35.
Jury, 86, 258, 358.
Justice, 16, 528.
Kant, 37.
Key, Ellen, 536.
Kropotkin, 359.
Labor, 165, 185, 250, 256, 289, 305, 429, 501, 533.
Land, 89, 251, 290, 294, 321, 343, 440, 522, 528, 536.
Land titles, 235, 295.
Law, 18, 85, 103, 194, 258, 285, 338, 527, 538.
Lecky, 56.
Libel, 526.
Libertarian, Definition of, 5.
Liberty, 11, 48, 51, 52, 154, 160, 168, 219, 253, 272, 281, 284, 291, 344, 398, 506, 520, 523, 527, 528, 529, 530, 532, 534, 535.
Liberty of assembly, 12.
Liberty of inquiry, 93, 105.
Liberty of the press, 12, 44, 48, 118, 531.
Liberty of speech, 11, 40, 46, 47, 118, 160, 531, 534, 535.
Liberty of thought, 11, 118, 160.
Lincoln, 253.
Lloyd, J. William, 37.
Love, 421, 454, 536.
Lowell, 33, 38, 43, 48, 49.
Lyttleton, Lord, 35.
Macauley, 52.
Macdonald, George E., 527.
Machiavelli, 34.
Machinery, 437.
Mackay, John Henry, 533.
Maine, Sir Henry, 17.
Majorities and minorities, 224, 520.
Majority rule, 25, 133, 193, 223, 335, 399.
Markham, Edwin, 42.
Marriage, 421, 448.
Medical freedom, 525.
Mexican revolution, 31.
Militarism, 29, 233.
Mill, John Stuart, 118.
Milton, 35.
Moderation, 154.
Modern school, The, 487, 494.
Money, 322, 341, 382, 533.
Montaigne, 58.
Montessori, Maria, 494.
Morals, see Ethics.
Morley, John, 43.
Morris, William, 54.
Morton, James F., 531.
Muller, Max, 36.

Music, Freedom in, 513.
Mutual aid, 359, 512.
Mutual banks, see banks and banking.
Mutual currency, 394.
Natural law, 19, 40.
Natural society, 60.
Nietzsche, Friedrich, 539.
Non-resistance, 156.
North, Luke, 537.
Norton, Edmund, 537.
Obscenity, 517, 527.
O'Connell, Daniel, 41.
Opinion, 52.
Opportunity, 532.
Originality, 138.
Paine, Thomas, 74, 529.
Parasitism (Woman), 461, 469.
Parker, Theodore, 35.
Pascal, 17.
Passive resistance, 32, 355.
Patent rights, 301, 344.
Patriotism, 37.
Pennsylvania, Constitution of, 35.
Persecution, 50, 56, 125. See also Religious liberty.
Phillips, Wendell, 160.
Poe, Edgar Allen, 39.
Politics, 398, 527.
Poole, J. P., 47.
Poor, 67, 367.
Post, Louis F., 528.
Power, 406, 409.
Prostitution, 443, 444.
Protection, see Free trade and protection.
Proudhon, 534.
Puck, 37.
Reason, 73.
Red Cross, 373.
Reedy, W. M., 538.
Reform, 162.
Reformation, The, 125.
Regicide, 313.
Religious liberty, 11, 53, 82, 90, 135, 227.
Renaissance, 485.
Renan, Ernest, 33.
Rent, 343, 522.
Representative government, 400.
Revolution, 45, 269, 520.
Riddle, Dr. Claude, 535.
Right and wrong, see Ethics.
Rights, 14, 527.
Robertson, John M., 37.
Rochefoucauld, 33.
Savages, 533.
Scherger, George L., 35.
Schopenhauer, 42.
Schreiner, Olive, 458.
Schroeder, Theodore, 517.
Servitude, 424.
Severance, Channing, 540.
Sex-relations, 444.
Sexual attractions, 463.
Shaler, N. S., 36.
Shaw, G. Bernard, 416.
Shelley, 41, 44.
Single Tax, 298, 536, 537.
Single Tax, Optional, 521.
Slavery, 75, 88, 253, 320, 323, 332.
Social contract, 339.
Society, 63, 75, 136, 144.
Society and government, 102.
Society, Primitive, 365.

Socrates, Charges against, 125.
Solidarity, 503.
Sovereignty, 135.
Spencer, Herbert, 210.
Spinoza, 33.
Spooner, Lysander, 258.
State, The, 46, 108, 183, 192, 220, 335. See also Government.
Statute law, 19.
Stirner, Max, 174.
Strikes, 350, 509.
Sudermann, 36.
Sufferage, 266. See also Ballot.
Sumner, Charles, 34.
Superstition, 61.
Swartz, C. L., 526.
Swift, 39.
Swinburne, 39, 40.
Syndicalism, 506.

Tacitus, 33.
Taine, 36, 46.
Tandy, Francis D., 531.
Tariff, see Free trade and protection.
Taxation, 193, 233. See also Single Tax.
Tilden, Samuel J., 39.
Thoreau, Henry D., 191.
Tolstoy, Lyoff N., 313.
Trade unions, 507.

Traubel, Horace, 46
Trial by jury, see Jury.
Trusts, 307.
Tucker, Benj. R., 334.
Turgot, 36.
Twain, Mark, 38.
Usury laws, 384.
Value, 349, 393, 431.
Violence, 31, 161.
Volney, 38.
Voltaire, 33, 45, 540.
Voluntary associations, 370.
Wages, 305, 342.
Wagner, Richard, 49.
Wallace, Alfred Russell, 533.
Walker, Edwin C., 530.
Walker, Dr. James L., 529.
War, 27, 75, 85, 101, 155, 286, 2 ?, 335.
Warren, Josiah, 168.
Washington, George, 53.
Wealth, 99.
Webster, Daniel, 34, 36.
Westermarck, Edward, 34.
Whitman, Walt, 41.
Wilde, Oscar, 472.
Witchcraft, 517.
Wollstonecraft, Mary, 50.
Woman, 50, 144, 419, 442, 458, 465, 539

www.ingramcontent.com/pod-product-compliance
Lightning Source LLC
Chambersburg PA
CBHW071641160426
43195CB00012B/1323